CENTRAL AND SOUTH AFRICAN HISTORY

Topics in World History
Edited by Patricia W. Romero

CENTRAL AND SOUTH AFRICAN HISTORY

VOL. III of African History: Text and Readings

by

Robert O. Collins
University of California, Santa Barbara

Markus Wiener Publishing
New York

For information write to: Markus Wiener Publishing, Inc.
225 Lafayette Street, New York, NY 10012

Library of Congress Cataloging-in-Publicaton Data

Collins, Robert O.
  Central and South African history / by Robert O. Collins.
        —(African history; v. 3) (Topics of world history)
  Includes bibliographical references.
  ISBN 1-55876-017-2:
  1. Africa, South—History—Sources.   2. Africa, Central–History—
Sources.   I. Title.   II. Series.   III. Series: Collins, Robert O.
African history: v. 3.
DT1.C55   1990 vol. 3
[DT1009]
968—dc20   89-70617
                                                                              CIP

Cover Design by Cheryl Mirkin

Printed in the United States of America

PREFACE

PREFACE

African history has come into its own. As we enter the 1990s, the old myths about the African past—that Africa had no history, or that no written records of that history existed—have been dispelled. The valuable discoveries about the continent that arose out of the study of archaeological remains and of the invaluable oral traditions have been extended and enriched through the analysis of documentary materials. The twenty years since I published the first edition of *African History* have seen a burgeoning of scholarly material on Africa, not only in monographs and journals, but also in textbooks. Research in African history has been established as a respected scholarly discipline. Surprisingly, however, there are relatively few anthologies that provide primary historical sources for the historian or student of Africa. This was the case twenty years ago, and it is still true. The present edition represents an updating of the 1970 volume, including text of documents dealing with the past thirty years in independent Africa. Its three-volume format reflects the fact that Africa is no longer regarded as an undifferentiated unity, and makes the materials for regional study more acceptable and affordable for teachers and students.

The original purpose of the volume prepared nearly twenty years ago was to demonstrate to the student the extent of the valuable documentary materials available for analysis and interpretation, while in no way minimizing the enormous importance of oral traditions. The aim of this volume on Central and South Africa has been to republish, revise, and add text and documents. I also introduce the reader to the long and rich history of Central and South Africa from the beginnings of recorded time to the present with a brief essay, and some of the principal documents that serve as landmarks in the history of Central and South Africa.

If my purpose has been to expose the student to source materials in African history, my objectives have been guided by two principles—the same principles which inspired the two earlier volumes. First, I have sought to embrace the full span of documentary records pertaining to Central and South Africa. Second, I have sought to cover the vast geographical sweep of the southern African continent. To achieve these two very ambitious goals in a single and modest volume has required an eclectic, if not ramdom, selection that betrays my own personal inclinations and interests. I am sure that anyone with a knowledge of the complex history of Central and South Africa might quarrel with the documents I have chosen, but I have endeavored to select those that describe Africans, and not just individuals who came to look or to rule. I have attempted to select passages from less well-known accounts and descriptions, as well as from the more standard authorities. I have also tried, where possible, to obtain passages of sufficient length to make them meaningful to the inquiring student. Finally, I have prepared a brief introduction to guide the beginner and to refresh the memory of the more experienced student. I have also made additions to the introduction in a attempt to overcome the twenty years that have passed since the publication of the first edition, and I have added documents more pertinent to the age of African independence and nationalism. In order to make the selections more understandable to the beginner, explanatory material has frequently been inserted directly into the text, either in brackets or as a footnote. All of the other footnotes and bracketed material found in the various selections are the work of editors who have preceded me and whose efforts need not be duplicated or deleted.

I wish to express my appreciation to Professor Patricia Romero who has been instrumental in reviving the text, and to the publisher, Markus Wiener, who has accepted the challenge of providing a volume for an increasing number of students interested in Central and South Africa.

I am also grateful for the suggests of Nell Elizabeth Painter and Martin Legassick, whose assistance on the original volume provided many improvements. I am equally grateful to my colleagues and students at the University of California, Santa Barbara—to Damazo Dut Majak and Kenneth Okeny, and to former colleagues, Jack Bermingham and Robert Shell, who have been of great assistance in improving the sections on Zimbabwe and, most especially, South Africa. And, of course, there has always been Dorothy Johnson, who for so many years has seen my manuscripts to conclusion.

Robert O. Collins
Santa Barbara, California
December, 1989

CONTENTS

SECTION I: CENTRAL AFRICA

SECTION II: SOUTH AFRICA   125

SECTION I

CENTRAL AFRICA

CENTRAL AFRICA
BY ROBERT O. COLLINS

THE KINGDOM OF CONGO

In the fourteenth century the son of a chief of Bungu, located near Boma on the north bank of the lower Congo, conquered the plateau of Congo south of the river, taking the title *mani Kongo* and establishing his capital at Mpemba, the present-day town of San Salvador in northern Angola. The kingdom of the mani Kongo was expanded steadily as a result of the conquest of the neighboring chiefdoms, and even territories beyond to the east, southeast, and south recognized the overlordship of Congo and would send tribute and presents to the king. North of Congo, however, the African states of Tyo near Kinshasa and Loango in the Kwilu Nyari basin maintained their independence. The Kingdom of Congo was divided into districts composed of numerous villages. The districts were governed by officials who were both appointed and removed by the king. These district officers carried out administrative duties and acted as judges. All the districts were either integrated into one of the six provinces— Soyo, Mpemba, Mbamba, Mpanga, Mbata, and Nsundi—or were dependent directly on the king. The provinces were ruled by governors who were also removable at the king's pleasure. In addition, there were officials with more specialized functions—such as the *mani lumbu*, who was responsible for the king's quarters in the capital. These officials possessed titles and formed a powerful aristocracy. At the apex of the Congo's political organization was the king, chosen after

1540 from the descendants of Affonso I by an electoral college of a dozen members. The king himself was protected by a permanent bodyguard, but war was carried out by the army, which was recruited by means of the instruction given by every territorial official to the headmen of his villages to rendezvous with all able-bodied men. The army lived off the land and could not therefore remain in the field for long. Consequently, a war was usually decided by a single battle, characterized by a general melée rather than by use of tactics or strategy. The government derived its income from taxation paid in raffia cloth, ivory, hides, and slaves. There were also the royal fisheries of Luanda Island, which provided shells used as currency whose value could be controlled by royal officials. Clearly, the Kingdom of Congo possessed a degree of centralization that few African states could match. Nevertheless, the very source of centralization, the king, proved the state's greatest weakness, for an ineffectual ruler would reduce the power of the state. Moreover, the conflicts over succession led to constant factionalism, strife, and intrigue, and the failure to establish clear rules for succession sapped the strength of the Congo just as it weakened many other African states (Olfert Dapper, *The Kingdom of Congo*).

THE COMING OF THE PORTUGUESE

In 1482 the first Portuguese caravels were sighted off the mouth of the Congo River, known to the Portuguese as Zaïre, the name immortalized in the great Portuguese epic poem, the *Lusiad*, for the mighty river emptying into the Atlantic from the center of Africa. In 1485 the Portuguese under the leadership of Diogo Cão returned, leaving four missionaries at the court of the mani Kongo in exchange for four nobles who sailed back with Cão to Portugal. The Portuguese came back again in 1487, and at that time Nzinga Kuwu, King of the Congo, sent a Congolese ambassador with a number of younger men to Portugal to request missionaries and technicians. After four years, the Congo embassy returned accompanied by missionaries and artisans. A church was constructed at Mpemba, the capital was christened San Salvador, and the king was baptized João I. The royal family and most of the nobility accepted Christianity as well. Although the king reverted to paganism after 1494, the queen mother and a son, Affonso, remained Catholic. Indeed, the religious rivalry reflected the opposition between two political factions in the struggle for the royal succession.

In 1506 Nzinga Kuwu died, and the rivalry between the pagan and Catholic groups erupted into open warfare, in which Affonso defeated the pagan faction and was crowned king (Rui de Aguiar, *King Affonso I*). Affonso was not only devoutly Catholic, but was in favor of increasing European influence. Consequently, contacts between Portugal and Congo developed rapidly between 1506 and 1512, and annual expeditions

3

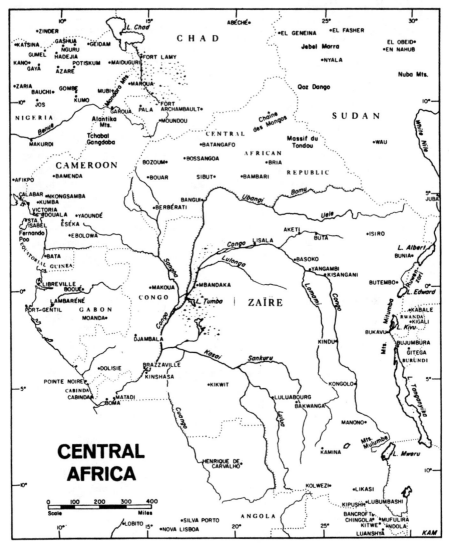

CENTRAL AFRICA

from Portugal carried priests, school-teachers, artisans, and technicians to the Congo. Young Congolese were sent to be educated in Portugal, and what seemed to be a mutually advantageous relationship was beginning. Unhappily, cooperation between Congo and Portugal was soon beset by numerous obstacles. First, the Portuguese traders at São Tomé hampered the exchange of goods and detained envoys between the Congo and Portugal in order to protect their trade monopoly. Second, some of the technicians proved undesirable and un-manageable, compelling Affonso to request that an official be sent from Lisbon with special jurisdiction over the Portuguese in Congo. Third, in 1512 Simão de Silva arrived with instructions, or *regimento*, to carry out the Christianization and Lusitanization of the Congo. The regimento proved a failure. Affonso accepted many of the suggestions while refusing others, but in the long run the failure of the regimento must be attributed to the real difficulties blocking cultural change on such an ambitious scale and the immediate greed of local

Portuguese traders. For a fundamental paradox conditioned Portugal's relations with the Congo which was never resolved and, in the end, greatly contributed to the collapse of the Congo kingdom: namely, that although they were willing to help Congo, the Portuguese wanted to exploit the country, and although they recognized Congo as an equal, they sought to limit its sovereignty. All the Portuguese in the Congo were inexorably drawn into the struggle to control the rapidly expanding trade in slaves, which soon compromised the more altruistic motives of the King of Portugal, and although Affonso also tried to limit the slave trade, he became increasingly powerless to do so. By 1526 the king's power throughout the country was being undermined by slave traders working with provincial officials. When he sought to restrict the European traders to the capital, they continued their raiding and trading through agents known as *pombeiros*. By 1530, 4,000 to 5,000 slaves were being exported annually, thus draining the kingdom of its vitality.

Just as Portuguese traders were eroding the power of the mani Kongo, the Portuguese government determined to prevent Congo from communicating with other powers. In 1532 and 1539 two embassies sent by Affonso to the Vatican were blocked in Lisbon, and Portugal did all in its power to restrict Congolese relations with other European states. By the end of Affonso's reign the dream of collaboration between Congo and Portugal had vanished. The Portuguese traders acted independently, and the king was powerless to control them. In 1545 Affonso died, and with the support of the local Portuguese, Dom Diego I, grandson of Affonso, was placed on the throne (Filippo Pigafetta and Duarte López, *The Successors to Affonso I*). His succession, however, did little to change the pattern of Congo affairs conditioned

by the coming of the Portuguese and fixed in Affonso's reign. The slave trade, the Portuguese factions, and the fitful efforts to educate and convert the Congolese continued for another dismal century.

The reign of Dom Diego was characterized by his unsuccessful attempts to control the white traders on the one hand and his more successful efforts to maintain his rule over his own people on the other. Supported by Portuguese traders at San Salvador, Diego was persuaded to go to war against the São Tomé traders, who were now dealing directly with the king's vassals and subjects. Diego's forces, however, were utterly routed, leading ultimately to the establishment of the colony of Angola. Although beaten by the São Tomé faction, Diego was able to enforce the ban on Portuguese traders going inland, but the pombeiros continued to carry out the wishes of the Portuguese traders. Diego was more successful at defeating internal rebellion, and in the spring of 1550 a plot by his principal rival was crushed. Nevertheless, his efforts to maintain internal security were always compromised by his failure to bring the white traders under close supervision and control (Monsignor Confalonreri, *São Tomé and the Slave Trade*).

THE JAGA INVASION

Diego died in 1561, and the Portuguese intervened to place Affonso on the throne. Affonso, however, was killed and was succeeded by numerous weak kings until 1568, when mauraders, known as the *Jaga*, fell on the kingdom. (See introduction to Andrew Battell, *The Jaga* for the scholarly controversy involving the Jaga). Erupting from the Kwango region to the south and east, the Jaga destroyed the Congolese Army and drove the king into exile on an island in the river Zaïre. Appealing for Portuguese assistance, the Governor of São Tomé, Francesco de

Gouvea, rallied the Congolese and with his harquebuses drove the Jaga from the kingdom in 1571. Although Gouvea virtually occupied the country until 1576, the centralized Congo state continued to be racked by revolts, foreign invasion, and internal discontent, resulting in near anarchy. The Jaga meanwhile established states to the east and south and from them continued to raid the Congo.

THE LAST OF THE CONGO KINGDOM

After the expulsion of the Jaga and the retirement of Gouvea, the King of Congo sought to reestablish his authority and to disengage himself from the Portuguese. Alvare I and his successor, Alvare II, were not entirely successful in maintaining their independence against attempts by Portugal, and later Spain, to restrict their freedom. Internally they were never able to re-create the centralized Congo of Affonso I and were continually hindered by internal revolts and intrigue. (Alvare II and Alvare III, *Relations Between the Kingdom of Congo and the Papacy*). Throughout the first half of the seventeenth century, the Congolese kings were unable to reassert their authority, having lost the support of the people and their chiefs while squabbling among themselves in endless disputes over succession. In 1641, however, Garcia II came to the throne. He was to rule for twenty years, during which he succeeded in checking the disintegration of authority but was unable to establish internal peace. The slave trade (now amounting to about 15,000 slaves a year), as well as a series of natural calamities, complicated Garcia's attempts to extend his authority. The reigns of Garcia and his successor, Antonio I, were the last stand of the Congolese kings. Upon the death of Antonio in 1665 the kingdom dissolved forever into anarchy, with faction against faction, province against province, and village against village.

When the kingdom was actually reunited in 1710, the king had lost all power, possessing only an empty title as a derisory memento of past greatness.

KING LEOPOLD'S CONGO

The disintegration of the Congo eliminated the last vestiges of Portugal's control, and although Portuguese slave traders continued to drain off the human resources of the Congo and the Portuguese crown continued to claim sovereignty over the region, Portuguese influence remained negligible. When Henry Morton Stanley arrived at the mouth of the Congo River in 1878, he found no trace of the Portuguese past in the Congo. Stanley's exploration of the Congo basin and his epic journey down the river excited the interest of King Leopold II of Belgium, who had taken an active interest in Africa since 1876 (Henry Morton Stanley, *The Great Rainforest of the Congo*). Leopold was eager to open up the Congo and in 1879 sent Stanley back up the river to make treaties with the chiefs that would transfer their sovereignty to the *Comité d'Études du Haut Congo*, which was organized by Leopold. Between 1879 and 1884 Stanley founded twenty-two stations and concluded over 300 treaties, firmly establishing the rights of the *Comité d'Études du Haut Congo* to the south bank of the river, while the French explorer de Brazza was laying claim to the territories along the north bank for France (Paul du Chaillu, *Trade in Gabon*).

Leopold's principal problem was to secure international recognition for the treaties concluded by Stanley, and after much skillful diplomacy and luck the king managed to convince the great powers at the Berlin Conference of 1885 to recognize the International Association of the Congo (formerly the *Comité d'Études du Haut Congo*) as a sovereign power. Called *État Indépendant du Congo*, or more commonly, the Congo Free

State, Leopold's Congo embraced nearly one million square miles of territory, dwarfing the old Kingdom of Congo by comparison. Although it was created by an international conference, which could theoretically "uncreate" the *État Indé-pendant du Congo*, in reality the Congo Free State was an absolute monarchy under the sole control of Leopold II. Although he established three departments (Foreign Affairs and Justice, Finance, and Interior) and a resident governor general in the Congo, the king himself managed the affairs of his state until just before his death in 1909. The creation of the Congo Free State provided an outlet for Leopold's energies and abilities, but although the ownership of nearly one million square miles of African real estate was a sop to his megalomania, it taxed his private fortune. By 1889 Leopold had spent over 31 million francs of his own fortune to establish his rule throughout the Congo basin and administer its territory. This sum was, of course, quite insufficient to rule the Congo, and a series of loans and grants from the Belgian government followed in 1887 and 1890. Gradually, as Leopold and his agents desperately sought to make the Congo pay its way, the Free State exploited the ivory and rubber resources of the Congo. Farming out huge tracts of territory to private concessionaires, the king even formed his own company in 1896 to exploit 112,000 square miles of land called the *Domaine de la Couronne* [Crown Lands].

The king's determination to make the Congo pay soon produced profitable results. In fifteen years he is estimated to have extracted nearly $15 million in profits on 11,345 tons of rubber, in addition to sums paid by concessionaires for the right to exploit other regions of the Congo. Ruthlessly driven to collect rubber at the expense of their fields and families, the Congolese, of course, were the ones who made these profits possible. Atrocities, hardships, and violence accompanied the Congo administration's lust for rubber, creating a wide discrepancy between the humanitarian aims professed at the founding of the state and the later malpractices (Edgar Canisius, *Rubber Collecting in the Congo*). As early as 1893 critics began to question Leopold's rule in the Congo, and, led by E. D. Morel, a British journalist and humanitarian, the criticism became so acute that in 1903 the British demanded an international inquiry on the strength of reports by Roger Casement, their consul at Boma. Bowing to the demands of the great powers, Leopold appointed a commission in 1904 to investigate. Although evidence was suppressed, the report could not hide the fact that the lofty principles of the Berlin Act had been forgotten and that if Leopold's regime was not tyrannical, it was certainly most harsh indeed. The Report of the Commission of Inquiry did not still the clamor against Leopold's rule, however, and in November 1908 the Belgian Parliament took over the Congo, paying its king 50 million francs in addition to the 45 million francs that were paid for the beautification of Belgium and annuities for the royal family.

THE BELGIAN CONGO

When Belgium took over the Congo Free State in 1908, she had no experience or tradition of colonial rule, and her colonial policy was shaped more to deal with the immediate problems of administration and development than the political future of the Congo. Practical considerations thus determined the main lines of Belgian policy, clearly reflected in the basic law of the colony, the *Carte Coloniale*, which made no reference to the political status of the Congo. Since Belgium had been forced to take over the Congo by the maladministration of Leopold, the Congo must therefore be administered to prevent such atrocities in the future. Moreover, Belgium had to give evidence that she was doing something for the Africans. These philanthropic themes fitted Belgian attempts to exploit the mineral resources of the Congo, which were first being tapped at the end of Leopold's rule. The development of the great mines of the Congo has led some to conclude that the Belgians sought to develop the economic potential of the Congo while neglecting the needs and services of her inhabitants. This picture, however, is inaccurate, for the mineral wealth permitted development of social and health services second to none in colonial Africa.

Belgium's administration of the Congo was never marked by a large influx of European settlers *(colons)*, and those who did come were equipped with large resources and capital. Thus the European settlers in the Congo never became sufficiently numerous to demand control of the government. But as the number of European settlers remained small, the growing urbanization marked by improvement in services to Africans resulted in nearly a quarter of the Congolese living in towns. The administration of the Congo was the responsibility of the Minister of Colonies, who issued the orders for his representative in the Congo—the Governor General. The Minister of Colonies in turn was advised by a council of nominated members, so that in fact that Congo was ruled by a small number of men—experts who scorned the political aspects of governing and steadfastly kept Belgian politicians out of Congo affairs.

The predominant characteristic of Belgian policy was economic development. As a heritage from the Congo Free State, economic policy guided all others so that over 50 percent of the wage-earning population was involved in 3 percent of the commercial enterprises, which in turn held over 86 percent of the capital investment. Labor policy was designed to provide a stable labor force for indus-

try without depleting the rural areas. Those Africans who were permitted to go to the industrial areas were educated and trained to become highly skilled technicians. The "stabilized labor policy," however, required careful control of the movements of Africans, which was frequently annoying if not oppressive. As a counterpart to industrialization, the administration in the Congo sought to create a peasant agriculture in an effort to increase African agricultural output. Such schemes were not always successful in the face of the shifting cultivation practiced by Africans in the Congo. Education under Belgian rule was guided by two principles. As in the British territories, instruction was given first in the vernacular, as opposed to schooling in the French colonies, where all instruction was carried out in French. Moreover, the emphasis on education in the Belgian Congo was practical. Education was designed to create a useful class of craftsmen or agriculturalists to provide the administration with clerks, and industry with technicians and artisans. As opposed to the practice in French and British colonies, no attempt was made to develop an African élite trained to occupy the higher administrative and political posts. Education did not identify the Congolese with Belgium, but concentrated on manual training. Many generations of Africans in French and British territories had passed through universities before the Congo possessed an institution of higher learning (Leon Pétillon, *Native Policy in the Belgian Congo*).

THE COMING OF INDEPENDENCE
Belgian rule in the Congo was thus a form of paternalism that tempered the technical training of the African with political suppression. The placid conditions that such a policy created were rudely disrupted in 1959 by widespread rioting in Léopoldville. Spurred on by the sentiments for independence expressed dur-

ing and after World War II, and excited by the example of other African territories that had received their independence, the African demand for a greater say in the administration of the Congo was not surprising (Patrice Lumumba, *Crisis of Confidence*). Unfortunately, no political élite or quasi-political organization existed through which this discontent could be constructively channeled into a nonviolent transfer of authority. Receiving little support either from the Western powers, which were beginning the process of dismantling their African empires, or from the Belgian people themselves, the small group of men who controlled the Belgian administration in the Congo precipitously promised elections and ultimate independence. The Congolese replied with demands for immediate independence, supported by rioting and violence, and the Belgian government had the choice of administering by force or granting the demands for independence. At the Congo Round Table Conference held in January 1960, the Belgians capitulated, agreeing to grant immediate independence to the Congo. Thus the Congo raced toward independence led by an army with no Congolese officers and possessing only a handful of Congolese with university training to advise the new government. On June 30, 1960, the Congo became independent, but celebrations were tempered by warnings and grim forebodings about the future of tropical Africa's largest state.

Unprepared for independence, the Republic of Zaïre was confronted by the enormous task of national integration in the face of the centrifugal forces of ethnic rivalries, mutiny within the army, and separatist movements throughout the state, with each province seeking to reap locally the spoils of the precipitous Belgian withdrawal. Katanga was the richest province by virtue of its copper and uranium mines; it seceded under the leadership of Moïse Tshombe on July 11, 1960, depriving the central government of critical revenue. In desperation, the Congo appealed to the United Nations to ensure the integrity of the new nation. The UN military forces responded with alacrity, imposing a modicum of stability and order on the sprawling and diverse country without seriously intervening in the political and military rivalries between Patrice Lumumba, the premier, and Joseph Kasavubu, the head of state. Lumumba favored a centralized, socialist government while Kasavubu, the chief of the influential Bakongo tribe who dominated Kinshasa [formerly Léopoldville], advocated the establishment of a Congo federation. The political stalemate between Lumumba and Kasavubu was broken in September 1960, when the armed forces, led by Colonel Joseph-Désiré Mobutu, the newly appointed chief-of-staff, took Lumumba prisoner. Lumumba was subsequently executed by Katangan authorities on the order of Moïse Tshombe in January 1961.

The death of Lumumba prompted UN and international action to end the Katangan secession. The concern increased with the death of the secretary-general of the United Nations, Dag Hammarskjöld, in a suspicious airplane crash in September 1961. His successor, U Thant, submitted a plan for national reconciliation in the Congo based on the creation of a federation. The plan was rejected by Tshombe, whose followers were subsequently overwhelmed by the UN peace-keeping mission; this action ended the secession of the Katanga on January 14, 1963.

The end of the Katangan rebellion against the central government was not, however, the end of insurrection in the Congo. Revolt soon erupted in the Kwilu region. In a desperate attempt to restore order, President Kasavubu recalled Tshombe from his exile when the UN forces were withdrawn on June 30, 1964. Tshombe, on his part, employed white mercenaries and Belgian paratroopers to reassert the control of the central government, at the expense of his own credibility among the Congolese. He was summarily removed as premier by Kasavubu on October 13, 1965; this precipitated a coup d'état by General Mobutu, now commander-in-chief of the Congolese National Army, who assumed the presidency and declared himself head of state on October 26, 1966. A new constitution was adopted in June 1967 which reaffirmed Mobutu's position as head of state by legally establishing a centralized presidential form of government reinforced by an establishment political party—the Popular Movement of the Revolution (Mouvement Populaire de la Révolution—MPR).

Thereafter, Mobutu moved relentlessly against all opposition. By 1970, the Congo, renamed Zaïre the following year, became not only a one-party state under the leadership of Mobutu Sese Seko, but a government committed to the Africanization of church and state through the identification of the administration with the single party—the MPR. The amalgamation between the civil service and the party was formalized by amendments to the constitution in July 1974 whereby Mobutu assumed complete power. He has maintained this power to the present day, to his personal enrichment and that of his followers in what has been described as the quintessential "kleptocracy."

THE ARRIVAL OF THE BANTU IN SOUTHERN AFRICA

Although the Bantu arrived in southern Africa approximately at the beginning of the Christian era, Bushmen, or Khosian-speaking peoples, and scattered bands of pygmies had long inhabited the plains and plateaus south of the Congo rain forest. These were Stone Age peoples,

hunters and gatherers, who retired before the advancing Bantu or sought refuge in isolated pockets bypassed by the Bantu immigrants. Moving down the spine of Africa, the vanguard of the Bantu probably reached the plateau country south of Lake Tanganyika a few hundred years before the birth of Christ, to be followed by additional migrants in subsequent centuries. The pattern of migration may have been that of the ravaging band of hunter-warriors moving far and fast without many women and children and settling where they pleased. More likely, the movement of the Bantu was conditioned by their shifting cultivation, in which groups would settle, slash, and burn the vegetation and carry on cultivation for a few years until the soil was exhausted, thus forcing them to move on. Equipped with iron implements, the Bantu carried iron-working techniques southward and brought central and southern Africa into the Iron Age. Always pressing southward, the Bantu crossed the Zambezi and settled on the plateau of Mashonaland in what is now Zimbabwe. By 1000 A.D. the Bantu were south of the Limpopo.

ZIMBABWE

Sometime around 1000 A.D., dry stone construction was begun on the Mashonaland plateau; the foundations of the impressive ruins at Zimbabwe were probably built in the eleventh century. Contemporaneous with the stone construction, gold mining activity increased to satisfy the demands of Arab traders from the East African coast. During the subsequent centuries, a thriving Bantu civilization developed in Mashonaland, and Great Zimbabwe was completed. Comprising an acropolis of a massive defensive fortification, the structure contains intricate passageways and rooms. The acropolis appears to have been the original building, but as late as the eighteenth century, an elliptical, or great, enclosure was constructed, with embankments and a conical tower below the acropolis in the valley. All the great walls and buildings were built of cut stone fitted without mortar, and dominated by the tragic solitude of the uninhabited valley. Indeed, Zimbabwe demonstrates such a high level of technological advancement that many of the Europeans who first saw the site in the nineteenth century refused to consider that it had been constructed by an African people. As a result, numerous theories were developed to explain its existence. Some argued that Zimbabwe was built by Phoenician sailors. Others attributed the ruins to southern Arabian origins or even, incredibly, early Portuguese adventurers. In 1929, Caton-Thompson investigated the Zimbabwe ruins and conclusively demonstrated that they were of Bantu origin. Although a few authorities continue to question where and how the Bantu acquired the Zimbabwe technology, all are in agreement that the Bantu built Zimbabwe.

THE MWANAMUTAPA

During the centuries in which the Zimbabwe ruins were being constructed, new Bantu migrants continued to pour into the high plateau between the Zambezi and Limpopo rivers, changing the ethnographic character of the region. The Sotho people probably crossed the Zambezi as early as the eleventh or twelfth century and remained for several hundred years until they were pushed south of the Limpopo into the northern Transvaal by the invasion of the *Shona* in the fifteenth century. The origins of the Shona are unknown, but they are a Bantu people who probably came, like other Bantu, from the north down the eastern highlands. The early Shona invaders consisted of related clans, such as the *Karanga*, *Zezuru*, and *Rozvi*. The Rozvi appear to have been a dominant

clan, whose King Mutota led the Shona nation on a military expedition south from Zimbabwe to the Matopo Hills in the mid-fifteenth century, subjugating the autochthons. He then turned northward to make his headquarters just south of the Zambezi, taking the name *mwana mutapa* (master pillager).[1] During the next half-century Mutota and his son Matope led a succession of conquests that spread the borders of Rozvi influence from the Zambezi to the Limpopo, and from the Indian Ocean to the Kalahari Desert. This was the short-lived empire of the mwanamutapa. By the end of the fifteenth century the empire began to fall apart. Matope tried to divide the administration of the confederation among brother, sons, and trusted vassals, but within a decade the southern provinces had broken away under their Rozvi ruler, a grandson of Mutota named Changa, who adopted the Arabic title amir and became the Changamir. Overextended communications, political intrigue within the ruling circles, and lack of cultural and ethnic homogeneity were factors too strong for the mwanamutapa to overcome. For another generation the mwanamutapa struggled in a series of wars to reassert his position over his rebellious vassals, principally the Rozvi. He failed and died about 1530 at the time of Portuguese penetration up the Zambezi.

The first European visitor to the mwanamutapa was the Portuguese *degredado* (outcast) Antonio Fernandez. In 1514 he reached the capital of the mwanamutapa and reported that the gold of Sofala originated in the land of the mwanamutapa. Consequently, for another half-century the Portuguese sought to establish direct contact with the interior. Sena was occupied by Portuguese

[1] The title *mwana mutapa* was frequently associated with his kingdom, which was known to the Portuguese as monomotapa or, more correctly, mwanamutapa.

troops in 1531, and a few years later Tete was founded. After 1550 a Portuguese trader resided at the court of the mwanamutapa as a free-lance adviser to the ruler. Ten years later the Jesuit Gonçala da Silveira reached the mwanamutapa, but was murdered on suspicion that he was simply spying for the Portuguese. Francisco Barreto sought to avenge Silveira's death, but his expedition was unsuccessful. Only in 1574, when Vasco Fernandes Homem marched from Sofala into the empire, did the Portuguese learn that the gold fields of the mwanamutapa could not be worked economically without machinery. Portugal subsequently lost interest in the interior until late in the nineteenth century, when the scramble for Africa had begun (Manuel de Faria e Sousa, *The Kingdom of the Monomotapa*).

Meanwhile the plateau south of the Zambezi was invaded by groups of wandering warrior peoples like the Jaga coming from the Kasai or the more terrifying Zimba, who roamed unchecked throughout the shrunken state of the mwanamutapa in the 1590s. In 1628, mwanamutapa Kapararidze unsuccessfully sought to rally the Shona nation to drive out the Arab and Portuguese traders. With Portuguese help, a puppet chief was installed; he was maintained by Portuguese support until his death in 1652. By this time the "mwanamutapa" had become a nominal title, which was made obsolete by the return of the Rozvi in the last part of the seventeenth century. At first, Rozvi relations with the mwanamutapa remained friendly, but at the end of the seventeenth century the ruling Changamir swept northward and established his hegemony throughout Mashonaland. Here the Rozvi ruled, occupying the stone forts in the south, including Great Zimbabwe, and even building new stone enclosures. Their work, however, never reached the quality of the mwanamutapa, and their

political and economic organization never rivaled that of the earlier period. Gold production declined, the Rozvi appearing content to raid rather than to develop.

THE LUNDA STATES

Zimbabwe was not the only area in Central Africa in which state systems developed. To the northwest of Zimbabwe beyond the Zambezi River, in the savanna regions below the Congo rain forest, complex states developed from the unification of a number of villages. The largest and most comprehensive were the Lunda Empire and its offshoots, the Kingdom of Kazembe and the Yeke kingdom. The Lunda Empire began from a nuclear territory north of its present location in the Kasai. To meet the demands of an increasing population, small villages broke off and settled in outlying areas. Nevertheless, the villages maintained relations with one another through the notion of perpetual kinship among their leaders, so that by the sixteenth century Lundaland was already a single, though loose, political unit. Subsequent Lunda rulers unified these villages either by sending royal emissaries to receive the submission of local headmen or, when necessary, by conquest. The Lunda continued to expand into Angola, Katanga, Zambia, and other territories where people did not recognize kinship ties with the Lunda. At first, small groups of Lunda adventurers would migrate to these areas and assume political control through the prestige associated with their name, the superiority and adaptability of their political system, and their own aggressive spirit. Political control by Lunda chiefs was later followed by large migrations of Lunda subjects. Thus the main agent for establishing Lunda hegemony was not military might but political skill. Indeed the Lunda did not even have a regular standing army, but depended entirely on irregular forces.

The foundation of the Lunda political structure was the village and its surrounding land. Villages were ruled by a council of elders and a hereditary headman who could be deposed only by the king. The villages were organized into groups according to the ties of perpetual kinship among their headmen. These groups of headmen were ruled by an elder, or *mbay*, and were grouped into districts under a *cilool*. The cilool was responsible for collecting taxes from his district for the king, and any report of dishonesty or inefficiency on the part of the cilool would bring a royal official called a *yikeezy* to supervise his activities. The central government was comprised of the king and his titleholders. The king's authority came from his power to nominate or dismiss officials and to create new titles. Tribute was paid to the king once a year and was the cement that held the empire together, for the provinces were free to do as they pleased so long as tribute was paid. The whole political structure of the Lunda Empire rested on the twin mechanisms of political succession and perpetual kinship. Each new official inherited the personal status as well as the office of his predecessor. In this way the political structure was divorced from the real descent structure and was not tied to any principle of descent in particular. Such a system could be diffused without necessitating any changes in the existing social structure, thus enabling many divergent cultures to be assimilated. Even after military defeat the local rulers were retained in honored and respected positions.

THE KINGDOM OF KAZEMBE

In the middle of the eighteenth century, a Lunda group migrated to the Lualaba and under its king, Kazembe, carved out a virtually independent Lunda state that embraced the territories from Lake Tanganyika to the Lualaba and to the south of Lake Bangweulu. Although the Kingdom of Kazembe was a state of the Lunda Empire, it remained the strongest Lunda kingdom until 1850, bringing security to the local population of the southern Katanga but also heavy taxation, some unwarranted cruelty by Lunda governors, and restriction on the freedom of many formerly independent clans (Father Pinto, *The Kingdom of the Kazembe*). The kingdom, which succeeded because of the great prestige of the Lunda political system, has been remembered for its trade contacts with the Portuguese on the East African coast (P. J. Baptista, *The Kazembe*).

THE BEGINNINGS OF ANGOLA

At the beginning of the sixteenth century, the small chiefdom of Ndongo was founded by a wealthy smith who imposed himself as king, with the title of *ngola*, on the people of the Cuanza River. By mid-century, successive ngola had expanded the kingdom north to the Dande River, and in 1556 it became independent from Congo. From the early years, the ngola appeared to have desired contacts with the Portuguese to enrich themselves by trade and to enhance their prestige. From the 1540s on, traders visited Kabasa, the capital of Ngola, and finally, in response to the requests of the Nadambi ngola, the Portuguese court sent four Jesuit priests to Kabasa under the leadership of Paul Dias de Novais. The party arrived in May 1560, but negotiations over missions and trade languished. In 1565 Dias was sent back to Portugal to secure military assistance for the ngola, and in the following year he returned, determined to obtain a trade monopoly in Angola. With the assistance of the Jesuits, Dias was granted a *donatario*, or feudal grant, with all its rights and responsibilities. In 1571, by the terms of this grant, he received the lands south of the Cuanza but agreed to colonize Angola at his own expense (Filippo Pigafetta and Duarte López, *Paulo Dias de Novais in Angola*).

In February 1575 Dias appeared off the island of Luanda with 400 men. He settled first on the island and then moved to the mainland, where he constructed the town of Luanda. Dias was convinced that huge silver mines existed in the interior in the territory of the ngola, and was determined to seize the mines. Dias marched against the Ndongo forces in 1579, plunging Angola into forty years of continual skirmishes, raids, plunder, and pillage that finally ended with the defeat of the ngola after the Jaga had joined the Portuguese as allies. By 1622 the Portuguese appeared to have triumphed, but Nzinga, the new queen of Ndongo, renewed the war and the struggle continued (Giovanni Cavazzi, *Queen Anna Nzinga*).

The Portuguese efforts to expand the colony were hindered by the clash of entrenched interests. The Jesuit priests wanted a theocracy, and the Portuguese soldiers and *conquistadores* sought only to profit from the trade in slaves, while the home government vacillated and was ineffectual in establishing its authority. The colony itself was populated largely by exiles, convicts, and criminals—hardly the types to bring the culture of Europe to Angola. In 1641 the Dutch allied themselves with the African powers opposing the Portuguese and captured Luanda, but their occupation was brief. In 1648 Salvador de Sá y Correa arrived with a fleet from Brazil, retook Luanda, and brutally crushed the African chiefs who had supported the Dutch. In 1656 Queen Nzinga made peace with the Portuguese, maintaining her independence but abandoning Ndongo territory west of the Lukala River. Although the peace between the Portuguese and Nzinga was kept until her death in 1663, thereafter the Angolan

settlers steadily expanded, their ambitions checked only by the power of the African states in the interior. By the end of the century the colony of Angola controlled over 50,000 square miles between the Dande and the Cuanza rivers inland to the Kwango, and from Benguela all the way to the southern tip of the highlands.

The Portugese divided Angola into *presidios* (captaincies), in which the military commander was the absolute ruler. As an absolute despot he controlled the chiefdoms that were formerly ruled by the old vassal chiefs of the ngola, by settled Jaga chiefs, or by previously independent chiefs. All were now vassals of the commanders of the presidios, whose principal policy was to exploit the Africans to the fullest extent without precipitating rebellion. In addition, the three towns of Luanda, Masangano, and Benguela were ruled by town councils. (That of Luanda, the *camara*, was particularly powerful.) Responsibility for the colony lay with the governor, who acted on orders from Portugal but had to consult closely with officials and the camara. Everyone in Angola was involved directly or indirectly in the slave trade, and little distinction was made between traders and officials. Graft and corruption characterized official life, drawing the colonists into the slave trade with its spiral of violence, as they urged expansion, war, and conquest in order to acquire slaves. During the eighteenth and nineteenth centuries Angola stagnated as none sought to exploit any but human resources. At the same time, it became a predatory state in its quest for slaves. For the African, life in Angola was one of terror and misery.

So deeply entrenched a system could not be easily uprooted, and although the rise of humanitarian interests in the nineteenth century forced Portugal to abolish the slave trade in 1836, the decree was ignored and was not fully enforced until

1845—and then only by a British naval squadron. Abolition soon followed in 1858, but the spirit of slavery in Angola died hard, continuing into the twentieth century under different names. Thus after 300 years, and in spite of the claims of Portuguese occupation regarding the ability of the Portuguese to adapt themselves to Africa and to Africans, in 1850 Angola was a land whose population had been plundered in return for a few crumbling fortresses, with scarcely any visible signs of Christianity or European civilization.

THE BEGINNINGS OF MOZAMBIQUE

In March 1498 Vasco da Gama anchored in Mozambique harbor and then sailed on up the East African coast to India. Vasco da Gama was followed by other Portuguese expeditions, which culminated in that of Don Francisco de Almeida, who sailed into Mozambique in 1505 with twenty-two ships and 2,500 soldiers and sailors, forced the ruler to acknowledge the suzerainty of Portugal, and then continued northward to establish Portuguese control over the city-states of East Africa. By 1507 the Portuguese had abandoned the pretense of rule through the local chiefs and established direct control over Mozambique, which soon became the center of Portuguese authority in southeastern Africa. Nevertheless, Mozambique, which is located on the tip of an African headland that juts into the Indian Ocean, remained chiefly a revictualing station on the sea road to India. Portuguese ships called here, and the small Portuguese community looked to the sea rather than inland to the interior of Africa. Further south, however, Sofala became the center from which Portuguese traders and adventurers moved into the interior. Sofala had been occupied in 1505, and in the following year Diogo de Alcaçova reported that Sofala derived its wealth

from the interior kingdom of the mwanamutapa. Although Antonio Fernandes reached the capital of the mwanamutapa in the sixteenth century, it was not until the Arabs began to drain off the gold trade that Portugal decided to protect the trade by intervention in the hinterland beyond their coastal settlements. Accordingly, in 1531 Portuguese troops occupied Sena on the Zambezi River and a few years later established Tete further upstream, not far from the capital of the mwanamutapa. Troops and traders were soon followed by Jesuits, but after the expedition of Vasco Fernandes Homem failed to find easily worked gold mines, few Portuguese ventured into the hinterland. Thereafter, until the nineteenth century, Portugal lost interest in the interior, leaving it to the half-caste settlers who lived in barbarian isolation on their estates and a few missionaries who competed for converts at Sena, Tete, and the court of the mwanamutapa (Antonio Suárez, *The Conversion of the Monomotapa*).

COLONIZATION AND SETTLEMENT

Portuguese attempts to colonize Mozambique and Angola were confined to sending *degredados*, beggars, thieves, and political exiles to Africa, for the industrious Portuguese never seriously considered going to the colonies. There were no white women and no attempt was made to attract them, so that a large half-caste population appeared, which in Mozambique created the *prazo* system in Zambezia. The *prazeros* were half-castes who carved out feudal estates for themselves in the Zambezi Valley. A typical prazero was Antonio Vicente da Cruz, known locally as Bongo (Charles Livingstone, *The Prazeros*). Illiterate, thieving, cruel, barbarous, and a drunkard, he was a sufficiently powerful baron to defeat a Portuguese army numbering over 1,000 men that was sent against him in 1850. Gradually, by the end of the nineteenth century, the prazeros were ousted from Zambezia in favor of Portuguese *colonos*, colonists who would work and develop the land, and the chartered companies that were given exclusive rights to trade and exploit mineral resources. Neither solution was a great economic success, but both were better than the prazo system. As for the Africans, they were no worse and probably no better off than they had been under the prazeros.

In Angola, colonization took much the same form as in Mozambique, and except in Luanda and Benguela, the Portuguese lost their identity. In 1845 Benguela had 600 houses, 38 white men, and one white woman (Hermenegildo Capello and Roberto Ivens, *Benguella in 1877*). By 1900, the white population of the whole colony was less than 9,000. Poverty and degradation are perhaps the most accurate terms to describe Angola and Mozambique in the nineteenth century.

MISSIONARY EFFORTS

The Christianizing of Africans had been a cardinal policy of Portuguese expansion since the days of Henry the Navigator. Portugal's historic combat with the Moors invested it with a traditional mission to implant the faith among the heathen, while the insularity of Portugal conditioned its Catholicism with a narrow and provincial outlook. Vasco da Gama's remark, "I seek Christians and spices," was not mere rhetoric, and the most Catholic of nations regarded with pride its mission to carry Christ to Africa. Unhappily, the performance of Portuguese missionaries never matched the visions of its statesmen, and Portugal lamentably failed to Christianize Africa. The climate certainly took its toll on priests, who were never numerous; many of them had come to Africa not for Christ, but to seek their own fortunes and to satisfy their passions. The prin-

cipal reason for the failure of Portugal's missionaries was that they offered nothing to the African but a disembodied doctrine, of which many of the disciplines and disciples were distinctly distasteful. Where were the superior advantages of European civilization that went with this faith? In the slave trade, in armed incursions into the interior, in the examples of Portuguese traders who were more African than European? By the mid-nineteenth century, Mozambique had only six missionaries, and the long involvement of the Jesuit missionaries of Angola in the slave trade was a mockery of their evangelism. By 1850 only five missionaries were left in the colony. Although the numbers of Catholic missionaries increased in the twentieth century, and even Protestants were allowed to proselytize, neither group has yet understood the basic requisite for spreading Christianity in Portuguese Africa. If the African is to be drawn into a Christian community, he must be treated with Christian dignity and understanding.

SLAVE TRADE, SLAVERY, AND CONTRACT LABOR

Portuguese participation in the slave trade was neither worse nor better than that of other nations, the only distinction being that Portugal was one of the first to participate and one of the last to give it up. Portugal exploited the African not because he was African, but because he was exploitable. Between 1680 and 1836, over two million slaves, acquired from African chiefs, from pombeiros, in wars against tribes, and as refugees from intertribal strife, were taken out of Angola. Slaves were held in barracoons on the coast before being carried to Brazil. Probably ten to twenty percent died during the middle passage. By the mid-nineteenth century the slave trade was largely curtailed by the British Navy, but slavery remained until 1869, when it was officially abolished. In fact, abolition meant little, and what had formerly been recognized as slavery was now euphemistically called "forced labor," "obligation labor," or "contract labor." Although colonial officials later argued that the African could best be "civilized" through work, there is no evidence to support this rationale.

REVIVAL OF PORTUGUESE INTEREST

The European exploration, scramble, and partition of Africa stimulated new Portuguese interest in its African colonies, an interest symbolized by the Colonial Act of 1895. The new era was characterized by efforts to consolidate the administration, devise a new native policy, and develop the resources of the colonies. The task of consolidating the administration was to execute in Africa the legislation that was drawn up in Lisbon. Although the Liberal government that took power in Portugal introduced humanitarian reforms, such reforms had little effect. The attitude of the governors was frequently opposed to liberal legislation and, for the most part, the European population of the colonies remained indifferent to proposals for the emancipation of Africans. Finally, many laudable projects died for want of trained personnel to execute them.

During this period the concept developed among Portuguese colonial officials that the African was a child who must be brought up slowly to civilized adulthood. No attempt was made to understand the African or his culture, which was dismissed with pious platitudes and conventional superficialities that in the end made the "native" problem less complex but more burdensome. From this attitude arose the practices of assimilation and miscegenation. If an African Europeanized himself (or, more correctly, became a black Portuguese), he would be accepted without prejudice, so a Portuguese could take an African wife or mistress without shame. Thus, although it never became official colonial policy, miscegenation was invested with moral dignity and egalitarian significance.

PORTUGUESE AFRICA IN THE TWENTIETH CENTURY

The interest in the African colonies that was aroused in Portugal at the end of the nineteenth century could not be sustained, and by the 1920s Angola and Mozambique had once more relapsed into the lassitude that had characterized their earlier centuries of rule. This condition did not last, however, and under the regime of Antonio Oliveira da Salazar, great efforts were made to turn Angola and Mozambique into assets for the mother country. Salazar first sought to whip up enthusiasm for the colonies by recalling the great maritime traditions of the golden age of Portuguese expansion mixed with historic traditions of Lusitanian overseas policy. The colonial mystique was compounded out of the cartographic sweep of Portuguese holdings, the heroic literature of the Portuguese epic poet Camoëns, and the lure of the hidden riches of the colonies for Portugal and her subjects. The Portuguese Empire was to be a far-flung, pan-Lusitanian community held together by the spiritual bonds of Portuguese culture.

The greatest task facing Portugal was to convert this vision into reality. The foundations of the new colonial administration were laid down in the Colonial Act of 1930, which sought to unify and center the administration of the colonies at Lisbon, to nationalize the economies of the colonies, and to emphasize the sovereignty of Portugal. The colonies became provinces of Portugal and the administration in the colonies was revised to conform to that of the metropolis. A governor general supervised each colony and was responsible for the administration and operation of government. He had extensive powers, which were executed by the governors in the districts into which the colony was divided. The key men were the local administrators, who combined the judicial, executive, and legislative authority all in one. Under this pyramidal administrative organization the African was under the closest possible control—peace and calm were preserved, but enterprise and initiative were discouraged and restricted.

Out of the authoritarian purpose and mystique of the Salazar regime evolved a policy of assimilation of the Africans, which, in the past, had taken place out of mere expediency. The purpose of the policy was to eliminate the African as a separate entity so that his identity would become completely Portuguese. As one Portuguese official put it:

Our whole policy has been and continues to be to improve the cultural, economic and social level of the Negro, to give him opportunities, to drag him from his ignorance and backwardness, to try to make him a rational and honorable individual worthy of the Lusitanian community.

The policy was based on legislation first fashioned in 1926 and reinforced in 1929, 1933, and 1950. Nevertheless, assimilation remained only a dream. In spite of its humanitarian language and its proposals for social and economic service, the policy was little more than an attempt to preserve the status quo. In 1950, only 30,000 *assimilados* existed in Angola out of a population of 4 million, and only 4,353 were registered in Mozambique out of a population of 2.5 million. Any policy designed for the population as a whole that affects less than .5 percent can hardly be described as a success, in spite of the fact that, in this case, the long and traditional acceptance of the African and the products of miscegenation favored assimilation. The

very poverty of Portugal worked against assimilation. Education, which was clearly the main instrument for making the Africans Portuguese, remained selective and open only to a few. Medical services were limited, and frequently discriminatory. Christianity, like education, was a cornerstone of Portuguese civilization. Yet the number of priests and converts remained small, in spite of the protection and encouragement of the state. Moreover, if the goal of the Portuguese was assimilation, it could be achieved only through work. Although slavery and forced labor had been ended or ameliorated, the attitude that produced them had changed little. The African was still regarded as a lazy child who must be disciplined, and the best way to instill discipline was considered to be through labor. A system evolved to coerce the Africans to work, but the recruitment and contracts were often abused by the government itself, as well as by companies. In an expanding economy the need for labor was so great that such abuses were tolerated by the home government, but neither the failure to eliminate corruption nor the system itself convinced the Africans of the value of Portuguese culture.

PORTUGAL'S COLONIES IN FERMENT

The poverty of Portugal's policies in Africa was first glaringly exposed by the forces of nationalism that swept through the continent in the mid-twentieth century. First the Sudan and Ghana, next the French territories, and then the Belgian Congo and Nigeria all experienced the rise of African nationalist groups whose determined opposition, both violent and nonviolent, to colonial rule led inexorably to self-government and independence. The Portuguese colonies of Angola and Mozambique could hardly have remained immune to the nationalism on their borders. Sparked by the granting of independence to the Congo in 1960, Angolan nationalism collided with the more determined nationalism of Portugal. Proud of her long, if inept, colonial rule and convinced of her mystical role as a governing power, Portugal was intent on remaining in control of her colonies. Violence was met by force, but supported from camps in the Congo, Angolan nationalists continue to remain in the field despite attempts by Portuguese military forces to crush them. The Portuguese were determined to retain their African holdings. The first Europeans to arrive in Africa, the Portuguese were the last to leave.

Independent Angola

Organized resistance to the Portuguese began in February 1961, when urban Africans in Luanda, led by Dr. António Agostinho Neto of the Popular Movement for the Liberation of Angola (MPLA), attacked the fortress of São Paulo and the police headquarters. The assault on Luanda by the MPLA precipitated rebellion further north, where rural guerillas of the Union of Angolan Peoples (UTA), which later became the National Front for the Liberation of Angola (FNLA), led by Holden Roberto, established a revolutionary government-in-exile in the Republic of Zaïre on April 3, 1962. A third and stronger insurgency was the National Union for the Total Independence of Angola (UNITA), led by Dr. Jonas Savimbi—which was the product of a division in the original revolutionary movement of which Savimbi had been the foreign minister. The divisions in the Angolan national movement were motivated as much by ethnic and personal rivalries as by ideology, but all factions were militarily active when on April 25, 1975, the coup d'état in Lisbon occurred. This insurrection established a government determined to put an end to Portugal's African empire. After complicated negotiations with the MPLA,

FNLA, and UNITA the Portuguese agreed, on January 15, 1975, to grant independence to Angola. Independence would commence on November 11, under a coalition government led by a three-man presidential council of António Neto, Holden Roberto, and Jonas Savimbi—an unholy alliance which was soon to collapse.

Independent Angola was now a tripartite state with three rival factions, which soon collapsed into two as the FNLA merged with UNITA to form the Democratic Republic of Angola, supported by the United States and South Africa, in opposition to the Marxist-oriented MPLA, which drew its support from Luanda, Moscow, and Cuba. Cuba supplied some 15,000 troops, permitting the MPLA to seize the initiative in the struggle for control. By mid-February of 1976, the MPLA had defeated the combined forces of the FNLA and UNITA and occupied their headquarters at Huambo. Their government was declared legitimate by the Organization of African Unity (OAU) on February 11.

Independent Mozambique

The hasty retirement of the Portuguese from Angola was matched by their precipitous departure from Mozambique, a sprawling country of some 302,329 square miles. Their departure after the revolution of April 1974 reduced the Portuguese presence, which had never been great, numbering at its height some quarter of a million, to less than 50,000 by 1976, leaving the Africans (the Thonga, the Makua-Lomwé-Meta, the Yao, and a variety of ethnic groups in the north—the Makonde, Nyanjam Chewa, and Achuabo) who revived historical hostilities. Their traditional rivalries, unleashed by the withdrawal of the Portuguese, hindered the development of national unity in Mozambique.

As in Angola, Africa resistance to Portuguese authority increased as Britain and France dismantled their African empires. Liberation movements usually emerged with ethnic associations, but in Mozambique they were forged into the Mozambique Liberation Front (FRELIMO) on June 25, 1962, under the charismatic leadership of Dr. Eduardo C. Mondlane. With guerillas trained in Algeria, FRELIMO formally inaugurated its insurgency on September 25, 1964, in the province of Cabo Delgrado. Thereafter, fighting spread to Niassa, and by 1968, FRELIMO forces were operating as far south as the Zambezi river near Tete. The Portuguese response was to commit more troops to quell the FRELIMO movement, operating from their bases in southern Tanzania. On February 3, 1969, Dr. Mondlane was assassinated in Dar es Salaam, and in December 1970 the acting leader of FRELIMO, Samora Machel, assumed the presidency of the movement.

Fighting between FRELIMO and the Portuguese army continued in a desultory and inconclusive fashion until the revolution in Portugal on April 25, 1974. The revolt precipitated negotiations between the revolutionary government in Lisbon and FRELIMO, leading to an agreement in September granting independence to Mozambique on June 25, 1975. Samora Machel was installed as the first president of the People's Republic of Mozambique; he advocated the nationalization of corporate enterprises in Mozambique, and support for the liberation movement in Rhodesia.

THE RETURN OF THE SOUTHERN BANTU

At the beginning of the nineteenth century, Central Africa was invaded by the northward march of Ngoni into the highland areas from the Limpopo to Lake Tanganyika. Between 1785 and 1789 a Ngoni chief, Dingiswayo, united the independent sections of the Ngoni peoples, including the Zulu, which occupied the present-day lands of Natal. In the early nineteenth century, Shaka obtained power in one of the regiments that Dingiswayo had organized for conquest, managed the death of Dingiswayo, and made himself chief. The people he ruled became known as the Zulu. Through the military despotism he founded and by the use of his Spartan military society, Shaka sought to impose his authority on other Ngoni, subjugating some and driving others away. Fleeing from Shaka, one group of Ngoni crossed the Limpopo and laid waste to Mashoaland in their northward march to the Zambezi. Another Ngoni group, the Ndebele (also known as Matabele), led by Mzilikazi, settled on the high veld north of the Limpopo and raided far and wide over the lands between the Kalahari Desert and eastern Nashonaland (Robert Moffat, *Mzilikazi*). Meanwhile, in 1835 the main group of Ngoni crossed the Zambezi and moved on through the highlands west of Lake Nyasa as dissident segments splintered in all directions—north into Tanzania, east to the Rufiji and Ruvuma rivers, and west through the territory of the Bemba and Bisa to what is now Zambia. During their march the Ngoni pillaged and ravaged the inhabitants of Trans-Zambezia, including the remnants of the Maravi (Malawi) confederacy (A. C. P. Gamitto, *The Maravi*), disrupting their social and political patterns and making easier the European conquest that soon followed.

The Ngoni chiefs created their states by adding the conquered to the original Ngoni nucleus, but frequently the Ngoni were a minority and took wives from subject tribes, the Ngoni language thus giving way to that of the non-Ngoni mothers. Not all the Ngoni, however, lost their identity. By 1840 Mzilikazi's Ndebele established themselves north of the Matopo Hills, where the previous Ngoni groups had broken the resistance of the indigenous inhabitants, who, like the Shona, were reduced to tribute-paying vassals, whereas others were assimilated by the Ndebele. Thus the Ndebele retained their own language and customs under Mzilikazi's autocracy. By 1870, when Lobengula succeeded Mzilikazi, the Ndebele had fashioned the strongest state in Central Africa, with a highly centralized political organization supported by a powerful and well-trained army.

THE LOZI KINGDOM

Northwest of the Ndebele in Barotseland the Lozi had occupied the floodplain of the upper Zambezi. From about 1833 to 1835, however, the Kololo, another Ngoni group fleeing from Shaka, moved north and west under the leadership of Sebitwane, crossed the Zambezi, and defeated the Lozi. So long as Sebitwane lived, he was able to control Barotseland, but his successors soon lost the confidence of their subjects, and under Njekwa, the Lozi threw off Kololo domination. Njekwa and his successors continued to expand the Lozi kingdom until, under Lewanika, the Lozi exerted control over the peoples of the upper Zambezi.

DAVID LIVINGSTONE

David Livingstone set out for Africa in 1840 as a medical missionary for the London Missionary Society. He established himself at Kuruman in Bechuanaland, but he soon began to look for new sites for mission stations in the north. His passion for exploration grew out of his missionary investigations, and in 1849 he crossed the Kalahari Desert. Determined to range even further afield, he set out in 1853 to march north to the Zambezi and with the help of the Kololo chief, Sekeletu, pressed on up the river and overland to Luanda, which he reached in 1854. He remained in Luanda but soon plunged back into Africa, traversed the continent, and emerged at Quilemane on the east coast in 1855.

Livingstone returned to England a fa-

mous man, and he used his fame to open an attack on the slave trade that he had seen both in Angola and on the lower Zambezi. In order to end the slave trade, Livingstone advocated new forms of commerce and Christianity to develop "civilization" in Africa. Not only did his explorations encourage others to seek answers to the many geographical riddles of Africa (foremost among them being the source of the Nile), but Livingstone himself returned to Africa to ascend the Zambezi, which he hoped would be a "highroad" into the interior. From 1859 to 1863 he and his companions of the government-sponsored expedition pressed up the Zambezi and Shire rivers. Although he was frustrated by the rapids at Tete, Livingstone was successful in discovering Lake Nyasa and the Shire highlands, but his expedition was a failure in its principal objective—to open a way to Central Africa. Nevertheless, in spite of its failure, Livingstone's Zambezi expedition made a profound impact on the public mind of Britain. The expedition's tragic record, its revelation of new and fertile country, and its discovery of how to cut the slave trade at its source fired the public imagination and inspired a host of missionary societies to establish themselves on the fringes of Central Africa—Lake Nyasa and the Shire highlands.

MISSIONARY BEGINNINGS IN CENTRAL AFRICA

Livingstone's example inspired missionary societies in England and France to press into Central Africa to end the slave trade and to introduce Christianity and European commerce. The Universities' Mission to Central Africa (UMCA) was a direct response to Livingstone's appeal. It failed. The UMCA first established itself in the Shire highlands, but as a result of the deaths of several of its members and the lack of African response, it soon transferred its operations to

Zanzibar. Even the advance of the London Missionary Society further west from Kuruman to Inyati on the borders of Matabeleland was stalled. Malaria and the geographical obstacles to penetration checked the efforts of the missionary societies.

The death of Livingstone in 1875 revived missionary interest in penetrating into Central Africa, and the *Société des Missions Évangéliques de Paris* sent a mission to Mashonaland led by François Coillard in 1877. Barred from Matabeleland by Lobengula, Coillard founded his first mission at Sefula on the edge of the Barotse plain, and, under the patronage of the great Lozi chief Lewanika, expanded his work among the Lozi. In 1893 Coillard was followed by the Methodist missionaries under Arthur Baldwin, who founded stations among the Lozi on the Nkala River. While Coillard's French Protestants and Baldwin's Methodists were carrying on in the west, the Free Church and the Established Church of Scotland sent missionaries to Lake Nyasa, where they were joined by a Scottish commercial concern, the Livingstonia Central Africa Company, in an attempt to end the slave trade by a mixture of Victorian commerce and Christianity. Finally, in 1890, the last of the early mission societies, the Roman Catholic White Fathers, entered Central Africa from its stations in the north, in Uganda and Tanganyika, and established a station at Mambwe between lakes Nyasa and Tanganyika.

Although few in number, the European missionaries had a profound effect on Central Africa. In general, they acted independently of either European or African control. They maintained their own supply routes to the coast and even acted as traders with the African population. They tried, not infrequently by force, to impose their own concept of law and order and even sought to extend political authority over the Africans. Few of the

missionaries, no matter how consciously they tried, could abstain from meddling in African politics. In return, the missionaries brought Christianity to Central Africa. Perhaps more importantly, they brought the beginnings of modernization in the form of hospitals, schools, and European products, which dramatically changed the life of the Africans who inhabited Central Africa.

THE DEFENSE OF TRANS-ZAMBEZIA

The influx of British missionaries into Central Africa, particularly Nyasaland, became of increasing concern to the Portuguese, who possessed long-standing and traditional pretensions to the hinterland beyond the East African coast. Consequently, after 1880 the Portuguese government sought to reassert its claims. At the same time the British, heeding the pleas of the Scottish missionaries for protection, refused to recognize Portugal's sovereignty in those parts of the interior that were neither occupied by Portugal nor operating under Portuguese jurisdiction. To support the missionaries, the British government sent a consul, Henry Hamilton (later Sir Harry) Johnston, to watch over British interests in Nyasaland and to take responsibility for British relations with the African chiefs. Johnston's appointment, however, only served to stimulate countermeasures by the Portuguese. After 1884 Portuguese officials made efforts to extend their real authority to Nyasaland, and in 1887 even obtained the recognition of Portuguese sovereignty by several African chiefs. Elsewhere the Portuguese sought to hinder the passage of goods and equipment to the African Lakes Company on Lake Nyasa. These supplies included guns and ammunition to carry on the war against the Arab slave traders in Nyasaland, which effort, of course, could not be separated from the

endeavors of the Scottish missionaries and traders to consolidate their control.

Meanwhile, in Britain, the representatives of the missionaries and traders urged the British government to declare Nyasaland a protectorate. They combined the usual arguments about the economic and strategic value of Nyasaland with the prospect of losing the Africans to Catholicism if the Portuguese succeeded in making good their claims to the interior. Although the British government expressed sympathy for the position of the missionaries and provided moral support for the campaign of the African Lakes Company against the slave trade, a succession of British foreign secretaries refused to declare a protectorate over Nyasaland. By 1889 the issue clearly remained in doubt.

CECIL RHODES

The British missionaries who led the advance into Central Africa were shortly followed by British trading firms. The African Lakes Company was the vanguard of British interests in Nyasaland, whereas south of the Zambezi, in Mashona and Matabeleland, the extension of the British Empire had become the personal mission of Cecil John Rhodes. Rhodes came from England in 1871 at the age of eighteen. He first tried cotton growing, but when diamonds were discovered in Griqueland he set out for the diggings. Rhodes made his initial capital by selling food and equipment to the miners and then began to buy up the small individual claims. In 1880, in partnership with Alfred Beit, he amalgamated these small holdings into the huge DeBeers Consolidated Mining Company. Rhodes used his wealth to carry out his political ambitions. He had a passionate faith in the destiny of Englishmen to carry the torch of Anglo-Saxon civilization throughout Africa and the world, and wanted to open new territory for English settlers to colonize and

to civilize. Such territory lay beyond the Boer republics of the Orange Free State and the Transvaal. The boundaries of these republics had been fixed by the Pretoria Convention, but the Boers sought to extend their control north of the Limpopo and west of the Transvaal, an action that would, of course, frustrate Rhodes' dream of empire in the north. In 1887, Paul Kruger, President of the Transvaal, sent Piet Grobler to the Matabele capital at Bulawayo to obtain permission for the passage of Boers beyond the Limpopo. Although he concluded a treaty with Lobengula in 1887, Grobler was later killed, and Rhodes' representatives at Bulawayo subsequently won over Lobengula to sign a treaty granting Rhodes mineral rights in Matabeleland. Once armed with the consent of Lobengula to enter Matabeleland, Rhodes sought a royal charter for his company in order to acquire administrative as well as commercial powers in Central Africa.

In the past the British government had been quite reluctant to extend its responsibilities to Central Africa, whether Nyasaland or Mashonaland. Protectorates were expensive and offered little hope of immediate return, but if a commercial company agreed to undertake the onerous financial and administrative burden in return for commercial exploitation, the British government welcomed such assistance to maintain British interests in the region. Thus, when Rhodes arrived in London in 1889, enormously rich and politically successful, he offered to pay for the colonization and administration of Bechuanaland and Matabeleland and to push telegraph and rail lines northward. He further agreed to obtain for Britain the territory north of the Zambezi, including Nyasaland. The British Prime Minister, Lord Salisbury, agreed to let Rhodes expend his fortune for the extension of the British Empire. Rhodes' company was chartered as the British

South African Company, with authority to colonize and govern the territories north of the Limpopo. In addition, Rhodes agreed to support the activities of Harry Johnston in Nyasaland.

NYASALAND, NORTHEASTERN, AND NORTHWESTERN RHODESIA

Between 1889 and 1890 Johnston traveled up the Shire Valley and along Lake Nyasa, making treaties with African chiefs and encouraging the British missionaries and traders. His efforts were rewarded in 1890 when Lord Salisbury sent a gunboat to Mozambique and ordered the Portuguese to remove their troops from Mashonaland and the Shire highlands. Portugal submitted, and Harry Johnston returned in 1891 as "Her Majesty's Commissioner and Consul General to the territories under British influence to the north of the Zambezi," with instructions to declare a British protectorate over the Shire highlands, thereby frustrating the designs of Portugal. With the assistance of Alfred Sharpe and the well-known African explorer Joseph Thomson, he negotiated a host of treaties with chiefs between Lake Nyasa and Mweru that could be used to support British claims if challenged by European rivals. While Johnston was extending the British Empire in the Shire Valley and Lake Nyasa, Rhodes' representative, Frank Lochner, obtained the signature of Lewanika, the Lozi king, to a treaty forfeiting control of Barotseland and its mineral rights to the British South Africa Company. Although Lewanika did not appreciate the full extent of his action, the Lochner treaty gave the company a claim to rule in western Trans-Zambezia and to exploit the rich copper deposits. Thus in 1891 Trans-Zambezia was divided into three protectorates: Nyasaland (known as the British Central African Protectorate), northeastern Rhodesia, and northwestern Rhodesia. Johnston governed both Nyasaland and

northeastern Rhodesia from Zomba in the Shire highlands, while agents of the British South Africa Company administered the land of the Lozi, Barotseland (northwestern Rhodesia). By employing Sikh soldiers recruited in India, Johnston was able to pacify and consolidate British administration in Nyasaland. He believed that tropical Africa "must be ruled by whites, developed by Indians, and worked by the Blacks." He therefore encouraged the settlement of European colonists and introduced Asians to organize the commercial life of Nyasaland. Meanwhile, the British South Africa Company gradually took over the administration of northwestern Rhodesia and, by governing directly, eclipsed the Lunda state of Kazembe and the Ngoni state under Mpexeni. By 1901 all the inhabitants of the lands north of the Zambezi were British subjects governed by the agents of the British South Africa Company.

THE CREATION OF SOUTHERN RHODESIA

Having extended British influence into Barotseland and northeastern Rhodesia, Rhodes was determined to occupy Matabeleland and Mashonaland. Despite the agreements and treaties he had signed with prospectors and Rhodes' agents, Lobengula retained undisputed control of the lands between the Limpopo and the Zambezi. His fearsome and powerful Ndebele *impis*, or raiding parties, ranged widely over Central Africa, exacting tribute and submission to Lobengula. Rhodes sought to break Lobengula's control of the Mashona plateau by sending in settlers who would consolidate British control against any attempts, either by the Portuguese to press inland from the east, or by the Boers to come from the south in the hope of discovering gold. Led by Colonel Leander Starr Jameson, and guided by the great hunter

Frederick Courtney Selous, the specially selected pioneer column guarded by some 500 company policemen marched into Matabeleland, bypassed Lobengula's capital of Bulawayo, and pressed northward to found Fort Salisbury in the heart of Mashonaland. Declaring Mashonaland British, the pioneers were soon joined by other white Europeans, who forcefully acquired *Shona* lands.

Mashonaland never fulfilled the expectations of the settlers. Its soil was unsuited to intensive farming or grazing, and workable gold deposits were not discovered. Moreover, the expense of transporting goods from South Africa was exorbitant, making the position of the settlers virtually untenable. Consequently, the pioneers began to press into Matabeleland, where they hoped to find the gold and grazing they had failed to discover in Mashonaland. Lobengula and his Ndebele opposed the probings of the settlers. They feared that the white prospectors would take their land, and they resented the protection the Europeans gave to the Shona, whom the Ndebele considered their traditional vassals. In 1893 a large Ndebele impi raided Mashonaland, pillaging not only the Shona but the farms and livestock of white farmers. Several Africans were killed, but no whites lost their lives, although the inhabitants of Fort Victoria were terrorized by roaming Ndebele warriors. Jameson, who was charged with administering the colony, ordered the impi to leave. When it tarried, the settlers attacked the Ndebele, driving them back to Bulawayo. Although the British government refused to encourage aggressive action, the settlers, supported by the British South Africa Company's mounted police, advanced into Matabeleland late in 1893. After several skirmishes and a few desultory battles, Bulawayo was captured and Lobengula was driven to the north, where he died in 1894. His followers made peace. This ended the Ndebele's first revolt, but not their resistance.

Although various assurances concerning their treatment had been given by Jameson at the time of their surrender, the Ndebele soon found themselves herded into reserves where the soil was the least fertile and water scarce, their best land having been taken by the settlers. The settlers also seized Ndebele cattle as reparations and forced the Ndebele to work on their farms so that they could pay the taxes imposed by the administration. Humiliated and resentful, the Ndebele were attracted to the leaders of a revitalized religious cult who used their widespread following to unite the Ndebele and Shona peoples behind a mass revolt against white rule in 1896. At first only the Ndebele rebelled, but their success in destroying European farms and besieging European towns led the Shona to rise in the north. The company and settlers fought back on two fronts to regain their undisputed control of Rhodesia. In July the Ndebele were crushingly defeated, but fought on from the safety of the Matopo Hills until Cecil Rhodes personally persuaded the Ndebele chiefs to surrender and accept the rule of the British South Africa Company (Ndansi Kumalo, *The Matabele Rebellion*). In the north, the Shona rebellion dragged on until the following year before the chiefs were captured and the Shona warriors were hunted down. By the end of 1897, the white settlers had demonstrated their superiority, Rhodesia had been conquered and occupied, and the settlers began to govern themselves under the paternal rule of the British South Africa Company - theoretically as a colony of the British Empire. Although the superior military power of the British almost ensured their defeat, the Ndebele-Shona uprising forced Rhodes to acquiesce to many of the demands of the Ndebele chiefs before they would surrender. Moreover, the limited success achieved by the united Ndebele people was not forgotten by subsequent nationalist leaders.

CENTRAL AFRICA UNDER COLONIAL RULE

Controlled by the British South Africa Company following the pacification, the Rhodesias were carved up into large reserves (usually of the least desirable land) for the Africans, while well-watered land near the railway was alienated for European settlement. The policy of the company was to segregate Africans and Europeans, assuming that those Africans who "squatted" on European lands or who sought employment on the farms or in the cities were temporary residents. To control the movements of Africans, "passes" or identification certificates were issued and laws were passed to maintain segregation. Although the number of Europeans in Nyasaland was never so great as in the Rhodesias, the alienation of land followed a similar process, so that the Africans soon found themselves paying rent on land where they had possessed security of tenure.

Once the white settlers had acquired large land holdings, they required labor to work their farms. As in East Africa, the settlers argued that the employment of Africans presented a "civilizing influence" and persuaded the government to institute means to force the Africans to work for the settlers. This was usually accomplished by taxing the Africans, who were then forced to labor for the Europeans in order to earn the wherewithal to pay their taxes. In Nyasaland tax defaulters' huts were burned or their wives seized as hostages. In Southern Rhodesia the company pressed the chiefs to supply labor for the European farms. Thus gradually throughout Central Africa the Africans offered their labor for European services to acquire cash for taxes and new wants.

Soon the European settlers began to form themselves into pressure groups— local chambers of commerce or planters' associations—to demand representation in the legislative councils of the colonial administration. Although the settlers were accorded a certain amount of satisfaction, in Northern Rhodesia and Nyasaland their demands for increasing authority were resisted by the colonial administrators, who were frequently the only defenders of African rights. In Southern Rhodesia, however, the white settlers had possessed a large say in governing the colony from its inception, and in 1907 they obtained a majority of seats in the legislative council and urged the company to administer the country on their behalf.

Although the Africans had been forced to submit to European rule, they continually protested their subordinate role. Throughout the Rhodesias and Nyasaland the principal means of protest were African separatist churches, where millennial preachers sought to lead their followers to the kingdom beyond colonialism and promised an independent, tax-free Africa. Perhaps the most influential was John Chilembwe of Nyasaland, who openly opposed the measures that he regarded as intolerable for the Nyasas. He spoke out against taxes and protested the use of African troops to fight Europe's wars. Establishing a chain of churches and schools, he led his followers in an unsuccessful uprising against British rule in Nyasaland in 1915. Although he failed, Chilembwe had made it perfectly clear to those who cared that in Central Africa the Africans were not happy under British rule. In Northern Rhodesia, the African Watch Tower or Kitawala movement acted as a similar organization of discontent, which spoke of the end of the world and the destruction of colonial rule. Although not openly rebelling, the Watch Tower movement continued to offer a millennarian solution to the economic, political, and social subordination to European colonial rule.

CENTRAL AFRICA BETWEEN THE WARS

Following World War I and the influx of veterans to Central Africa, white settlers in each of the territories sought greater control. In Southern Rhodesia the settlers had voted in favor of home rule in 1922, and in the following year the British government formally annexed the colony, ending the rule of the British South Africa Company. Permitted to rule their own internal affairs, the settlers sought to frame racial policies designed to meet the interests of the settler community. Thus in the Land Apportionment Act of 1930, Africans were prohibited from living in European areas, except singly or in specific locations. Beyond in the reserves, pressure on the land continued to mount at an alarming rate. In 1931 half of the 96 million acres of Southern Rhodesia were controlled by 50,000 whites, whereas about a million Africans possessed rights to 28 million acres. Yet without African labor, Central Africa could not have been developed. The Africans dug for minerals and harvested the tobacco crop that provided Southern Rhodesia with capital for development but nevertheless remained second-class citizens. Dr. Godfrey Huggins (later Lord Malvern), Prime Minister of Southern Rhodesia from 1933 to 1953, was the creator of the "two pyramid" scheme of racial development based on strict segregation, which was enforced by the "pass" laws (Lord Bledisloe, *Native Policy in Rhodesia*, *1938*).

During the years before World War II the settlers of Central Africa sought to amalgamate the Rhodesias and Nyasaland. In 1936 representatives of the settler community met at Victoria Falls and agreed to work toward that end. Although Huggins and others urged amalgamation, a royal commission sent to study the matter found that liberal Europeans and Africans opposed any arrangement that would allow settlers to rule the protected peoples of Northern Rhodesia and Nyasaland. The issue was deferred.

While the south fell increasingly under the control of its European settlers, Northern Rhodesia was dramatically transformed by the beginning of a great mining industry. After 1924 the development of the rich copper deposits created mining towns that attracted both European and African labor. New towns sprang up; the industry boomed, survived the depression, and during World War II brought great wealth to Northern Rhodesia. Yet the growth of the copper belt created as sharp a pattern of discrimination as that experienced in the agricultural south.

THE STIRRINGS OF AFRICAN NATIONALISM IN CENTRAL AFRICA

Despite the bitter opposition of African leaders, the two Rhodesias and Nyasaland were at last forged into a federation in which there was to be a partnership between white and black. There were, to be sure, great economic advantages in the federation of Central Africa, but politically it meant the entrenchment of white rule throughout Nyasaland and Northern Rhodesia as well as in the south. In the autumn of 1953, the federation was made official, but ironically, instead of ensuring white domination, it hastened the time when Nyasaland and Northern Rhodesia would govern themselves.

In 1958 nationalists from all over Africa met at Accra to attend the first All-African Peoples' Conference. Both Hastings Banda and Kenneth Kaunda attended and departed determined to break up the Central African Federation and struggle for independence by force if necessary. Throughout 1959 tension and

militant agitation swept through Nyasaland and Northern Rhodesia. Mission
buildings were burned, property was destroyed, and police were stoned. Discontent escalated into open violence, which
was stopped only by the appearance of
Rhodesian troops in Nyasaland and the
arrest of Banda. Nevertheless, the violence marked only the beginning, not
the end, of African nationalism. Banda,
leading his new Malawi Congress Party,
and Kaunda, with his United National
Independence Party, soon won victory in
the elections, toppling in the process the
structure of the Central African Federation, and leading to the complete independence of Northern Rhodesia, called
Zambia, and Nyasaland, known as Malawi, in 1964.

INDEPENDENT ZAMBIA

Unlike Southern Rhodesia, the other
creation of Cecil Rhodes, Northern Rhodesia never attracted any significant European population; the whites there
numbered less than 4,000. Demands for
self-government could never be justified,
as they might be by the Europeans of
Southern Rhodesia. In fact, Northern
Rhodesia proved a constant liability, if
not an embarrassment, to Rhodes' British South Africa Company, which was
only too willing to transfer its jurisdiction
and administrative expenses to the British Colonial Office at the end of the First
World War.

Nevertheless, Cecil Rhodes' infatua-
tion with the northern territories across
the Zambezi served as proof of his pres-
cience long after his death in March
1902; in 1925, extensive deposits of copper were discovered in Northern Rhodesia, establishing the fabled "Copperbelt." The Copperbelt may not have
been as impressive as the holdings of the
DeBeers Consolidated Mining Company
or the gold of the Witswatersrand, but it
transformed what was regarded as an
economic backwater into a source of the

astounding productive mineral wealth of
southern Africa. The technology needed
to extract the copper not only brought in
an influx of Europeans, but the capital to
exploit and develop the mines and to
expand the colony's economy. The development of the copper-mining industry created, however, the two central
issues of modern Zambia: the relationship between the expanding European community and the Colonial Office
on the one hand; and the Europeans'
relationship with the Africans on the
other. As in all the settler colonies, land
was the principal issue, for, just as in
Southern Rhodesia, Europeans drifted
away from the mines to farm the land.
The differences between concepts of African land tenure and the freehold principles of the Europeans were made more
acute with the federation of the three
territories of Northern Rhodesia, Southern Rhodesia, and Nyasaland (Malawi)
in 1953. The federation may have made
economic sense, but it was vigorously
opposed by an overwhelming majority of
Africans, who ultimately prevailed upon
the British Government to terminate the
ill-fated venture on December 31, 1963.

During the years of federation, however, the government of Northern Rhodesia underwent increasing Africanization. The process began, as is usual, with
a modest African representation in the
Legislative Council in 1948, but the African presence in the Council steadily
expanded, ultimately leading to a review
of the constitution in December 1960.
After protracted negotiations in September 1962, a new constitution was instituted; it decreed the dissolution of the
federation on December 31, 1963. Elections for the new government followed
swiftly thereafter, and the United National Independence Party (UNIP), led
by Kenneth Kaunda, rose to power, still
under the terms of the new constitution.
On October 24, 1964, Northern Rhodesia became the Republic of Zambia

under President Kaunda, who remains the republic's president to this day.

INDEPENDENT ZIMBABWE

In Zimbabwe the major issues before independence had been land and the monopoly of power by the white settlers. The settlers, who started arriving in the 1890s, had seized about half the land owned by Africans. By the time of independence, they controlled huge estates producing tobacco, maize, tea, cattle, and other products, and employing several hundred thousand landless black farm labourers.

Meanwhile, the other, generally poorer, half of the country had been designated as Tribal Trust Lands by the settler regime. About four million people lived on small plots in these lands. Most of the families there were unable to make a living from their plots alone, so they were forced to send family members to the mines or the towns in order to make ends meet. Thus, the migratory labour pattern that is characteristic of South Africa also developed in Zimbabwe.

This state of affairs had led in the 1950s to the emergence of the first nationalist movement, which was called the African National Congress and led by Joshua Nkomo. Its name was later changed to the Zimbabwe African Peoples Union (ZAPU). ZAPU agitated for peaceful change, but the whites, though at first flirting with moderation, became intransigent and moved to the right as African demands became more and more insistent. They supported the Rhodesian Front led by Ian Smith, who vowed never to allow majority rule in his lifetime.

Upon the dissolution of the Central African Federation in 1963, Southern Rhodesia sought to formalize its independent status under the name of Rhodesia. Tensions with Britain were exacerbated by the fact that the British

government was also negotiating about independence with Malawi and Zambia, the two other former members of the abortive federation. The white-settler community of Rhodesia was determined to remain in control after independence; the African nationalists were equally eager for autonomy, but on the condition of universal suffrage—which would, of course, mean African majority rule. The British government assumed its usual compromise position; it was in favor of the gradual extension of the franchise, leading ultimately to African rule. This policy, which was framed in amendments to the Rhodesian constitution, was anathema to the white community.

Meanwhile, on the nationalist side, younger people, such as Robert Mugabe, became concerned about the moderate stance taken by Nkomo. In 1963, they broke away from ZAPU and formed the Zimbabwe African National Union (ZANU); subsequently they began to prepare for guerrilla warfare. It was against this background that the white parliament voted on November 11, 1965 for the Unilateral Declaration of Independence (UDI). The ostensible reason for UDI was, of course, the preservation of the system of white domination. Both ZANU and ZAPU responded by sending guerrilla raids in the hope that Britain would intervene to stop the resulting chaos, as it had in Guyana, Malaya, and other colonies. Britain did not, however, intervene; the guerrillas were crushed and their leaders detained.

The declaration of UDI had also precipitated intense demands by the African states that the British government restore the original unamended Rhodesian constitution, by force if necessary. These demands were rejected by the British government, which resorted to limited economic sanctions, a palliative which satisfied no one. Once again, protracted but futile negotiations were conducted, with the Rhodesians rejecting the constitutional compromise of the British Prime Minister, Harold Wilson, in late 1966. Negotiations continued, but resulted only in embarrassing failure as the Rhodesian electorate, which consisted of 92% white residents, approved the establishment of the Republic of Rhodesia. The founding of the republic was officially announced on March 3, 1970. The British government condemned the action as illegal, and the Security Council of the United Nations called on its members not to recognize any actions by the Rhodesian government.

During UDI, the Rhodesian Government had been dominated by the Rhodesian Front Party (RFP), which advocated racial separation and the defense of white-settler political and economic privileges. Although there had been a moderate, multiracial Center Party established in 1968, it never commanded any significant support, as political power in Rhodesia shifted increasingly to the African nationalists. The Africans, however, were more divided among themselves than the more monolithic white community. African political parties included not only ZAPU and ZANU, but the Front for the Liberation of Zimbabwe (FROLIZI). They were consolidated in a tenuous alliance on December 7, 1974, as the African National Council, under the leadership of Bishop Abel Muzorewa, who was later replaced by Joshua Nkomo, leader of ZAPU, in September 1975 (*Zimbabwe Declaration of Unity*, Lusaka, December 7 and 11, 1974).

By 1971 the Rhodesian government had found itself increasingly isolated and besieged by regional and international political pressure, the demands of African nationalists, and the increasing activity of African guerillas operating on the borders and within Rhodesia itself. In late 1972, the second Chimurenga, or war of national liberation, began in earnest. (The first was the 1896-7 revolt.)

Fruitless discussions continued with the British government, while members of the African National Council (ANC), who formed the core of the African opposition to Ian Smith's regime, were subjected to increasing harassment and imprisonment. Riots followed at the University of Rhodesia, and there was general unrest throughout the countryside. Nevertheless, negotiations between Ian Smith and the ANC continued throughout 1974, 1975, and 1976, but without success, while external pressure upon the Rhodesian government intensified as guerilla forces operated from Mozambique and Zambia with increased intensity.

The destabilisation caused by guerrilla activity aroused concern in both Britain and the U.S. They were not motivated merely by humanitarian considerations, but also by the concern that continued conflict in the region might be exploited by the Eastern bloc for its own purposes. It was felt that a prolonged war might very well result in the emergence of a radical regime which would pose a threat to foreign investment. Both countries, therefore, saw the person of Ian Smith as an obstruction to an orderly transition to moderate black rule. South Africa also wanted to do away with Smith so as to secure a larger national market for its manufactured and agricultural products.

All these pressures combined in late 1976 to force Smith to the negotiating table. He had earlier been compelled to release leading nationalists, including Mugabe and Nkomo, from detention. Meanwhile ZANU and ZAPU had joined in an alliance as the Patriotic Front (PF) that same year. They refused to consider any settlement that did not guarantee radical land reforms and political reform based on universal suffrage. Smith, on his part, was not negotiating in good faith; his army was at the same time launching raids on ZANU camps inside Mozambique.

In an attempt to come to a settlement with Smith, Bishop Abel Muzorewa signed the so-called "Internal Settlement" agreement. In the early 1970s, while the major ZANU and ZAPU leaders were either in detention or in exile, the bishop had attained genuine stature as a nationalist. But after the release of Robert Mugabe, Joshua Nkomo, and other nationalist leaders, his popularity, as well as that of the Rev. Ndabaningi Sithole, one of the first militant nationalists, began to wane. It was against this background that they decided to reach out to Smith. In March 1978, Muzorewa signed the "Internal Settlement" agreement, which gave him the trappings of political power, while the substance remained with the white minority.

After coming to power, Muzorewa abolished some remaining petty apartheid restrictions. He did not, however, make significant advances toward land reform. Muzorewa had hoped that fighting would stop if a black government came to power, but the war continued to drag on. In the event, Britain decided to bring both parties to a negotiating table at the Lancaster House conference in London in 1978. Muzorewa and Smith attended in a joint delegation.

Both sides were reluctant to go to the conference. Despite the reluctance, however, Lord Carrington, the British Foreign Secretary, was determined to reach agreement among all parties on a new constitution. Muzorewa and Smith agreed to the new constitution because it was to their mutual advantage. The Patriotic Front objected, especially to the reservation of twenty seats (out of 100) in the new parliament for whites, to be elected only by whites, who at that time consituted only three or four percent of the population. The PF was forced, however, to accept the constitution because Rhodesian raids were becoming ruinous, and their African collaborators were applying pressure on them to come to a settlement.

Following the signing of the Lancaster House agreement, Britain assumed control of Rhodesia in mid-December 1979, and Lord Christopher Soames was placed in charge as governor of the breakaway colony. Joshua Nkomo returned in mid-January 1980; two weeks later, Robert Mugabe followed him. Both ZANU and ZAPU opened offices immediately and began campaigning soon afterwards. White Rhodesians, as well as the British, were surprised at the level of support the two parties were attracting—especially ZANU, which was considered the more radical of the two. They, therefore, began to conspire to keep ZANU from power. The opportunity came when ZANU's Central Committee turned down Nkomo's plea that the PF wartime alliance be maintained through the election period.

The division within the PF gave the British authorities and the Rhodesian whites their chance. They expected that ZANU would win thirty to thirty-five seats, and Nkomo and Bishop Muzorewa twenty to twenty-five each, while the whites would have their twenty seats reserved for them. Lord Soames would then put together a coalition among Nkomo, Muzorewa and Smith, with Nkomo as Prime Minister. According to this plan, ZANU would then be kept from power even if it won forty or more of the eighty black seats. When the election results were announced on March 4, 1980, however, Lord Soames had no choice but to ask Mugabe to form the first government of independent Zimbabwe. His ZANU had won fifty-seven seats, while ZAPU had won twenty, and Bishop Muzorewa only three seats.

Mugabe formed a government of national unity that included ZAPU and the whites. The most pressing task facing him at independence was the reconciliation of the three separate armies. With the assistance of some senior white officers and British military instructors, the government was able to integrate these forces into a National Army of Zimbabwe. The government also promoted reconciliation to prevent the kind of white exodus that had taken place in the former Portuguese colonies of Mozambique and Angola. A wholesale departure of whites would have resulted in chaos, as the white population monopolized the skilled technical and managerial positions in the economy.

The result of this policy was that the economy grew by eight percent in 1980, and five percent in 1981. In 1982, when the world recession and a continent-wide drought hit Zimbabwe, its economy was strong enough to survive the crisis. This economic stability and growth enabled the government to carry out many reforms. It abolished school fees, provided increased facilities for secondary education, and rebuilt the rural schools which had been destroyed during the war of independence. In the first year alone the number of school children increased from 800,000 to 1.3 million. The government also abolished fees for health care for the very poor, and implemented a minimum wage. Despite this initial success, the government faced enormous problems. By 1982 its land reform program had not yet been fully implemented; only ten thousand families had been resettled. This constituted a continuing source of concern to the government.

Far more serious than the slow progress in land reform was, however, the 1982 split between ZANU and ZAPU. In February 1982, the Prime Minister announced that huge caches of arms were uncovered on farms that belonged to Joshua Nkomo's ZAPU; he accused Nkomo and ZAPU leaders of planning to overthrow his government. This was followed up by the dismissal of Nkomo from his cabinet post. Immediately after this, former Zapu guerrillas deserted from the army and began to carry out campaigns of violence and killings. Meanwhile, after briefly fleeing the country, Nkomo returned on the assurance that the government intended no harm to him. Apart from this unfortunate incident, reconciliation between blacks and whites was remarkably successful, demonstrating that liberation is not inevitably accompanied by an apocalyptic racial bloodbath and economic collapse.

1 OLFERT DAPPER
THE KINGDOM OF CONGO

Olfert Dapper (1636–1689) was a Dutch geographer who wrote one of the best seventeenth-century accounts of Africa. He acquired his information firsthand from Dutchmen who had traded and fought along the coast of western Africa. He describes in this selection three critical periods in the history of the kingdom of Congo: the introduction and impact of Christianity, the invasion of the Jaga, and the rebellion of the Count of Soyo at the time when the kingdom was disintegrating. The introduction of Christianity into the kingdom of Congo was one of the most fascinating but futile experiments in European-African relations. In 1568 the Jaga crossed the Kwango River, defeated the Congolese army, and destroyed the capital of San Salvador. Although their origins are still unknown, the Jaga probably had some connection with the Luba-Lunda peoples of the interior. The Jaga were cannibals but not savages, for after sacking the kingdom of Congo, they retired to the south and east, where they founded states. Located at the mouth of the Congo River, Soyo was one of the six provinces of the kingdom of Congo that was ruled by a governor who was originally removable at the king's pleasure, but after 1491 the office became hereditary in the lineage of the then-ruling governor, who later took the Portuguese title of count.

CHRISTIANITY IN THE CONGO

Before the Portuguese entered the land of Congo, the inhabitants were extremely idolatrous, and each one fabricated a god to his own fancy. The Congolese adored dragons, serpents of a prodigious girth, billygoats, tigers, and other ferocious beasts, imagining that the honors they accorded them would stop them from doing harm. Birds, grass, trees, even the skins of animals filled with straw were the object of their cult. Their religious ceremonies consisted of genuflections and prostrations. They covered their heads with dust and offered to the idols whatever was most precious to them. Finally, about two centuries ago, Christianity (or at least a semblance of the Christian religion) was introduced into the kingdom.

In the year 1484 Dom João II, the Portuguese king who sponsored the discoveries of the coasts of Africa and the route to India, had a fleet equipped under the leadership of Diogo Cão, who, having ar-

From Olfert Dapper, *Description de l'Afrique* (Amsterdam: Wolfgang, Weesekerge, Boom, and Van Someren, 1686), trans. by Nell Elizabeth Painter and Robert O. Collins, pp. 355–358. Material in brackets has been supplied by Professor Collins.

rived at the mouth of the Zaïre [Congo] and having learned from the signs made by the few Negroes whom he met on the coast that there was a powerful king in the interior, sent some of his people to him. But seeing that they did not come back, he took with him four Congolese who seemed intelligent and promised to bring them back in fifteen moons. The King of Portugal looked kindly upon these foreigners, and having had them taught the language and religion, he sent them back with presents under the same pilot. When he was once again anchored at the mouth of the Zaïre, Diogo Cão sent one of these Negroes to the King of Congo to beg him to send back his Portuguese to him because he had brought back the Congolese, as he had promised.

During their stay in that land, the Portuguese had so put themselves in the good graces of the Count of Soyo, the uncle of the king, and had impressed him with such a great horror of idolatry and such a vivid interest in our mysteries that the prince went to find his nephew, the king, and strongly encouraged him to abandon pagan superstitions and to embrace Christianity. Because the king was half-convinced, he asked Diogo to bring Cacuta, one of the four Negroes who had been with him in Portugal, so that, acting as his ambassador, Cacuta would ask King Dom João for priests to instruct his people. Cacuta learned Portuguese and Christianity so well that he was baptized with his followers. He left King João, after having received a thousand signs of friendship, and brought back with him priests, images, crosses, and other church ornaments, whose novelty was received by the Negroes with great admiration and pleasure.

The first to receive baptism in the country were the Count of Soyo and his son, who were baptized on Christmas Day of the year 1491. The count was given the name Emmanuel and his son was named Anthony. The king, his wife, and the younger of their children did the same and took the names of the House of Portugal. Thus, the king was named João, the Queen Eleonor, and their son Affonso. A great many people of both sexes followed the example of their princes, and since then the Portuguese have expended much effort to banish pagan idolatry among these people. That is why they established several posts for schoolmasters who would teach reading, writing, and the principles of religion and that is why they support many Portuguese and mulatto priests who celebrate the mysteries according to the ceremonies of the Latin Church. But even though the majority of these Negroes outwardly profess to be Christians, the greater number are still idolatrous in their hearts and secretly worship false gods, tigers, leopards, and wolves, imagining that in this way they will escape feeling the effects of their fury. They are straightforward hypocrites who act like Christians only in the presence of Europeans and who have more respect for their king than they do for the true God. Those who live around the churches and under the gaze of the Portuguese have their marriages blessed by the priest, but they are not willing to go very far to seek this benediction; furthermore, even those who receive it do not in the least admit to the condition under which it is given, and they take as many concubines as they can feed.

The Negroes of Soyo are Christians of the same strength; they all have two strings in their bows—the Catholic religion and paganism, and when the saints do not answer their prayers, they invoke the fetishes. Yet to see them all covered with crosses and rosaries one would take them for sanctimonious people. Many churches and many Negro and mulatto priests are found in their province. When the Count of Soyo goes to mass, he dresses himself superbly and wears golden chains and collars of coral. He marches pompously to the sound of drums and horns, surrounded by guards among whom there are five or six musketeers who fire from time to time and others who carry flags and are followed by a great crowd of people.

Between 1644 and 1647, at the request of the King of Congo, the Pope sent a mission of Capuchins from Sicily and Cabis to that country. As the Capuchins entered Soyo, the count kept a few of them, and the others spread throughout the kingdom of Congo. The Negroes of the province of Oando [Luanda] are good Christians, according to what they say; at least great care is taken to make good Catholics of them. There are churches, Negro schoolmasters, and priests who baptize and say mass.

THE JAGA INVASION, c.1570

During the time of Alvarez I, successor and son-in-law of Dom Diogo, the last prince of the old family of the kings of Congo, the Jagas of Ansico and Angola brought the kingdom close to ruin. These Jagas are people without faith, king, or religion—wandering nomads of the plains, or rather robbers of the open road, like the Arabs. First they crossed the province of Mbata and put it all in blood and flames.[1] Then they came to camp on the plain before San Salvador. They defeated Dom Alvarez in an ordered battle and forced him to retreat into the city with great losses. But the prince, not feeling safe within the walled city, abandoned his capital to be pillaged and fled to a small island called *Ilhas das Cavallas,* because horses are found there. He took with him a great many Portuguese and the principal lords of the land. As masters of the city, the barbarians reduced it and the churches to ashes and took a great many men prisoners and subsequently killed and ate them. During these disasters, the land was uncultivated and the peasants hid themselves in the forests and mountains; consequently, food became so expensive that a slave worth ten crowns was sold for a loaf of bread. Most of the peasants died of hunger and the others sold themselves to the Portuguese, who shipped them to the island of São Tomé. Thus princes of the blood and lords of the kingdom found themselves reduced to the condition of slaves. Of those who sought refuge on the island, nearly all died of sickness because of the stench of the air. The king contracted dropsy, from which he never fully recovered, and which left him with swollen legs for the rest of his days.[2]

Seeing no other remedy for his miseries, the king finally resolved to send an ambassador to Portugal to implore King Dom Sebastian to send help, which he agreed to do, preparing a regiment of six hundred men. When several gentlemen and volunteers had joined the group, the captain of the squadron, Francisco de Gouvea, set out for Africa. Having called at the island of São Tomé and having furnished themselves with arms and provisions, they went to get the King of Congo, his men, and a few horses that were found on the

Ilhas das Cavallas. They immediately put down on dry land. There were several battles between the Jagas and the Portuguese, in which the barbarians suffered more and fled, frightened by the discharges of the muskets and the noise and fire of the cannon. Even so, one-and-one-half years were needed to clear the country of these brigands and to reestablish the King of Congo to his kingdom. Put back on his throne, this prince was so grateful to the King of Portugal, his benefactor, that he sent him an ambassador to thank him and to ask for priests to reestablish Christianity in the lands belonging to him. He gave them letters in which he offered to become a vassal of the Portuguese crown and to pay an annual tribute in slaves, but Dom Sebastian graciously refused and sent him a very obliging response in which he addressed him as brother and said that he would be satisfied if only he would constantly preserve the Christian religion. After four years had passed and Francisco de Gouvea saw that he was no longer necessary in Congo, he left several Europeans who had come there with him and returned to Portugal.

WAR BETWEEN THE KING OF CONGO AND THE COUNT OF SOYO

The Count of Soyo is the most powerful vassal of the King of Congo, but he is not the most faithful or the most subject. Because the forest of Findemguolla encompassing his states serves as a strong bulwark and renders him nearly inaccessible to a great army, this count no longer wants to recognize the King of Congo as his sovereign and believes that he should be given the status of an ally. This was the count who, at the instigation of the Portuguese, set fire to the stores of the Dutch East India Company; but when the States-General [of the Netherlands] made themselves masters of Luanda São Paulo in the year 1643, he was obliged to reestablish these stores.

---

[1] Mbata was the eastern province of the kingdom of Congo (ed.).
[2] Probably edema of swelling caused by an abnormal accumulation of fluid in the interfibrillar tissue (ed.).

In the year 1636, a war took place between the King of Congo, Dom Alvarez II by name, and the Count of Soyo. Having raised troops and received a reinforcement of eighty Portuguese commanded by the Governor of Luanda São Paulo, the king wanted to invade the lands of the count, but this invasion was not as easy as he had thought, because the people of Soyo set up an ambush in the woods, surprised him, cut his army to pieces, and took the king to their master as a prisoner. To buy back his freedom, the king was forced to cede divers lands to the count. Of these the most important was the principality of Mocato. The following year, the king wanted revenge and put a new army into the field but was defeated a second time. These two victories gratified the people of Soyo and their count, but the self-esteem of the Congolese was undiminished, and they blamed their misfortune on the imprudence of Dom Alvarez, who despised his enemy out of false bravado. Instead of overwhelming him with a multitude of countless soldiers, which he could have raised from his lands, Dom Alvarez attacked his foe with weak forces. Thus these two battles, instead of producing peace, sowed the seeds of a longer and more bloody war between these two princes in the year 1641, the occasion of which I will describe.

Dom Daniel de Silva, son of Dom Michel, Count of Soyo, seeing himself excluded from paternal succession by a powerful intrigue, retired into the lands of the Duke of Bamba [province of kingdom of Congo], where he was poorly received. In time, the enemies of Dom Daniel died, and he was recalled and reestablished himself in Soyo with the good wishes of all the people. Dom Daniel may have wanted revenge or he may have been using the bitterness between himself and the Duke [of Bamba] as a pretext to break away and become independent; in any case, Dom Daniel neglected to go pay homage and did not ask for confirmation from the King of Congo, saying that his birth and his free election by his subjects gave him sufficient right to the throne. Irritated by this disdain, the king invested Prince Dom Affonso, his son, with the principality of Mocato, which Dom Alvarez had ceded to Count Michel. Because Dom Affonso had raised troops to go and take possession of his new state, the Soyolese did the same. The two sides came to blows on April 29 of the year 1645. The royal army was cut to pieces, the prince and his principal chiefs were made prisoners, and, according to the custom of these barbarous people, all their heads were cut off and were carried triumphantly on the end of long poles, amid much dancing and jumping about. Only Prince Affonso was spared, by order of the count, his cousin, who treated him in a manner consistent with his rank.

One can imagine the state in which this defeat and capture put the King of Congo. The following year he gathered as many people as he could and put an army in the field that was so large that it seemed to flood the province of Soyo. He gave command to the Duke of Bamba who, followed by nearly all the nobility of the kingdom and three or four hundred mulattoes, approached the enemy's frontiers. However, the count's people, who were in ambushes scattered throughout the Findemguolla forest, charged them spontaneously and with so much valor that the general, the nobles, and the most courageous soldiers were left dead on the field; the others sought their safety in flight. Such a great loss reduced the King of Congo to the most trying extremes. He realized that he was no longer able to obtain his son's liberty by force of arms and that he would have to buy it with a fat ransom and cede new provinces to the count. The moment the prince was free, the Congolese could no longer suffer their vassals congratulating themselves on their victories and tried to seek all means imaginable to revenge themselves and ruin their vassals. Thinking that the Soyolese would be more afraid of a foreign militia than of his own, the king sent letters and ambassadors to Brazil to Count

Maurice, Governor of the States-General in the West Indies, with two hundred slaves and a good chain for the governor and other slaves for the counselors of state. Having been warned by this action, the Count of Soyo also sent three ambassadors. One ambassador went to Holland and the other two went to Maurice to beg him to remain neutral. The Dutch governor, who was allied to the princes, thought that the best course would be not to get involved but rather to preserve his position as mediator. That is why, after having written to his lieutenants in Congo and Angola to bring about a satisfactory peace between the two nations, he assembled their ambassadors and gave them presents for themselves and their masters. To the King of Congo he sent a red velvet coat with gold and silver braid, a coat of silk, and a beaver hat with a cord of gold and silk. To the Count of Soyo he sent a chain covered with silk embroidered in gold and silver, a coat, a beaver hat, and a saber whose shoulder belt was decorated with a silver fringe. Nevertheless, the King of Congo and the Duke of Bamba were not content. They sent new ambassadors to Count Maurice, who again gave them a warm welcome and sent them to Holland. They took letters from their master to the States-General, to Prince Frederic Henri, and to the intendants of the East India Company. These men were very black, robust, and agile, and in order to make themselves more supple, they rubbed themselves regularly with palm oil. They seemed to be born tightrope walkers and gladiators, for they knew how to do prodigious jumps and fence in a surprising manner. Some of the gentlemen of the States-General, having invited them to dinner, had the pleasure to see them demonstrate the manner in which the King of Congo sits on his throne and shows his majesty by profound silence. They also saw how the Negroes adore their prince, according to ancient pagan superstition.

2   RUI DE AGUIAR
KING AFFONSO I

Rui de Aguiar, a Portuguese missionary, worked in the Congo as Vicar-General during the second decade of the sixteenth century. The following description of the greatest King of Congo, Affonso I (Mvemba Nzinga), who ruled from 1506 to about 1545, is contained in a letter dated May 25, 1516 from Rui de Aguiar to King Manuel of Portugal. A genuine and devout convert to Christianity, Affonso sought to establish Catholicism and to carry out a program of westernization in the Congo. Only a shrewd and able king could have abandoned the traditional sanctions of divine kingship and introduced new customs to challenge the old without disrupting the kingdom or losing his throne.

This king, Dom Affonso, has nothing else in mind but Our Father and His

Rui de Aguiar to King Manuel of Portugal, May 25, 1516, in Willy Bal, *Le Royaume du Congo aux XVième et XVIième Siècles. Documents d'Histoire* (Kinshasa: Éditions de l'Institute National d'Études Politiques, 1963), pp. 71–72. Trans. by Nell Elizabeth Painter and Robert O. Collins. Bracketed material has been supplied by Professor Collins.

manifestations. He has presently ordered that every man in all his kingdom pay the tithe,[1] saying that the light must be carried in front and not behind.

In his quality as a Christian, Your Highness will know, it seems to me, that

[1] A tax, usually ten percent, for the support of the church (ed.).

he is not a man but an angel whom God has sent to this kingdom to convert it, according to the things he says and expresses. For I swear that he teaches us, and he knows the prophets and the gospel of Our Lord Jesus Christ and all the lives of the saints and all the things of our sacred mother the church better than we ourselves know them. I swear that such a sight would greatly astonish Your Highness. He says things so well phrased and so true that it seems to me that the Holy Spirit always speaks through him, for he does nothing but study, and many times he falls asleep over his books, and many times he forgets to eat and drink for talking of Our Lord, and he is so absorbed by the things of the Book that he forgets himself, and even when he is going to hold an audience and listen to the people, he speaks of nothing but God and His saints. He studies the sacred gospel, and when the priest finishes saying mass, he begins to preach to the people with great love and charity, asking these people and begging them, for the love of Our Lord, to convert and turn themselves toward God—so much so that his people are taken by amazement and we, even more so, by his virtue and the faith he has in Our Lord. And he does that every day, and he preaches, as I have described to Your Highness.

Your Highness will also know that he is very just and that he greatly punishes those who adore idols and that he burns them with their idols, and that he has, throughout his kingdom, ministers of justice to seize all those of whom it is learned that they possess idols or carry on sacrilege or any other bad actions touching our saintly Catholic faith. And again,

throughout his kingdom he has sent many men, natives of the country, Christians, who have schools and teach our saintly faith to the people, and there are also schools for girls where one of his sisters teaches, a woman who is easily sixty years old, and who knows how to read very well and who is learned in her old age. Your Highness would rejoice to see it. There are also other women who know how to read and who go to church every day. These people pray to Our Lord at mass and Your Highness will know in truth that they are making great progress in Christianity and virtue, for they are advancing in the knowledge of the truth; also, may Your Highness always send them things and rejoice in helping them and, for their redemption, as a remedy, send them books, for they need them more than any other things for their redemption.

I am not speaking [here] of the great love and friendship that the King of Congo has for Your Highness. I have heard him say, in fact, that he asked Our Lord not to let him die before having seen Your Highness. I also have heard him say that Your Highness was King of the Congo, and he, King of Portugal. These things he says often to whomever wants to hear them. By that, Your Highness will know that all that I say is very true, and if I write a lie to Your Highness, may God destroy me, body and soul. And may Your Highness remember the very great good that has begun and for that Our Lord will give him the retribution he deserves.

Done today, the twenty-fifth day of the month of May of the year MDXVI.

3   FILIPPO PIGAFETTA AND DUARTE LÓPEZ
THE SUCCESSORS TO AFFONSO I

Filippo Pigafetta (1533–1604) was an Italian writer and humanist. His popular Relatione del Reame di Congo *drew European attention to the kingdom of Congo. Pigafetta's informant was Duarte López (c. 1550–c. 1623), a merchant who visited the Congo on a trading voyage in 1578. In 1583 the King of Congo, Alvaro I, sent López as an ambassador to the pope with a mining concession for the Vatican in return for papal support to counter Portuguese influence. The pope refused the concession. In Rome López collaborated with Pigafetta on the* Relatione. *Whether or not he returned to the Congo is unknown.*

While these works undertaken in the service of God were being carried on [in 1543] and Christianity, still in its beginnings, was spreading in such a favorable way, it pleased God to call King Dom Affonso to him. The manner in which he died heightened the merits of his past life. His faith was great, he showed that his time had come and he spoke of the Christian religion with such favor that the cross and the true belief in Our Savior Jesus Christ were shown to be deeply ingrained in the depths of his heart. To Dom Pedro, his son and successor, he recommended principally the keeping of the Christian doctrine. The son followed the example of the father, for he maintained and defended the religion.

During his reign a greater number of boats began to navigate these waters and, by the order of the king, the island of São Tomé was populated with Portuguese. Up to that time the interior had been deserted; only the coasts were inhabited by a few navigators who frequented the neighboring regions. In time the island was well populated by Portuguese and people from other nations who came there with the authorization of the king. There was much trade. The people cultivated and planted, as has been said above. Then

From Filippo Pigafetta and Duarte López, *Description du Royaume du Congo et des Contrées Environnantes (1591)*, trans. and annotated by Willy Bal (Louvain: Editions Nauwelaerts, 1963), pp. 100–105. Trans. from the French by Nell Elizabeth Painter and Robert O. Collins. Reprinted by permission. Bracketed material has been supplied by Professor Collins.

the king sent a bishop to govern the Christians of the island and those of Congo. He arrived at São Tomé and then proceeded to the kingdom of Congo, where he took possession of his charge [1543].

When the bishop disembarked, the king and the whole population welcomed him with incredible joy. From the sea to the capital (that is, for a distance of one hundred and fifty miles), the king had the roads smoothed and widened. He even had them covered with mats, the people having received an order to take charge of a particular portion [of the road]. Thus the bishop never put his foot on a bit of ground that was not decorated. But even more admirable was the sight of the spaces bordering the road as well—the trees and hills, which were covered with men and women who ran to see the bishop, whom they took for a saint, an envoy of God. One would offer him lambs, another kids, another chickens, still another guinea fowl, game, fish and other food in such abundance that he did not know what to do with it and had to leave much behind him. In this way the great zeal and obedience of these new Christians were made known. The memorable event should be especially noted that countless men and women, girls, boys, old people of eighty years and more, came to meet him, throwing themselves across the road asking him for the water of holy baptism and making the singular signs of the true faith, not wanting to let him pass without having received it. Thus the bishop had to stop a great deal to satisfy them, and he had provided himself with water contained in certain containers, salt, and other necessities.

Let us now leave the narrative of the welcome made to the bishop by the populations of each region, the vivid manifestation of joy, as much general as particular, and speak of his arrival in the city of San Salvador. The priests, the king, and all the court came to meet him. He was led to the church in a procession; then after he had rendered grace to God, he was taken to the home set aside for him. Immediately he began to set the organization of the church and the clergy—monks and secular priests—in order. He gave rank of cathedral to the Church of the Holy Cross, which then had about twenty-eight canons and their chaplains, a musical director and chorus, an organ, church bells, and all the objects of worship.

But this bishop, in cultivating the vine of the Lord, now in the kingdom of Congo, now in São Tomé, coming and going with twenty days at sea each time, and always leaving his vicars on the spot, ended by dying. He was buried on the island of São Tomé.

Another bishop succeeded him in the Congo. He was a black man of the royal family whom King Affonso had first sent to Portugal, then to Rome. There he had learned Latin and Christian doctrine. He came back to the Congo, and shortly after having disembarked, while on his way to his bishopric of San Salvador, he died. After that the kingdom remained without a pastor for some years. Then the king died also; he had no children. His brother, Dom Francisco, succeeded him, but his reign was short [reign ended in 1545]. A fifth king mounted the throne. His name was Dom Diogo [1545–1565], and he was the closest to the royal line. He was a man with a noble soul, magnificent, ingenuous, of good judgment and wise counsel, and above all a guardian of the Christian faith. A great warrior as well, he conquered several neighboring countries in a few years. He liked the Portuguese very much and put aside the

traditional costume to dress himself in their manner. He sought to be pleasing in his dress as well as in the ornamentation of his palace. He was liberal and courteous and gave generously to his own people as well as to the Portuguese. He bought ornaments that pleased him at great expense, saying that rare things should belong to no one but kings. He wore a suit of clothes only two or three times and then gave it to his people. The Portuguese, who saw that he appreciated golden brocades, tapestries, and other precious things, brought them to him from Portugal, and thus tapestries, cloths brocaded in gold, and lordly ornaments of that nature began to be appreciated in the kingdom.

During the reign of this king there was a third bishop of São Tomé and Congo who was of Portuguese nationality. On the road and at the court of San Salvador he was welcomed with the habitual ceremonies. But the devil, who was very annoyed by the happy progress of the Catholic religion, began to sow the seeds of discord among the monks, secular priests, and the bishop. The discord grew from the long period of liberty—the many years when the people had had no pastor. Each of them considered himself not only a bishop but even more, and did not want to obey his prelate. This tendency gave rise to grave dissension, and serious scandal followed. The king, a faithful Catholic, always took the bishop's side, and to put an end to these troubles he sent some of the priests as prisoners to Portugal, others to São Tomé. Others went away of their own accord, taking their goods with them. For this reason, instead of progressing, the religion regressed by the fault of its own ministers.

But the enemy did not stop there. In addition he stirred up disturbances between the princes and their subjects. In fact, after the death of the king, three people declared themselves pretenders to the throne. The first was the son of the king. He only had the favor of a small number of people because they wanted someone else. He was put to death. Two others of royal blood were left. One of them was made king by his partisans with the support of the majority of the people but against the will of the Portuguese and a few lords who aimed at placing the third pretender on the throne. They went to the church to murder the one who had just been crowned, reasoning that if they killed him, the other contender would necessarily become king. But at the same time, those of the opposing party assassinated the one favored by the Portuguese, thinking that after his death their prince would no longer have any difficulty in taking possession of the kingdom, for there would no longer be any other possible pretender to the royal scepter. In this manner, at the same hour, in different places, the princes were murdered.

The people saw that because of these conspiracies and murders, there was no longer any legitimate pretender to the throne. Placing the blame for all these evils on the Portuguese, they turned on them. Those who were found on the spot were massacred. The priests and Portuguese living in other places were not touched.

As there was no one of royal blood left to place in power, a brother of the deceased King Diogo, Dom Henrique, was chosen. Intending to make war on the Anzincas,[1] Dom Henrique left Dom Alvaro behind as governor with the title of king. Dom Alvaro was a young man of twenty-five years and the son of the wife of Dom Henrique by another marriage. Dom Henrique died in the war a short time afterward [1567]. Dom Alvaro [1568–1587] was chosen and recognized as sovereign by the people, the ancient line of the kings of Congo thus having ended with Dom Henrique.

Dom Alvaro was a man of good judgment who combined authority with gentleness. He immediately calmed all the

troubles of the kingdom. He reunited the Portuguese, the monks, and the laymen who had dispersed into the neighboring provinces following the past wars. Thanks to them his Catholic faith was well reconfirmed. He pardoned them, demonstrating that they had not been the cause of the evils of the past, which was clearly seen by all. He decided to furnish ample written information on these events to the King of Portugal and the bishop of São Tomé and had letters delivered to them by certain persons. The bishop had not dared risk a visit to the kingdom during the height of the disturbances. As soon as he received this news, he embarked for the Congo and used all his authority to calm the dissension and restore order to all the affairs concerning the divine cult and ministry of the priests. Shortly afterward he returned to his residence in São Tomé, where sickness ended his days. For the third time, these regions remained without a bishop.

The absence of a pastor meant that the Christian faith cooled somewhat in the heart of the king, as well as in the hearts of his lords and his people. All of them let themselves be drawn into carnal licentiousness—especially the king, led by other young men of his age who were his everyday companions, in particular by a lord named Francisco Bulamatari (which means "breaker of rocks"), who was one of his relatives. Because he was a great lord, he led a dissolute life already parted from Christian teaching. He declared publicly that to have only one wife was stupid and that it was better to go back to ancient custom. Thus, by this intermediary, the devil opened the door to the destruction of the temple of Christianity in this kingdom, which had up to then been built at the cost of so much trouble. This man divorced himself so much from the way of the truth that, from sin to sin, he abandoned the true faith almost entirely.

Meanwhile, he died, and as he was a noble lord, he was buried in the Church of the Holy Cross, although he was mani-

[1] Probably the people of the kingdom of Ndongo in Angola, which seems to have recognized the suzerainty of the kingdom of Congo in the sixteenth century (ed.).

festly suspect and tainted with heresy. An extraordinary event took place, calculated to reconfirm the good in the holy faith and frighten the devil. At night, malicious spirits opened part of the roof of the Church of the Holy Cross where he was interred, making a great din heard by the whole city, and drew him out of the tomb and carried him off. The next morning the doors were found closed, the roof bro-ken, and the sepulcher empty of his body.

This event was a warning intended to show the gravity of the fault that had been committed by the king and by those who followed him. But as there was still no bishop in the kingdom, the sovereign, who was young and unmarried, while remaining firm in his faith, persisted in carnal license until God inflicted severe punishment on him.

4 ANDREW BATTELL
THE JAGA

Andrew Battell (1565–1614) was an English sailor who was seized from a British privateer operating in South American waters and imprisoned at Luanda by the Portuguese authorities. After numerous adventures, Battell lived with the Jaga for twenty-one months; his account of these mysterious and warlike people is the most authoritative. As is the case for the Funj of the Sudan, the origins of the Jaga are unknown, if they existed at all. In one of the more interesting debates among Africanists, in 1973 Joseph Miller published an article suggesting the Jaga never existed. Later, John K. Thornton refuted Miller on this question, declaring that not only had the Jaga existed, but they were just as Battell described them. Miller's rejoinder, "Thanatopsis," upheld his earlier argument; but later, Anne Hilton, in "The Jaga Reconsidered," supported Thornton's "resurrection" of the Jaga. If indeed the Jaga were present in the Congo in this period, they probably had cultural connections with the Luba-Lunda peoples of the interior of Central Africa. In any event, according to Battell, they suddenly appeared in 1568, overran the kingdom of Congo, and destroyed the capital, San Salvador. Originally, the Jaga were probably small in number, but like the Zulu in the nineteenth century, they rapidly assimilated conquered peoples. Their military superiority was irresistible, and they roamed widely, spreading terror from the Congo River to the Cunene River. A few military units settled and founded states on the Kwango, Cuanza, and Cunene Rivers.

In our second voyage, turning up along the coast, we came to the Morro, or cliff of Benguele,[1] which standeth in twelve degrees of southerly latitude. Here we saw a mighty camp on the south side of the river Cova.[2] And being desirous to know what they were, we went on shore with our boat; and presently there came a troop of five hundred men to the waterside. We asked them who they were. Then they told us that they were the Gagas, or Gindes, that came from Sierra de lion [Serra Leoa],[3] and passed through the city of Congo, and so travelled to the eastward

From *The Strange Adventures of Andrew Battell of Leigh in Angola and the Adjoining Regions,* edited by E. G. Ravenstein and reprinted from *Purchas His Pilgrimes* (London: Hakluyt Society, 1901), pp. 19–35. Reprinted by permission of Cambridge University Press on behalf of The Hakluyt Society. Bracketed material in this selection is supplied by E. G. Ravenstein. See Joseph C. Miller, "Requiem for the 'Jaga'" *Cahiers d'Études africaines,* 49, XIII-1, 1973, pp. 131–155. See also John K. Thornton, "A Resurrection for the Jaga" *Cahiers d'Études africaines,* 69–70, XVIII-1-2, 1979, pp. 223–27. Joseph C. Miller, "Thanatopsis" *Cahiers d'Études africaines,* 69–70, XVIII-1-2, 1979, pp. 229–31. For support for Thornton's findings, see Anne Hilton, "The Jaga Reconsidered" *Journal of African History,* Vol. 2, no. 2,

1981, pp. 191–202. I am grateful to Joseph Miller for his generous assistance with the continuing sage of the Jaga.

[1] The Morro, or bluff, of Old Benguella, in lat. 10° 48′ S., is a conspicuous headland, presenting a perpendicular cliff towards the sea, its summit being covered with cactus trees. Here Antonio Lopez Peixoto, a nephew of Paulo Dias, in 1587, had built a presidio, which was soon afterwards abandoned.
[2] The river Cuvo (Kuvu) enters the sea in 10° 52′ S.
[3] *Sierra de lion,* or mountains of the lion, is of little help in identifying the origins of the Jaga, because there are many possible mountains of the lion (ed.).

of the great city of Angola, which is called Dongo.[4] The great Gaga, which is their general, came down to the waterside to see us, for he had never seen white men before. He asked wherefore we came. We told him that we came to trade upon the coast. Then he bade us welcome, and called us on shore with our commodities. We loaded our ship with slaves in seven days, and bought them so cheap that many did not cost one real, which were worth in the city [of Loanda] twelve milreis.[5]

AMONG THE JAGAS

Being ready to depart, the great Giaga staid us, and desired our boat to pass his men over the river Cova, for he determined to overrun the realm of Benguele, which was on the north side of the river Cova. So we went with him to his camp, which was very orderly, intrenched with piles of wood; we had houses provided for us that night, and many burthens [loads] of palm-wine, cows, goats and flour.

In the morning, before day, the general did strike his *gongo,* which is an instrument of war that soundeth like a bell, and presently made an oration with a loud voice, that all the camp might hear, that he would destroy the Benguelas, with such courageous and vehement speeches as were not to be looked for among the heathen people. And presently they were all in arms, and marched to the river side, where he had provided *Gingados.*[6] And being ready with our boat and *Gingados,* the general was fain to beat them back because of the credit who should be first.

We carried over eighty men at once, and with our muskets we beat the enemy off, and landed, but many of them were slain. By twelve of the clock all the Gagas were over.

Then the general commanded all his drums, *tavales,*[7] *petes, pongos,* and all his instruments of warlike music to strike up, and gave the onset, which was a bloody day for the Benguelas. These Benguelas presently broke, and turned their backs, and a very great number of them were slain, and were taken captives, man, woman and child. The prince, Hombiangymbe, was slain, which was ruler of this country, and more than one hundred of his chief lords, and their heads presented and thrown at the feet of the great Gaga. The men, women and children that were brought in captive alive, and the dead corpses that were brought to be eaten, were strange to behold. For these Gagas are the greatest cannibals and man-eaters that be in the world, for they feed chiefly upon man's flesh [notwithstanding of their] having all the cattle of that country.

They settled themselves in this country and took the spoil of it. We had great trade with these Gagas, five months, and gained greatly by them. These Gagas were not contented to stay in this place of Benguela, although they lacked almost nothing. For they had great store of cattle and wheat, and many other commodities; but they lacked wine, for in these parts there are no palm-trees.

After the five months were expired they marched toward the province of Bambala,[8] to a great lord that is called Calicansamba, whose country is five days up into

---

[4] Ndongo is the name of the kingdom of Ngola (Angola). Its old capital was at Pungu-a-Ndongo, a remarkable group of rocks, popularly known as Pedras Negras.

[5] *Real* and *milreis* were Portuguese monetary units in use before 1911 after which they were superseded by the escudo (ed.).

[6] "Gingado," elsewhere spelt "Iergado," is evidently a misprint for *Jangada,* a Portuguese word meaning "raft." Such a raft is called *Mbimba,* and is made of the wood of the *bimba,* which is identical with the *Ambaj* of the Nile, and grows abundantly on the swampy banks of the rivers. Battell himself, at a critical point of his career, built himself such a *jangada.*

[7] *Tavale.* Mr. Dennet suggests that *tavale* corresponds to the *libala* of Loango, a word derived from the Portuguese *taboa* (table), for the instrument of this name consists of a board supported by two sticks of wood, and kept in its place by wooden pegs driven into the ground. The player beats this board with his two index fingers. A. R. Neves, *Mem. da Epediçao a Cassange,* p. 110, calls *tabalha* a drum, which is beaten to make known the death of a Jaga Cassange.

[8] Mbala or Embala merely means town or village. . . .

the land. In these five months' space we made three voyages to the city of San Paul, and coming the fourth time we found them not.

MARCH INTO THE INTERIOR

Being loth to return without trade, we determined to go up into the land after them. So we went fifty on shore, and left our ship riding in the Bay of Benguela to stay for us. And marching two days up into the country we came to a great lord which is called Mofarigosat; and coming to his first town we found it burnt to the ground, for the Gagas had passed and taken the spoil. To this lord we sent a negro which we had bought of the Gagas, and [who] lived with us, and bid him say that he was one of the great Gaga's men, and that he was left to carry us to the camp. This lord bade us welcome for fear of the great Gaga, but he delayed the time, and would not let us pass till the Gaga was gone out of his country. This lord Mofarigosat, seeing that the Gagas were clear of him, began to palter with us, and would not let us go out of his land till we had gone to the wars with him, for he thought himself a mighty man having us with him. For in this place they never saw [a] white man before, nor guns. So we were forced to go with him, and destroyed all his enemies, and returned to his town again. Then we desired him that he would let us depart; but he denied us, without we would promise him to come again, and leave a white man with him in pawn.

LEFT AS AN HOSTAGE

The Portugals and Mulatos being desirous to get away from this place, determined to draw lots who should stay; but many of them would not agree to it. At last they consented together that it were fitter to leave me, because I was an Englishman, than any of themselves. Here I was fain to stay perforce. So they left me a musket, powder and shot, promising this lord, Mofarigosat, that within two months they would come again and bring

a hundred men to help him in his wars, and to trade with him. But all was to shift themselves away, for they feared that he would have taken us all captives. Here I remained with this lord till the two months were expired, and was hardly used, because the Portugals came not according to promise.

The chief men of this town would have put me to death, and stripped me naked, and were ready to cut off mine head. But the Lord of the town commanded them to stay longer, thinking that the Portugals would come. And after that I was let loose again, I went from one town to another, shifting for myself within the liberties of the lord. And being in fear of my life among them I ran away, purposing to go to the camp of the Gagas.

HE JOINS THE JAGAS

And having travelled all that night, the next day I came to a great town which was called Cashil, which stood in a mighty overgrown thicket. Here I was carried into the town, to the lord Cashil. And all the town, great and small, came to wonder at me, for in this place there was never any white man seen. Here were some of the great Gaga's men, which I was glad to see, and went with these Gagas to Calicansamba, where the camp was.

This town of the lord Cashil is very great, and is so overgrown with *Olicondie* [*baobab*] [9] trees, cedars, and palms, that

[9] The baobab is indifferently called by Battell *alicunde, licondo, elicondi, olicandi,* or *alicunde,* all of which are corruptions of *nkondo,* by which name the tree is known in Congo. The Portuguese know this characteristic tree of the coast-land and the interior as *imbondeiro* (from *mbondo* in Kimbundu). Its inner bark yields a fibre known as *licomte,* is made into coarse cloth, and is also exported to Europe to be converted into paper. The wood is very light. The pulp of the fruit is refreshing, and was formerly esteemed as a remedy against fever and dysentery. The seeds are eaten. The shell (*macua*) is used to hold water (hence the popular name of Calabash tree). Ficalho distinguishes three species, viz., *Adansonia digitata,* Linn., the fruit of which is longish; *A. subglobosa,* bearing a bell-shaped fruit; *A. lageniformis,* yielding a fruit shaped like a cucumber. . . .

the streets are darkened with them. In the middle of the town there is an image, which is as big as a man, and standeth twelve feet high; and at the foot of the image there is a circle of elephants' teeth, pitched into the ground. Upon these teeth stand great store of dead men's skulls, which are [were] killed in the wars, and offered to this image. They used to pour palm oil at his feet, and kill goats, and pour their blood at his feet. This image is called Quesango,[10] and the people have great belief in him, and swear by him; and do believe when they are sick that Quesango is offended with them. In many places of this town were little images, and over them great store of elephants' teeth piled.[11]

The streets of this town were paled with palm-canes, very orderly. Their houses were round like a hive, and, within, hanged with fine mats very curiously wrought. On the south-east end of the town was a mokiso [*mukishi*] which had more than three tons of elephants' teeth piled over him.

From this town of Cashil I travelled up into the country with the Gagas two days, and came to Calicansamba, where the great Gaga had his camp, and was welcome to him. Among the cannibal people I determined to live, hoping in God that they would travel so far to the westward that we should see the sea again; and so I might escape by some ship. These Gagas remained four months in this place, with great abundance and plenty of cattle, corn, wine, and oil, and great triumphing, drinking, dancing, and banquetting, with man's flesh, which was a heavy spectacle to behold.

At the end of four months they marched towards the *Serras,* or mountains of Cashindcabar, which are mighty high, and have great copper mines, and

they took the spoil all the way as they went. From thence they went to the river Longa,[12] and passed it, and settled themselves in the town of Calango,[13] and remained there five or six months. Then we arose and entered into the province of Tondo,[14] and came to the river Gonsa [Coanza],[15] and marched on the south side of the river to a lord that was called Makellacolonge, near to the great city of Dongo. Here we passed over mighty high mountains, and found it very cold.

Having spent sixteen months among these cannibals, they marched to the westward again, and came along the river Gonsa, or Gunza, to a lord that is called Shillambansa,[16] uncle to the King of Angola. We burnt his chief town, which was after their fashion very sumptuously builded. This place is very pleasant and fruitful. Here we found great store of wild peacocks,[17] flying up and down the trees, in as great abundance as other birds. The old lord Shillambansa was buried in the middle of the town, and had a hundred tame peacocks kept upon his grave, which peacocks he gave to his *Mokeso,* and they were called *Angello Mokeso,*[18] that is, the Devil's or Idol's Birds, and were accounted as holy things. He had great store of copper, cloth, and many other things laid upon his grave, which is the order of that country.

From this place we marched to the westward, along the river Coanza, and came right against the *Serras* or mountains of Cambambe, or Serras de Prata.[19]

[10] Kizangu, in Kimbundu, means fetish. . . .
[11] The so-called fetishes (from *feitiço,* a Portuguese word meaning sorcery) are not idols, but charms and amulets, generally known as *nkissi, nkishi,* or *mukishi.* . . .
[12] The river Longa [Lungu] enters the sea in lat. 10° 20′ S.
[13] A soba Calungo is shown on the most recent maps as residing north of the river Longa.
[14] Perhaps we ought to read *Tunda,* the bush, the East. . . .
[15] The Gonsa or Gunza (Ngunza) of Battell is undoubtedly the Coanza. A river Ngunza enters the sea at Novo Redondo.
[16] *Shila,* nasty; *mbanza,* towns.
[17] According to Duarte López, the feathers of peacocks and of ostriches are used as a standard in battle. Hence, peacocks are reared within a fence and reserved for the king.
[18] *Njilo* (in Kimbundu), bird; *mukishi,* a charm.
[19] Cambambe (*Ka,* diminutive; *mbambi,* gazelle), a village on the north bank of the Coanza, below the

Here is the great fall of water, that falleth right down, and maketh a mighty noise that is heard thirty miles. We entered into the province of Casama,[20] and came to one of the greatest Lords, which was called Langere. He obeyed the great Gaga, and carried us to a Lord called Casoch,[21] which was a great warrior, for he had some seven years before overthrown the Portugals camp, and killed eight hundred Portugals and forty-thousand negroes, that were on the Portugals side. This Lord did stoutly withstand the Gagas, and had the first day a mighty battle, but had not the victory that day. So we made a sconce of trees after their fashion, and remained four months in the wars with them. I was so highly esteemed with the great Gaga, because I killed many negroes with my musket, that I had anything that I desired of him. He would also, when they went out to the wars, give charge to his men over me. By this means I have been often carried away in their arms, and saved my life. Here we were within three days' journey of Massangano, before mentioned, where the Portugals have a fort: and I sought means, and got to the Portugals again with merchant negroes that came to the camp to buy slaves.

MILITARY ORGANISATION OF THE JAGAS

There were in the camp of the Gagas twelve captains. The first, called Imbe Calandola, their general, a man of great courage. He warreth all by enchantment, and taketh the Devil's counsel in all his exploits. He is always making of sacrifices [22] to the Devil, and doth know many times what shall happen unto him. He believeth that he shall never die but in the wars. There is no image among them, but he useth certain ceremonies. He hath straight laws to his soldiers: for, those that are faint-hearted, and turn their backs to the enemy, are presently condemned and killed for cowards, and their bodies eaten. He useth every night to make a warlike oration upon an high scaffold, which doth encourage his people.

It is the order of these people, wheresoever they pitch their camp, although they stay but one night in a place, to build their fort, with such wood or trees as the place yieldeth: so that the one part of them cutteth down trees and boughs, and the other part carrieth them, and buildeth a round circle with twelve gates.[23] So that every captain keepeth his gate. In the middle of the fort is the general's house, intrenched round about, and he hath many porters to keep the door. They build their houses very close together, and have their bows, arrows, and darts standing without their doors; and when they give alarm, they are suddenly all out of the fort. Every company at their doors [gates?] keep very good watch in the night, playing upon their drums and *tavales*.

---

falls formed by the river in forcing its way through the Serra de Prata. Silver, however, has never been found there (at least not in appreciable quantities), nor anywhere else in Angola or Congo. Still we are told that the King of Congo, in 1530, sent the wife of King Manuel two silver bracelets which he had received from one of his chiefs in Matamba, and that among the presents forwarded by Ngola Nbande, the King of Ndongo, to Paulo Dias in 1576, there were several silver bracelets, which the Regent of Portugal, Cardinal Henrique, had converted into a chalice, which he presented to the church at Belem. According to Capello and Ivens, silver ore is plentiful in Matamba, although they never saw any *in loco.*

[20] Battell's Casama is the wide province of Kisama (Quiçama), to the south of the Coanza.

[21] This Casoch (a misprint for Cafoch) is the Cafuxe (Cafuche) of the Portuguese, who defeated Balthasar de Almeida on April 22, 1594. On August 10, 1603, the Portuguese, led by Manuel Cerveira Pereira, retrieved this disaster.

[22] Human victims are still sacrificed by the diviner when consulting departed spirits.

[23] Cavazzi gives a plan of a Jaga camp, or Kilombo. It is formed of a square stockade, having in its centre the quarters of the Commander-in-chief, within a triple hedge of thorns. Between the stockade, which has only a single gate, and the inner enclosure are the quarters of the six principal officers, including the Golambolo (*ngolo,* strength *mbula,* a blow), or Lieutenant-General, the Tendala, or Commander of the Rear-guard, and the Mani Lumbo (*lumbu,* a stockade), or Engineer-in-chief.

A RIVER OF GOLD

These Gagas told us of a river that is to the southward of the Bay of Vaccas,[24] that hath great store of gold: and that they gathered up great store of grains of gold upon the sand, which the fresh water driveth down in the time of rain. We found some of this gold in the handles of their hatchets, which they use to engrave with copper; and they called it copper also, and do not esteem it.

PALM WINE

These Gagas delight in no country, but where there is great store of Palmares, or groves of palms. For they delight greatly in the wine and in the fruit of the palm, which serveth to eat and to make oil. And they draw their wine contrary to the Imbondos.[25] These palm-trees are six or seven fathoms high, and have no leaves but in the top: and they have a device to go up to the top of the tree, and lay no hands on it, and they draw the wine in the top of the tree in a bottle.

But these Gagas cut the palm-trees down by the root, which lie ten days before they will give wine. And then they make a square hole in the top and heart of the tree, and take out of the hole every morning a quart, and at night a quart. So that every tree giveth two quarts of wine a day for the space of six and twenty days, and then it drieth up.

JAGA RAIDS

When they settle themselves in any country, they cut down as many palms as will serve them wine for a month: and then as many more, so that in a little time they spoil the country. They stay no longer in a place than it will afford them maintenance. And then in harvest-time they arise, and settle themselves in the fruitfullest place they can find; and do reap their enemy's corn, and take their cattle. For they will not sow, nor plant, nor bring up any cattle, more than they take by wars. When they come into any country that is strong, which they cannot the first day conquer, then their General buildeth his fort, and remaineth sometimes a month or two quiet. For he saith, it is as great wars to the inhabitants to see him settled in their country, as though he fought with them every day. So that many times the inhabitants come and assault him at his fort: and these Gagas defend themselves and flesh [26] them on for the space of two or three days. And when their General mindeth to give the onset, he will, in the night, put out some one thousand men: which do ambush themselves about a mile from their fort. Then in the morning the great Gaga goeth with all his strength out of the fort, as though he would take their town. The inhabitants coming near the fort to defend their country, being between them, the Gagas give the watchword with their drums, and then the ambushed men rise, so that very few escape. And that day their General overrunneth the country.

DRESS AND ORNAMENTS

The great Gaga Calando [27] hath his hair very long, embroidered with many knots of Banba [28] shells, which are very rich among them, and about his neck a collar of *masoes,*[29] which are also shells, that are found upon that coast, and are sold among them for the worth of twenty shillings a shell: and about his middle he weareth *landes,* which are beads made of the ostrich eggs.[30] He weareth a palm-cloth about his middle, as fine as silk. His body is carved and cut with sundry works, and every day anointed with the fat of

26 "Flesh" in the sense of encourage.
27 Calando should be Calandola.
28 Mbamba, a whelk or trumpet-shell.
29 Mr. Dennet suggests *msose,* a turritella, popularly known as screw-shell.
30 No ostriches are met with in Angola, and as to beads made of ostrich eggs, I can give no explanation.

24 Bahia das Vaccas, old name for Benguella Bay. . . .
25 The Imbondos are clearly the Nbundu of Angola, who draw the palm wine from the top, whilst the Jagas cut down the tree.

men. He weareth a piece of copper cross his nose,[31] two inches long, and in his ears also. His body is always painted red and white. He hath twenty or thirty wives, which follow him when he goeth abroad; and one of them carrieth his bows and arrows; and four of them carry his cups of drink after him. And when he drinketh they all kneel down, and clap their hands and sing.[32]

Their women wear their hair with high *trompes* full of bamba [*mbamba*] shells, and are anointed with civet.[33] They pull out four of their teeth, two above and two below, for a bravery. And those that have not their teeth out are loathsome to them, and shall neither eat nor drink with them. They wear great store of beads about their necks, arms, and legs; about their middles, silk cloths.

INFANTICIDE

The women are very fruitful, but they enjoy none of their children: for as soon as the woman is delivered of her child, it is presently buried quick [alive], so that there is not one child brought up in all this generation.[34] But when they take any town they keep the boys and girls of thirteen or fourteen years of age as their own children. But the men and women they kill and eat. These little boys they train up in the wars, and hang a collar about their necks for a disgrace, which is never taken off till he proveth himself a man, and bring his enemy's head to the General: and then it is taken off and he is a freeman, and is called *Gonso* or soldier.[35]

This maketh them all desperate, and forward to be free, and counted men: and so they do increase. In all this camp there were but twelve natural Gagas that were their captains, and fourteen or fifteen women. For it is more than fifty years since they came from Serra de Lion, which was their native country. But their camp is sixteen thousand strong, and sometimes more.

HUMAN SACRIFICES [36]

When the great Gaga Calandola undertaketh any great enterprise against the inhabitants of any country, he maketh a sacrifice to the Devil, in the morning, before the sun riseth. He sitteth upon a stool, having upon each side of him a man-witch: then he hath forty or fifty women which stand round about him, holding in each hand a *zevra* [zebra] [37] or wild horse's tail, wherewith they do flourish and sing. Behind them are great store of petes, ponges, and drums, which always play. In the midst of them is a great fire; upon the fire an earthen pot with white powders, wherewith the men-witches do paint him on the forehead, temples, 'thwart the breast and belly, with long ceremonies and inchanting terms. Thus he continueth till sun is down. Then the witches bring his *Casengula*,[38] which

---

[31] The practice of wearing such nose ornaments exists to the present day in Lunda, among the Bangala and other tribes.

[32] Marginal note by Purchas: "They use this ceremony in Florida."

[33] Civet-cats are numerous in this part of Africa.

[34] I am inclined to believe, from what we learn from Cavazzi and other missionaries, that only those children were killed which were born within the *Kilombo*. On the other hand, at the Court of the ferocious queen Jinga, we are told by Captain Füller, a Dutchman, that, on two days in 1648, 113 newborn infants born *outside* the camp were killed.

[35] *Ngunza*, according to Cordeira da Matta, means all-powerful; according to Bentley a herald, who speaks on behalf of a chief.

[36] Human sacrifices among the Jaga are even now [1900] of frequent occurrence. They are made at the installation of a Jaga, one year after his election (when the sacrifice and its accompanying banquet are intended to conciliate the spirit of Kinguri, the founder of the Dynasty), at his death, on the outbreak of war, etc. The ceremony witnessed by Battell was an act of divination. The soothsayer summons the spirit of Kinguri, who is supposed to foretell the results of any enterprise about to be undertaken. In 1567, the Jaga Ngonga Kahanga, of Shela, having been advised by his soothsayers that he would suffer defeat in a war he was about to enter upon against the Portuguese, declined the arbitration of the sword, and submitted voluntarily. The body of the victim is cooked with the flesh of a cow, a goat, a yellow dog, a cock and a pigeon, and this mess is devoured (ceremoniously) by the Jaga and his *makotas* (councillors).

[37] The handle of this switch contains a potent medicine, which protects the owner against death.

[38] Casengula, called Kissengula, was perhaps a trombash, for *sangula* means to kill at a long range.

is a weapon like a hatchet, and put it into his hand, and bid him be strong against his enemies: for his *mokiso* is with him. And presently there is a man-child brought, which forthwith he killeth. Then are four men brought before him; two whereof, as it happeneth, he presently striketh and killeth; the other two he commandeth to be killed without the fort.

Here I was by the men-witches ordered to go away, as I was a Christian, for then the Devil doth appear to them, as they say. And presently he commandeth five cows to be killed within the fort, and five without the fort: and likewise as many goats, and as many dogs, and the blood of them is sprinkled in the fire, and their bodies are eaten with great feasting and triumph. And this is used many times by all the other captains of their army.

BURIAL OF THE DEAD

When they bury the dead they make a vault in the ground, and a seat for him to sit.[39] The dead hath his head newly embroidered, his body washed, and anointed with sweet powders. He hath all his best robes put on, and is brought between two men to his grave, and set in seat as though he were alive. He hath two of his wives set with him, with their arms broken, and then they cover over the vault on the top. The inhabitants when they die are buried after the same fashion, and have the most part of their goods buried with them. And every month there is a meeting of the kindred of the dead man, which mourn and sing doleful songs at his grave for the space of three days, and kill many goats, and pour their blood upon his grave, and palm-wine also; and use this ceremony as long as any of their kindred be alive.[40] But those that have no kindred think themselves unhappy men, because they have none to mourn for them when they die. These people are very kind one to another in their health; but in their sickness they do abhor one another, and will shun their company.

[39] The Jagas are still buried sitting, and wives are sacrificed. In Ngois, likewise, the dead are occasionally buried in a sitting posture.

[40] These feasts are intended to secure the goodwill of the deceased, so that he may not injure the living. Human beings are occasionally sacrificed, in addition to goats and fowls.

5   ALVARE II AND ALVARE III, KINGS OF CONGO
RELATIONS BETWEEN THE KINGDOM OF CONGO AND THE PAPACY

After the Jaga *attack had been subdued, the kings of Congo, Alvare I (1568–1587), Alvare II (1587–1614), and Alvare III (1614–1622) sought to reassert their authority and to disengage themselves from dependence on the Portuguese. Alvare I had sent Duarte López to Rome in 1583, hoping to enlist Vatican support against Portugal. In 1590 Alvare II allied himself against the Portuguese in Angola and in 1604 sought to make the Congo a papal vassal. The Vatican rejected this proposal but agreed to intercede with the King of Spain on behalf of Congo. The appointment of Monsignor Vivès inaugurated an era of close relations between Rome and San Salvador. Acting on the appeal of Alvare III for support, the Vatican remonstrated with the King of Spain to check Portuguese who invaded the Congo from Angola.*

From J. Cuvelier and L. Jadin, *L'Ancien Congo d'après les Archives Romaines (1518–1640)* (Brussels: Académie Royale des Sciences d'Outre-Mer, 1954), pp. 329–331, 333–335, 348–351. Trans. by Nell Elizabeth Painter and Robert O. Collins. Reprinted by permission. Bracketed material has been supplied by Professor Collins.

ALVARO II TO POPE PAUL V SAN SALVADOR (CAPITAL OF THE KINGDOM OF CONGO) 27 FEBRUARY 1613

Dom Alvaro II by divine grace, augmenter of confession to the faith of Jesus Christ and defender of that same faith in these lands of Ethiopia, king of the very ancient kingdom of Congo, Angola, Matamba, Ocango, and of the Ambandu, and also of many other kingdoms and sovereignties that are subject to him this side and beyond the marvelous river Zaïre. Written from his royal city of San Salvador, the 27th of February 1613.

To the very Holy Father, Pope Paul V, at present head of the Church of God Our Lord.

He expresses the desire that he has to come personally to kiss the feet of His Holiness.

He acknowledges the reception of the letter from His Holiness, received in the year 1611. He thanks him for the title of Majesty, which was given to him in that letter, which was read from the pulpit by a father of Saint Dominic who was here at that time.

He expresses his thanks for the welcome made for Dom Antonio Manuel, his ambassador, who died in Rome.

Dom Antonio Manuel, not being able to be admitted as ambassador and thus unable to kiss the feet of His Holiness, having been taken away by death; the king not being able to come himself, nor send others at short notice, has chosen for his ambassador to Your Holiness Monsignor Jean-Baptiste Vivès, prothonotary of the number of participants and referendary [arbitrator] of the one and the other signature, so that with all the solemnity of ambassadors of kings, he may kiss the feet of His Holiness in his name, swear allegiance and express the joy which he feels about his elevation to the Sovereign Pontry. Monsignor Vivès will be able to take care of the business entrusted to D. Antonio Manuel. . . .

He chooses the Cardinal of Saint Cecilia as protector of his kingdom. If both should die, His Holiness may replace them as he sees fit.

He has been informed that the Portuguese in this country seek to bring about a division between himself and the King of Spain, so that the latter would be prompted to conquer the kingdom of Congo. For his own part, he has always shown friendship to this king and he has favored his subjects.

He has always treated the churches and priests well and has made sure that the tithes are paid. He has had the tithes collected by his servants in specie because foodstuffs could not be transported due to the size of the kingdom and could not be taken out of the villages. They have agreed on a certain number of measures of *Nzimbu*, the word that designates their money.

He has not received the brief mentioned in the letter.

He asks that by means of a brief, everyone would be prohibited, on pain of censure, from encroaching on the lands of his kingdom or taking possession of the mines. . . .

He asks for a brief in order to be able to defend himself against the attacks of the bishops. If he is not treated justly, may he notify them by a priest or cleric, because the bishop threatens to interdict him and deprive him of priests. This suggests to him that the Portuguese desire to conquer his kingdom. In the past pontiffs accorded very ample briefs, but these briefs were lost during the wars with the "Giacchi" [Jaga]. . . .

He is very badly treated by the Portuguese and the prelates. He is very ashamed of this. He hides it so that the pagan kings may not be glad of it and because he expects protection from Rome. If his authority is maintained these other kings may be converted.

He suffers many vexations because of the distance from the King of Portugal and because his business is sent to Portugal, where the relatives of the Portuguese who are in the Congo occupy certain offices.

The Christian religion is making no progress because there are no priests. . . . The foreign priests who come to the Congo have no preoccupation other than that of enriching themselves and returning to their countries; they take no interest in gaining souls for heaven. If religious personnel are sent, may they be like the "Mariani" [Monks of Mary], or Carmelites, who came during his father's time. They got very good results because of the example they set, their doctrine, and their charity.

As for the Dominican fathers requested from the King of Portugal, of the four he sent, two died during the course of the trip and the two who arrived at their destination are hardly useful.

They interfere in the foreign affairs of the kingdom and in the plans and duties of the king at their own bidding. May those fathers who will come in the future be ordered to keep to their own duties.

He begs that a brief be accorded the bishop giving him the faculty of dispensing with irregularities of notable persons wanting to be ordained and also the faculty to dispense with the impediment of consanguinity and affinity, with the order that the bishop not make difficulties in according them and not do so according to his own desires, but that he carry out what Your Holiness commands and what the king asks.

At the time of the first vacancy of the episcopal seat, there was much dispute and disorder among the members of the chapter. They abused themselves publicly at mass and in the offices in the presence of the king, imposing conflicting censures. If the situation had not been remedied, it would have become aggravated. The remedy (there was no other means) was to threaten them with expulsion from the kingdom. Then they calmed down.

He begs that remedies be found for other similar cases, for they take excessive liberties. The king asks that the vicar, who at that time did not conduct himself according to law, be sent away and another chosen by means of a brief that he requests and that the new one be of the best group and chosen from among those who are in agreement with him.

ALVARO III TO POPE PAUL V SAN SALVADOR, 25 OCTOBER 1617

Very Holy Father,

Myself, Dom Alvaro the Third, by divine grace, augmenter of the faith of Jesus Christ and defender of the faith in these lands of Ethiopia, king of the very ancient kingdom of Congo, Angola, Matamba, Ocanga, and of the Ambandu, here and beyond the marvelous river Zaïre [Congo], and of many other kingdoms and neighboring sovereignties. . . .

As the very humble and very obedient son of Your Holiness, I kiss his very holy feet in my name and of my royal person as well as in the name of all my kingdoms and states, I give him the allegiance due him as the universal pastor of the flock of Christ. I beg Your Holiness with all possible ardor to accept the above-said allegiance, which I have given and offered by the intermediary of my procurer, Dom Jean-Baptiste Vivès of Valencia. The prothonotary and referendary [arbitrator] of Your Holiness will remit it, according to the mode and manner which the other Catholic Kings are accustomed to in dealing with the apostolic Holy See. I give him all necessary faculties to pledge allegiance as well as to treat affairs in my name to Your Holiness and to all the Roman pontiffs, his successors. If for any reason he cannot do so, we would like Your Holiness and his successor to have the power to name other procurers in my name and in the name of my kingdoms. In this way the designs of King Dom Alvaro II, my lord and father whom God has, in His glory, taken up again. This is what he had in mind when he sent Dom Antonio Manuel, who died in Rome, to the apostolic Holy See. He entrusted letters to him, affairs to be discussed and commissioned him with an embassy. It is necessary that these projects be developed for the greater service of God and for the greater good of Christianity.

I reconfirm the instructions he gave and the business he negotiated, and I humbly beg Your Holiness to give orders so that old requests and those which more recently have been addressed to the above-named procurer, to be submitted by him to Your Holiness, may be examined. All these affairs are contained in instructions that I have sent, signed by my hand, which manifest that my goal is to promote the divine cult for the greater glory of God, the exaltation of His Church, the confusion of barbarians and pagans, and the consolidation of Catholics.

By other routes I have written to Your Holiness, to the Seignior Cardinal, protector of these kingdoms, and to the above-named procurer, my ordinary ambassador resident at that Roman court, Dom Jean-Baptiste Vivès.

In those letters I announced the death of King Alvaro II, my lord and father. I related that after his death, given my young age, the kingdom was put in the possession of Dom Bernard, my uncle, bastard half-brother of the above-named king, with the help of a few important people. But after less than a year, the kingdom, seeing the injustices done to me, scandalized by some disorders indicative of little Christian religion, took up arms against him without my knowing. This was under the command of Dom Antonio da Silva, Grand Duke of Mbamba, a province of the kingdom, and general of the kingdom, to whom the above-named king, my lord and father, before dying, had given over my person, as executor of his will. Dom Bernard was deprived of the kingdom and his life, and I was reestab-lished in power to the great joy of all, and I was recognized by all the states as their king and their universal lord.

I beg Your Holiness to deign to send many favors and spiritual graces to me and to all my subjects, to deign to let us rejoice in his letters, which will bring us many benefits and much honor, and the courage to resist the barbarous pride of paganism by which, from all sides of our kingdom, we are besieged.

We also beg Your Holiness to deign to receive us forever under the protection and defense of the apostolic Holy See and to make his Catholic Majesty, King Dom Philippe [of Spain], whom we greatly esteem and honor as our well-loved brother, favorable to us, recognizing the great benefits that I and all these kingdoms and this Christianity owe to his magnificence. These benefits have cost His Majesty great expenditures, which he has not ceased to make in favor of this Christianity whose culture he assures. Even so, we are under the weight of injustice on the part of his captains-general and governors who reside in Angola. They enter the lands belonging to our crown and make themselves masters there, as if it were enemy territory, without receiving any such orders from His Majesty. On the contrary, the king orders them in his instructions, which he gives them, to aid and serve us in all instances. They do not do this, having only their own interests in mind. They commit numerous unjust acts, making alliance with a nation of extremely barbarous men called Gindas and Ingas [Jagas], who live on human flesh.

May Your Holiness deign to find a remedy for this. I beg him to accord me his immediate protection.

May the Lord care for the very holy person of Your Holiness in the measure that his very humble and very obedient son desires. . . .

6 MONSIGNOR CONFALONRERI
SÃO TOMÉ AND THE SLAVE TRADE

By the donatarios* *of 1486 and 1493, the Portuguese who had settled on the island of São Tomé had been granted the privilege of trading in slaves along the western coast of Africa. Although the donatario of 1493 was withdrawn in the regimento of 1512, the São Thomistas, under their Governor, Ferrão de Mello, acted quite independently of Portugal and used their strategic position between the kingdom of Congo and Europe to subvert Congolese-Lusitanian relations to their own advantage. Throughout the sixteenth century, the São Tomé party and its supporters carried on a vigorous trade in slaves, ignored the commands of the King of Portugal, and undermined the authority of the King of Congo. Their subversive activities did much to bring about the disintegration of the kingdom of Congo. The following description was probably compiled by Monsignor Confalonreri, who used the* Relatione *of Pigafetta and López and the firsthand accounts of two Carmelite fathers who were missionaries in Congo and São Tomé from 1584 to 1587.*

THE WAY OF LIFE OF THE MERCHANTS WHO GO IN THESE REGIONS FOR COMMERCE AND THE GREAT ABUSES THERE ARE ON THE ISLAND OF SÃO TOMÉ CONCERNING THE SLAVES POSSESSED BY THE PORTUGUESE THERE

The Portuguese merchants in these countries have been reprimanded and corrected many times by diverse preachers secretly and publicly in lessons and in sermons. They are reproached for the numerous abuses and customs and sins that they practice and live in this land, and because there has been no evidence of change up to the present time, it is necessary to notify the church. . . . Where there are many Spaniards [Portuguese] in these areas, some are merchants and go to the Congo and other places to trade. They are of two types: some are called *pombeiros,* who go to the interior of the country and trade with pagans as well as with Christians. They buy and sell the

merchandise that they bring. They buy slaves whom they send to Congo (San Salvador) or to Pinda, and to others of their associates. The latter embark them on ships coming to the port of the island of São Tomé, where they take care of feeding them until the return of the slave owners. The others are inhabitants of the city of Congo or of the port of Pinda and have the job of receiving the slaves that the pombeiros send them. They own slaves, and they send those whom they trust into the interior of the country with merchandise to trade as the pombeiros do.

There are others living on the island of São Tomé and they are also of two sorts: some are inhabitants, but they are occupied only with feeding and receiving slaves, who are sent to them by the pombeiros up to the time they are embarked for Portugal, or else they keep the slaves until they come, according to what they have agreed upon between them.

Others live on the island and have sugar factories; many slaves cultivate the plantations.

Here the way of life will be described. The country is very hot and humid, but not, however, as much as is said. And this they take as a pretext to live with the greatest latitude and liberty in their persons, concerning (food) and so they all indiscriminately eat meat, on Fridays and

From J. Cuvelier and L. Jadin, *L'Ancien Congo d'après les Archives Romaines (1518–1640)* (Brussels: Académie Royale des Sciences d'Outre-Mer, 1954), pp. 152–156. Trans. by Nell Elizabeth Painter and Robert O. Collins. Reprinted by permission. Bracketed material has been supplied by Professor Collins.

* A royal grant of land or privileges.

on other fast days; Lent, they do not know what it is. . . .

The monks stayed a long time without eating meat on forbidden days, not giving up fasting, even though the bishop had commanded them not to fast and to eat meat, so much has this perverse custom been accepted. But they still do not do it because of their scruples, and they are still in good health and do not accord themselves other dispensations that were in vogue but that are illicit.

I will abstain here from discussing their trade, about which there is much to be said, particularly of their trickery and the exorbitant prices that they demand for their wares. There are very few of them who do not do everything possible for gain. From this these traders can become rich in two days, although this be counter to their conscience.

Similarly, their houses are full of Creoles who are the children of the whites and Negroes, and there are no other whites to whom the children could belong if not to them. Finally, because the major part of those who go in these lands are not people of pure blood (they are Jews, half-castes, mulattoes), as soon as they find themselves at liberty with no one to control them, they live as they please without performing the sacraments or giving signs of being good Christians, which would be necessary to do where the faith begins.

In particular, the pombeiros, who are those who go among the pagans, communally take with them three or four Negroes as slaves—those with whom they can do whatever they please—and at the end of the year there are that many Creoles. Besides that, years pass when they do not attend mass, or listen to a sermon, or go to confession, or carry out the other duties of a Christian. And what is even [worse], many of them go to the pagans without having confessed or taken communion or put their souls in order. . . .

The merchants [established] on the island of São Tomé and who live there have many plantations, from which they harvest much sugar and other products. . . . The person directing these plantations has a recreation house there and near it an enclosure, and in the interior of this enclosure are the slaves, men and women, who cultivate these plantations. They have their camps and in one line one hundred men slaves and in the other one hundred women slaves . . . [others are arranged] so that each man has a woman slave or two as concubines, and thus they live in concubinage, as though they were married in a cabin. The masters see this and not only do they not reprimand them but they are glad of it, because at the end of the year they have their lands cultivated and half again more slaves because of the births. Every Negress infallibly gives life to a black child each year. Besides this, the masters do not teach the doctrine or the faith to these slaves. They remain ignorant of such things as if they had stayed in their country and were pagans. The masters do not care about Sundays or holidays, and they neither hear mass nor confess. They do not even give the slaves the time necessary for that. They only care about one thing: that the slaves work the land and increase their number. The masters do not support them, giving them nothing to eat all week. The slaves have to procure their nourishment themselves, and thus it is necessary for them to work on Sundays and holidays to sustain themselves. When they are sick they are not given what is necessary. Finally, they are treated like so many cattle—even worse than that, because cattle are cared for where no account is taken of slaves at all. And all this was introduced to this island as though it were consistent with reason. On the island of Principe [in the Gulf of Guinea], conditions are the same. Neither sermons nor admonitions nor even the interventions of bishops I think could remedy or procure protection against these abuses, because they say that if the slaves did not have their concubines they would revolt or join with the blacks who are already in a state of rebellion and would no longer work. They say that it is good that each man slave has his woman slave and that it is necessary that they be united thus, because if these slaves married, they could no longer separate them. As for food, they say that their plantations would no longer be kept up if it were necessary to feed them. It is a surprising thing that such a great abuse exists that does not exist among the pagans or among the Turks. . . . A remedy must be found for this abuse, which offends all law, divine and human. Those who do it or permit it, being obliged to remedy it, are in a bad spiritual state. May great attention be paid. The prelates who go in these lands cannot do much unless they are aided by the king, who draws a great deal of profit from these islands, which are part of their patrimony. The ecclesiastics, who receive a payment from the king, also have the obligation to remedy these abuses, and it is not possible that such a Christian and Catholic king would not support them in these things, which he could easily remedy.

Of great importance for this end would be that the king pass a law for the slave trade, a law prohibiting all merchants from entering the interior to trade. The merchants would be established only at the ports where they embark or disembark. They are a great source of scandal and a hindrance to the conversion of souls, for how can one persuade them to hear mass and not to have a great many wives, when they see that the Europeans do the contrary.

It would also be a great remedy if slaves were prohibited to live in concubinage. . . . Slaves should be accorded one or two days so that they might be able to see to their own sustenance. At the least His Majesty should see that no one keeps male and female slaves together in the same cabin unless they are married. . . .

7 FILIPPO PIGAFETTA AND DUARTE LÓPEZ
PAULO DIAZ DE NOVAIS IN ANGOLA

The kingdom of Ndongo was probably founded at the beginning of the sixteenth century. The king took the title of ngola. *From 1519 on, the ngola sought to make contact with the Portuguese. In 1560 four Jesuit priests and a young nobleman, Paul Diaz de Novais, arrived at the capital of Kabasa. Diaz returned to Portugal in 1565 and sought to obtain a commercial monopoly of the silver mines that he believed were in the interior. He obtained a* donatario, *or land grant, from the Portuguese crown in 1571, allowing him to colonize Angola at his own expense and to receive land and a commercial monopoly. Diaz appeared off the island of Luanda with 400 men in February 1575. He moved into the interior in 1576 and began a long series of campaigns that culminated in a great victory in 1583 and the construction of the Fort of Masangano at the confluence of the Lukala and Cuanza. Diaz died in 1589.*

In the direction of the sea several lords are found who accord themselves the title of king but whose domains are tiny. There are no suitable ports on these

From Filippo Pigafetta and Duarte López, *Description du Royaume du Congo et des Contrées Environnantes (1591)*, trans. and annotated by Willy Bal (Louvain: Éditions Nauwelaerts, 1963), pp. 39–41,

44. Trans. from the French by Nell Elizabeth Painter and Robert O. Collins. Reprinted by permission. Bracketed material has been supplied by Professor Collins.

coasts. Already many times we have made mention of the kingdom of Angola. That is why it is now time to talk of it in more detail. We have said that in the past a governor of the King of Congo ruled this territory. This governor proclaimed himself king long before the conversion of the king [of Congo] to Christianity. In this way he usurped absolute power in the whole area under his administration, and then in time he conquered other neighboring territories so that he has now become a great and rich prince, hardly less powerful than the King of Congo, to whom he pays or refuses tribute as he pleases.

It came about that King João II of Portugal implanted the Christian faith in the Congo and that the king of this land converted [to Christianity]. Since that time the Lord [King] of Angola has always been his friend and, so to speak, his vassal, sending him a present every year. The people trade with each other. With the permission of the King of Congo, the Portuguese traded with the people of Angola at the port of Luanda. Slaves were brought there and were traded for various sorts of merchandise, and all were sent to the island of São Tomé. In this way the trade of Luanda was linked with that which was carried on in the island. First the boats landed at São Tomé before going to Luanda. Because the commerce continually increased, they began to send boats from Lisbon expressly for Angola. A governor was sent there [in 1575]; his name was Paulo Diaz de Novais. The trade belonged to him because his ancestors had discovered its beginnings. The King of Portugal, Dom Sebastian, awarded him the right to conquer thirty-three leagues of coast from the mouth of the Cuanza toward the south and in the interior all that he could conquer entirely at his expense for himself and his heirs. Diaz left with many boats and began a prosperous trade in Angola, always directing it from the already-mentioned port of Luanda where the boats were unloaded. Little by little he penetrated into the interior and established himself in a village called Anzelle, one mile from the river Cuanza, for convenience and to get closer to his market in Angola. The traffic increased even more; the Portuguese as well as the Congolese freely brought the merchandise that they wanted to sell or trade to Cabaza, which is situated 150 miles from the sea and where the court of the Lord of Angola is to be found.

The Lord of Angola gave the order to massacre all the merchants and seize their wealth, on the pretext that they came to spy and invade his state. It is believed that in reality the Lord of Angola simply wanted to appropriate their goods, which were considerable, for himself. These people, whose business was trade, were merchants and had nothing to make war. The massacre took place the same year that King Sebastian suffered a defeat from the Berbers [1578].

Seeing this, Paulo Diaz took arms against the King of Angola. He assembled as many Portuguese as he could find in the region. With two canal barges and some other boats that were anchored in the Cuanza, he ascended the river, conquering both banks. By force of arms he subjugated many lords and rendered them vassals and friends.

Seeing that his vassals surrendered to Paulo Diaz, who was continually gaining ground, the King of Angola raised a great army to destroy the Portuguese. Then Paulo Diaz asked for help from the King of Congo, who sent reinforcements of 60,-000 men, led by one of his cousins, Dom Sebastian Manibamba, and a captain with 120 Portuguese soldiers who were in the region and whom he had hired for this campaign.

This army was to join the forces of Paulo Diaz in order to combat the King of Angola. When the army arrived at the river Bengo twelve miles from Luanda, the numerous embarkations caused the army to be late in coming. For this reason and because a good deal of time had been lost in trying to move so many men, the army ascended the river along the bank. Advancing in this way it encountered the troops of the King of Angola, whose mission was to prevent the Congolese penetration of the country. . . .

.   .   .

A few advances were made by each side. From the first battles the Congolese emerged victorious. In the combats that followed, the losses were equal on both sides. Already food had become short. Some men became sick and died. The army of the King of Congo dissolved as the soldiers returned to their homes.

Not being able to join the friendly army, Paulo Diaz marched at that moment. He passed the river and stopped at Lukala because this place, naturally fortified, could permit him to resist the King of Angola. Lukala is situated at the confluence of the Cuanza and the Lukala, 105 miles from the coast. A little upstream from the confluence, the two rivers are separated by just the distance of a shot of

a harquebus and thus form a peninsula. At its end, where the two waterways meet there is a hill. Paulo Diaz occupied it and fortified it for more security. The place was not inhabited when he arrived. Now a small congregation of Portuguese has formed there.

From this place called Lukala, which Paulo Diaz occupied, one can go down the river as far as the sea in small boats. By land there are 105 miles to cover and the way is not dangerous. Not far from there are the mountains called Cambambe. An infinite quantity of silver is extracted from them. Diaz is still trying to conquer these mountains and that is why the people of Angola oppose him. They know as a fact that the Portuguese prize these mountains because of the numerous silver mines. Thus they apply more force to repulse the Portuguese. Fighting takes place in other areas as well because the Portuguese cross the river and make continual incursions into the territory belonging to the King of Angola.

8   GIOVANNI CAVAZZI
QUEEN ANNA NZINGA

Father Cavazzi was a Capuchin missionary, originally from Modena, who went to Angola in 1654. He returned to Rome in 1658 and, with Father Alamandini di Bologna, wrote the History of Ethiopia. *He returned to Angola in 1670. Queen Anna Nzinga came to the throne of Ndongo in 1623 after having poisoned her brother, the king. Thereafter, this able and determined woman began her long struggle against the Portuguese. She allied with the* Jaga *and induced Portuguese vassal chiefs to rebel. The Portuguese retaliated by proclaiming Aidi Kiluanji the rightful king of Ndongo in 1625. For the next fifteen years, Nzinga and the Portuguese fought indecisively for control of Angola until the Dutch, in their struggle against the combined empires of Portugal and Spain, captured Luanda in August 1641. Allied with the Dutch and the King of Congo, Garcia II, Nzinga's armies consistently defeated the Portuguese, destroying their field army in 1648 and besieging the fortress of Masangano. Masangano probably would have fallen had not the Dutch suddenly withdrawn. The Africans could not defend themselves against a strong Portuguese expeditionary force from Brazil under Salvador de Sa. After protracted negotiations Nzinga signed a peace treaty in 1656, by which she lost much territory but retained her independence. Peace prevailed between the Portuguese and Queen Nzinga until her death in 1663.*

In 1641 a Dutch fleet composed of twenty-two warships with good land troops appeared in the port of Luanda. The Portuguese defended Luanda so badly that the town was taken, along with a goodly part of the kingdom.

Having learned of these advantageous events, Queen Zingha [Nzinga] thought that the time had arrived for her to revenge herself against the Portuguese. She had always remembered in her heart how they had affronted her by proclaiming Ngola Arij [Aidi Kiluanji] the King of Dongo [Ndongo]. She sent them [the Dutch] ambassadors to congratulate them on their victories and to invite them to join their troops to hers so as to get rid of their common enemies once and for all. She assured them that she would be happy to have them as neighbors because she knew of their justice and politeness, whereas she could no longer bear the proud and haughty manner of the Portuguese.

The Dutch accepted these propositions with joy; these were offers that they had not expected. The King of Congo [Garcia II] entered the alliance so that the Portuguese found themselves attacked in three different places all at once. They faced them all. They had some advantages, but they were so closely pressed that they lost all the flat country and were besieged in their fortresses of Massangano, Muzzima, Cambamke, and Embacca, as well as in a few little islands in the Cuanza.

Queen Zingha had a few encounters with them that were not favorable to her. This made her think again. She wanted

From Giovanni Antonio Cavazzi, *Relation Historique de l'Ethiopie Occidentale,* trans. by J. B. Labat (Paris, 1732), pp. 80–86. Trans. from the French by Nell Elizabeth Painter and Robert O. Collins. Bracketed material has been supplied by Professor Collins.

to consult the demon about the outcome of the war she had entered. She did it because of a superstition that is common to the Negroes of that country. They use two cocks, one white and the other black. From the outcome of the combat, they judge whether the whites or the blacks will gain victory. Thus two cocks were prepared, one black and the other white, and they had them fight. They saw wonderful things. The black one always came out on top. Finally on the third day he pulled out all the white one's feathers and killed it.

For those people, the victory absolutely decided the outcome of the war and there were great celebrations. Without waiting any longer they went to attack the fortress of Massangano, but the queen's army was almost completely defeated. The Portuguese took a great many prisoners, and among them were the two sisters of Zingha, Cambo and Fungi, and it was only by luck that she herself escaped a trap that they had set for her.

This defeat did not discourage her but curbed her desire to attack such places and obliged her to decimate the countryside, which the Portuguese had carefully cultivated and which she made a desert.

It is true that she once surprised a few Portuguese troops and defeated them, taking a rather sizable number of prisoners. This made her think that she could surprise a frontier fort that the Portuguese had on the borders of one of her tributary vassals. She attacked it with a vigorous assault, and she was vigorously thrown back, losing part of her army on that occasion, so that comparing her losses with her gains, she found that the losses were infinitely more considerable than the advantages, despite the fact of the information she had of the Portuguese, even in the fortress of Massangano where her sister Fungi was prisoner.

That princess had been given the freedom of the town out of respect for her birth, and she abused it by winning over a large number of Negro subjects of the Portuguese and other discontented people. By means of presents and promises, she had them agree to seize one of the gates of the fortress and relinquish it to the troops of Zingha, who were to approach on a certain day with a new army that she had assembled. The treason was discovered, Fungi was tried and strangled, and her body was thrown in the river.

Meanwhile the war continued between the Portuguese and the Dutch, but the Dutch, having been defeated on several occasions, were so closely pressed by the victors that at the end they were forced to abandon the country and even the city of Luanda, which the Portuguese reentered and fortified better than it had been before.

Queen Zingha was deeply upset by the defeat of her allies. She could easily see that she missed the help of Europeans and would be exposed to all the vengeance of the Portuguese with even less hope of resisting, for the King of Congo had also made a settlement with them.

God took advantage of this misfortune to touch her and bring her back to herself. In her heart she had always kept some of the kind sentiments that she had had when she was outwardly a Christian. These good thoughts came to her, and she thought seriously of the crimes she had committed. She cried over them in secret, beginning to show signs of repentance. Here are some events that mastered her conversion.

Her army was in the province of On-nando, which it sacked. A priest named Dom Augustine Floris was taken and killed by one of the soldiers. This miserable cannibal, along with a few of his companions, resolved to eat the cadaver, but at the first cut he made to take a piece and eat it, it fell off dead stiff, which destroyed the desire of the others to taste such meat.

The queen was advised of this and was possessed by a very great fear of the judgments of God. She published an edict that forbade, under threat of very vigorous punishment, the killing of the priests of the whites. She even ordered that the sacred ornaments of the deceased should be conserved.

Dom Jerome Segueira, a priest in the Portuguese Army, was wounded and was taken in battle. She ordered that he be carefully taken care of and that all that had been taken from him be returned to him. She saw that he was well fed, and when he was cured, she permitted him to come and go at liberty in her camp. When he went out, whether on foot or carried in a hammock by the slaves whom she had given him, those who accompanied him cried out from time to time, "This is how we respect the Ganga, or the Priest of the God of the Catholics."

She did more than that. She permitted the building of a church to which she gave some carpets for decoration, as well as all that had been taken from the priest killed at Onnando. It is true that she never entered the church. She still had political reasons for not doing so, but every time she passed by it, she gave signs of the respect that she had for the Sovereign Master of the Universe, to whom it was dedicated.

9 MANUEL DE FARIA E SOUSA

THE KINGDOM OF THE MONOMOTAPA

At the beginning of the fifteenth century, a group of patrilineal Bantu clans known collectively as the Karanga *occupied southwestern Rhodesia. They were organized under a dominant clan, the* Rozvi, *which, under the leadership of Mutota, sought to secure control of the whole of Central Africa from the Kalahari Desert to the Indian Ocean, between the Zambezi and the Limpopo rivers. Known as* Mwana Mutapa, *"the great plunderer." Mutota swept northward and established the center of the kingdom of the Mwanamutapa in northeastern Rhodesia. Mutota's son and successor, Matope, continued to expand the empire, but upon his death in about 1480, Changa, a Rozvi vassal, took the title of* changamir *and asserted his independence in southwestern Rhodesia. Although the empire of the Mwanamutapa was thus beginning to disintegrate within two generations of its founding, the kingdom continued to exist until the end of the nineteenth century. The Mwanamutapa had, in fact, been dominated by the Portuguese since the beginning of the seventeenth century. Manuel de Faria e Sousa (1590–1649), author of* Asia Portuguesa, *was regarded as one of the most learned men of his time. His description of the kingdom of the Mwanamutapa in 1569 is based on an account of the expedition of Francisco Barreto. Barreto was sent to avenge the murder of Father Gonçalo da Silveira, who had been killed by the Mwanamutapa at the instigation of Muslim traders at his court. At this time the Mwanamutapa were only beginning to confront the challenge of the Portuguese newcomers.*

The empire of Monomotapa from the mouth of Cuama in the east runs two hundred and fifty leagues, is divided by the great river Zambesi, which falls into that of Chiri [Shire—ed.], running through the country of Bororo, where are many other large rivers, and on their banks many kings, some absolute, some subjects of Monomotapa. The greatest of the first is Mongas, bordering on Sena and the Zambesi, which falls into the sea between Mozambique and Sofala, to the south-east by four mouths: the first that of Quilimane, 90 leagues from Mozambique, the second Cuama, 25 to the southward, the third Luabo, 5 leagues lower, and the fourth Luaboel, 15 more to the south.[1] Between them are fruitful and large islands, whereof one is sixty leagues in compass. The river is navigable the same number of leagues up to the town of Sena, inhabited by Portuguese, and as many more to Tete, a colony of theirs also. The richest mines are those of Masapa, called Aufur, the Ophir where the queen of Sheba had her riches, when she went to Jerusalem.[2] In these mines has been found a lump of gold worth twelve thousand ducats. It is not only found among stones, but grows up within the bark of several trees to the top where the branches spread.

The mines of Manchica and Butica are not much inferior to these. There are many others not so considerable. There are three fairs or markets, whither our people trade for this gold from the castle of Tete on the river Zambesi, 120 leagues from the sea: the first is Luane, four days' journey up the inland; the second Buento, farther distant; and Masapa the third, yet farther off. This gold was purchased for

From Manuel de Faria e Sousa, *Asia Portuguesa* (first published in Lisbon in 1666), trans. and reprinted by George McCall Theal in *Records of South-Eastern Africa, Collected in Various Libraries and Archive Departments in Europe* (London, 1898), II, 22–25.

[1] Leagues. A unit of measure varying from 2.4 to 4.6 miles (ed.).

[2] Some scholars have identified the gold mines of Rhodesia and the port of Sofala with the Biblical land of Ophir, whence came the gold for the Queen of Sheba (ed.).

cloth, glass beads, and other things of no value among us. At Masapa resides a Portuguese officer appointed by the commander of Mozambique, by consent of the emperor of Monomotapa, but upon condition not to go into the country without his leave upon pain of death. He is judge of the differences that arise there. There are churches of the Dominicans at Masapa, Bocuto, and Luanze.

The original number and time of the reign of the kings is not known; it is believed there were several in the time of the queen of Sheba, and that they were subject to her, for thence she had her gold. In the mountain Afur, near Masapa, are seen the ruins of stately buildings, supposed to be palaces and castles. In process of time the empire was divided into three kingdoms: Quiteve, Sabanda, and Chicanga, this last the most powerful, as possessing the mines of Manchica, Butua, and others. It is believed the blacks of Butua of the kingdom of Chicanga are those that carry the gold to Angola, because it is thought there are but one hundred leagues distance between those two places. This country bears rice and what we call Indian wheat, has abundance of all sorts of cattle, fowl, and gardening. Their chief care is pasturage and tillage. This empire is divided into twenty-five kingdoms, which are Mongas, Baroe, Manica, Boesa, Macingo, Remo, Chique, Chiria, Chidima, Boquiza, Inakanzo, Chiruvia, Condesaca, Daburia, Macurumbe, Mungussi, Anturaza, Chove, Chungue, Diza, Romba, Rassini, Chirao, Mocaranga, and Remo de Beza. There are many lordships that have not the title of kings.

The emperor has a great palace, though of wood; the chief apartments in it are three: one for himself, another for his wife, and a third for his menial servants. It has three doors into a court: one for the queen to go in and out at, another for him and the servants that attend his person and are sons of his noblemen, the third for his cooks, who are two great men and his

relations, and the under-cooks who are also men of quality. None of these must be above twenty years of age, for till that age they do not believe they have to do with women, and if any do they are severely punished; after that time they are preferred to great employments. Those within doors are governed by a captain, and those without by another, as formerly in Spain.

The principal officers about the king are Ningomoxa, governor of the kingdoms; Macomoaxa, captain-general; Ambuya, great steward, to him it belongs when the Mazarira, or the king's principal wife, dies, to name another in her stead, but it must be one of the king's sisters or nearest relations; Inhantovo, the head musician, who has many under him, and is a great lord; Nurucao, captain of the vanguard; Bucurumo, which signifies the king's right hand; Magande, the chief conjuror; Netambe, the apothecary that keeps the ointments and utensils for sorcery; Nehono, chief porter. All these offices are executed by lords. There is no delicacy in cookery used; they only eat boiled and roasted; they eat the same as is usual with us, with the addition of mice, which they esteem as good as partridge or rabbit.

The king has many wives, only nine called great queens, which are his sisters or near relations, the others the daughters of nobles. The chiefest is called Mazarira, and mother of the Portuguese, who often present her, because she solicits their business with the king, and he sends no ambassador to them without some servants of hers; the second is Inahanda, that solicits for the Moors; the third Nabuiza, that lives in the same apartment with him; the fourth Navemba; the fifth Nemangore; the sixth Nizingoapangi; the seventh Negangoro; the eighth Nessani; the ninth Necarunda. Each of them lives apart, with as great state as the king, and have several revenues and kingdoms for their expense. As soon as one dies, another succeeds in place and name. They have power to reward and punish, as well as the king. Sometimes he goes to them, some-times they come to him. There are many women waiting on them, of whom he makes use as he pleases.

The principal people of Monomotapa, and whereof the emperor is, are the Moca-ranga, not warlike, nor furnished with any other arms but bows, arrows, and jave-lins. They have no religion nor idols, but acknowledge one only God, and believe there is a devil, that he is wicked, and they call him Muzuco. They believe their kings go to heaven, and call them Muzi-mos, and call upon them in time of need, as we on the saints. They speak of things past by tradition, having no knowledge of letters. They give ear to the doctrine of Christianity: the lame and blind they call the king's poor, because maintained by him with great charity, and if they travel the towns they go through are obliged to maintain and furnish them guides from one place to another: a good example for Christians.

Every month has its festival days, and is divided into three weeks, each of ten days; the first day is that of the new moon, and the festivals the fourth and fifth of each week. On these days they put on their best apparel, the king gives public audience to all, holding a truncheon [club —ed.] about three quarters of a yard long in each hand, as it were leaning upon it; they who speak to him lie prostrate; this lasts from morning till evening. If he is

indisposed Ningomoxa stands in his place; nobody can speak to him or go to court on the eighth day of the new moon, because it is held most unlucky.

On the day the new moon appears, the king with two javelins runs about in his house as if he were fighting, the great men are present at this pastime, and it being ended, a pot full of Indian wheat, boiled whole, is brought, which he scatters about the ground, bidding them eat, because it is the growth of the earth; they know how to flatter, for every one strives to gather most, knowing that pleases him, and they eat it as savourly as if it were the greatest dainty.

Their greatest holy day is the first day of the moon of May, they call it Chuavo. On this day all the great men, which are a great number, resort to court, and there with javelins in their hands run about representing a fight. The sport lasts all day. Then the king withdraws, and is not seen in eight days after, during which time the drums never cease beating. On the last day he orders the nobleman he has the least affection for to be killed; this is in the nature of a sacrifice to his Muzimos or ancestors; this done, the drums cease, and every man goes home. The Mumbos eat man's flesh, whereof there is a public butchery. Let this suffice for the customs of this empire, for it would be endless to relate all.

10 ANTONIO SUÁREZ
THE CONVERSION OF THE MONOMOTAPA

During the mid-fifteenth century, a vast empire that included most of what is now Rhodesia and part of Mozambique was created by Mutota and his son and successor, Matope. Known to the Portuguese as the Monomotapa, the empire of Mutapa began to disinte-grate and finally broke up in the early sixteenth century during the successful revolt of a provincial chief, Changa. While Changa established an independent center of power at Zimbabwe in the south, the Mutapa empire in the northeastern part of the country contracted. Here the Mwanamutapa became increasingly dependent upon the Portuguese, whose influence was moving steadily up the Zambezi valley. Father Gonçalo da Silveira baptized the Mwanamutapa in 1560 but was assassinated soon thereafter. To avenge the death of Father da Silveira, the Portuguese sent punitive expeditions against the Mwanamutapa in 1572 and 1574. Although these expeditions failed to establish permanent Portuguese control, Portuguese influence in the seventeenth century reduced the Mwanamutapa to a puppet king. Upon the death of such a puppet king, Mavura, in 1652, the Mwanamutapa were baptized by Dominican missionaries, as described in the following account.

Dom Dominic Manamotapa, by the grace of God king and lord of Mocharanga, Boessa, Boronghá, Quiteve, Monghos, Inhaxamo, &c., make known to all to whom these presents shall come, that during the life of our father and lord the king Philip, we, being prince of these kingdoms, were brought up by the Religious of St. Dominic, to whose care the said king, our father, consigned us in the days of our early youth, and by them we were instructed and catechised and many times persuaded, until we desired to embrace the holy faith of Jesus Christ, and to receive the waters of holy baptism, and though we fervently desired the fulfilment of this our longing, being firmly convinced that this was the true path, in which the fathers walked; nevertheless we deferred the effect of our desire until such time and season as God our Lord should have done us the grace of bringing us to the actual possession of this our kingdom, wishing to imitate in this particular all that was done by the king our father, who being instructed and catechised in the doctrines of the holy faith, by Friar Emanuel Sardigna, of the said order of St. Dominic, would not receive holy baptism until he was in possession of his kingdoms, the Divine Majesty being after-

wards pleased to call the said king our father to his holy glory on the 25th of May 1652, immediately the fathers of St. Dominic and the nobles of the kingdom, who were present at court, informed us of his death, and several of these religious, although they were assisting the vicar of the court in person, Friar Ignatius of St. Thomas and others in his company came to us in the place where we resided, many leagues distant from the court, such being the custom and usage of these kingdoms, and after they had arrived we immediately prepared to depart with all possible haste, fearing some disturbance upon our succession on the part of Caprasine the tyrant king, who for his oppressions was expelled from the kingdom, and whose turbulent risings have brought forth many evils to these realms, in particular the death of many of our Portuguese vassals and of several religious, during the space of three years that the rising lasted. Therefore, before setting forth from the retreat where we resided, we caused the captain of Dambarare to see that the Portuguese were in order and readiness for any event which might occur. Afterwards there came Friar Giovanni de Melo, to whom our father gave our person in charge to instruct and make learned in letters, which charge the said Father ever fulfilled with the utmost diligence and zeal, and therefore we hold him in great consideration and esteem, keeping him next our person in the place of a father, being confident that if in this our government he assists us with his good counsel and aid we shall govern it with the same

"Authentic testimony of the baptism of the emperor and king Manamotapa, signed by the said emperor, sealed with the royal seal, signed by his secretary and interpreter, and sent to the Father Provincial Friar Dionysio de Lancastro of the Portuguese province of the Order of Preachers." Trans. by Miss A. de Alberti in George McCall Theal, *Records of South-Eastern Africa, Collected in Various Libraries and Archive Departments in Europe* (London, 1898), II, 445–448.

peace and tranquillity with which it was ever governed by the king our father with the assistance of Friar Emanuel Sardigna. And treating with the said Friar Giovanni de Melo of grave matters, he did not fail to remind us that the time was now come to receive holy baptism, in order to procure the assistance of God our Lord in our government, which is what the said father places above everything. We were well pleased with his reminder, agreeing in every way with his wish that we should receive holy baptism, to which end we greatly desired to keep him in our company as far as the court, but it was not possible to gratify this wish, it being necessary that the said father should go to Dambarare in person to treat of different matters of great importance to our person. He therefore hastened his journey thither, and on arriving, in a few days he successfully dispatched the business with which we had charged him, and there also overcame the difficulties which might have deferred the fulfilment of our desire of receiving holy baptism, and returned directly to this court, in company with the Presentado Friar Salvador of the Rosary, and arrived at court on the 1st of July of the year aforesaid. We rejoiced greatly at his coming, great signs of joy being also shown by all the nobles of our court, who were all ready, owing to the zeal of the said fathers, to receive the waters of holy baptism. We omitted no occasion of encouraging the holy work of the said fathers, and hearing that some of our nobles showed some reluctance to receive the waters of holy baptism, we ordered them to be summoned to our presence, and making use of the doctrine learned from the said fathers, we made them an exhortation by means of which they were fully convinced and resolved to become Christians. The fathers did not fail, for many days following, in catechising the said nobles, and their instructions came to an end on the feast of St. Dominic. On this day we issued from our palace with great pomp, accompanied by all the no-

bles, the soldiers of the garrison, and by the aforesaid religious who walked on each side of our person. On arriving at their church, richly decorated and prepared with great magnificence, we prescribed the order in which the waters of baptism were to be administered, which was in this manner following: we caused Friar Giovanni de Melo to baptize us and the queen our consort, Friar Salvador of the Rosary being godfather and bestowing upon us the name of Dom Dominic, the day being consecrated to that saint, and upon the queen the name of Dona Louisa. Then we ordered the two chief nobles of our kingdom to be baptized, Inigomaxa receiving the name of Dom John, and Inevinga that of Dom Sebastian, and after these two Inhamapa was baptized by the name of Dom Ferdinand, and Inhamafunhe our friend by the name of Dom Peter, who five or six months before dreamed that a religious of St. Dominic was baptizing him and making him a Christian, as he himself related to us in the presence of the said fathers. All the above named are nobles of our kingdom, lords of many lands, and nearly related to ourself. This baptism was celebrated with great rejoicing, especially by those of our court, who with musical instruments and festive dances gave incredible signs of joy. The said fathers are continuing their religious and Christian office, by which it is held as certain that in a few days there will be another baptism of other nobles, who are all ready and disposed to receive holy baptism. From all that has been said it cannot be denied that glory and the greatest praise are due to the Order of St. Dominic and the friars thereof, who are ministers in these our realms. We have therefore commanded Antonio Suárez, interpreter and secretary in this our court, faithfully and well to draw up an authentic document with the royal seal, confirmed by which these presents may come to the Superiors of the said Order, that they may certify the same to the Most Serene Majesty of Portugal, our brother, that this kingdom may remain under his protection, and that he may be pleased to command the Superiors of the said fathers to recognise their labours and the great services they have rendered to God, his Majesty, and ourself, in these realms.

Given at our court of Zimbaoe, signed by us and the aforesaid secretary, and sealed with the royal seal, the 14th of August 1652.

MANAMOTAPA, THE KING.

ANTONIO SUÁREZ,

Secretary and interpreter in the faith.

11 FATHER PINTO
THE KINGDOM OF THE KAZEMBE

Francisco José Maria de Lacerda e Almeida (d. 1798) was Governor of Sena (on the Zambezi River) when he was ordered to open a transcontinental route from Mozambique to Angola. His expedition reached the Kazembe capital, where Lacerda died. A record of the expedition had been kept by its chaplain, Father Pinto. The kingdom of the Kazembe originated in the early eighteenth century when the Lunda adventurer, Nganda Bilonda, was invested with the title of kazembe and organized a state on the upper Lualaba. His successors expanded eastward, and under Kazembe III, or Lukwesa (c. 1760–1850), the kingdom reached its height, becoming the strongest of all Lunda states and embracing southern Katanga and parts of northeastern Zambia. Kazembe III had established trade relations with the Portuguese settlers around Tete. Although he refused to permit Lacerda's expedition to proceed westward, trade developed with the coast, and the Kazembe capital became a major terminus for routes to Kilwa and Tete.

February 17, 1799—At 8 A.M. the Sana Muropúe returned to my house, and, in presence of all the whites, delivered a message from the Cazembe, that, as there was no more talk of Angola, he wanted the now superfluous presents intended for the Muropúe and the Mueneputo.[1] I put it to the vote of all: they were in a panic lest I should refuse: knowing the demand would be made, they augured the worst; some, for fear of being plundered and stripped, could not sleep at night. Lieut.-

Colonel Pedro Velasco (sic pro Nolasco) Vieira d'Araujo, the chief sergeant Pedro Xavier Velasco, and Antonio José da Cruz, were the only officers who did not show fear.

All being of one opinion, namely, that refusal would be dangerous, I was obliged to consent; but before doing so, I inquired of the Sana Muropúe what the Cazembe meant by such a claim; he replied it was all done in good friendship. I added that the presents should be put into his hands, not into those of the Fumo Anceva, as the latter had received a considerable gift in the name of our sovereign, and we did not know whether it had reached its destination. Moreover, that besides plundering what was given to his master, he robbed what the Cazembe sent to his friends and relatives (buenozes). But I insisted that in presence of the king the first present

From *Lacerda's Journey to Cazembe in 1798*, trans. and edited by Captain R. F. Burton, and *Journey of the Pombeiros P. J. Baptista and Amaro José Across Africa from Angola to Tette on the Zambeze*, trans. by B. A. Beadle (London: Royal Geographical Society, 1873), pp. 124–136.

[1] This was one of the strongest reasons for the transit not being allowed. The message was delivered by the apparent friend of the party, the Sana Muropúe, after the bully Fumo Anceva had been allowed to frighten them. All was perfectly *en règle*.

should be referred to. The Fumo Anceva changed colour, now denying that he had received the gift, then affirming that he had given up all to his master. The Sana Muropúe confirmed this last assertion, and relieved the Caffre whose guilt was evident; either to please the Cazembe who much affected his minister, or to draw him from a confusion which also fell upon all the nation (Murundas). Yet I persisted that the present gift should be reported before delivery, and to that purpose I sent the lieutenant, Antonio José da Cruz, who could not, however, find the Cazembe at home. The poor king has the *naïveté* to believe that over-zeal for his interests makes the Fumo Anceva, who is the greatest thief in his dominions, suffer from our false charges. I was therefore obliged to deliver the present without further ado, and without verifying the delivery of the former gift, a fact committed to paper and signed by all the party.[2] In the evening I began to inquire into the misdemeanour of Pedro Xavier Velásco.

18*th*–21*st*—There was drumming and dancing (tombocacao), which other Caffres of these parts call "Pembe-raçao,"[3] between Prince Muenebuto and his brother-in-law Chibuery, already alluded to on January 20th. The Cazembe was present with his usual dignity, but guarded by armed Caffres, as the prince danced with his large knife drawn in order to touch with it that of his father, a sign of honour and respect. The Cazembe, however, thus favoured only his son. The ceremony took place in the open space before the principal gate of the palace, a great crowd of people having instruments collected, and there also were our troops, for whom the Cazembe sent, and whose

discharge of musketry he himself directed. It was said that this fête was to celebrate his having closed once for all the Angola road, so as to increase his connection with Tete, whence their best things came. This was not confirmed, as they do not wish to break off with Angola.

I will now describe Muenebuto the prince, and his Murundas. Muenebuto is tall, good-looking, and well proportioned; his expression is pleasing, nay, almost always cheerful and smiling; he cares only for amusement, and his age—twenty years—permits nothing else. On the contrary, the Cazembe shows gravity and inspires respect; he also is tall, and well built, and his age may be about fifty. As he has many wives—the greatest sign of Caffre dignity—he becomes every year the father of two, three, or four children. He is very generous at times in giving slaves and pieces of cloth to his vassals, as well as to strangers and whites, when he is not set against them; and every day he sent the Muzungos money and different presents of provisions, captives, ivory or copper bars, in proportion to their offerings of cloth and beads, and according to his regard for them.

He is severe; death, or at least amputation of the hand, being the usual punishment. He is barbarous; every new moon he causes a Caffre to be killed by his medicine-man, and with the victim's blood, heart, and part of the entrails, they make up his medicine, always mixing it with oil. When these charms are prepared, they are inserted into the horns of various animals, and even into scrivellos, which are closed with stoppers of wood or cloth. These fetishes are distributed about his palace and courts; they are hung to the doors, and for fear of sorcery the king never speaks to any one without some of these horns lying at his feet.[4]

He holds assemblies of his chiefs, who are invited to drink pombe, or millet-beer,

---

[2] Those who have not travelled in Africa often wonder at all the importance attached to these trifling presents. But the fact is that without supplies the journey is brought to a dead stop, not taking into account the hardships and sufferings of return. The explorer, therefore, must fight for every cubit of cloth, and this is, perhaps, the severest part of his task.

[3] Native festivities, including drinking and cancan.

[4] Small horns of goats and antelopes are thus used in Unyamwezi, stuffed with thin iron wire; in Congo with strips of cloth.

which is mixed with other pulse or not, as each man's taste is. These drinkings begin with the full moon, and continue to the end; they commence daily at or before 1 P.M., and they last two hours. All those present drink as much as they please, but should any one vomit in the assembly, the wretch is instantly put to death. Though superstition-ridden, like all these people, the Cazembe is not so much so as are others. He visits no one in person, and never leaves his palace to walk; he has the name of being proud, but his people make him inconsistent.

The subjects (Murundas), who say that sixty years ago they came from the Western regions and established themselves in the lands of the conquered Vaciras (Messiras), are of the same nation as the Cazembe, whose rites and customs they follow.

Usually the men are tall, dark, well made, and good-looking; they tattoo (incise), but do not paint their bodies, nor do they jag their teeth. Their dress is a cloth extending from the waist to the knees, which are exposed by the garment being raised in front; it is girt by a leathern belt, 4 to 10 fingers broad. Their gala-dress is called "Muconzo;" it is of woollen or cotton, but it must be black. To make it they cut a piece $5^1/_2$ fathoms, or a little less in length, and if it be too short they add a bit of the same quality; the breadth is $2^1/_2$ hands, and if wider it is reduced to that size. It must be finished with a full edging, which increases it in all parts; this border is made of three strips of a different cloth, each 4 fingers broad. When the colour is red, for instance, the middle is white; it is yellow if the middle be red or white. Finally, they diversify these strips as they please, always taking care that the colour differs from the body or the principal part of the cloth. When putting on the "Muconzo," they cover the waist and legs, finishing at the front of the person with a great band of artificial pleats; and the larger it is, the grander is the garb. For arm-ornaments they use strings of fine beads like bracelets; their feet are covered with strung cowries, large opaque stoneware beads (pedras de côres), and white or red porcelains (velorios). Over their combed head-dresses, which are of many braids, large and small, they wear a cap (carapuça), covered with exquisite birds'-plumes; the locks are also striped (barradellas) with a certain clay, which, when dry, resembles the levigated sandal-wood used by the Moors and Gentoos (Hindus); the stripes, however, are only on the crown and temples (molleira). Others rub their bodies upon the waist and upwards to the hair with a certain vermilion (vermelhao),[5] here common.

Such is the gala dress. Their every-day clothing is a little cloth, $1^1/_2$ to 2 fathoms long, with or without a border of a single strip; others wear bark cloth, like the Muizas, or edgeless cotton; and finally, coarse native cotton (maxilas de Gondo),[6] as each one has or can afford.

As usual the women dress better than the men, as to the kind of cloth, which is of wool (collomanha) or similar stuff. They also use, like the males, strings of many sorts of beads, to cover their ankles, but they are not so fond of cowries or porcelain (velorio). Their coiffure is unlike that of the men; they cut off all the hair, leaving a little lock in the middle, which in time, growing long, serves to support a kind of diadem [ornamental headband—ed.]; the rest of the hair, when it grows, forming sundry lines of short braid. Their ordinary dress is extremely poor, consisting of one very small cloth. These women, who also can be sold by their husbands, lead the lives of slaves, doing all the labour of domestic slavery.

The Murundas,[7] like other peoples of

---

[5] It has previously been described as being wood-powder.
[6] The expression is fully explained in the diary of June 20–23. Dr. Kirk says that a "Maxila de garda" is a hammock of native cloth. "Maxila de Gondo" is a stuff so coarse that hammocks can be made of it. Hence Monteiro and Gamitto call the coarse cotton cloth made by the Marave, "Manxila."
[7] In the original misprinted "Mosundas."

this country, have no (practical) religion. They recognize the existence of a sovereign creator of the world, and call him "Reza," but they consider him a tyrant that permits his creatures' death. They have great veneration for their Azimos (murimos), or dead, whom they consult on all occasions of war or good fortune. The Caffre servants of any Moçaza,[8] or place in which a king is buried, have many privileges. The Azimos require offerings of provisions, as dough (massa), a food made of manioc flour, to stew with the porridge, which in the Brazil is called Angú; of quiriaça (any mess of meat, fish, or herbs), and of pombe, the millet-beer before described. They greatly respect what the oracle says to them. Their sons are circumcised between the ages of fourteen and eighteen,[9] and they affect polygamy, which they regard as their greatness, much wondering at the one-wife marriage of the whites.

Their unions are effected without ceremony: the would-be husband goes to the father or guardian of the girl, who may be quite a child, and with him arranges the dowry in cloths, which, if great, may reach a dozen. After this arrangement, called betrothal (roboracção), the payment being left to the bridegroom's convenience, they arrange a day for leading home the bride, who, until of nubile years, remains with her parents. Consummation is done thus: carried by the horse of some Caffre, and accompanied by her female relations and friends, beating drums, the bride is escorted to near the bridegroom's house, and when close to it they send him word that they bring his wife. This done, they drum and dance till some velorio beads are sent to them, after which they advance two paces or so, and stop till they get more. Thus, on his marriage-day, the poor Caffre must not only strip himself, but also go out borrowing, to show that he has given all his own. Seeing nothing more come, they inspect the sum offered them, then they advance nearer, and at length they hand over the bride to the chief wife and her companions, and retire to their homes, leaving her in tears. As the Caffres may buy an unlimited number of spouses, even their slaves being wives to them, they choose one, and call her the great woman, and she is the most respected. Her peculiar duties are to preserve the husband's wardrobe and medicines, and to apply the latter when required; without using them no one goes to war, to hunt, or to travel, or, indeed, on any important business.

The funerals of these people are proportioned to the means of the deceased. Their pomp consists in the great cortége by which the body is borne to the grave, and in the quantity of food and drink expended upon the crowd of people, who sing and dance to the sound of drums. If the deceased be a king, he must carry with him all that he possesses, with slaves to serve him and women for his pleasures. Throughout his dominions robberies and disorder (cleirero) are allowed for ten or fifteen days, or even more. Their deadliest crimes are witchcraft, adultery, and theft. The first, and the most enormous, is always punished capitally; the second sometimes, but more often by mutilation of the hands, the ears, and the offending member. They are less severe with the women, as a rule, but some plaintiffs are not satisfied except by death. Although they cut off the thief's hands and ears, many wretches have exposed themselves to such mutilation.

The soil of this land is fertile, and would produce all that the people want; there are many kinds of food, but the principal is manioc. They eat it in dough, toasted and boiled and even raw; and they drink it in pombe with a little mixture of millet. Manioc flour for dough is easily made in the following way: after gathering

---

[8] Mussassa is a camp: here it must be the burial-place before called Mâxâmo.
[9] In Dahomey this rite is deferred often till the twentieth year, and then it becomes dangerous. I have repeatedly recorded my opinion that it is of African origin, borrowed by the Jews from the negroid race.

the root, they peel it, and soak it in a stream, for three days; on the fourth, when it is almost rotten, they dry it in the summer sun, or in winter over a fire which they light under the cots used for this purpose; and, finally, they pound it in a tree-trunk mortar. We may say that they are collecting and sowing this root all the year round, but the harvest is when provision is wholly wanting. At such times they dig up a small quantity to last for a few days, and in its stead they bury a few bits of stalk which act as seed. The rains are abundant and regular. Fruits are few, except bananas of many kinds: of live stock, poultry is the most plentiful and goats are rare. Game and fish suffice, but they cannot salt their provision, so to keep it they dry it with fire and smoke, making it unfit for us to eat. The black cattle is well flavoured, but only the king keeps them in certain places, to show his greatness: he does not eat their flesh, saying that they are Fumos [black in color—ed.], like himself; also he does not milk them, not knowing how, so the cows are almost wild. Here we find traces of the Metempsychosis theory.[10] With this idea the king sends his cattle as gifts to his guests, and when they die or are killed for injuring millet fields—these animals pasture by night and sleep by day—he divides the meat amongst his people, who, not considering them, like their king, great Fumos, eat them unscrupulously. Cow leather makes their girdles, that of other horned cattle their dress, and cows' blood enters into their medicines. Therefore they sent us only dead and skinned animals.

There may be many articles of trade, but it is now confined to two—ivory and slaves. A tusk of 32 lbs. to 48 lbs. costs 2 to 3 pieces of cloth, the piece being 1 1/2 to 2 fathoms long, and ten couros.[11] The tusk of 80 lbs. to 96 lbs. is worth 5 to 6 pieces, with a little couro or velorio. There are copper bars sold for four common cloths, or pagnes (pannos de fato), or 40 to 50 couros; the small bars cost as a rule one cloth's worth of missanga. Uncut greenstone (malachite)[12] of different sizes is sold cheap, but the two latter articles are not indigenous.

22nd—The Sana Muropúe took away, in presence of all the whites, the gifts destined for the Muropúe and the Mueneputo, as was promised at our assembly on the 17th instant.

23rd—Having ordered Lieutenant Antonio José da Cruz, commandant of the troops, to chastise a soldier with forty blows, he not only disobeyed me, but he also falsely reported having carried out my orders.

February 24th to *March 1st*—The men, instigated by their officers, demanded an advance of three months' pay, which I sent to them without receiving any reply.

2nd–4th—I gave Pedro Xavier Velasco leave to go back to Tete, not only at his request, but because I wished to avoid the disgust shown by all the Expedition to the Cazembe, with whom, it is said, this arrangement of return had been made in anticipation of my desires. José Rodrigues Caleja, hearing this, wished to interfere and exceeding his duties as guide and Receiver of the Treasury, he addressed me a note in which, after a fashion, he made himself accessory to the command. As I took no notice of his false reasonings, he began to show me aversion and to seek his revenge.

5th—The manioc grown in the land which the Cazembe had offered to the whites (muzungos) on the 27th January was divided, but their carelessness prevented them sending their slaves (checun-

---

[10] Superficial observers often confound the highly philosophical and complicated theory of metempsychosis with the vulgar metamorphosis of the savage African. [Metempsychosis is the passing of the soul at death into another body either animal or human —ed.]

[11] From the context it would appear that these couros are some kind of bead.

[12] Monteiro and Gamitto mention malachite "malaquites," which the Cazembe call "chifuvia." I have seen fine copper from the Cazembe's country.

das) to receive the portion appertaining to them.

6th–9th—Loud murmurs arose about the Expedition arriving at the Cazembe's city—which it could not at once leave—during the early month of January, when the evils caused by the wet season and the country rendered a long rest necessary. As José Rodrigues Caleja, by declaring me to be the cause of the delay and of their consequent sufferings, showed signs of stirring up against me even the most indifferent, I assembled all the whites. They knew what were my reasons for wintering here, so I resolved that each should separately declare his opinion touching our inaction, whether it could have been avoided or not and how. I told the writer, or notary, to take the paper in which all had recorded their opinions, to draw it up in legal form, and to get their signatures. It was late when we separated, and the scribe was not skilled enough to draft the deed without the aid of others. He went to José Rodrigues Caleja, being of that party, and with him falsified not only Caleja's vote but also that of Vasco Joaquim Pires, as is proved in the forged paper. I was disregarded by Captain João da Cunha Pereira, and when I wished to punish him there and then he would not be arrested, nay, with threats he declared that His Excellency, the Captain-General of Mozambique, should not deprive him of his receivership, as had been done to Lieut. Manoel dos Santos Silva.

As I had little power, nothing was effected. I asked Gonçalo Caetano Pereira, the first guide, how to ascertain from Chinhimba and Mossindassaro the deficiency of the loads entrusted to them for carriage to the Cazembe's court. He replied, in the presence of many, that this must be done with the beneplacet of the king, whose vassals they were. Finding the answer reasonable, I entrusted to him the business, which he undertook promptly and with good will.

10th—Lieutenant Antonio José da Cruz, when ordered to attest in writing the refusal of Captain João da Cunha Pereira to submit to arrest yesterday, gave in his attestation which denied all that had happened.

11th–14th—Gonçalo Caetano Pereira, whom I had resolved to send on the 8th instant to the Cazembe in the matter of Mossindassaro and Chinhimba, when asked by José Rodrigues Caleja not to delay, excused himself by means of his Caffre Inharugue, saying that the latter did not wish to bear any message to the Cazembe. The most embarrassing thing is, that they try to lay the blame upon me, when at the same time they bar my road to the king, and they prevent the two Caffres obeying all my summons. At last I tried every effort to send some other person on this errand to the king, who deferred it till the morrow.

15th—Sending back to the Cazembe the messenger who had returned yesterday, I heard to-day that the king was pleased with my calling up and examining the two Caffres before mentioned. When they declined to obey my summons I reported the fact to the king, begging that his messenger would conduct them into my presence. He promised but he never performed, which I attributed to the intrigues of Caleja. This man, under colour of benefiting D. Francisca Josefa of Tete, whose niece he had married, declared that the late Governor de Lacerda, who had taken charge of that lady's venture, and whose death had caused the goods to be confused, had concealed by means of the Mossindassaro, six bales (moteros) [13] of cloth, and had changed the mark or mixed the articles, removing 150 pannos and two bags (guissapos) [14] of velorio beads. These he had wished to make over to D. Francisco's slave, Candeone, in order to exchange for ivory. And this was done with the knowledge of the gover-

---

[13] This is afterwards explained to be one-third of 456 cloths, that is to say, each 152 cloths.
[14] The word "guissapo" means a bag of bamboo rind or grass cloth. Monteiro and Gamitto speak of "um Quissápo, sacco feito de palma."

nor's managing man, whose duty it was to take charge of those articles, pretexting the report spread by José Rodrigues Caleja that the manager had wished to appropriate the said spoils. This trick of José Rodrigues Caleja's was very ingenious, for not only was that Caffre encouraged to conceal 912 more cloths (pagnes) of royal property, but Chinhimba, the other Caffre messenger, also took heart successfully to embezzle from the Crown 456 cloths, three bags (guissapos) of velorio, two ditto of (red) beads, and one of cowries.

16th–28th—José Rodrigues Caleja was always imposing upon them the necessity of giving the Cazembe time to prepare for our departure. The others being sick, I directed him to go with a "mouth" or parcel of cloth and to make preparations, at the same time reviving the matter of the two Caffres. The Cazembe received him well, and said that he knew—the winter now being over—that the Expedition would wish to return to Tete. As regards the defaulting Caffre, he said that the whites had allowed a long time to pass in silence, and had finally received everything. The first part of this reply could not have come from a Caffre, who all hold that the palaver (milando) never dies, nor wastes, but is kept up till "settled" from generation to generation. So I resolved either that the king had not said it, or had been taught to say it by José Rodrigues Caleja. The affair was not pushed further, because it was not advisable to call Chinimba to account until the appearance of Mossindassaro, who would hear of it from the Cazembe and conceal himself.

29th–30th—I gave the said Caffres some small quantity of clothing for which they asked, thus hoping to assemble them and to elicit something about the hidden goods.

31st—The Cazembe sent me the chair enclosed in his present (mirambo), begging me to have it lined with "cherves," which was done at once.

April 1st–7th—By an accidental fire eight of my slaves were burned in their own huts; many of the Expedition rejoiced thereat, and a certain José Thomaz Gomes da Silveira, openly wished that the accident had taken place in my house. I report this and other things, which do not exactly relate to the service of the Crown, both to carry out my instructions and to show the character of my subordinates.

8th–9th—The Cazembe forbade the whites, who had begun their cabals greatly to his disgust, all intercourse with him, thus avoiding their impertinences, and he wondered at our disunion.

10th—José Rodrigues Caleja, an old enemy of Lieutenant Manoel dos Santos e Silva, with whom he appeared friendly only when wishing to insult me, after visiting him in his sickness, declared to me that he wished for death, and that if he knew of anything to end his life he would take it.

11th–12th—I had some inklings that the crime charged upon Pedro Xavier Velasco was a mere imputation, and Lieutenant José Vicente Pereira Salema confessed that he had been intimidated to give false witness by José Rodrigues Caleja. I also learned that Captain João da Cunha Pereira, after his deposition, went to Pedro Xavier Velasco's quarters, and told him that I wanted to drink his blood, which was my reason for drawing up papers against him, but that no depositions made by himself or his colleagues would do him any injury.

13th—José Rodrigues Caleja convoked, in the house of Gonçalo Caetano Pereira, to debate over the affair of the 9th of March, all those of his party, viz., Captain João da Cunha Pereira, Lieutenant Manoel dos Santos e Silva, Captain José da Cruz, José Thomaz Gomes da Silva, Lieutenant José Vicente Pereira Salema, and Ensign José Joaquim Pires; they agreed to outrage me in that business, first by word and then by deed. The Lieut.-Colonel Pedro Nolasco Vieira de Araujo and the chief sergeant Pedro Xavier Velasco were sick, and not of the league.

I had no testimony whereby to convict them, thus they could insult me with impunity. The former of these two, however, came unexpectedly upon them, and the project fell to the ground. All this was told to me by Lieutenant José Vicente Pereira Salema, whom as the most timorous they sent to me with a paper of their requisitions.

14th–15th—José Rodrigues Caleja, who was in the habit of troubling me morning and evening, came early to report that messengers were expected from Tete to recall the troops, as there was great alarm of the French.

16th—José Rodrigues Caleja required me to assemble the members in order to determine how to sell the Crown stores remaining in the receiver's hands. My reply was that I had reasons for not convening any more of such assemblies. He went at once and wrote me a letter representing the loss that would result from taking the goods back to Tete. In view of all this trouble I at once ordered the stores to be valued.

17th—The effects were valued by the arbitrators at only double their cost-price at Tete, and the receiver, with sundry impertinences, demanded permission to sell them. I ordered them to be sold for the sums offered, finding that nothing more advantageous could be obtained.

18th–19th—I sent to compliment the Cazembe, who was then a great friend of mine; he sent back that he wanted to see me.

20th—I returned an answer to the Cazembe's message, declaring that I would call upon him personally.

21st—José Rodrigues Caleja, angry because, without consulting him, I had allowed Pedro Xavier Velasco to return to Tete, and because I would not be made the tool of his private enmities, did all he could to annoy me. He teazed me with requests to smuggle out the cloth required for our return march, as the Cazembe would never allow it, after once entering, to leave the country. Fearing his malice,

I appointed him and the guide, Gonçalo Caetano Pereira, to fix upon the quantity and the place. The former was settled, the latter they refused to tell me, pleading that, as we had travelled together, I—a chaplain—must know as much as they (the guides) did.

22nd–23rd—I again ordered the two aforesaid guides to tell me the "cache," and they refused.

24th—The Cazembe consented to receive me on the morrow, and to send a household officer to conduct me, as the Fumo Anceva wished all the whites to be purely dependent upon himself. José Rodrigues Caleja happened to be present, and, dissimulating his jealousy of my getting an audience when he had failed, begged me to forward the departure of the Expedition, which, depending upon the Cazembe, would easily be forgotten unless often brought to mind.

25th—After a short delay I was admitted to the Cazembe, who received my compliments kindly, responding briefly after the country fashion. This over, I earnestly prayed him to forward the time of our return; to which he also replied favourably. I then submitted to him that on reaching Tete there would be a difficulty in explaining to my superiors the prohibition of passing over to Angola; he bade me leave two members of the party to proceed there after our departure. The Fumo Anceva wrested this into a demand that each of the whites should leave behind one or two Cheundas.[15] Knowing that the slaves would be pawns for our future communication, and that the Caffres being scarce, and many of them sickly, the whites would not consent to the measure. I replied that when Catára and Chinimba had come with friendly messages to Tete, we had at once set out without hostages. Hearing me speak to the soldier-linguist in the Sena dialect, the Cazembe at once explained that he did not want hostages, but two persons to go to

---

[15] This, I presume, is "checunda"—a slave.

Angola. I could not reply to so sudden and unexpected a permission, so I told the king that the presents destined for the Muropúe and the Muenebuto having been given away, and the treasury being exhausted, my confusion prevented my returning an answer. The Cazembe at once said that he would manage about the presents, and that all I had to do was to look after the subsistence and the means of travel. I finally answered that the matter should be thought over. He then spoke of the opaque stoneware beads (pedras de côres) which he wanted from the whites, who still, he knew, had good things. I contented him as well as possible, and left deeply preoccupied about Angola. After my return, José Rodrigues Caleja, on hearing the affair, malignantly remarked, that if I had proposed Pedro Xavier Velasco as envoy to the Cazembe, he would soon close the road with a new prohibition; and much of the same kind to throw obstacles in my way.[16]

26th—José Rodrigues Caleja came, and insultingly showed me a paper in which the lieutenant-colonel Pedro Nolasco Vieira de Araujo and Pedro Xavier Velasco had complained of him, and charged him with being their informant. As if a secret between nine persons could be kept, especially when of the many councillors are Captain João da Cunha Pereira and Lieutenant José Vicente Pereira Salema, who do nothing but tittle-tattle. I tried to avoid a scandalous rupture, but from that day forward he did nothing but oppose me, wishing to commit all the goods to the Cazembe, and thus to frustrate the transit to Angola.

27th—The Fumo Anceva came from the Cazembe, refusing passage to Tete for Lieut.-Colonel Pedro Nolasco Vieira de Araujo, who wished to leave these bad men. I answered that he was not going, because I had not given him leave. This reply closed the Caffre's mouth. He doubtless had been taught to oppose this departure, though not by his friendship for the departer. It was José Rodrigues Caleja's plan, in opposing the going of the two Pedros, Nolasco and Velasco, to forewarn all those who might be useful to him at Tete, adding as many lies as possible, and well knowing that the thing first heard, though false, is generally credited in preference to truth.

Not satisfied by this mischief, that perverse man went with Lieutenant Antonio José da Cruz to the Cazembe, designing to traduce me and Pedro Nolasco, but the Cazembe, who hated his mutinous disposition, refused him access. He must indeed be a bad white man who is hated by Caffres. He reported to the Fumo Anceva that the Lieut.-Colonel Pedro Nolasco and the other whites had so well hidden many fine cloths and coloured stoneware beads (pedras pintadas), that these could be discovered only by opening their boxes. The Cazembe, despite his generosity, was persuaded to give this order, or the Fumo Anceva fabricated it. I sent for the lieutenant-colonel, Pedro Nolasco, to hear the message: he excused himself, but he could not prevent the search. I positively refused to sanction it in the case of other whites, knowing that the Fumo Anceva wanted only to enter the receiver's house and to carry off everything for his king.[17]

[16] This permission for two of the party to proceed to Angola was a sham, to see if any presents had been withheld, and to try the perseverance of the whites. The Cazembe must have thought unfavourably of the leader when he hesitated at once to reply—a thing ever to be avoided in Africa. The two soldiers were eventually left behind as was proposed, but they never, it need hardly be said, reached Angola. In 1806 the Angolan Pombeiros found one man still waiting for permission.

[17] There is a Fumo Anceva at every African court, who thinks only of recommending himself to the king by giving any amount of trouble to strangers. Of course it is a shallow, short-sighted policy, but nothing better can come from the negro's brain. It is, however, dangerous, and must be carefully watched, as it is calculated to cause disagreeables between the members of an expedition, and then everything goes to ruin.

12 P. J. BAPTISTA
THE KAZEMBE

In 1806 two pombeiros (African traders), P. J. Baptista and Anastasio José, arrived at the capital of Kazembe and there met Lukwesa's successor, his son Kibangu Keleka, or Kazembe IV. After a prolonged residence at the capital, Kazembe IV permitted the pombeiros to complete their trans-African journey in 1810. The following excerpts are from Baptista's diary.

[74th.] *Saturday, 20th*—Halted in the Cazembe's sister's farm, by her own order. At two in the morning, she sent for us, and we went inside her walls. She asked whence we came. We replied, from Angola and the court of Muropue, who had given us the guide. That we had come to speak with her brother King Cazembe, to get permission to go on to the town of Tette. She replied it was very good on the part of Muropue to send white people to speak with her brother; that none of Muropue's predecessors had done so; that it was a very great fortune for her brother Cazembe's heir to the State. She offered us a large she-goat, forty fresh fish, two bottles of a drink called "pombe," and six quicapos of dry mandioca flour. We presented her with thirty-two xuabos, a blue glass, and a "mozenzo" of a hundred white stones. She said she was much pleased with our gifts. We waited there that she might send notice of our arrival to her brother, King Cazembe, as it is obligatory on her part when travellers come to report them to her brother. With this end we waited six days at her farm, when the carriers came in search of us.

[75th.] *Saturday, 27th*—Got up and left the farm of Cazembe's sister at 7 A.M. Had no rain. We followed down the course of the Luapula. Passed a river of two fathoms' width, name unknown, which runs into the Luapula. During the

From *Lacerda's Journey to Cazembe in 1798*, trans. and edited by Captain R. F. Burton, and *Journey of the Pombeiros P. J. Baptista and Amaro José. Across Africa from Angola to Tette on the Zambeze*, trans. by B. A. Beadle (London: Royal Geographical Society, 1873), pp. 186–188.

journey we came to the farm of a black named Murumbo: we reached it at midday. We met no one, and marched with the sun on our right. We lodged in the houses of the farm, and saw nothing rare or important.

[76th.] *Sunday, 28th*—We got up at 2 A.M., and started from the farm of Murumbo. We marched down with the above-named river on our left. We passed two rivers, Lufubo and Capueje, which run into the above-named river. During the journey we came to the farm of a black named Gando, near a river called Gona, here we gave no presents. We reached it at six in the afternoon. We marched with the sun as before.

[77th.] *Monday, 29th*—At 5 A.M. we got up and started from the farm of Gando, near the river Gona. We passed two rivers, one called Belenje, the other's name not known; during the march we came to the place of a black named Canpungue. We reached this place at three in the afternoon, and met a good number of King Cazembe's people carrying firewood. We presented this black, Canpungue, with a chuabo of "Zuarte" or Indian cloth; he told us to continue our journey, as the Cazembe was expecting us.

[78th.] *Tuesday, 30th*—At seven A.M. we started from the place of the black, Canpungue—had no rain; we passed no river, and during the journey came to the place of a black named Luiagamára, of the Cazembe. Reaching this place at four in the afternoon, we lodged in the houses near a river called Canengua, narrow, and running into the river called Mouva, near which Cazembe's city is situated. We gave no present to the owner of this place; we halted there, and sent forward a day's notice of our arrival; we waited a little time, when the King Cazembe's messenger arrived, bringing us, as guest-gift, four murondos of a drink called "pombe," one hundred pieces of fresh meat, with some manioc flour for our consumption, and also a message from King Cazembe, asking us to remain at present where we were, that he would send for us later. Day breaking directly, and it being two o'clock in the morning, he sent for us by his chief, with orders that on our arrival near the walls of his chiefs (ancestors?), we should fire off all our guns, as a signal that we had arrived at his capital. He ordered us to lodge with one of his gatekeepers, named Fumo Aquibery. We did nothing respecting our journey on this day: he sent us for our people, however, some provisions, manioc flour, fish, fresh meat, and "pombe," she-goats, and meats already prepared; he said he would see us with great pleasure. When morning broke, he sent word for us to come and tell him what brought us there. We found him seated in the public highway, where he was accustomed to deliver his judgments to his people, surrounded by all the great potentates of his councils. He was robed in his silks and velvets, and had beads of various kinds on his arms and legs; his people surrounded him, and he had all his instruments of barbarous grandeur round about him. He sent to say that the guide who had come with us from his Muropue should speak. The guide said, "I bring you some white men here from the king they call Muenuputo; they come to communicate with you, King Cazembe; treat them well, without malice, and execute the wishes entrusted to them: grant them, King Cazembe, permission, together with some guide, who you may see able to conduct them, to go to the town of Tette, to deliver a letter to the Most Illustrious Governor of that town, they being entrusted with this mission in Angola,

whence they came. Muropue also strongly recommends you will do all necessary to despatch the travellers where they wish to go, and afterwards send them back to Muropue, in order that he may return them whence they came." The King Cazembe said that he esteemed it much, and not a little, his Muropue's having sent travellers from afar; that for a long time past he had entertained the idea of opening the road to Senna; that he was very pleased to see travellers from Muropue, none of whose predecessors had similarly acted before; that he would do all in his power—not only provide a guide, but go with us himself as far as the Warcamp, to fight the highwaymen and robbers who meet with and intercept people on the road coming to communicate with him, King Cazembe. We had gone with King Cazembe as far as a farm of his people, about half a league from Cazembe, with numerous troops to escort us on the road; after this, a perturbation spread among his people, who did not wish to fight, so the attempt was frustrated; we returned to the farm with him against his wish. He began to cast out his chiefs; he cut the ears of some, others he mulcted in slaves and manilhas (bracelets); and on the second month he handed us over to his chief named Muenepanda to accompany us with more people. On our reaching a desert-lodging called Quipire, he turned back, saying that the town of Tette was a long way off; that the force he (Muenepanda) had to oppose to the potentates he might meet on the road was very small; that he did not wish to run any risk. We returned with him, and after waiting another half month, the black, named Nharugue, belonging to Gonçalo Caetano Pereira arrived, and we started and marched in his company till we reached this town of Tette.

King Cazembe is very black, a fine, stout young man, with small beard, and red eyes; he is very well accustomed to white traders, who come to his court to buy and sell such articles as seed, manioc flour, maize, millet, haricot beans, a good many "canas" (sugar-cane?), and fish which the people catch in the river near there called Mouva. Ivory comes from the other side the river Luapula, and is brought as tribute by the people; green stones (malachite) are found in the ground, called "catanga"; traders from the Muizas people come and buy ivory, in exchange for tissues and merchandise; another nation, named Tungalágazas, brings slaves and brass bracelets, cowries, palm-oil, and some goods which King Cazembe has, come from the Cola (Angola?), a land of Muropue, also fine large beads. There is a good deal of salt in that part, which they get from the ground; there is also another kind of rock-salt which is brought as tribute from the salt district, on the road to Muropue's territory, called Luigila, where he has a chief and a relation, named Quibery, who takes account of the Salina, and sends tributes of salt to his Muropue, besides buying it of the travellers who come from Muropue. I have made no entry of the rainy days we stopped, or of those when we were detained by sickness. I saw nothing more at the Court of King Cazembe which I have forgotten to write; I saw nothing but that already stated.

13   A. C. P. GAMITTO
THE MARAVI

A. C. P. Gamitto (1806–1866) was second in command of the Monteiro expedition that set out to open a transcontinental route from Mozambique to Angola between 1831 and 1832—an abortive mission that Lacerda similarly had failed to accomplish a generation before. The Maravi *described by Gamitto are one of the principle groups in the modern state of Malawi, which takes its name from the former chiefdoms of the Maravi west of Lake Malawi. The Maravi claim to have originated in Lubaland, and although the Portuguese believed that the Maravi built a great empire, the probability is that no one chief became paramount, as was the case in the kingdom of the* Kazembe.

· · ·

The territory occupied by these people is one of the largest in this part of Africa. Its inhabitants, who are in continual warfare among themselves, are the subjects of a great number of small chiefs or princes who are forever trying to destroy one another; this is one reason for the poor opinion that foreigners hold of this country in

From A. C. P. Gamitto, *King Kazembe and the Marave, Cheva, Bisa, Bemba, Lunda, and Other Peoples of Southern Africa, Being the Diary of the Portuguese Expedition to that Potentate in the Years 1831 and 1832,* trans. by Ian Cunnison (Lisbon: Junta de Investigações do Ultramar, 1960), I, 63–73. Reprinted by permission.

spite of its size and population. The land, properly known today by the name of Marave, is bounded in the west by the Shombwe stream, which divides it from the Cheva; and in the east by the Mukakamwe torrent, which separates it from the Portuguese dominions of Tete district which extend on the left bank of the Zambezi as far as the Lupata. In the north, the boundary is with the Bororo and the Maganja; and in the south the boundary is the Zambezi, which divides it from the Munhaes of Monomotapa and the Portuguese territory of the district mentioned.

The part which we traversed, which is not its widest part, would be about 59 leagues. Its length from north to south comprises a very great extent, but not knowing how much I am unable to calculate the total area. In the east, north and south these people border Portuguese lands.

Formerly this region was divided into two dominions, Munhaes and Maraves; and today these people have taken various names. Those referred to above are prope·ly the Marave; Bororos are those who dwell on the left bank of the Zambezi and are bordered by the territory of Quelimane and on the west by the Shire. Between these and the Lupata are the Maganjas. And from the north to the coast at Cape Delgado are the Makwa. West of the Marave, as far as the river Luangwa, live the Cheva, and to the east of these and near the mouth of that river are the Senga and between these and the Portuguese territories of the left bank of the Zambezi are the Mogoa. East of the Makwa, and on the shores of the river or lake Nyanja, are the Yao or Nguru. All these people today are totally independent of each other, and each is known by its own name. Nevertheless it is beyond dispute that all are of the same Marave race, having the same habits, customs, language, etc.

This country is of very vast extent, and according to my information there are many impassable regions in it, because of the bad treatment received from the savage inhabitants, and the thick forests covering it. The Nguru are of ferocious appearance, and do not agree to penetration by strangers into their land beyond the western margin of the aforesaid lake or river. It is only there that commerce with them takes place.

II

It is still not known whether the Lake Marave of the geographers, called Nyanja-Mukulu (Rio Grande) by the Blacks, and Rio Nyanja by the Portuguese, has communication with the sea. It seems certain however that it forms a mighty river which has its mouth on the Zanzibar coast, being perhaps the Koavo, which debouches opposite Kilwa. It seems it was visited by the early Portuguese,[1] but I have no information that it has been visited by any European traveller, but only by Moors and Blacks who have gone there from Mozambique to trade, and Bisa who are today the merchants of those regions. From all of these I have received the following unanimous information.

The river Nyanja-Mukulu, or great Nyanja, has an extraordinary breadth. Embarking in canoes to cross it, it is necessary to sleep two nights on islands, with which it is sprinkled, before arriving on the third day in the afternoon on the opposite shore: a distance which, according to my calculation, must be about nine leagues. It has a strong easterly current. The many islands it contains, some of which are very large, are for the most part inhabited, those on the west by the Marave, and those on the east by the Yao or Nguru. This is the story that mer-

[1] Father Manoel Godinho, in his Voyage from India to Portugal by Land in 1663, says as follows:

"The road from Angola to India by land is not yet discovered; but it certainly will be, and the passage will be easy, because from Angola to Lake Zachaf (which is in the middle of Ethiopia and is fifteen leagues broad, although its length is not yet known) is less than 250 leagues. Cosmographers put this lake at 15° 50', and according to a map I have seen, made by a Portuguese who went many years to the kings of Monomotapa, Manica, Butua and others of Kaffraria, this lake is not far from the Zimbawe, or court, of Mesura or Marabia. There issues from it the river Aruvi which flows into the Zambezi above our fort of Tete. And also the river Chire which, cutting through many lands, and latterly through those of the Rondo, joins the river Cuama below Sena. This assured I now say: he who would make this journey from Angola to India by way of Mozambique, crossing the interior of Kaffraria, should ask for the said Lake Zachaf, and on finding it, descend by the rivers to our forts of Tete and Sena and from there to the Quelimane delta; from Quelimane by land and sea to Mozambique, and from Mozambique to Goa in a month. That there is such a lake is stated not only by the Kaffirs, but also by Portuguese who already went there, navigating up the rivers and who, for lack of funds, have not yet discovered this route."

chants who have been there generally give.

There is another river called by the Africans Nyanja-Panono, or little river, and which the Portuguese call Nyanja-Pequeño. I cannot say if it comes out of the Rio Grande, from which at some places it is several days away.

On this point, and on the matter of its shores being inhabited by Marave and Yao, I can affirm nothing positively, because these were not things I observed.

To this information on the two Nyanjas we may add what is read in the diary of the march made to Kazembe in 1798 by Dr. Lacerda, "On September 21st he found himself in the village of the Fumo Mouro-Achinto, situated 10° 20′ 35″ lat. S., and 39° 10′ 0″ long. E. of Lisbon according to observations made on the sun and two eclipses of Jupiter's satellites: and he mentions that he was told there that to the north, between the Sukuma nation which reaches the banks of the Shire or Nyanja, and the Bisa, lay the Bemba nation: and that the lands to the south were peopled by the Lamba and Ambo, and that these two nations do commerce with the Africans in the neighbourhood of Zumbo."

I have said already that the Bisa today have no land of their own, it having been conquered by the Muembas, who are probably the Bemba (Uemba) mentioned above. As to the Shire being the same as the Nyanja, we add nothing to what is already stated.

It would not be difficult to confirm the truth about the Nyanja Grande if a small expedition left the Sena Rivers, another left Mozambique and another left the isles of Cape Delgado, without military equipment but with all possible trade goods, each taking a man capable of making an exact description to satisfy the aims of the exploration. It would be best to leave from these three points, making arrangements to communicate and inform each other of discoveries made, because in this way, if one or two of them miscarried

through various obstacles (of which the main is the desertion of Kaffirs who have to be taken as carriers), one of them would probably arrive at its destination and this would be enough. All should be ordered to make for the River, and there buy canoes in sufficient number to provide transport for all, or a part, and navigate downstream to its mouth. A craft appropriate to the task would have to be sent from Mozambique to where its mouth is supposed to be, in order to bring them back. This should be easy and would involve little expense.

I calculate the width of the great Nyanja at nine leagues because, according to my information, it has a strong current; therefore the canoes have to go obliquely and so they have to spend three days on a journey which, with a slow current, they could do in half the time. The same width in slightly different circumstances takes longer.

The best season for such an exploration would be spring, and it should not begin before the end of April or even May.

The Portuguese rule in Cape Delgado by right, but by the neglect which this territory has suffered it has been left to the Arabs of the Imam of Muscat to profit by all its commerce; this they do mainly through contraband, without the Portuguese government of the district having the power to embarrass them; and so they monopolise the trade and take all the profits. As this is another subject I shall keep what I have to say for another memorandum on Portuguese East Africa; but just now I felt it was necessary to explain about these explorations.

III

In the middle of Marave land is a small area occupied also by some Marave who are known as Chupeta; and their district has the same name. Although they have the same habits, etc., they live quite independently. Each village has a supreme chief, who belongs to the family composing it, and who recognises no political superior: it is better to let oneself be annihilated or destroyed completely, than to give obedience to another. In case of a dispute or outbreak of war between two chiefs, which is very frequent, the members of the two villages fight one another but it never finishes with the first fight. He who weakens retreats and gets another one to help him, and thus the two factions grow incessantly to the point where often all the chiefs are eventually involved in the contest. On each occasion, the quarrel is brought to an end by the appointment of arbitrators to judge the matter, which may be nothing more than the purloining of a millet stalk. Often enough war breaks out again if the guilty party does not agree to pay an indemnity which appears too exorbitant, or if the innocent party is not satisfied with it. In such cases when fighting has been heavy, the quarrel is brought to an end and the condemned party pays war damages to the satisfaction of all the chiefs who helped the winning side, who assess all the damage since the start of the fighting. It usually happens that the lives of all those who died are indemnified if there are deaths on only one side; but if both sides lost lives, then deaths on the losing side are discounted. These payments go to the profit of the chiefs of both sides and are usually made in livestock, i.e. cattle, sheep and goats, or in slaves.

These people are much more warlike and industrious than other Marave, but are also bigger liars and thieves. The land of the Chupeta is flat, with few trees, and those that exist are very small. Hence they lack firewood, and use instead millet stalks, dry shrubs, and particularly cattle dung which they are careful to keep dry. They have peat, but do not know its use. They keep many cattle, sheep and goats, and in other respects they are like the Marave.

IV

The climate in summer—i.e. May to September—is agreeable, being mild rather than hot. In the rains the sun is burning.

In general, Marave country is much cut about with rivers and has plenty of water; and there are many mountain ranges and hilly districts which the people prefer for their dwellings: in the valleys, they have few villages, and these they use as keeps or outposts. Generally the gardens are on the hills and slopes, and as I mentioned they inhabit one of the hilliest regions of East Africa. I saw no navigable rivers on my march.

V

The population of this country is enormous, although the populated districts are smaller than the deserted ones. If the chiefs were united they would constitute a respectable nation. The Marave busy themselves for the most part with agriculture, from which they gain their livelihood. Weavers, smiths, and basket makers, and those that practise other trades, do so mostly for amusement rather than as a way of life. They have also a large number of lazy people and highway robbers.

VI

Government is despotic and hereditary, succession going to sister's son, and never to brother's son; if there is none, then the dead man's brother succeeds. A Fumo or Mambo is rarely recognised before months, or even years, have elapsed in civil war, brothers and kinsmen fighting one another until one side is triumphant and, having the advantage, supplants all the others. It is from these continual wars and expulsions that the sale and killing of prisoners and outlaws, who are all themselves Marave, result. The chief of the nation has the title Unde; his orders are executed without question or delay in all the dominions in which he is obeyed; but no important matter is decided without being heard by a council composed of elders, or of those in whom he has equal trust. On rare occasions this council meets in secret session; it gathers usually under a great tree in the Muzinda (the name of the village in which the Mambo or Fumo resides), against whose trunk Unde sits back with the council about him; round the council are seated the people who want to listen to the case. The spectators who do not belong to the council often speak and are heard as if they belonged to it. When the subject has been talked over, Unde declares that he agrees with the council's deliberations, or amends them, as he thinks fit. The councillors always follow Unde's opinion if they know it beforehand; and if any speak against it, it is because they do not know it; for as soon as it is known, everyone assents. But Unde usually opens the council. The village in which he lives is called Muzinda-a-Unde.

The whole of Marave country is divided into territories or provinces governed by Mambos, and these are subdivided into districts whose chiefs are the Fumos. Both are hereditary and succession takes place in the same way as for Unde. Neither he nor the Mambos and Fumos wear insignia of any kind to mark them off from other Marave; they usually go dressed in a skin or a Nyanda, a kind of cloth, not woven but made from the inner bark of certain trees. The form and process of government is the same throughout the Marave. Alliances are of short duration, and often broken; any new interest may persuade Mambos and Fumos to change their allies, or become neutral or hostile. These changes often occur when they are in the process of negotiating with their allies. The wars, in which they are at most times involved, often start from bagatelles. All affairs can be judged by arbitrators, but if they are not satisfied, they litigate before the authorities, appealing from one Fumo to another, and then to the Mambo; but at times, if they are not satisfied with the judgment of the Mambo in council, they have resort to arms, and this gives rise to a small war which may spread. This happens sometimes, but not very often.

When the Fumos are at war, the Mambos to whom they are subordinate do not interfere, and at the end receive the tribute due to them. If one of the Fumos is killed, his place is usurped by his enemy, who pays the Mambo and receives recognition and rules in peace as if he were the legal heir. This happens in all ranks. The Marave authorities are Unde, the paramount chief of the nation; and the Fumos and Mambos in their districts and provinces, who all exercise in them the same arbitrary power. All legislation is traditional. In judgments and sentences they look to sentences already given in similar cases, which custom has made law: all the same, some judgments are invariable and do not change, as those relating to sorcery, adultery, theft and homicide, the most important being directed against sorcerers and adulterers. They have no statute law.

VII

The strength of these people consists in their great number. They know no elements of attack or defence apart from courage. Although continually engaged in small civil wars, the result in no way alters the general state of the nation because the victor is always a Marave and is subject to the same laws and customs. When Unde is attacked, a rare enough eventuality, the whole nation takes up arms without regard to age, as many as can manage; those unable to fight take to the hills and forests with everything they possess. The number of fighting men is great, but there is no discipline or military plan. In time of peace there are no standing armies, but when war breaks out, people gather in groups, called Mangas, of which the Mambos or Fumos of the districts they belong to are the leaders. If they are large, each one acts on its own; if they are small, two or more may join together. The word Manga, though used by the Portuguese in this part of Africa, is certainly African, and has no other meaning than a column or group of armed men. Perhaps the Portuguese adopted it from them.

As Unde is nearly always in a safe place with a large population, he is seldom subject to a close attack; but he engages in frequent distant wars, and only gets notice of them when they are over or nearly so.

As they have no formal military organisation into armies, so they have no recruitment; but in each Muzinda there is a big drum called Ngoma which can be heard a great way off, and which is used as a call to arms when the enemy is expected or imminent or when the spies or Sopozos, who are distributed around the roads to get news from travellers, come and give information that armed men are near. At the sound of the alarm, there come armed as many as belong to the district under the Muzinda; and in the next district also the alarm is sounded, and people gather, and so on successively until all are up in arms. Warriors arm themselves and maintain themselves at their own cost during a war, and this they do mainly by pillage.

There is no other way of calling up, and no way of finding out if anyone capable of fighting is missing, even if he is one of those obliged to turn out. But it is only those who are totally incapable of fighting who fail to present themselves, because the hope of plunder moves them all.

VIII

Their legs are their only defensive weapons and they put them to good use. Offensive arms are bows, poisoned arrows, spears, axes and knives. The bow is carried in the left hand with the spear, the arrows being in a leather quiver called Mutumba. The bow is Uta, the spear Dipa, the arrow Miseve, the axe Bazo and the knife Shisu. Axe and knife are worn in the belt, one on each side. The arrows have very small heads, but are entirely barbed; they are inserted into canes which they use for shafts in such a way that when an arrow hits its mark the head enters the body and the shaft falls, and

within two hours the poison has taken effect and has killed. But if a certain kind of oil, called by the Portuguese "Frei Pedro" and by the Africans Mafuta, is used upon it, no harm results. I do not know the composition of this antidote—it was not divulged.

Africans come with it for sale, but much of it is not genuine, and the only way to be sure is to see the effect it produces. This syrup was discovered by a Portuguese friar of that name in Zumbo [a town 600 miles up the Zambezi River —ed.], who found it to be a swift and efficacious anti-toxin. It is from Zumbo that this discovery has spread to all parts.

They say that among other things the poison contains certain substances considered essential—crocodile gall, hippopotamus brain, a kind of kapok, and the sap of some grasses. The effect produced is to stop the circulation of the blood, making it coagulate immediately.

The Marave are completely ignorant of any military operational planning, and of the division of armies into corps, and the formation of lines for defense and attack. On the contrary, the crowds march against the enemy as a body and as soon as they see him they become completely disorganized, utter the Tunguro cries and start letting off their arrows at random, without revealing themselves or leaving the shelter of the trees which defend them. There is no command, every warrior fights as he likes and because it appears the safest thing for him to do he attends mainly to his self-preservation. They use the spear only to finish off the wounded, and the axe and knife only to cut heads off the dead bodies. As superstition is at the base of all their beliefs, the Mambos and Fumos propagate the notion that the safety and prosperity of their lands depend upon their being sorcerers, and so they are all thought to be; they are feared and respected by their people and by strangers alike. The higher they stand in the hierarchy, the more they seek to inculcate the superiority of their medicines, of which they boast. The most important thing is to have in one's dominions under one's protection the most renowned magicians, to whom the public attributes supernatural powers by means of their Mankwaras, or magic. Nothing is done which has not the approval of the magic.

The Ganga or Surjao is the one who divines and makes the supposed magic or divination. The latter term may be a corruption of the Portuguese word Cirurgião.[2]

In times of war it is the Gangas who go in front of the Mangas, much attired with feathers, bones, tails of various animals, horns, etc. etc. They make long speeches in which they exhort the warriors to trust their medicines, because they are efficacious and infallible, and assert that they alone will be able to conquer the enemy.

The Marave place complete faith in these charlatans. If the outcome is fortunate, the Gangas attribute it entirely to themselves; and if it is adverse they blame someone for the breach of the elaborate taboos they impose, which consist usually in abstinence from certain foods, from cohabitation with someone of the other sex, etc. When they fight the Portuguese, these try first to procure the death of the Ganga who is reckoned infallible. This obtained, victory is not far ahead, because resistance then is weak, since they think that the Europeans have better magic than they, which it would be useless to resist. But in an internecine war this does not happen; all avoid shooting at the Ganga for fear that if they killed or wounded him they would be lost for his blood would fall upon the man who spilt it and the Muzimos would thus have to take vengeance.

[2] Surgeon. (Trans.).

IX

The Mambos or Fumos, according to their rank, receive Chipatas, or presents for safe conduct, from all traders passing through their lands; fees, or costs, for hearing and judging cases; Mouths (Muromos) and tribute from the land, etc. The only way they spend this is by sharing it out among the people about them, and the more liberal they are, the greater the number of followers, the larger the Muzindas, the stronger their cause and the greater their power. They spend it also in making new houses for their wives, and in paying the debts they contract; these are all personal expenses. But apart from them the Fumos pay tribute to the Mambos to whom they are subordinate, and the Mambos pay to Unde.

The Chipata, or safe-conduct, is a tribute which has to be paid in merchandise to the Mambos and Fumos through whose country one passes. Its size should correspond to the category of chief to whom it is made and to the wealth of the person making the payment. The safe-conduct gives right of transit and obliges the authorities on the land to guarantee the life and property of the merchants. There is no sure rule about the value of this tribute; the traveller can only learn from practice. Nearly always the chiefs ask for more, however much is given, and it is always necessary to take this into account when the Chipata is made up.

The Muromo, a word signifying mouth, is the fee for asking to speak to an African authority, and this cannot be done without first presenting something, this being the "morsel for the mouth," whose value should be relative to the nature of the business or discussion desired. There is no set price.

14 CHARLES LIVINGSTONE
THE PRAZEROS

David Livingstone (1813–1873) was the greatest Christian missionary-explorer of the nineteenth century. Between 1853 and 1856 he traveled overland from Kuruman, the mission station of his father-in-law, Robert Moffat, to the Victoria Falls, which he was the first white man to see, and thence to Luanda and back across Africa to the mouth of the Zambezi River. His Missionary Travels and Researches *aroused great enthusiasm in Victorian England for the opening of the interior of Central Africa to Christianity and commerce. With the support of the Royal Geographical Society and the assistance of the British government, Livingstone returned to Portuguese East Africa in 1859 with a large expedition that included his brother, Charles, and that aimed to establish the Zambezi as a highway into the interior. The Zambezi proved unnavigable beyond Tete, but Livingstone's descriptions of the slave trade and the Prazeros of Zambezia continued to excite humanitarian and commercial interests in England.*

By the eighteenth century, a group of half-caste Portuguese had carved out for themselves great feudal estates in Zambezia. These Prazeros were warlords beyond the reach of any authority, African or European, and dominated vast areas. From the profits of their plantations and the slave trade they equipped large private armies that terrorized the countryside. The Portuguese were unable to root out the Prazo system until the 1890s. A typical Prazero was Antonio Vincente da Cruz, commonly known as "Bonga." Like his brother, Mariano, he was an illiterate, thieving, cruel, barbarous drunkard.

On reaching Mazaro, the mouth of a narrow creek which in floods communicates with the Quillimane River, we found that the Portuguese were at war with a half-caste named Mariano, *alias* Matakenya, from whom they had generally fled, and who, having built a stockade near the mouth of the Shire, owned all the country between that river and Mazaro. Mariano was best known by his native name Matakenya, which in their tongue means "trembling," or quivering as trees do in a storm. He was a keen slave-hunter, and kept a large number of men, well armed with muskets. It is an entire mistake to suppose that the slave-trade is one of buying and selling alone, or that engagements can be made with laborers in Africa as they are in India; Mariano, like other Portuguese, had no labor to spare. He had

From David and Charles Livingstone, *Narrative of an Expedition to the Zambesi and its Tributaries; and of the Discovery of the Lakes Shirwa and Nyassa, 1858–1864* (New York: Harper and Brothers, 1866), pp. 26–30, 38–43.

been in the habit of sending out armed parties on slave hunting-forays among the helpless tribes to the northeast, and carrying down the kidnapped victims in chains to Quillimane, where they were sold by his brother-in-law Cruz Coimbra, and shipped as "Free emigrants" to the French island of Bourbon. So long as his robberies and murders were restricted to the natives at a distance, the authorities did not interfere; but his men, trained to deeds of violence and bloodshed in their slave forays, naturally began to practice on the people nearer at hand, though belonging to the Portuguese, and even in the village of Senna, under the guns of the fort. A gentleman of the highest standing told us that, while at dinner with his family, it was no uncommon event for a slave to rush into the room pursued by one of Mariano's men with spear in hand to murder him.

The atrocities of this villain, aptly termed by the late governor of Quillimane a "notorious robber and murderer," became at length intolerable. All the Portuguese spoke of him as a rare monster of inhumanity. It is unaccountable why half-castes, such as he, are so much more cruel than the Portuguese, but such is undoubtedly the case.

It was asserted that one of his favorite modes of creating an impression in the country, and making his name dreaded, was to spear his captives with his own hands. On one occasion he is reported to have thus killed forty poor wretches placed in a row before him. We did not at first credit these statements, and thought that they were merely exaggerations of the incensed Portuguese, who naturally enough were exasperated with him for stopping their trade and harboring their runaway slaves; but we learned afterward from the natives that the accounts given us by the Portuguese had not exceeded the truth, and that Mariano was quite as great a ruffian as they had described him. One expects slave-owners to treat their human chattels as well as men do other animals of value, but the slave-trade seems always to engender an unreasoning ferocity, if not bloodthirstiness.

War was declared against Mariano, and a force sent to take him; he resisted for a time, but, seeing that he was likely to get the worst of it, and knowing that the Portuguese governors have small salaries, and are therefore "disposed to be reasonable," he went down to Quillimane to "arrange" with the governor, as it is termed here; but Colonel da Silva put him in prison, and then sent him for trial to Mozambique. When we came into the country his people were fighting under his brother Bonga. The war had lasted six months, and stopped all trade on the river during that period. On the 15th of June we first came into contact with the "rebels." They appeared as a crowd of well-armed and fantastically-dressed people under the trees at Mazaro. On explaining that we were English, some at once came on board and called to those on shore to lay aside their arms. On landing among them we saw that many had the branded marks of slaves on their chests, but they warmly approved our objects, and knew well the distinctive character of our nation on the slave question.[1] The shout at our departure contrasted strongly with the suspicious questioning on our approach. Henceforth we were recognized as friends by both parties.

At a later period we were taking in wood within a mile of the scene of action, but a dense fog prevented our hearing the noise of a battle at Mazaro; and on arriving there immediately after, many natives and Portuguese appeared on the bank.

Dr. Livingstone, landing to salute some of his old friends among the latter, found himself in the sickening smell and among the mutilated bodies of the slain; he was requested to take the governor, who was very ill of fever, across to Shupanga, and just as he gave his assent, the rebels renewed the fight, and the balls began to whistle about in all directions. After trying in vain to get some one to assist the governor down to the steamer, and unwilling to leave him in such danger, as the officer sent to bring our Kroomen did not appear, he went into the hut, and dragged along his excellency to the ship. He was a very tall man, and as he swayed hither and thither from weakness, weighing down Dr. Livingstone, it must have appeared like one drunken man helping another. Some of the Portuguese white soldiers stood fighting with great bravery against the enemy in front, while a few were coolly shooting at their own slaves for fleeing into the river behind. The reb-

---

[1] Toward the close of the eighteenth century, a small group of high-principled Englishmen organized a campaign against slavery and the slave trade. Outraged by the horror and injustice of the trade, the abolitionists were convinced of its moral wrongness, and through their influence slavery was declared illegal in England in 1772. In 1807 an act of Parliament prohibited British subjects from engaging in the African slave trade, and finally in 1833 another act abolished slavery throughout the British Empire. Thereafter Britain used its diplomatic and military power to persuade other nations to abandon the trade (ed.).

els soon retired, and the Portuguese escaped to a sand-bank in the Zambesi, and thence to an island opposite Shupanga, where they lay for some weeks, looking at the rebels on the main land opposite. This state of inactivity on the part of the Portuguese could not well be helped, as they had expended all their ammunition and were waiting anxiously for supplies; hoping, no doubt, sincerely that the enemy might not hear that their powder had failed. Luckily, their hopes were not disappointed; the rebels waited until a supply came, and were then repulsed after a three and a half hours' hard fighting. Two months afterward Mariano's stockade was burned, the garrison having fled in a panic; and as Bonga declared that he did not wish to fight with this governor, with whom he had no quarrel, the war soon came to an end. His excellency meanwhile, being a disciple of Raspail, had taken nothing for the fever but a little camphor, and after he was taken to Shupanga became comatose.[2] More potent remedies were administered to him, to his intense disgust, and he soon recovered. The colonel in attendance, whom he never afterward forgave, encouraged the treatment. "Give what is right; never mind him; he is very (*muito*) impertinent;" and all night long, with every draught of water, the colonel gave a quantity of quinine: the consequence was, next morning the patient was cinchonized and better.

.   .   .

Bonga, the brother of the rebel Mariano, and now at the head of the revolted natives, with some of his principal men, came to see us, and were perfectly friendly, though told of our having carried the sick governor across to Shupanga, and of our having cured him of fever. On our acquainting Bonga with the object of the expedition, he remarked that we should suffer no hinderance from his people in our good work. He sent us a present of rice, two sheep, and a quantity of firewood. He never tried to make any use of us in the strife; the other side showed less confidence by carefully cross-questioning our pilot whether we had sold any powder to the enemy. We managed, however, to keep on good terms with both rebels and Portuguese.

Being unable to take the steamer up the shoal channel along which Senna stands, we anchored at Nyaruka, a small hamlet of blacks, six miles below, and walked up to Senna next morning. The narrow winding footpath, along which we had to march in Indian file, lay through gardens and patches of wood, the loftiest trees being thorny acacias. The sky was cloudy, the air cool and pleasant, and the little birds, in the gladness of their hearts, poured forth sweet strange songs, which, though equal to those of the singing birds at home on a spring morning, yet seemed, somehow, as if in a foreign tongue. We met many natives on the road. Most of the men were armed with spears, bows and arrows, or old Tower muskets; the women had short-handled iron hoes, and were going to work in the gardens; they stepped aside to let us pass, and saluted us politely, the men bowing and scraping, and the women, even with heavy loads on their heads, courtesying—a courtesy from bare legs is startling!

Senna is built on a low plain, on the right bank of the Zambesi, with some pretty detached hills in the background; it is surrounded by a stockade of living trees to protect its inhabitants from their troublesome and rebellious neighbors. It contains a few large houses, some ruins of others, and a weatherbeaten cross, where once stood a church; a mound shows the site of an ancient monastery, and a mud fort by the river is so dilapidated that cows were grazing peacefully over its prostrate walls. This grieves not the villagers, for its black garrison was wont to keep within doors when the foe came near, leaving the merchants to settle the

[2] François Vincent Raspail (1794–1878), French chemist and revolutionary (ed.).

strife as best they could; and they therefore consider that the decay of the fort has not caused them to be any more helpless than they were before.

The few Senna merchants, having little or no trade in the village, send parties of trusted slaves into the interior to hunt for and purchase ivory. It is a dull place, and very conducive to sleep. One is sure to take fever in Senna on the second day, if by chance one escapes it on the first day of a sojourn there; but no place is entirely bad. Senna has one redeeming feature: it is the native village of the large-hearted and hospitable Senhor H. A. Ferrão. The benevolence of this gentleman is unbounded. The poor black stranger passing through the town goes to him almost as a matter of course for food, and is never sent away hungry. In times of famine the starving natives are fed by his generosity; hundreds of his own people he never sees except on these occasions; and the only benefit derived from being their master is, that they lean on him as a patriarchal chief, and he has the satisfaction of settling their differences, and of saving their lives in seasons of drought and scarcity. His father, a man of superior attainments, was formerly the Portuguese governor of Senna, and acquired a vast tract of rich country to the southward, called Chiringoma, in a most honorable manner; but the government ordered it to be split up, and reserved two leagues only for the heir, apportioning the rest in free grants to emigrants; the reason assigned for the robbery was that "it would never do for a subject to possess more land than the crown of Portugal." The Landeens soon followed, took possession of the whole, and spoiled the spoilers.

Senhor Ferrão received us with his usual kindness, and gave us a bountiful breakfast. During the day the principal men of the place called, and were unanimously of opinion that the free natives would willingly cultivate large quantities of cotton, could they find purchasers. They had in former times exported largely both cotton and cloth to Manica and even to Brazil. "On their own soil," they declared, "the natives are willing to labor and trade, provided only they can do so to advantage: when it is for their interest, blacks work very hard." We often remarked subsequently that this was the opinion of men of energy; and that all settlers of activity, enterprise, and sober habits had become rich, while those who were much addicted to lying on their backs smoking invariably complained of the laziness of the negroes, and were poor, proud, and despicable. We dined with another very honorable Portuguese, Major Tito A. d'A. Sicard, who quoted the common remark that Dr. Livingstone's discovery of the Kongone Bar had ruined Quillimane; for the government had proposed to abandon that fever-haunted locality, and to found a new town at the mouth of the Kongone. It was not then known that householders in the old village preferred to resign all offices rather than remove. The major had a great desire to assist Dr. Livingstone in his enterprise; and said that when the war was past he would at once take up his goods to Tette in canoes; and this he afterward most generously did. While returning to Nyaruka, we heard a bird like a nightingale pouring forth its sweet melody in the stillness of the evening.

15 HERMENEGILDO CAPELLO AND ROBERTO IVENS

BENGUELLA IN 1877

Two officers of the Portuguese Royal Navy, Hermenegildo Capello and Roberto Ivens, led an expedition to Central Africa during the years 1877–1880 that produced the first survey of the Bié region and the upper reaches of the Okovanggo River. In 1884 they were sent once more into the interior by the Portuguese government in order to discover a trans-African route connecting Angola and Mozambique and to assert Portuguese rights in Central Africa at a time when other European nations, particularly Great Britain, were challenging Portuguese claims.

In latitude 12° 34′ 17″ of the southern hemisphere and longitude 13° 22′ 30″ east of Greenwich, lies upon the west coast of Africa, at the bottom of a spacious bay, the ancient and well-known city of Benguella.

The capital of a vast territory, it possesses as subdivisions the districts of Dombe Grande and Dombe Pequeno, Egito, Novo Redondo, Catumbella, Quillengues, Caconda, &c.; embracing an approximate area of 15,000 square miles of the southern portion of the Portuguese province.

Its custom-house revenues amount, at the present day, to some 25,000£. A delegation of the central government, the seat of which is at Loanda, its administration is entrusted to an official, who can only be appointed by the government of the mother country.

A traveller, on arriving there, may, in the course of a day's wandering about the city and its environs, get a general impression of the place, which the following narrative must, to a certain extent, reproduce.

A sufficiency of houses, among which rise the public buildings, somewhat larger than the rest, without any pretension to elegance, but spacious, clean, and set in

right lines in broad streets, bordered with trees, and connected together by garden-ground, constitute the commercial ward, properly so called, where the authorities and numerous merchants have their habitations.

A custom-house, a hospital, barracks, a palace (the residence of the governor), and a fortress on the seashore, where, in the evening, the tired wayfarer can breathe the pure air of the ocean, observe the splendid spectacle of the setting of a tropical sun, and watch the waves as they roll into the beautiful bay, closed in at the south-west by a lofty mount called the *Sombrero,* constitute the most remarkable features of the landscape, and form altogether an agreeable picture.

Scattered here and there, the observer will note a good many isolated establishments, where the most important business of Benguella is carried on. The aspect of these buildings is singular and antiquated. In the foreground appears the classical wooden balcony, either blackened by time or painted blue, surrounded by massive benches piled up with every kind of cotton goods, striped stuffs, beads, caps, and mirrors; the whole crowned by well-ordered rows of bottles containing various liquors, all of them articles of a nature to excite the cupidity and warm the imagination of the aborigines. On penetrating farther in, the curious traveller will find spacious store-houses, where the first object that meets his eye, suspended from a beam, is

From Hermenegildo Capello and Roberto Ivens, *From Benguella to the Territory of Yacca: Description of a Journey into Central and West Africa,* trans. by Alfred Elwes (London: Sampson Low & Co., 1882), pp. 10–19.

the old wooden balance, supported by eight ropes, with square scales. These magazines are full of the most varied products of the interior, among which prominently figure wax, india-rubber and ivory; and waiting their turn at the weighing-machine, stands a numerous band of natives, who, lank, bony, and emaciated, suck at the long and traditional calumet, the while their roving glances are turned incessantly to the coveted European goods.[1]

This quarter of the town has other features of a less agreeable character. These are tortuous lanes, lined with miserable huts, amidst which are vast enclosures, called *quintaes,* surrounded by walls of a sufficient height to intercept the heat and light, within which are frequently huddled together some hundreds of negroes who have travelled from the interior. The utmost disorder and squalor exist in these enclosures. Calcined stones upon which are still standing the earthen pipkins that have been used for cooking the recent meal; wretched old rags serving as beds; gourds scattered all over the place among tobacco-pipes, bows, and assagais; the inevitable black glass bottle, with a small cord round the neck, by which it is suspended in the long country-basket called a *muhamba;* two or three dozen negroes in the garb of our first parents, with long tresses reeking with oil and *tacúla* (a vermilion powder obtained by triturating tiny morsels of the trunk of an acacia), lying asleep in every direction, are the more salient objects which distinguish these habitations of the natives' ward. And if we throw in some five or six hundred Ban-dombes, Bailundos, Bihenos, and Ganguellas, promenading the streets, with skins hanging from their girdles, some far gone in intoxication, others well upon the road, talking, gesticulating, shrieking; if we frame in the town with a belt of thin and wiry vegetation; draw a line of blue mountains at some twenty to

twenty-five miles' distance from Benguella, and set the whole in a clear, grey atmosphere, we shall have the general aspect presented by this celebrated city on one of its busy market-days.

The effluvia emanating from this accumulation of black humanity, from monstrous head-dresses anointed with rancid oil, from reeking pipes, and the fumes of *aguardente,*[2] must be taken into account to make our sketch complete, and which, out of a feeling of delicacy, we have reserved for the close, though the aroma thus created is perhaps the first thing which strikes the recently arrived traveller from Europe.

Shortly after sunset the profoundest silence falls upon the place, broken only by the occasional tramp of a couple of natives carrying their master in a *muchila,*[3] through the deserted streets, or a group or two of aborigines, directing their steps towards the *quintaes,* where the reflection of ruddy light hints at the preparation of some meal.

The darkness is, otherwise, complete; the silence interrupted only in the manner we have stated, or by the occasional roar or howl of a wild beast, followed by the barking of the dogs, becomes, in the intervals, supreme; until the obscurity is gradually dissipated, the terrors of the night begin to vanish, and within an incredibly short time one of nature's most brilliant aspects, the break of day, entrances the observer.

The earth reacquires all its brightness and freshness, and dons its verdant mantle; the birds fill the air with melodious song; the limpid atmosphere and soft temperature invite the traveller abroad, and the general stir of humanity recommences.

The negro is on foot, armed with his fishing-tackle; the trader opens his store; the women proceed to their washing-places; the thirsty souls, rousing them-

---

[1] A calumet is a highly decorated ceremonial pipe (ed.).

[2] Any strong, distilled alcoholic liquor (ed.).
[3] A sort of elongated chair, suspended from a pole, having a rectangular tester, from which curtains fall all round.

selves from their beds of foul rags, where they have been shivering with cold, shuffle off to the neighbouring tavern, there to imbibe the fiery *aguardente*.

The climate of Benguella is mild during a great part of the year; still, it must not be considered as fine, and is very far from being the best on the coast. The improvements effected during these latter years, the irregularity of the rains since 1870, and the more restricted gathering of the natives within its precincts, in consequence of the diversion of many of them to the mart at Catumbella, somewhat more to the northwards, are the causes of the alteration in climatic circumstances; so that Benguella finds, mainly among the merchants and traders there established, numerous advocates of its salubrity.

Still, the fact remains that there are many victims to various fevers, but as the dead cannot offer an opinion upon the subject, the causes which brought about their end are soon forgotten amid the hurry and absorption of trade. The Bandombes, who are always seen about Benguella, are almost exclusively the inhabitants of a good part of the district. Long accustomed to dealing with Europeans, they are of infinite service to the latter, chiefly as regards transport, for they are not much given to trade.

The language spoken in the town is very different to the *n'bunda* of Loanda, and is known by the name of *n'bundo*[4] of the Bihé, which is understood in the neighbouring districts and in the regions extending eastward as far as the Ganguellas, where it begins to undergo alterations in consequence perhaps of the introduction of *lulundo* words and phrases.

The life of a European in Benguella is purely and exclusively a commercial one. The caravans which come in, the tidings which arrive, the products that are brought forward, the prices made through the competition of others, and his negotiations with the natives absorb every mo-

ment of daylight. It is no uncommon thing for the latter, after haggling, for two or three hours with a merchant, suddenly to break away and carry the rest of the troop with them, to seek a more liberal purchaser elsewhere.

In the Benguella market, where the trade is in the hands of the Portuguese, almost all the important products of the interior of Africa are exposed to view, and ivory, wax, walrus's teeth, *abbuda* (unicorn) horns, gums, resins, *licomte,*[5] skins, feathers, india-rubber, and canes appear in considerable quantities, and are bartered for arms, powder, cotton goods, and other similar products.

The Bihenos, the great African traders, are, not unnaturally, the chief habitués of the market, as they are exactly upon the line which connects this city with the inland producers. On completing their transactions, they carry off with them their European wares, travelling in caravans into the interior, where they again exchange their purchases in still remoter regions.

These men know how to drive very hard bargains, and having learned how much is to be gained by competition among the Europeans, they have gone on constantly raising the standard of value until they have succeeded in establishing the following prices upon the sea-board:

One pound of ivory	
standard	6s. 9d.
medium	6s. 1d.
small	4s. 0d.
One pound of wax, clean	0s. 9¹/₂d.
A quarter hundredweight of india-rubber	38s. 3d.
A panther's skin	9s. 0d.

In times not so very remote, travellers or *aviados,* as they were called, were despatched by firms established on the coast into the interior; and inland traders, gen-

[4] A dialect of the *lu-nano* language, generally denominated *quinbundo* (*t'chinbundo*).

[5] Fibre of the *Adansonia digitata* [the monkey bread tree—ed.].

erally styled *funantes*, still make their way thither on their own account.

The marts in the interior that were most frequented by these enterprising men were: *Alucusso*, one of the earliest travellers to which was Candimba (Gonçalves), a Portuguese from the main, recently deceased: *Garanganja; Canunguessa* and *Catanga*, to the west of Bangueolo, frequently visited by José Alves, and recently by the sons of Major Coimbra, Tiberio and others; *D'jengi*, the valley of the Zambese, and finally *Liniani* for many years frequented by Silva Porto, that old and honoured Portuguese citizen, long established at the Bihé in Belmonte, and whose journeys are so well known that his itineraries may be seen traced upon many maps published abroad, where the name of the veteran traveller figures so justly, as a testimony of his merit.

We spent with this old gentleman several agreeable hours, during which he had the kindness to read to us the most important portions of his diaries, containing facts which though now no longer new, had all the charm of novelty then. They proved in the most conclusive manner how great was the industry of this bold traveller in collecting data that he might some day turn to account, notwithstanding the difficulties which his business as a trader entailed upon him, amid peoples hotly opposed at that period to the advance of any European, and frequently at open hostility to himself.

It was this Portuguese who had the honour to meet, in the heart of Africa, with David Livingstone during his first journey across the continent, and whose friendly services the celebrated English explorer could not at the time accept.

In this place we may also name as worthy of special mention, a remarkable Portuguese *funante*, João Baptista Ferreira, who for many years scoured the country, and was well known for the boldness and venturesomeness of his journeys, until, some years ago, they terminated in

his destruction at the hands, it is surmised, of some petty sovereign of the interior or of the Arabs, either Janima Mericani or Sheik Abed-ben-Salim in the north.

He was the first European who, as it would appear, starting from Benguella, arrived at the dominions of the Cassongo Calombo, and became acquainted with Imbarri, the residence of Tibu-tib, Sheik Hamed-ben-Mohammed; subsequently crossing the Samba, passing through Quilemba, and penetrating nearly to Niangué.

Tired of wandering about the Garanganja, and presuming this region to be in great part commercially explored, João Baptista began to turn his attention to the Samba, where, during one of his journeys, he was informed that there existed in the territory of Ulua, to the east of the Lunda do Muata-Janvo, a track which would lead him to the markets of the north, which abounded in ivory.

Adventurous and fearless, he determined at once to follow it, notwithstanding the objections raised by his native followers, and towards the close of 1870 and beginning of 1871 he entered Cassongo's territory in company with a son of Major Coimbra who, two years later, elected to reveal to José Alves this identical route.

After rendering important services to Cassongo, João Baptista returned to the coast, in order to procure a further supply of goods, as had been arranged with the king, and subsequently return to his dominions with a view to barter.

José Alves, however, started on the same occasion, and Coimbra having, as above mentioned, undertaken to guide him by a track known at that time only to himself, the former accepted the offer, and the two great traders met one another in the coveted territory in 1874.

Nowadays the travellers or *aviados* of European houses are few. The death of some, the flight of others, have so disenchanted the merchants on the coast with the system of sending goods into the interior, that they have given it up almost entirely, so that the trade at this present time is almost exclusively carried on by the natives themselves, working on their own account.

The time of our departure now drew near, and after a sojourn of a fortnight in Benguella, the Portuguese expedition was in readiness to start upon its journey into the interior.

16 ROBERT MOFFAT

MZILIKAZI

Chief of the Khumalo Nguni *and one of Shaka's most trusted generals, Mzilikazi defied Shaka's authority about 1821 and marched up to the highveld of the Transvaal, where he settled with his followers. None of the tribes of the Transvaal could stand against Mzilikazi's regiments, and between 1825 and 1834 prisoners from defeated Sotho-speaking tribes swelled the ranks of Mzilikazi's people, evolving into the Ndebele* nation. The Ndebele nation crystallized along the lines of a typical Nguni military state but soon found itself under assault from half-caste Korana and Griqua peoples from the south who were equipped with firearms. Mzilikazi was able to defeat the half-caste Africans, but in 1837 Boer commandoes successfully defeated the Ndebele and convinced Mzilikazi to take his people north across the Limpopo River to the upland pastures of Rhodesia. The Ndebele rapidly recovered in their new home, and their state developed under their king until his death in 1868.*

A pioneer missionary and the father-in-law of David Livingstone, Robert Moffat (1795–1883) went to South Africa on behalf of the London Missionary Society in 1817. In 1825 he settled at Kuruman, where he lived and worked for nearly half a century. He first visited Mzilikazi in 1829 and established a profound influence over the Ndebele monarch. Mzilikazi probably found in the stern, uncompromising missionary the qualities of a father figure that he had not experienced in his youth since the execution of his own father, Mashobane, by the Khumalo overlord, Zwide. Mzilikazi's devotion to Moffat was repaid, and the two shared a deep, lifelong friendship.

. . . Umbate and two of his relations, whom he wished to introduce to my notice, remained behind till a late hour. One of these appeared to be a man of superior intellect, and put rather striking questions on the subjects which I had brought before the attention of the great man. The stillness of a serene night, far from the

dance and war song, which echoed from the neighbouring hills, inspired confidence in these chieftains, who spoke in whispers, as if afraid that their king should hear their liberty of speech. Umbate repeated to his friend much that he had heard from me on the road about divine things. Though extremely cautious in their remarks, it was evident that they were not insensible of the rigours of the despotism under which they lived. I had been struck with the fine, open counte-

From Robert Moffat, *Missionary Labours and Scenes in Southern Africa* (London: J. Snow, 1842), pp. 539–546.
* Ndebele is frequently spelled Matabele.

nances of many of the warriors, who, though living amid the bewildering mazes of ignorance and superstition, debased, dejected, and oppressed under the iron sceptre of a monarch addicted to shedding blood, possessed noble minds; but, alas! whose only source of joy was to conquer or die in the ranks of their sovereign. The following morning was marked by a melancholy display of that so-called heroism which prefers death to dishonour. A feast had been proclaimed, cattle had been slaughtered, and many hearts beat high in anticipation of wallowing in all the excesses of savage delight; eating, drinking, dancing, and singing the victors' song over the slain, whose bones lay bleached on the neighbouring plains. Every heart appeared elate but one. He was a man of rank, and what was called an Entuna, (an officer,) who wore on his head the usual badge of dignity. He was brought to head-quarters. His arm bore no shield, nor his hand a spear; he had been divested of these, which had been his glory. He was brought into the presence of the king, and his chief council, charged with a crime, for which it was in vain to expect pardon, even at the hands of a more humane government. He bowed his fine elastic figure, and kneeled before the judge. The case was investigated silently, which gave solemnity to the scene. Not a whisper was heard among the listening audience, and the voices of the council were only audible to each other, and the nearest spectators. The prisoner, though on his knees, had something dignified and noble in his mien. Not a muscle of his countenance moved, but his bright black eyes indicated a feeling of intense interest, which the moving balance between life and death only could produce. The case required little investigation; the charges were clearly substantiated, and the culprit pleaded guilty. But, alas! he knew it was at a bar where none ever heard the heart-reviving sound of pardon, even for offences small compared with his. A pause ensued, during which the silence of death pervaded the assembly. At length the monarch spoke, and, addressing the prisoner, said, "You are a dead man, but I shall do to-day what I never did before; I spare your life for the sake of my friend and father"—pointing to the spot where I [Moffat—ed.] stood. "I know his heart weeps at the shedding of blood; for his sake I spare your life; he has travelled from a far country to see me, and he has made my heart white; but he tells me that to take away life is an awful thing, and never can be undone again. He has pleaded with me not to go to war, nor destroy life. I wish him, when he returns to his own home again, to return with a heart as white as he has made mine. I spare you for his sake, for I love him, and he has saved the lives of my people. But," continued the king, "you must be degraded for life; you must no more associate with the nobles of the land, nor enter the towns of the princes of the people; nor ever again mingle in the dance of the mighty. Go to the poor of the field, and let your companions be the inhabitants of the desert." The sentence passed, the pardoned man was expected to bow in grateful adoration to him whom he was wont to look upon and exalt in songs applicable only to One to whom belongs universal sway and the destinies of man. But, no! holding his hands clasped on his bosom, he replied, "O king, afflict not my heart! I have merited thy displeasure; let me be slain like the warrior; I cannot live with the poor." And, raising his hand to the ring he wore on his brow, he continued, "How can I live among the dogs of the king, and disgrace these badges of honour which I won among the spears and shields of the mighty? No, I cannot live! Let me die, O Pezoolu!" His request was granted, and his hands tied erect over his head. Now my exertions to save his life were vain. He disdained the boon on the conditions offered, preferring to die with the honours he had won at the point of the spear—honours which even the act that condemned him did not tarnish—to exile and poverty among the children of the desert. He was led forth, a man walking on each side. My eye followed him till he reached the top of a precipice, over which he was precipitated into the deep pool of the river beneath, where the crocodiles, accustomed to such meals, were yawning to devour him ere he could reach the bottom! This was a sabbath morning scene such as heathenism exhibits to the view of the Christian philanthropist, and such as is calculated to excite in his bosom feelings of the deepest sympathy. This magnanimous heathen knew of no hereafter. He was without God and without hope. But, however deplorable the state of such a person may be, he will not be condemned as equally guilty with those who, in the midst of light and knowledge, self-separated from the body, recklessly rush into the presence of their Maker and their Judge. We have often read of the patriotism of the Greeks and Romans, and heard that magnanimity of soul extolled which could sacrifice honour, property, and life itself, for the public good, rather than become the vassals of a foe, and live divested of the poor trappings of human glory; if this be virtue, there are, even among Africa's sons, men not inferior to the most illustrious of the Romans. The very monarch who was thus influenced by the presence of the Christian missionary, needed only to ask his warriors, "Who among you will become a sacrifice for the safety of the state, and the country's good?" and his choicest men would have run upon the thick bosses of the enemy's buckler.

Moselekatse's [Mzilikazi—ed.] conduct in this affair produced a strange impression among his people, some of whom regarded me as an extraordinary being, who could thus influence one more terrible to them than the fiercest lion of the forest. His government, so far as I could discover, was the very essence of despotism. The persons of the people, as well as their possessions, were the property of their monarch. His word was law, and he

had only to lift his finger or give a frown, and his greatest nobles trembled in his presence. No one appeared to have a judgment of his own; none dared negative an opinion breathed by his sovereign. When any were permitted to approach his person, they crouched softly, muttering his great names. Messengers from the distant out-stations of his dominions were constantly arriving. These laid down their shields and spears at a distance, approached, and then kneeled about thirty yards from his royal person; and when it was his pleasure to receive the communication, it was conveyed by one of his chiefs in waiting. Some of these brought the news of the attacks of lions on some parts of his distant herds, but no one presumed to be the reporter without bringing the head and paws of the animal which had dared to assail the possessions of its mighty namesake.

Although his tyranny was such, that one would have supposed his subjects would execrate his name, they were the most servile devotees of their master. Wherever he was seated, or wherever he slept, a number of sycophants, fantastically dressed, attended him, whose business was to march, jump, and dance about, sometimes standing adoring his person, then manoeuvring with a stick, and vociferating the mighty deeds of valour performed by himself and Machobane. The same things are repeated again and again, often with a rapidity of articulation which baffles the understanding of their own countrymen. After listening many times, I was able, with the assistance of one of these parasites, to pick up the following expressions: "O Pezoolu, the king of kings, king of the heavens, who would not fear before the son of Machobane, mighty in battle! Where are the mighty before the presence of our great king? Where is the strength of the forest before the great Elephant? The proboscis is breaking the branches of the forest! It is the sound of the shields of the son of Machobane. He breathes upon their faces; it is the fire among the dry grass! His enemies are consumed before him, king of kings! Father of fire, he ascends to the blue heavens; he sends his lightnings into the clouds, and makes the rain to descend! Ye mountains, woods,ʼand grassy plains, hearken to the voice of the son of Machobane, king of heaven!" This is a specimen of the sounding titles which incessantly meet the ear of this proud mortal, and are sufficient to make the haughty monarch believe that he is what the terror of the name of Dingaan convinced him he was not; for, notwithstanding all his vain boasts, he could not conceal his fears of the successor of the bloody Chaka, against whose iron sway he had rebelled.

It may be necessary to notice here, very briefly, the origin of this great man. When a youth his father was the chief of an independent tribe. His people were attacked by one more powerful, and routed. He took refuge under the sceptre of Chaka, who was then rendering his name terrible by deeds of crime. Moselekatse, from his intrepid character, was placed at the head of a marauding expedition, which made dreadful havoc among the northern tribes; but, instead of giving up the whole of the spoils, he made a reserve for himself. This reaching the ears of Chaka, revenge instantly burned in the tyrant's bosom, who resolved to annihilate so daring an aggressor. Moselekatse was half prepared to take flight, and descend on the thickly peopled regions of the north, like a sweeping pestilence. He escaped, after a desperate conflict with the warriors of Chaka, who killed nearly all the old men, and many of the women. His destructive career among the Bakone tribes has been noticed; but dire as that was, it must have been only a faint transcript of the terror, desolation, and death, which extended to the utmost limits of Chaka's conquests. Though but a follower in the footsteps of Chaka, the career of Moselekatse, from the period of his revolt till the time I saw him, and long after, formed an interminable catalogue of crimes. Scarcely a mountain, over extensive regions, but bore the marks of his deadly ire. His experience and native cunning enabled him to triumph over the minds of his men, and made his trembling captives soon adore him as an invincible sovereign. Those who resisted, and would not stoop to be his dogs, he butchered. He trained the captured youth in his own tactics, so that the majority of his army were foreigners; but his chiefs and nobles gloried in their descent from the Zoolu dynasty. He had carried his arms far into the tropics, where, however, he had more than once met with his equal; and on one occasion, of six hundred warriors only a handful returned, who were doomed to be sacrificed, merely because they had not conquered, or fallen with their companions. Abject representatives came, while I was with him, from the subjugated tribes of the Bamanguato, to solicit his aid against a more distant tribe, which had taken their cattle. By means like these, it may be said, "He dipped his sword in blood, and wrote his name on lands and cities desolate." In his person he was below the middle stature, rather corpulent, with a short neck, and in his manner could be exceedingly affable and cheerful. His voice, soft and effeminate, did not indicate that his disposition was passionate; and, happily for his people, it was not so, or many would have been butchered in the ebullitions of his anger.

The above is but a faint description of this Napoleon of the desert,—a man with whom I often conversed, and who was not wanting in consideration and kindness, as well as gratitude. But to sympathy and compassion his heart appeared a stranger.

17 NDANSI KUMALO

THE NDEBELE REBELLION

Defeated and bitterly discontented over the loss of land and cattle, the Ndebele rebelled in March 1896, when the military resources of the British South Africa Company were preoccupied in the Jameson Raid in the Transvaal. Over a hundred Europeans were killed in the revolt, and the remainder were besieged until a relief force under Major Plumer reached Bulawayo. The Ndebele rebels were then defeated by the superior fire power of Maxim guns and driven into the Matopo Hills, where Cecil Rhodes personally arranged the surrender of the principal Ndebele Ndunas (chieftains) and their followers.

So we surrendered to the white people and were told to go back to our homes and live our usual lives and attend to our crops. But the white men sent native police who did abominable things; they were cruel and assaulted a lot of our people and helped themselves to our cattle and goats. These policemen were not our own people; anybody was made a policeman. We were treated like slaves. They came and were overbearing and we were ordered to carry their clothes and bundles. They interfered with our wives and our daughters and molested them. In fact, the treatment we received was intolerable. We thought it best to fight and die rather than bear it. How the rebellion started I do not know; there was no organization, it was like a fire that suddenly flames up. We had been flogged by native police and then they rubbed salt water in the wounds. There was much bitterness because so many of our cattle were branded and taken away from us; we had no property, nothing we could call our own. We said, "It is no good living under such conditions; death would be better—let us fight." Our King gone, we had submitted to the white people and they ill-treated us until we became desperate and tried to make an end of it all. We knew that we had very little chance because their weapons were so much superior to ours. But we meant to fight to the last, feeling that even if we could not beat them we might at least kill a few of them and so have some sort of revenge.

I fought in the rebellion. We used to look out for valleys where the white men were likely to approach. We took cover behind rocks and trees and tried to ambush them. We were forced by the nature of our weapons not to expose ourselves. I had a gun, a breech-loader. They—the white men—fought us with big guns and Maxims and rifles.

I remember a fight in the Matoppos when we charged the white men. There were some hundreds of us; the white men also were many. We charged them at close quarters: we thought we had a good chance to kill them but the Maxims were too much for us. We drove them off at the first charge, but they returned and formed up again. We made a second charge, but they were too strong for us. I cannot say how many white people were killed, but we think it was quite a lot. I do not know if I killed any of them, but I know I killed one of their horses. I remember how, when one of their scouts fell wounded, two of his companions raced out and took him away. Many of our people were killed in this fight: I saw four of my cousins shot. One was shot in the jaw and the whole of his face was blown away—like this—and he died. One was hit between the eyes; another here, in the shoulder; another had part of his ear shot off. We made many charges but each time we were beaten off, until at last the white men packed up and retreated. But

From Margery Perham, *Ten Africans* (London: Faber and Faber Ltd., 1963), pp. 72–75. Reprinted by permission of Northwestern University Press and Faber and Faber Ltd.

for the Maxims, it would have been different. The place where we have been making the film is the very place where my
cousins were killed.

We were still fighting when we heard
that Mr. Rhodes was coming and wanted
to make peace with us. It was best to
come to terms he said, and not go shedding blood like this on both sides. The
older people went to meet him. Mr.
Rhodes came and they had a discussion
and our leaders came back and discussed
amongst themselves and the people. Then
Mr. Rhodes came again and we agreed at
last to terms of peace.

So peace was made. Many of our people
had been killed, and now we began to die
of starvation; and then came the rinder-
pest and the cattle that were still left to
us perished. We could not help thinking
that all these dreadful things were
brought by the white people. We struggled, and the Government helped us with
grain; and by degrees we managed to get
crops and pulled through. Our cattle
were practically wiped out, but a few were
left and from them we slowly bred up our
herds again. We were offered work in the
mines and farms to earn money and so
were able to buy back some cattle. At
first, of course, we were not used to going
out to work, but advice was given that the
chief should advise the young people to
go out to work, and gradually they went.
At first we received a good price for our
cattle and sheep and goats. Then the tax
came. It was 10s. a year. Soon the Government said, "That is too little, you must
contribute more; you must pay £1." We
did so. Then those who took more than
one wife were taxed; 10s. for each additional wife. The tax is heavy, but that is
not all. We are also taxed for our dogs;
5s. for a dog. Then we were told we were
living on private land; the owners wanted
rent in addition to the Government tax;
some 10s., some £1, some £2 a year.
After that we were told we had to dip our
cattle and pay 1s. per head per annum.

Would I like to have the old days back?
Well, the white men have brought some
good things. For a start, they brought us
European implements—ploughs; we can
buy European clothes, which are an advance. The Government have arranged
for education and through that, when our
children grow up, they may rise in status.
We want them to be educated and civilized and make better citizens. Even in
our own time there were troubles, there
was much fighting and many innocent
people were killed. It is infinitely better
to have peace instead of war, and our
treatment generally by the officials is better than it was at first. But, under the
white people, we still have our troubles.
Economic conditions are telling on us
very severely. We are on land where the
rainfall is scanty, and things will not grow
well. In our own time we could pick our
own country, but now all the best land has
been taken by the white people. We get
hardly any price for our cattle; we find it
hard to meet our money obligations. If
we have crops to spare we get very little
for them; we find it difficult to make ends
meet and wages are very low. When I
view the position, I see that our rainfall
has diminished, we have suffered drought
and have poor crops and we do not see
any hope of improvement, but all the
same our taxes do not diminish. We see
no prosperous days ahead of us. There is
one thing we think an injustice. When we
have plenty of grain the prices are very
low, but the moment we are short of grain
and we have to buy from Europeans at
once the price is high. If when we have
hard times and find it difficult to meet our
obligations some of these burdens were
taken off us it would gladden our hearts.
As it is, if we do raise anything, it is never
our own: all, or most of it, goes back in
taxation. We can never save any money.
If we could, we could help ourselves: we
could build ourselves better houses; we
could buy modern means of travelling
about, a cart, or donkeys or mules.

18 LORD BLEDISLOE
NATIVE POLICY IN RHODESIA, 1938

The Bledisloe Commission was a Royal Commission appointed in 1938 under the chairmanship of Lord Bledisloe to investigate the feasibility and desirability of closer association between Northern and Southern Rhodesia and Nyasaland. The commission found the differences in the aims of the racial policies to be of very great importance. By this time, Southern Rhodesia's policy of strict racial segregation was closer to that of South Africa than to the policies of the other two territories. The commission recommended the formation of a territorial council to study the possibility of economic coordination.

SOUTHERN RHODESIA

392. In Southern Rhodesia native policy is more complicated by reason of the more extended development of white settlement. In the absence of any official statement of policy, we venture to quote certain passages from a public speech which the Prime Minister made in the Colony on the 30th March, 1938, to an audience composed largely of natives, and which he brought to our notice shortly after our arrival in Salisbury:

In common with several other African States, the most important question in Rhodesia is the regulation of the relations between Europeans and natives. For nearly four centuries African administrators and statesmen have found this matter so beset with difficulties that for the most part they have shelved it. Meanwhile it has steadily grown more acute. Because of the presence of the white man the Bantu is, with accelerating speed, lifting himself out of his primitive conditions. His inter-tribal wars have been prohibited, and his once frequently recurring epidemics checked. His numbers are increasing. Tribes once separated by traditional animosities are developing the idea of racial unity—an idea fostered by the development of Bantu newspapers and the publication of books in their own dialects. The Bantu is resolved to learn, and within as yet undetermined limits, is capable of learning. To forbid him opportunities is contrary to natural justice, but are we to allow him to develop and in the course

From *Rhodesia-Nyasaland Royal Commission Report* (Bledisloe Report) (London: H.M. Stationery Office, 1939), pp. 170–175. Reprinted by permission.

of time, because his requirements are so small, gradually to oust the European?

While there is yet time and space, the country should be divided into separate areas for black and white. In the native areas the black man must be allowed to rise to any position to which he is capable of climbing. Every step of the industrial and social pyramid must be open to him, excepting only—and always—the very top. For what can be done we may point to Uganda, for what must be avoided we may look at Haiti and Liberia. The senior administrative officer must be white. The native may be his own lawyer, doctor, builder, journalist or priest, and he must be protected from white competition in his own area. In the European areas the black man will be welcomed, when, tempted by wages, he offers his services as a labourer; but it will be on the understanding that there he shall merely assist, and not compete with, the white man. If he wishes to stop in his own area, let him. The two races will develop side by side under white supervision, and help, not hinder, each other's progress. The interest of each race would be paramount in its own sphere.

The policy I suggest enables the two races to live side by side to the benefit of both.

393. The policy as a whole is based on the Land Apportionment Act, the main features of which we have already described. In order to ensure to the natives security of tenure in the land available to them, the native reserves themselves are vested in a Board of Trustees, and no portion of them can be alienated without the approval of the Secretary of State for Dominion Affairs. In the area set aside for

purchase by individual natives (the "Native Purchase Area") no person other than an indigenous native may hold or occupy any land. The natives have therefore fixity of tenure of the land available to them.

394. The native lands comprise some 30 per cent. of the total land area of the Colony, but it may be anticipated that a considerable portion of the Unassigned Area (some 19 per cent. of the total) will eventually be added to that presently available to the natives. Certain disadvantages attach to the native lands. For example, as map No. 5 annexed to this Report will show, they are widely scattered in comparatively small patches and are not, generally speaking, well served by communications. Of 1,350 miles of railway approximately only 60 miles traverse native land, and the position as regards main road communications is little better. It was contended by certain of our witnesses specially interested in native welfare, and possibly with some justification, that in many cases the native lands are inferior in respect of both soil and rainfall, and that, judged from the standpoint of the present density of the native population, without taking into account the possibilities of its increase, they are inadequate. In our opinion the position in this respect has been materially aggravated by wasteful methods of cultivation and by over-grazing, resulting in excessive soil exhaustion and erosion. This the Government is now attempting to check by education and demonstration in more approved methods of husbandry.

We realise that it is impossible to say with confidence, at the present time, that the land set aside is or is not sufficient to provide for the reasonable needs of the native. Until all the reserves have been dealt with, both by the development of irrigation and water conservation schemes, where practicable, and by the adoption of a more prudent and economical system of husbandry, and until it has been possible to replace the present herds of inferior cattle by smaller numbers of improved stock, it is admitted that the land at present available cannot with any certainty be said to be sufficient. It is, however, claimed that the land potentially available for natives should prove adequate, when proper steps have been taken for its maintenance and proper treatment, to provide for their reasonable needs.

We do not regard ourselves as qualified, without a much more detailed examination of the subject on the spot, to express a definite opinion on the general question whether the natives in Southern Rhodesia will in the long run prove to have been adequately provided for in the matter of land. We feel justified in concluding, however, that in so far as there may be defects in this respect, these are due to mistakes in the past, when the necessity of providing for prospective native requirements was not so clearly appreciated as it is to-day. The record of the Colony in recent years shows that genuine efforts are being made to meet the land requirements of the native.

395. As regards the political aspects of native policy in Southern Rhodesia, we have described how in 1937 provision was made for the constitution of Native Civil Courts and the establishment of Native Councils. These Native Courts and Councils represent a delegation of power from the Central Government to Chiefs or Headmen selected by that Government. This presents a marked contrast to the principle of "indirect rule" in Nyasaland and Northern Rhodesia, under which the government of the natives is (within the narrow limit of the functions so far assigned to the Native Authorities) carried on by the traditional tribal authorities. This difference in approach to the native problem is explained largely by the view current in Southern Rhodesia that, as a result of the rebellions of 1896 and 1897, and of forty years of subsequent direct rule, it is impracticable to build up a system of native administration based on tribal discipline.

396. The present social policy of Southern Rhodesia as regards the native areas is progressive. We have, in our review of the social services commented upon the absence of any systematised attempt, prior to 1936, to provide medical facilities for natives in the reserves. Since then the Medical Department has addressed itself to the problem with energy, and has successfully initiated an excellent scheme for the extension of medical services. In the spheres of education and agriculture a considerable advance has been made in the course of the last ten years. In the former respect the missions, as in Northern Rhodesia and Nyasaland, have played a noteworthy part, the main work of primary education being entrusted to them. In the agricultural sphere the Government is making determined efforts to arrest the deterioration of the soil by improved methods of cultivation and rotation of crops, and to expand and render more productive the cultivable areas in various ways, especially by water conservation and irrigation. The steps being taken to reduce the numbers of native cattle in order to limit the ill effects of over-grazing appear to be causing concern in some reserves, and care will be needed to see that the objects of such measures are fully understood.

397. The provision of medical services and schools for natives in the European areas is not being overlooked by the Government and other interested agencies. Native labour in the mining and other industrial centres is housed in compounds provided by the employers, in conformity with the practice in other African countries. In most cases, especially where the compounds are provided by the larger industrial companies, the natives are better fed and cared for than when living in their villages. The standard, however, varies. In the larger towns Africans are confined to urban locations provided by the municipalities. The conditions in some of these (especially the lack of recreative facilities and the terms charged for accommodation) leave room for improvement and amendment. The Government is setting a commendable example in the relatively high standard of housing, sanitation and amenities provided in its model native villages at Highfield, near Salisbury, and Luveve, near Bulawayo. In establishing such model villages proximity to the towns is an important consideration.

398. The Pass Laws of Southern Rhodesia are of a complicated nature. The following are their main provisions. As regards *indigenous natives* they require that adult males, with certain special exceptions, shall carry a registration certificate. In the principal towns every native is compelled to have, in addition to the registration certificate, one of the following:

(a) a pass to seek work in the town; or

(b) a certificate to show that he is employed within the town; or

(c) a certificate signed by a Native Commissioner to the effect that he is earning a living in the town by lawful means; or

(d) if he is employed outside the town, a written permit from his employer; or

(e) a visiting pass.

Section 14 (1) of the Natives Registration Act, 1936, provides that any native who is found in a town without being in possession of one of these documents shall be guilty of an offence. The provisions of this sub-section do not apply to wives and minors living with their families, but this does not free such persons from liability to be challenged by the Police, and this feature of the system is much disliked by the natives.

No native living on his employer's premises in a town, or living in a native location, may be absent therefrom between 9 P.M. and 5 A.M. without a written permit. Every native who is seeking employment in, or visiting, a "proclaimed" township must, if he wishes to remain for the night within the township, spend the hours of darkness in a township hostel. No township had been so proclaimed down to the date of our visit.

Non-indigenous natives are subject to the same requirements, as regards both the registration certificate and the special town passes. In addition, adult males, unless they are employed under a contract of service entered into outside the Colony which provides for their return on the completion of their service, are required to possess either a "visiting pass" or a pass to seek work in the Colony. This requirement applies to non-indigenous male natives throughout the Colony, and not only in the towns.

399. Under the Agreement [1] relating to Migrant Native Labour signed at Salisbury in August, 1936, male natives of Northern Rhodesia and Nyasaland entering Southern Rhodesia are required to possess certificates in a form adequate for identification purposes. Upon presentation of this proof of identity such immigrants are furnished with Southern Rhodesia certificates of registration, of a colour different from those issued to indigenous natives of the Colony. Where there exists no doubt that a native has previously been registered in the Colony, this certificate of registration is issued by the Pass Officer at the point of entry. In other cases particulars are forwarded to the Native Foreigners Identification Bureau, the native receiving a temporary Protection Pass until his identity has been verified, after which a registration certificate can be issued by the Pass Officer in the district where he intends to seek work.

400. The economic prospects of the native in the European areas are limited owing to the policy of segregation. In these areas no career is open to natives, the pursuit of which would adversely affect the opportunities of employment, or the standard of living, of Europeans. Native unskilled labour is, however, indispensable for the economic prosecution of any industrial enterprise, and the native is therefore free to offer his services as a worker on the condition that he shall merely assist, and not compete with, the European.

This policy finds expression in an agreement made under the Industrial Conciliation Act, 1934, between the parties constituting the Industrial Council of the building industry. This agreement, which applies in the areas of, and immediately around, the principal European centres, stipulates that no employee shall receive wages at less than certain rates. The object of this provision is to prevent the under-cutting of European skilled labour in the areas in question by the employment of less highly paid Africans. This legislation does not specifically disentitle the native to be employed as a skilled labourer, provided that he is paid at the same rate as the European; but where it is put into practice it operates to the exclusion of the native from employment in the industry to which it applies, since employers who are compelled to pay a specified rate of wages will obviously prefer to employ the more efficient European worker. Pending the development of opportunities within the native areas, this limitation of employment is calculated to act as a deterrent to the development by the native of his efficiency as a skilled worker. A further handicap is imposed by the limitation of opportunities for the employment of natives in clerical and other subordinate posts in the central Government service. Employment in similar capacities in the native areas is however open to them without restriction.

[1] This Agreement [is] usually referred to as the "Salisbury Agreement."

19 PAUL DU CHAILLU

TRADE IN GABON

Paul Belloni du Chaillu (1831–1903) spent eight years in Africa—four as a trader and four as a naturalist and explorer. During his travels between 1856 and 1859, he explored Gabon, Congo (Brazzaville), and areas that are now in the Spanish colony of Rio Muni, hitherto unknown to Europeans. As a trader he well knew the methods of commerce then in use in equatorial Africa, as well as the role of the African trader in the systems of controlled barter and exchange with European traders along the coast and in the interior.

. . . Each of these tribes assumes to itself the privilege of acting as go-between or middle-man to those next to it, and charges a heavy percentage for this office; and no infraction of this rule is permitted under penalty of war. Thus a piece of ivory or ebony may belong originally to a negro in the far interior, and if he wants to barter it for "white man's trade," he dares not take it to a market himself. If he should be rash enough to attempt such a piece of enterprise his goods would be confiscated, and he, if caught, fined by those whose monopoly he sought to break down, or most likely sold into slavery.

He is obliged by the laws of trade to intrust it to some fellow in the next tribe nearer to the coast. He, in turn, disposes of it to the next chief or friend, and so ivory, or ebony, or bar-wood, passes through probably a dozen hands ere it reaches the factory of the trader on the coast.

This would seem to work against the white trader by increasing the price of products. But this is only half the evil. Although the producer sold his ivory, and though it was resold a dozen times, all this trade was only a *commission* business with no advances. In fact, the first holder has *trusted* each successive dispenser with his property without any equivalent or "collateral" security. Now, when the last black fellow disposes of this piece of ebony or ivory to the white merchant or captain, he retains, in the first place, a very liberal percentage of the returns for his valuable services, and turns the remainder over to his next neighbour above. *He,* in turn, takes out a commission for *his* trouble and passes on what is left; and so, finally, a very small remainder—too often nothing at all—is handed over to the poor fellow who has inaugurated the speculation or sent the tusk.

Anyone can see the iniquity of this system, and the fatal clog it throws on all attempts at the building up of a legitimate commerce in a country so rich in many products now almost indispensable to civilized nations. The poor interior tribes are kept by their neighbours in the profoundest ignorance of what is done on the coast. They are made to believe the most absurd and horrid stories as to the ferocity, the duplicity, and the cunning of the white traders. They are persuaded that the rascally middle-men are not only in constant danger of their lives by their intercourse with the whites, but that they do not make any profit on the goods which they goodnaturedly pass on to a market; so that I have known one of these scoundrels, after having appropriated a large share of the poor remainder of returns for a venture of ivory, actually, by a pitiful story, beg a portion of what he had handed over to his unsuspicious client. Each tribe cheats its next neighbour above, and maligns its next neighbour below. A talent for slandering is, of course, a first-rate business talent; and the harder stories one can tell of his neighbours below the greater profit he will make on his neighbour above.

From Paul Belloni du Chaillu, *Explorations and Adventures in Equatorial Africa* (London: J. Murray, 1861), pp. 10–16.

The consequence is that the interior tribes—who own the most productive country—have little or no incentive to trade, or to gather together the stores of ivory, bar-wood, ebony, &c., for which they get such small prices, and these at no certain intervals, but often after long periods, even years elapsing sometimes before a final settlement is found convenient. Thus they are discouraged, and perforce remain in their original barbarism and inactivity.

The trade in slaves is carried on in exactly the same way, except that sometimes an infraction of trade-laws, or some disturbance on account of witchcraft, causes a war between two tribes in the commission business, when, of course, each side takes all it can of the opposite and ships them direct to the coast—to the barracoons or slave-depôts, of which I shall have something more detailed to say farther on.

There are, however, other obstacles to the prosecution of a regular commercial enterprise even by the shrewder among the negroes. It is not permitted that any member of a tribe shall get into his hands more than his share of the trade. It occurred some years ago to a shrewd Mpongwe fellow that in trade transactions honesty might be the best policy, and he followed the suggestion so well that presently both the whites and the interior natives threw a very considerable trade into his honest hands. But no sooner was this observed than he was threatened with poisoning, accused of witchcraft, and such a hullaballoo raised about his ears that he was forced to refuse the trade offered him, and, in a measure, retire from business to save his life.

More recently still, there were three or four men in the river who had obtained by long good conduct quite a character for honesty, and also, in consequence, got a good deal of business. At last a captain came for a load of bar-wood, and declared that he would trust only the three or four men in question, to the bitter disappointment of other traders. The vessel was quickly filled and departed; and there arose a great "palaver"—the Mpongwe cant for a quarrel—in which the kings and chiefs and all the disappointed trading fellows met together at Glass Town—the residence of my honest friends—to advise about such an outrage. The men were called up for trial. They had been educated at the American mission, and knew how to write; and the charge made against them now was that they had written to the white man's country to say that there were no good men in Gaboon but themselves.

To this the accused shrewdly replied that the white men would not believe men who should thus praise themselves.

But reply was useless. They were threatened that if they took the next ship that came, the malcontents would "make a boondgi," or work a spell of witchcraft upon them, and kill them. Fortunately, in this case, the honest fellows had learned at the mission not to fear such threats; and the French commander for once stepped in and protected them against their envious fellows, so that for this time, on the West Coast of Africa, honesty seems likely to get its reward.

Again, through the anxiety of white traders to secure "trade," there has sprung up along the coast an injurious system of "trust." A merchant, to secure to himself certain quantities of produce *yet to come down* from the interior, gives to such black fellows as he thinks he can depend upon advances of trade goods, often to very considerable amounts. In this way, on the Gaboon and on the coast, often many thousand dollars' worth of goods are in the hands of natives, for which no consideration has been received by the white trader, who meantime waits, and is put to trouble and expense, and thinks himself lucky if he does not eventually lose a part of his investment.

This system of "trust," as it is called, does great injury to the natives, for it tempts them to practise all sorts of cheats, for which they are sharp enough—indeed, much too shrewd often for the white man.

Of course, *his* only dependence lies in the knowledge of his black debtor that if he cheats too badly his future supplies will be stopped entirely. But the practice develops all kinds of overtrading as well as rascality—negroes seldom hesitating to contract to supply much greater quantities of produce than they can hope to procure during a season.

Even the slave-trade, I found, on my visit to Cape Lopez, is burdened with this evil of "trust," and some of the Portuguese slavers, I was told, get preciously cheated in their advances on shipments of slaves sold "to arrive," but which do not come to hand.

I have heard the negroes called stupid, but my experience shows them to be anything but that. They are very shrewd traders indeed; and no captain or merchant who is a new hand on the coast will escape being victimized by their cunning in driving a bargain.

Say that to-day the good ship *Jenny* has arrived in the river. Immediately every black fellow is full of trade. The ship is boarded by a crowd of fellows, each jabbering away, apparently at random, but all telling the same story.

Never was there such dearth of ivory, or whatever the captain may want!

Never were the interior tribes so obstinate in demanding a high price!

Never was the whole coast so bare!

Never were difficulties so great!

There have been fights, captain!

And fever, captain!

And floods, captain!

And no trade at all, captain!

Not a tooth!

This point settled, they produce their "good books," which are certificates of character, in which some captain or other white trader who is known on the coast vouches for the honesty—the great honesty and entire trustworthiness—of the bearer. It is not worth while for a fellow to present himself without a certificate, and the papers are all *good*, because when "the bearer" has cheated he does not apply for a "character." Now these certificates help him to cheat. When he finds the need of a new set of papers, he conducts himself with scrupulous honesty towards two or three captains. These, of course, "certify" him, and then he goes into the wildest and most reckless speculations, upheld by the "good books," which he shows to every captain that comes.

Now, while they are pretending that nothing is to be bought, that there is no ivory on the coast, all this time the lying rascals have their hands full, and are eager to sell. They know the captain is in a hurry. The coast is sickly. The weather is hot. He fears his crew may fall sick or die, and he be left with a broken voyage. Every day is therefore precious to him; but to the black fellows all days are alike. They have no storage, no interest account, no fever to fear, and, accordingly, they can tire the captain out. This they do. In fact often, if they have an obstinate customer to deal with, they even combine and send all the trade a day's journey up river, and thus produce a fair show of commercial scarcity. At last, when high prices have been established, when the inroads of fever on his crew or the advance of the season have made the poor captain desperately willing to pay anything, the ivory comes aboard, and the cunning black fellows chuckle.

Even then, however, there are tedious hours of chaffering. A negro has perhaps only one tooth to sell, and he is willing —as he must live on this sale for a long period of idleness—to give much time to its proper disposal. He makes up his mind beforehand how much more he will ask than he will eventually take. He brings his tooth alongside; spends the afternoon in bargaining, and probably takes it back ashore at dusk, to try again the next day; till at last, when he sees he cannot possibly get more, he strikes the trade. I have known several days to be spent in the selling of a single tooth or a single cask of palm-oil.

Of course the captain protests that he is not in a hurry—that he can wait—that they shan't tire *him* out. But the negroes know better; they know the fatal advantage their climate gives them.

When it is supposed that a captain or trader will return to the coast no more after his present voyage, then he is properly victimized, as then the native has no fear of future vengeance before him; and I have known many individuals who, by the system of "trust," were all but ruined—getting scarce any return at all.

It is much to be wished that white traders would combine to put down at least this abuse. But until the spread of commerce shall break down the scoundrelly system of middle-men in this land, there will be no really prosperous trade there. And this will not happen till the merchants themselves visit the headquarters whence the produce is brought, and until the rude tribes shall be somewhat civilized by lengthened contact with the whites. At present things are in a state of utter disorganization, and the "trust" abuse seems a real necessity. For so hardly and often have the interior tribes been cheated of all returns for their wares, that now they have come to demand at least part payment in advance; and, of course, this advance is exacted of the white trader on the coast, to lure whom great rumours are spread through the tribes of teeth of a marvellous size lying ready for purchase, &c. Too often, when an advance has been made for a specific purchase—of a tooth, say— it is, after all, seized for some intermediate party's debt on its way down, and thus the poor trader is again victimized.

So eager are the Mpongwe for trade that they have even set up a regular coasting business. Every considerable negro trader owns several canoes; but his great ambition is to buy or build a larger vessel, in which he may sail along the coast, and, getting goods on trust from white merchants, make his regular voyage, or establish his little factory on some out-of-the-way point on the shore. The splendid harbour of the Gaboon has made them tolerably fearless on the water, and their rage for trade leads them to all manner of adventures.

Their coasting-vessels are only large boats, but I have seen some of so considerable size as to hold conveniently eight to ten tons. To make one of these they cut down an immense tree, sharpen it at the ends, then burn out the interior, guiding the fire so as to burn the heart of the tree and leave them the shell they need. For this hull, which is then scraped smooth, and otherwise finished and strengthened, they next make masts and sails, the latter being of matting, and then they are ready for sea. These cockle-shells stand the wind and sea remarkably well, as is evident when the squally and blustery weather of this country is considered, and when we know that they make voyages from the Gaboon as far as Cape St. Catherine's south, and as far as Banoko and Cameroon north.

The start for one of these voyages is a great occasion. Guns are fired, and the people shout and wish a pleasant voyage; and the lucky vessel is received at her port of destination with similar ceremonies.

The great aim of a Mpongwe trader, however, is to get "trust" from a white man, with authority to go off up or down the coast and establish a factory. Then there is double rejoicing. But the poor white trader is generally sadly victimized; for his agent goes to some spot where he thinks he can get ivory and other trade and settles down. Then, first, he mostly picks out the best and most valuable of the goods with which he has been intrusted, and secretes these for his own use. His next step is to buy himself some slaves and to marry several wives; all which being accomplished, it is at last time to think of the interests of his principal. Thus, after many months, perhaps he makes returns on his sales, or perhaps he fails altogether to make returns, if he thinks he can cheat so far with impunity.

These fellows understand all the dialects spoken on the coast, as well as English, French, Spanish, and Portuguese.

On their voyages, as they go poorly provisioned, and depend more on luck than real skill, they often suffer extreme hardships, but they are seldom drowned.

The chief product of the Gaboon country is its ivory. This is said to be the finest on the western coast. It produces also bar-wood, a dye-wood, from which is obtained a dark red dye, and ebony, the last taken from the great forests of this wood which abound near the head-waters of the Gaboon River. I have seen very large sticks brought thence, but the supply is not yet large. The bar-wood tree is found in great plenty along the shores of the river and its numerous tributary creeks. It is also found on the Moondah and Danger rivers. Copal is another product of this country, but it is of inferior quality, and is not sought.[1]

Ivory comes down the river from the

interior by inland journeys in great quantities. Upwards of 80,000 pounds are taken from the Gaboon River yearly when home prices are good; for the ruling prices here are so high that traders cannot buy to advantage unless the home demand is very brisk. I suppose that the country from Banoko to Loango furnishes in brisk years at least 150,000 pounds of ivory.

But however important may be these commercial resources of the Gaboon country, I am convinced that the people will never prosper till they turn their attention more to agricultural operations, for elephants must finally disappear. This, indeed, is the great evil of all the nations of Western Africa. The men despise labour, and force their women and slaves to till the fields; and this tillage never assumes the important proportions it deserves, so that the supply of food is never abundant; the tribes, almost without exception, live from hand to mouth, and, with a fertile soil, are half the time in a state of semi-starvation.

[1] Copal is a resinous substance exuded from various tropical trees that is used in making varnishes and lacquers (ed.).

20 HENRY MORTON STANLEY
THE GREAT RAINFOREST OF THE CONGO

Sir Henry Morton Stanley (1841–1904) was a famous journalist who was commissioned by his employer, James Gordon Bennett, owner of The *(New York)* Herald, *to march into the interior and find Dr. David Livingstone, whose whereabouts were unknown. Stanley's subsequent meeting with Dr. Livingstone at Ujiji in 1871 brought him greater fame, and upon the death of Livingstone in 1873, Stanley returned to Africa to resolve the geographical riddle of the sources of the Nile and Congo rivers, which Dr. Livingstone had failed to untangle. Stanley circumnavigated Lake Victoria, proving that John Hanning Speke had been correct in his assumption that Lake Victoria was a single lake and the source of the Nile. Stanley then circumnavigated Lake Tanganyika, proving that Sir Richard Burton had been wrong—the lake had no outlet and was thus divorced from the Nile system. Finally, Stanley struck west through the great tropical rainforest of the Congo basin to make his way down the Lualaba/Congo River to the Atlantic. His descriptions of the rainforest did much to confirm the image of Africa that was common throughout the Romantic and Victorian eras—that the continent was indeed the heart of darkness—mysterious, brooding, remote, and terrifying.*

From Henry Morton Stanley, *Through the Dark Continent* (New York: Harper and Brothers, 1878), pp. 130–133, 136–140.

On the 6th November we drew nearer to the dreaded black and chill forest called Mitamba, and at last, bidding farewell to sunshine and brightness, entered it.

We had made one mistake—we had not been up early enough. Tippu-Tib's heterogeneous column of all ages were ahead of us, and its want of order and compactness became a source of trouble to us in the rear.[1]

We, accustomed to rapid marching, had to stand in our places minutes at a time waiting patiently for an advance of a few yards, after which would come another halt, and another short advance to be again halted. And all this time the trees kept shedding their dew upon us like rain in great round drops. Every leaf seemed weeping. Down the boles and branches, creepers and vegetable cords, the moisture trickled and fell on us. Overhead the wide-spreading branches, in many interlaced strata, each branch heavy with broad thick leaves, absolutely shut out the daylight. We knew not whether it was a sunshiny day, or a dull, foggy, gloomy day; for we marched in a feeble solemn twilight, such as you may experience in temperate climes an hour after sunset. The path soon became a stiff clayey paste, and at every step we splashed water over the legs of those in front, and on either side of us.

To our right and left, to the height of about twenty feet, towered the undergrowth, the lower world of vegetation. The soil on which this thrives is a dark-brown vegetable humus, the debris of ages of rotting leaves and fallen branches, a very forcing-bed of vegetable life, which, constantly fed with moisture, illustrates in an astonishing degree, the prolific power of the warm moist shades of the tropics.

The stiff clay lying under this mould, being impervious, retains the moisture which constantly supplies the millions of

tiny roots of herb, plant, and bush. The innumerable varieties of plants which spring up with such marvellous rapidity, if exposed to the gale, would soon be laid prostrate. But what rude blast can visit these imprisoned shades? The tempest might roar without the leafy world, but in its deep bosom there is absolute stillness. One has but to tug at a sapling to know that the loose mould has no retentive power, and that the sapling's roots have not penetrated the clays. Even the giants of the forest have not penetrated very deeply, as one may see by the half exposed roots; they appear to retain their upright positions more by breadth of base than by their grasp of earth.

Every few minutes we found ourselves descending into ditches, with streams trending towards the Kunda River, discharged out of leafy depths of date-palms, Amoma, Carpodinae, and Phrynia. Climbing out from these streams, up their steep banks, our faces were brushed by the broad leaves of the Amomum, or the wild banana, ficus of various kinds, and climbing, crawling, obstructing lengths of wild vines.

Naturally our temper was not improved by this new travelling. The dew dropped and pattered on us incessantly until about 10 A.M. Our clothes were heavily saturated with it. My white sun-helmet and puggaree appeared to be weighted with lead. Being too heavy, and having no use for it in the cool dank shades, I handed it to my gun-bearer, for my clothes, gaiters, and boots, which creaked loudly with the water that had penetrated them, were sufficient weight for me to move with. Added to this vexation was the perspiration which exuded from every pore, for the atmosphere was stifling. The steam from the hot earth could be seen ascending upward and settling like a grey cloud above our heads. In the early morning it had been so dense that we could scarcely distinguish the various trees by their leafage.

At 3 P.M. we had reached Mpotira, in

---

[1] A well-known and powerful Swahili trader who built up a large commercial empire in the eastern Congo and western Tanzania in the 1870s and 1880s (ed.).

the district of Uzimba, Manyema, twenty-one miles and a half from the Arab depot on the Lualaba.

The poor boatmen did not arrive until evening, for the boat sections—dreadful burdens—had to be driven like blunted ploughs through the depths of foliage. The men complained bitterly of fatigue, and for their sake we rested at Mpotira.

The nature of the next two days' experiences through the forest may be gathered by reading the following portions of entries in my journal:

"*November* 8. N. ¹/₂ W., nine miles to district of Karindi, or Kionga, Uregga.

"We have had a fearful time of it to-day in these woods, and Bwana Shokka, who has visited this region before, declares with superior pride that what we have experienced as yet is only a poor beginning to the weeks upon weeks which we shall have to endure. Such crawling, scrambling, tearing through the damp, dank jungles, and such height and depth of woods! . . . Once we obtained a side-long view from a tree on the crown of a hill, over the wild woods on our left, which swept in irregular waves of branch and leaf down to the valley of the Lualaba. Across the Lualaba, on the western bank, we looked with wistful eyes on what appeared to be green grassy plains. Ah! what a contrast to that which we had to endure! It was a wild and weird scene, this outlook we obtained of the top of the leafy world! . . . It was so dark sometimes in the woods that I could not see the words, recording notes of the track, which I pencilled in my note-book. At 3.30 P.M. we arrived in camp, quite worn out with the struggle through the intermeshed bush, and almost suffocated with the heavy atmosphere. Oh for a breath of mountain air!"

"*November* 9, 1876. N. ¹/₂ W., ten and a half miles' march to Kiussi, Uregga.

"Another difficult day's work in the forest and jungle. Our Expedition is no longer the compact column which was my pride. It is utterly demoralized. Every man scrambles as he best may through the woods; the path, being over a clayey soil, is so slippery that every muscle is employed to assist our progress. The toes grasp the path, the heads bear the load, the hand clears the obstructing bush, the elbow puts aside the sapling. Yesterday the boatmen complained so much that I organized all the chiefs into a pioneer party, with axes to clear the path. Of course we could not make a wide road. There were many prostrate giants fallen across the path each with a mountain of twigs and branches, compelling us to cut roads through the bush a long distance to get round them. My boatbearers are utterly wearied out."

.   .   .

From Kiussi, through the same dense jungle and forest, with its oppressive atmosphere and its soul-wearying impediments, we made a journey of fourteen miles to Mirimo. Four streams were crossed, all trending westward to the Lualaba, the two principal being the Rugunsi and Rumuna rivers. Mirimo is a populous settlement, and its people are good-natured.

The boatmen did not arrive at all on this day, the obstacles having been too great, but on the 12th, about noon, they appeared, utterly disheartened at the delays which had deprived them of their food and rest.

On the 13th we moved to Wanekaman-kua, crossing *en route* the Kariba River and two small streams.

Our next march was to Wane-Mbeza, in Uregga, eight miles in a north-westerly direction. We crossed the Kipembwé, a river 40 yards wide, deep and swift, which flows westward.

Uregga, it appears, occupies a broad belt of country lying north-east and south-west. Its people know nothing of the immediate settlements contiguous to them, and though within twenty miles of the Lualaba, many adult males at Wane-Mbeza had never seen it. They have been imprisoned now for some five or six generations within their almost impenetrable forest fastnesses, and the difficulty of travelling, and the danger that would be incurred unless they united in strong bands, are the causes of their knowing nothing of the world outside, and the outside world knowing nothing of them.

The Wangwana began at this place to murmur loudly, while the boatmen, though assisted by a dozen supernumeraries and preceded by a gang of pioneers, were becoming perfectly savage; but the poor fellows had certainly cause for discontent. I pitied them from my soul, yet I dared not show too great a solicitude, lest they should have presumed upon it, and requested me either to return to Nyangwé or to burn my boat.

Even Tippu-Tib, whom I anxiously watched, as on him I staked all my hopes and prospects, murmured. Sheikh Abdullah was heard to growl ominously, and Bwana Ibrahim was particularly severe in his remarks upon "the pagans' forest." The evil atmosphere created sickness in the Arab escort, but all my people maintained their health, if not their temper.

At this camp we parted from Bwana Shokka and his 300, who were about to penetrate some eight or ten marches more to the north-east to Tata country. I have a suspicion that "Tata" is not a proper name, but that it simply signifies "farther in."

On the 15th we marched six miles and a half to Wane-Kirumbu. From this village, which, like all the villages that we had passed, crowned a hill, we obtained the most extended view we had enjoyed since entering the forest. Towards the north and north-east the outlook was over a jumble of forest-clad hills separating narrow and deep valleys. The view was indeed most depressing and portentous.

Our march, short as it was, was full of incidents. The constant slush and reek which the heavy dews caused in the forest through which we had travelled the last ten days had worn my shoes out, and half of the march I travelled with naked feet. I had then to draw out of my store my last pair of shoes. Frank was already using his last pair. Yet we were still in the very centre of the continent. What should we do when all were gone? was a question which we asked of each other often.

The faces of the people, Arabs, Wangwana, Wanyamwezi, and the escort, were quite a study at this camp. All their courage was oozing out, as day by day we plodded through the doleful, dreary forest. We saw a python 10 feet long, a green viper, and a monstrous puff-adder on this march, besides scores of monkeys, of the white-necked or glossy black species, as also the small grey, and the large howling baboons. We heard also the "soko" or chimpanzee, and saw one "nest" belonging to it in the fork of a tall bombax. A lemur was also observed; its loud harsh cries made each night hideous.

The path presented myriapedes, black and brown, 6 inches in length; while beetles were innumerable, and armies of the deep brown "hot-water" ants compelled us to be cautious how we stepped.

The difficulties of such travel as we had now commenced may be imagined when a short march of six miles and a half occupied the twenty-four men who were carrying the boat sections an entire day, and so fatigued them that we had to halt another day at Wane-Kirumbu, to recruit their exhausted strength.

The terrible undergrowth that here engrossed all the space under the shade of the pillared bombax and mast-like mvulé was a miraclé of vegetation. It consisted of ferns, spear-grass, water-cane, and orchidaceous plants, mixed with wild vines, cable thicknesses of the *Ficus elastica,* and a sprinkling of mimosas, acacias, tamarinds; llianes, palms of various species, wild date, *Raphia vinifera,* the elais, the fan, rattans, and a hundred other varieties, all struggling for every inch of space, and swarming upward with a luxuriance and density that only this extraordinary hothouse atmosphere could nourish. We had certainly seen forests before, but this scene was an epoch in our lives ever to be remembered for its bitterness; the gloom enhanced the dismal misery of our life; the slopping moisture, the unhealthy reeking atmosphere, and the monotony of the scenes; nothing but the eternal interlaced branches, the tall aspiring stems, rising from a tangle through which we had to burrow and crawl like wild animals, on hands and feet.

About 9 A.M. Tippu-Tib and the Arabs came to my hut at Wane-Kirumbu. After a long preamble, wherein he described the hardships of the march, Tippu-Tib concluded by saying that he had come to announce his wish that our contract should be dissolved!

In a moment it flashed on my mind that a crisis had arrived. Was the Expedition to end here? I urged with all my powers the necessity for keeping engagements so deliberately entered into.

"It is of no use," Tippu-Tib replied, "to have two tongues. Look at it how you may, those sixty camps will occupy us at the rate we are travelling over a year, and it will take as much time to return. I never was in this forest before, and I had no idea there was such a place in the world; but the air is killing my people, it is insufferable. You will kill your own people if you go on. They are grumbling every day more and more. This country was not made for travel; it was made for vile pagans, monkeys, and wild beasts. I cannot go farther."

"Will Tippu-Tib then return to Nyangwé, and break his word and bond? What will all the Arabs at Nyangwé, Mwana Mamba, and Kasongo's say when they hear that Tippu-Tib, who was the first Arab to penetrate Rua, proceeded only a few days with his friend, and then returned?"

"Show me a man's work, and I will do it."

"Well, look here, Tippu-Tib. The land on the west bank of the Lualaba is more open than this, and the road that Mtagamoyo took to go to the Lumami is on that side. Though the land is more open, I hear that the people are worse there than on this side. However, we are not Mtagamoyo, and they may behave better with us. Let us try the other side.

"Now, I will give you choice of two contracts. Accompany me to the river, and wait while I transport my people across, and I will give you 500 dollars; or accompany me twenty marches farther along the west bank, and I will give you 2600 dollars. At the end of that time, if you see your way clear, I will engage you for another journey, until I am quite satisfied that I can go no farther. Provisions will be given your people until we part, and from that point back to Nyangwé."

For two hours I plied him with arguments, and at last, when I was nearly exhausted, Tippu-Tib consented to accompany me twenty marches farther, beginning from the camp we were then in. It was a fortunate thing indeed for me that he agreed to this, as his return so close to Nyangwé in the present dispirited condition of my peoples' minds would have undoubtedly ensured the destruction of all my hopes.

21 EDGAR CANISIUS
RUBBER COLLECTING IN THE CONGO

In 1885 King Leopold II of Belgium became sovereign of the Congo Free State and set out to establish the state's authority throughout the Congo basin and beyond. The task soon absorbed the king's private resources, and despite loans from Belgium, by the early 1890s the Congo Free State was on the verge of bankruptcy. It was saved from financial collapse by the rubber industry. King Leopold leased vast territories of the Congo to concessionaire companies while exploiting the royal domain with his own agents. Soon rubber was exported from the Congo in ever increasing quantities, to the profit of the companies and the king. Unhappily, rubber could be collected only by employing brutal and repressive methods against the Africans who derived no profit from tapping the vines and collecting the sap and consequently had no wish to work. The atrocities that were perpetrated to force the Africans into the forest to tap the vines soon caused an international scandal and ultimately resulted in the transfer of the Congo Free State to Belgium. Edgar Canisius was a young American who joined the service of the Congo Free State in 1896 and was stationed in the Province Orientale. *After completing his tour of duty, he joined the* Société Anversoise du Commerce au Congo *and, as an agent of that concessionaire company, he was able to describe at first hand the methods employed to collect rubber.*

There are, or were, in the immediate vicinity of N'Dobo about a dozen villages, the people of which were obliged to bring in rubber every fifteen days. On these occasions the natives crowded into the post, each village in charge of a "capita," or headman, whose most important duty it was to ensure that the demanded amount of rubber was collected. These capitas usually belonged to tribes settled in other districts of the State, and were as a general rule, armed with muskets of the gas-pipe variety, although some had breech-loaders. They were paid by the company, but the villagers were expected to supply them with food, and this Mr. "Capita" was never remiss in deciding should be of the best and of sufficient quantity.

The natives carried to the muster small baskets supplied by the post, and supposed to be full of rubber. When all had arrived, the people were ranged by the capitas according to their villages. The agent, who had their names inscribed in

From Edgar Canisius, "A Campaign Amongst Cannibals," in Captain Guy Burrows, *The Curse of Central Africa* (London: R. A. Everett & Co., 1903), pp. 74–80.

a book kept for the purpose, then called the people forward, first by villages, then individually. As each man stepped up I noticed that he carried, attached to his neck by a cord, a small disc of metal evidently cut from the zinc lining of a packing-case, and that each disc bore a number corresponding with that entered in the book opposite the man's name. The soldiers having ranged the people in lines, each man with his basket before him, the agent proceeded to verify the individual numbers—not without some difficulty, however, for the natives by some means or other frequently get their "tags" mixed, and much time and a fearful amount of shouting and gesticulation are required, on the part of both natives and white man, to set matters right.

As each man or boy presented his basket, the agent carefully inspected the quantity of rubber it contained, and paid the bearer accordingly in *mitakos*—pieces of brass wire about six inches long, the estimated value of which at N'Dobo was about a half-penny. I calculated that the rubber was paid for at the rate of rather less than one penny per pound, which certainly could not be considered excessive in view of the fact that at that time the product in Europe was fetching from two to three shillings a pound. Those natives who had brought in quantities which the agent deemed insufficient were ordered to one side, and as soon as the entire village had been thus inspected and paid, these delinquents were seized by some of the "soldiers" attached to the post, thrown upon the ground, and soundly flogged. Some received twenty-five lashes, others fifty, but I have occasionally seen even 100 lashes administered, the instrument used being the "chicotte," a heavy whip of hippopotamus hide. This proceeding—inspection and eventual punishment—was repeated until all the villages had been dealt with. Then the natives started off for their jungle homes, usually at a sharp trot, apparently only too glad to escape with life from a place which no doubt they looked upon much as the Belgians' forefathers regarded the torture-chambers to which they were oftimes led by their Spanish masters. They, of course, carried with them their baskets and their *mitakos,* which they did not want but were forced to accept. The manager of the post had accumulated perhaps no less than a thousand pounds of rubber at the cost of about £4 sterling, including presents to the chiefs and capitas. Thus was rubber "gathered" twice each month at N'Dobo.

I found that it was usual to "tag" not all, but only three-fourths or so of the male villagers. Those "tagged" at once became mere slaves to the company, for rubber-making occupied all their time, the victim having to search far and wide for the giant vines from which the sap is extracted. They were not even fed by their taskmasters, their only remuneration being merchandise or *mitakos* distributed in ridiculously small quantities, as already described.

The cruel flogging of so many men and boys would probably have had a peculiar effect upon a new-comer, but I was in a measure case-hardened. My experience in the State service during three years had made me familiar with many such, and worse incidents of Congolese life. For instance, at the Government post where I was for a long time stationed, a man had died as the result of an exceptionally severe castigation at the hands of a white official, and elsewhere I had seen blood drawn from the backs of women.

At N'Dobo I found many brick houses and magazines in course of construction under the direction of an ex-architect and builder. At that time, it was evident, the company's officials at Mobeka entertained keen hopes that the fierce and hitherto intractable Budjas of the interior were about to tumble over each other in their eagerness to bring in rubber—an idea which proved very erroneous, as will later be seen.

The Brazilian rubber-gatherer has no reason to envy the people engaged in a similar occupation in the wilds of Africa, for his work in comparison is a mere picnic. The great rubber-trees of the Amazonian forest yield to him their precious sap after but a few blows of the axe, and fill the bucket of the collector without entailing upon the latter any necessity of raising himself above the ground. Nor does the extraction of a few quarts of sap deprive him of another supply from the same source later on.

Not so, however, with the Congolese rubber-gatherer. In the African jungle the sap is drawn from a giant creeper (often six inches in diameter at the base), which, shooting upward towards the life-giving light of heaven, twists about the surrounding vegetation—its rivals in the struggle for existence. After reaching the crown of the highest monarch of the forest (often a hundred feet above the ground), the vine rises still further until it is bent back by its own weight to the topmost branches of its original support. Then it climbs along these branches, and those probably of half-a-dozen other great trees, until the machete of the rubber-gatherer cuts short its career.

The Congo native, when about to

gather rubber, generally goes with his fellow-villagers far into the jungle. Then, having formed a rough, shelterless camp, he begins his search for the creepers. Having found one of sufficient size, he cuts with his knife a number of incisions in the bark, and, hanging a small earthenware pot below the vine, allows the sap to slowly trickle into it. Should the creeper have been already tapped, the man must climb into the supporting tree at more or less personal risk and make an incision in the vine high above the ground where the sap has not been exhausted; and here he will remain, perhaps the whole of the day, until the flow has ceased. Not unfrequently the natives slumber on their lofty perches, and, falling to the ground, become victims to the white man's greed. Few Africans will imperil their lives in rubber-gathering unless under compulsion. The natives, if pressed for time, as they usually are in the Congo in consequence of the threats of the white man and the fear of the Albinis of the soldiers and the muskets of the capitas, cut down long lengths of the giant creepers and then subdivide them to make the sap ooze out more quickly.

Of late, the people have been compelled to so frequently tap the vines that the latter soon dry up and die. Each tribe has only a limited extent of forest which it can call its exclusive domain, and it consequently very frequently happens, when their own "bush" is worked out, that natives from one village penetrate the territory of the other in defiance of tribal usage. Such an invasion is naturally resented by their neighbours, who, equally pressed no doubt by circumstances and the white man, are themselves experiencing difficulty in making up the quota of rubber definitely fixed for each village, and a deficient production of which may entail dire punishment and even death. In consequence, disputes arise between villages which heretofore, perhaps for quite a long period, have been at peace; and then come wars, involving more or less loss of life, destruction and cannibalism. Natives, I may add, have often come to me with bitter laments over the disappearance of their brothers after accidents when rubber-gathering, or the attacks of leopards or hostile tribesmen.

The coagulation of the sap is effected in a variety of ways. In some regions, the natives smear the latex over their chests, and with their hands rub it until a small ball is formed. This process is repeated until the ball is the size of a small walnut. These balls have often a reddish hue, the result of the powdered camwood with which the natives usually smear their bodies. In other parts, the juice is poured into a pot in which is boiling water, and is then allowed to boil until all the water has evaporated and the rubber forms a kind of cake over the bottom of the pot. This product, when brought to the stations, is cut into fine strips and hung upon battens in a drying-shed for several months. In the Province Orientale the natives generally pour the sap into an oblong form of box, made of flat-sided sticks laid upon the ground. The heat of the sun is utilized to coagulate the sap, a thin layer of latex being poured on the top from time to time until the whole forms a solid mass of rubber some fifteen to twenty inches long, eight inches wide, two or three inches thick, and weighing from eight to ten pounds. After reaching the stations, these slabs are cut into small strips or *vidoles* (fingers), and then placed in sheds to dry upon shelves made of poles.

I have seen it stated in official documents, and in books written by persons represented to have travelled through the African forests, that there are regions where the jungle is literally a tangled mass of rubber-vines. Such stories are ridiculous, for nowhere does the creeper exist in such luxuriance; like all tropical jungle vegetation, it is scattered over large areas with many other similar plants, which may belong to the same genus but are not the true rubber-vine. On an acre of jungle one rarely finds two trees of a kind, and the same may be said of the large creepers, or lianas, with which the tropical bush abounds.

That the stock of rubber-vines in those parts of the Congo which have been worked for any length of time is being rapidly exhausted is evidenced by the ever-increasing difficulty experienced in inducing the natives to exploit it. Wherever I have been in this vast territory, always excepting, of course, the Budja country, which has never been much worked, the natives bitterly bemoaned the scarcity of the rubber-producing lianas, and piteously begged to be allowed to perform other service than rubber-gathering. In some places they brought in large quantities of "false rubber," a resinous matter much resembling caoutchouc, from which, indeed, when freshly-made, it cannot be easily distinguished. In the course of drying, however, the false rubber assumes a glossy appearance, unlike that of the genuine article.

22   LÉON PÉTILLON
NATIVE POLICY IN THE BELGIAN CONGO

In his speech before the Government Council of the Belgian Congo in Léopoldville on July 18, 1955, Governor General Léon Pétillon outlined a revised native policy, according to which the Belgians hesitantly agreed to begin to train Africans for a greater role in the administration of the colony. The tardy awakening of Belgian colonial policy is in striking contrast to the relatively mild demands of Patrice Lumumba put forth in his book, Le Congo, *a portion of which is the subject of the following selection.*

THE TASK OF THE OLD CHIEFS
In their great majority, the traditional chiefs are elements of value; even among those who lack education, there are those who enjoy great prestige; many of them establish, in a satisfactory manner, the contacts between the European administration and the populations whose resources, needs and aspirations they know. They are among the most precious collaborators that Belgium has on African soil. They have worked under often difficult circumstances, executing orders whose scope exceeded their understanding, in a spirit of trusting submission. Therefore, we have decided that it was

From *Belgium's Policy in the Belgian Congo* (New York: Belgian Government Information Center, 1956), pp. 18–22, 26–27. Reprinted by permission of the author.

necessary to compensate them in relation to the importance of their responsibilities, present and future, and have just raised their salary.

Far be it from me to minimize their merit or to slight the importance of their services. But we have to admit that except for a very small number, they are rooted in the tradition that they personify, and envision only with reserve and anxiety an order of things different from that over which they preside. It is up to us to make them, and especially their successors, understand that we wish only that their institutions develop in such a way as to make of them instruments of progress.

Moreover, the ever-increasing multiplicity and the diversity of the tasks of the chief call for the creation of administrative machinery and, as far as possible, the separation of the executive and judicial powers. The collection of duties and taxes, the preparation of the cadastral survey (plan of commune), the registration of the vital statistics, the administration of public thoroughfares, the execution of social works, the setting up and running of the record office of the provinces require a specialized and trained personnel. Besides, the chief no longer has the peace of mind nor the necessary time to fulfill his function of judge; therefore, whenever custom permits, he must be relieved of this obligation.

TRAINING THE ELITE FOR ADMINISTRATIVE TASKS

That is why we thought that, in order to instruct the future rural authorities and their assistants in their tasks, it was necessary to create a system of instruction which might give an authentic administrative and civic training to the sons of chiefs and notables and to all the young natives called upon to exercise a function in their rural milieu.

Furthermore, it is not exclusively a matter of specialized instruction; the pupils must be assured a solid general training which will permit them eventually to request other functions or to attempt other activities. But it is deemed necessary that this program be organized in the very districts where the functions taught are to be exercised, in order to inculcate in their officials a spirit of healthy regionalism and to familiarize them with the tangible aspects of public office.

Two levels of education are planned, corresponding to the minor and the responsible positions. These schools will be directed by an experienced member of the territorial service, assisted by a pedagogue chosen from the teaching personnel.

A first step has been envisaged for the near future: three schools of administration will be opened in the provinces for which the need is the most pressing: Equator, Kasaï and the East Province.

At the same time we shall anticipate an adaptation of the program of the existing secondary schools, especially as regards civic formation, in such a way as to permit their pupils to become oriented in communal occupations, if they so desire.

2. To encourage or increase the participation of the populations in public life also implies that it is necessary to confer upon the districts communal autonomy to the extent that the formation and popular control of those whom they administer would allow.

To be autonomous, is above all to control one's own finances.

Through a series of measures that your Permanent Delegation has recently approved, the legislator will allow additional quotas in the duty to be increased from 40 to 70% and will authorize the creation of non-compensatory taxes. It is a first step towards fiscal autonomy.

COMMUNAL DOMAIN

Besides, it is necessary that the districts possess a domain. The assignment to the advanced centers of the lands in their jurisdiction had already been decided. The Royal Decree of December 19, 1949 for the center of the Katanga and the projected decree of the Cities were resolutely conceived in this view.

The existence of a private domain calls for strict regulations and the capacity to extract from them the benefit that a prudent administration would authorize. This problem must be initiated and resolved without particular apprehension.

The setting up of assets and the creation of receipts to tend to financial autonomy without contrivances would necessitate the total suppression of imposed works not having an educational nature, in such a way that the obligations which the districts met by means of a noncompensated manpower may henceforward have to be paid for with their money. Shortly, it will also be an accomplished fact.

However, we must see to it that the

burdens of the native communities are bearable.

The maintenance of the road network of local interest such as it was conceived up to now might exceed the means of most people. Therefore, the State undertook on its own account a part of the expense since the beginning of this year; besides, we have placed under study, to be applied starting next year, a reclassification of the roads reducing the proportion of those which we call "of local interest."

Furthermore, the development of the communal administration will considerably increase public expenses. It was, therefore, fitting to provide, a priori, that each district be able to fulfill its tasks properly, and to conceive of an adequate system of subsidization until, after a long initial period which is beginning, complete financial autonomy can be foreseen and instituted. That is why the system of subsidies has been re-examined and will in the future be based on new principles which will go into effect in 1956. We are expecting notably a simplification of the duties of the territorial administrator as manager of the credits of the Colony, more faithful respect for financial soundness, a calmer management of the coffers of the chefferies,[1] an activity becoming more and more predominantly that of native authorities.

But, it will not suffice for native communities to manage their ordinary receipts and expenses from day to day. As every public administration, they will have to be able to proceed with community investments and with the equipment that our reform calls for. Communities, like men, need starting capital. Therefore, the districts are authorized to contract loans under certain conditions.

The National Savings Bank, which collects the available funds of the richest communities, is normally indicated to lend to the poorest the funds which they

need. Later, it will be necessary to establish an institution which would have a statute similar to the Communal Bank of Belgium, founded on the principle of the coöperatives. The first step will be accomplished without difficulty; the scope that the credit will have, and which will be the reflection of the desired evolution, will tell us when the establishment of an autonomous organism is justified.

3. It thus appears that we intend henceforward to substitute a regime of guardianship for the paternalism that we have practiced up to the present: the representatives of European authority will only continue to intervene as animators, advisers and inspectors.

A balance must be established between the two elements which serve as counterweights for the liberal administration of the communities: popular control on one side, European guardianship on the other. Proportionately, as the first falters, it is essential that the second be more closely exercised. One should not have any illusions in this regard: a careful guardianship will have to compensate for the insufficiency of popular control for a long time to come. Nevertheless, is it to be expected that it will ever disappear entirely since, as everywhere, the local powers here remain subordinate to the higher instances of authority?

As the decree of July 14, 1952 on the political organization of Ruanda-Uruandi already provides, the action of territorial authority will be exercised a priori, by means of councils and a posteriori, by means of veto. The text which is submitted to you specifies the duties and the powers of the authority in this respect: the success of the new regime evidently depends in large measure on the tact with which the administrator of the territory and his assistants exercise their tutelary function. Just as they will have to remain vigilant toward the backward communities and be uncompromising when, as must be anticipated, abuses develop, so they must be discreet and unobtrusive,

---

[1] A chefferie is a community under the administration of a local chief.

when the communal authorities merit their confidence.

COOPERATION ON A HIGHER PLANE

The third point with which our plans deal is to create a favorable climate for collaboration on the higher plane of the Belgo-Congolese community.

For the cities, we have visualized a regime which makes allowances for the duality in fact which exists between the African and the European cities, a duality which dominates and tempers administrative unity in all that concerns the general interest and towards which we wish to tend more and more.

For still more evident reasons, it is inconceivable that on the level of the native communities of the interior, the assemblies be homogeneous for still a long time. But it is necessary, here also, to anticipate a level of coordination and of cooperation of the local administrations, on the one hand with those which surround them, on the other hand with the European population.

That will have to be accomplished with the flexibility desirable, in creating mixed councils in the territories and the districts, councils whose essential and local competency will have to be within the range of understanding and capacity of the men who compose them. There would be certain danger in the beginning, to create these organs abstractly and to impose them everywhere with the same methods. It will therefore be necessary that the local authorities experiment with a theory, adapted to the necessities of each region, in several places judiciously chosen, and put it to the test.

The program that I outlined in 1952 would thus be realized, little by little, as a foundation, on which is to be constructed later—the last step of our reform—the pyramid of the Territorial and District Councils, crowned by the Provincial and Government Councils.

.   .   .

NATIVES TO ACQUIRE REAL ESTATE

We have been, the very first in this respect, to burn with impatience, realizing how much this delay would retard the progress of the native middle class and, more generally, the installation of one of the most innovative measures and one most likely to bring about profound changes, that has been applied in recent times.

For, its economic and social scope will be considerable. "To grant to the Congolese," as the texts proclaim, "the enjoyment of all the real estate rights provided by written law," is to confer upon them the possibility of becoming title holders of actual guaranteed rights, to use them freely and conveniently within the limits which only the law may fix; to settle and mortgage their heritage economically; to have recourse to mortgage credit.

But it was certainly necessary to yield to the evidence and admit the reasons which the heads of service brought forth to justify the impossibility of going more quickly. It is not, indeed, without infinite precautions that one can put into effect, in an immense territorial area, a precise system or organization of real estate rights, with all the legal, economic and social implications that it embodies at a time when nothing was yet provided for in this domain, when all the indispensable opinions remained to be gathered, the collaboration to be obtained and the specialized personnel to be recruited.

Oddly enough, in the centers where the problem was most urgent, it was necessary to organize the cadastral survey, set up the administration and train the personnel.

In large measure, the difficulties are today surmounted and resolved in the following manner.

The Office of the African Cities—whose cooperation has been sought in the settlements where it is established because of its related activities and its more flexible organization—is charged with the surveying and the demarcation of boundaries of the lands placed at its disposal; it will do this according to a plan and an order decided by mutual agreement between the Administration and itself. The conditions and the methods of this collaboration have been agreed upon in the belief that the Office will give the maximum of efficiency to the accomplishment of its task.

For the lands other than those of the Office, we shall go forward, starting from the basis which we have. In the chief provincial towns, the urbanistic studies are advanced enough to permit land development, if not by districts, at least by blocks limited by public thoroughfares; there, the Cadastral Service will establish its land developments and will proceed with the surveying and parceling according to the directions of the town-planners. Besides, the land developments would be best completed with the means and personnel that the local authorities have at their disposal; the parcels of land will be delimited provisorily and sold or rented without guarantee of area.

This work—I am sketching here only the outstanding features—will be executed everywhere with the maximum of precision that circumstances will permit, if it is not perfect, the excuse will be found in the will which animates us not to wait and in the obligation to resign ourselves sometimes to the "almost" when one cannot do better.

As for the administration of the real estate domain, it will be assured, according to the case, either by the Colony, or by the native communities as soon as they will have become owners of their land grants.

We shall have thus done the maximum that is necessary and sufficient to satisfy urgent necessities, to resolve in a practical way the problem of accession of natives to private real estate property.

Henceforward and everywhere where they will usefully desire it, the Congolese people will be in a position to acquire real estate, fully and completely, to dispose of it prudently, to exhaust all its economic possibilities and, notably through mortgage credit, to have recourse to a new efficient and flexible means of amplifying their activities and giving a more competitive luster to their enterprises.

23 PATRICE LUMUMBA
CRISIS OF CONFIDENCE

The following selection is taken from the book originally entitled Le Congo, Terre d' Avenir, Est-Il Menacé?, *written by Patrice Lumumba (1925–1961) before he became the first Premier of the Congo and before he was committed to the needs of a Congolese national consciousness and pan-Africanism. Moderate in tone and in demands, Lumumba criticizes the Belgian leaders for their failure to understand, let alone appreciate, Congolese nationalism.*

Ever since the Belgians first came to Africa, the Congolese have shown themselves to be docile, obedient and grateful to their mentors. Their confidence has been put to the test for over seventy-five years.

The social peace which reigns in the Congo and which foreigners call the "Bel-

From Patrice Lumumba, *Congo, My Country*, trans. by Graham Heath (London: Pall Mall Press, 1962), pp. 160–166. Reprinted by permission of Frederick A. Praeger and Pall Mall Press.

gian Miracle in Africa," is a dazzling sign of good administration and of the high morale of the native population.

The first stage of the colonisation has been completed: the stage of the conclusion of treaties, construction of roads, liberation of the people, etc. After these three-quarters of a century of hard work, of groping steps which have now led to success, the people of the colony put forward a confident and dignified plan to leave this stage, which has been out-dated by the course of development, and to enter stage two.

Will Belgium disappoint them? I do not think so, because there is no valid reason to justify such a refusal and because Belgian policy as a whole is sincerely moving towards the steady emancipation of the Congolese under Belgian trusteeship.

What is this *second stage?* It is the stage of *integration* (not of assimilation which involves the absorption of one people by another) of the *democratisation of the country* and of the *Africanisation of the leadership.*

This integration is the task of our rulers, in whom I have every confidence. In this book, I have mentioned some transitional stages which may facilitate the immediate advancement of the Belgian Africans.

In their co-existence with the Whites, the Africans are greatly worried, not by the fact of living alongside them, but by the idea that they may never be able to attain complete emancipation and liberty whilst under European domination.

Hence the African's dream of independence does not arise from hatred for the Whites or a desire to drive them out of Africa, but simply from the wish to be not merely a free man but also a citizen in the service of his country and not perpetually in the service of the European. He believes, moreover, that, even if he is able to obtain complete emancipation under white domination, it will only come after centuries, because the European will hamper that emancipation by all sorts of tricks and political schemes, and that the Blacks will therefore be kept in a state of inferiority as long as possible. Finally, he believes that once the country becomes independent, the emancipation of the inhabitants will be much more rapid than it would have been under the system of tutelage and colonialism.

"We shall certainly have difficulties at the beginning—like every other nation—but we shall overcome them thanks to the help of the Europeans to whom we shall appeal and who will come, in this case, not to dominate us but to help us and to serve Africa. With these Europeans we shall always maintain neighbourly and fraternal relations."

This is what the Africans think in their heart of hearts.

This general impression prevailing among the Congolese, which they do not pass on to Europeans for fear of reprisals—a fear which is often imaginary—arises out of the following considerations:

Since the European occupation began, some eighty years ago, no African in the Congo has been accepted for any post —even the lowest—of European officer grade in the administrative services, the law and the army, even if he has had a full secondary education and studied philosophy for several years. (I am leaving out of account the two Congolese from Leopoldville who recently finished their studies in Belgium and the native priests.) A European (I refer here to temporary officials, some of whom have had no secondary education) is *always* superior to an African even if the latter has studied longer and hence is better educated.

There are, in fact, some cases of this kind.

Except for the priests and the two or three Congolese who have studied in Belgium, no native, however competent, occupies the post which is his due and which he could have occupied long ago or could take over now *if the leading administrative posts were Africanised.* Even if he holds a responsible position, he does not have the same prestige as a European official. He is only a minor assistant, always dependent on a European official.

As a justification for refusing him the position which should by rights be his, the African will be told that he does not hold the European secondary education certificate or some other academic document, or that he must go to university, even though everyone cannot go to university even in Europe or America; or, if he is employed in the Government Service, he will have to wait twenty, twenty-five or thirty years before getting to the rank of chief clerk, Grade I, assistant drafting officer or assistant territorial officer, although a short three- or five-year course would be amply sufficient to give a really capable person the competence to do the work of a territorial officer or drafting officer. Many people can do these jobs long before completing five, ten, fifteen or twenty years of service.

Example: A Congolese with six years of secondary education is at present taken on in the rank of a clerk, third class. He must have a minimum of eighteen years' service (with good reports and regular promotion) in order to enter the grade of chief clerk, first class; to become an assistant territorial officer or assistant drafting officer, he must serve for a further three years, making a total of twenty-four years. Thus, it is only after twenty-four years of good and loyal service that a Congolese with a certificate of secondary education can take his place among the European officers, just when he has reached the end of his career or is about to do so.

At the moment when the Congolese is admitted to the lowest grade in the European hierarchy, a European who has had the same education (secondary) and who was initially engaged in the rank of area officer or drafting officer, will, after the same period of service of twenty-four years, be a director or head of some department.

And yet the same Congolese could very well carry out the duties of a territorial officer or drafting officer immediately on recruitment, or at least after a normal probationary period; there is no need for him to wait for this excessively long period of twenty-four to thirty years.

The fact that Ruanda-Urundi, a territory which has been under Belgian mandate since 31st August 1923, is more favourably situated than the Congo from the administrative point of view is not without influence on the Congolese.

"Whereas Ruanda-Urundi, which had the great good fortune to be placed under international trusteeship in 1923, is taking giant strides towards autonomy, we Congolese, who have been under the *same Belgian administration* for more than three-quarters of a century—much longer than Ruanda-Urundi—are far behind our neighbour. In Ruanda-Urundi, the position of the chiefs and underchiefs has been *enhanced,* their authority is respected and there are two kings, but, in the Congo, the authority of the native chiefs is reduced to the point where they are no longer real chiefs in the etymological sense of the word but mere V.I.P.s, government servants working under the authority of territorial officers and agronomists." That is the authentic view of the Congolese on this matter.

There is a contradiction in methods, particularly between the political principles enunciated by the Government and the higher authorities in all their official statements on colonial policy, and the application of those principles—sometimes in a contrary sense—*by the executive* officers. Some lower-grade officers apply these principles in a reactionary fashion *whenever* they are not personally in favour of a particular measure planned and enacted by their superiors for the benefit of the African.

These contradictions have created, and are still creating, a most regrettable confusion in the minds of the Congolese who draw the illogical conclusion that "The Government is scheming and intriguing with its officials to hoodwink us. The Government promises us this or that, enacts its laws and regulations and makes spectacular speeches, but the Government officials go in the other direction; perhaps they have received secret instructions. Even at school in Europe, they are taught to be cunning in dealing with the Blacks. Before they come to Africa, they are told that they must always live a long way away from the Blacks. This is proved by the sharp line of demarcation between the European and African quarters. The so-called green belts which separate the European and African quarters are barricades but, in order to fool us, they plant trees and flowers there to look like nursery gardens. If what they tell us is true, it should be put into practice by the high-ups and by the lower-ranking officials."

Let me explain: If, for example, the Governor General gives instructions to European officials, advising them to behave towards the natives with all due correctness, and if no change takes place in the behaviour of a large number of these officials, so that the Africans still do not obtain satisfaction, the latter follow this train of reasoning: "It is inconceivable that a minor official can ignore the instructions and recommendations given by the Head of the colony. As these instructions do not always give the results which we expect them to give, we doubt their sincerity. The policy is designed to trick us."

When some Congolese find difficulty in obtaining a loan from the Colonial Advancement Fund to purchase a decent dwelling, they reason as follows: "They don't want us to have nice houses to suit our taste. They refuse us loans so as to compel us indirectly to live in the houses of the African Townships Department, houses which are not to the taste of most people but for which funds are provided without any hesitation. All this is so that

the Blacks shall not have houses of the same taste and style as those of their 'masters' (the Whites)."

When the "King's Fund" [1] does not give the satisfaction which Congolese families expect, their reaction is the same: "Our dear King has seen with his own eyes that we are poor and badly housed and he has SENT money to enable us to have decent dwellings. The Whites have misappropriated this money and are using it for projects which are of benefit only to them. We are being deceived."

I note that quite a number of settlers (though there are exceptions) hesitate or even protest sometimes whenever the Government or the high-ups decide on the smallest increase in salaries or confer some benefit on the Congolese in the economic or social sphere or elsewhere.

There is an impression that anyone, be he minister, governor-general, governor, administrator, or mere official, in the public or private sector, who concerns himself actively with native interests and interracial relations and lives in close contact with the Africans, often ends up by being looked at askance by the others, *simply* because he takes a greater interest in the advancement of native society and has no axe to grind. Thus there are some people who pay dearly for espousing the cause of the natives and who forfeit sympathy in many quarters.

This idea can be illustrated by a few notable examples: "M. Jungers, who, in the opinion of the Congolese, was the first Governor General to advocate, in his historic speech to the Government Council in 1952 (the last Council over which he presided at the end of his term of office), the establishment of the Belgo-Congolese Community and the total assimilation of the Congolese *immatriculés,* was hotly

[1] *King's Fund: Fonds du Roi*—instituted on 18th October, 1955 by King Baudouin to promote social welfare in the Congo. The number of beneficiaries from the Fund in 1955 was 777 on a budget of about £60,000; in 1958 it provided for 2,608 beneficiaries from a budget of more than £4,600,000.

criticised, regarded with disapproval in some quarters and described as a *madman* by certain organs of the Press" (I have irrefutable proof of this in the form of Press articles) "because he was bold enough to express progressive ideas in front of people with conservative ideas."

Then Governor General Pétillon, who won the approval and appreciation of the protagonists of African advancement, was frowned on by a considerable number of people because of his moving speech at the opening of the Government Council of 1955, dealing with human relations between Whites and Blacks, and also because of the authorisation which he gave to the Blacks to enter public premises which had previously been reserved for Europeans only.

One section of the Press threw back at M. Pétillon the idea which he had put forward in his speech that "Anyone who disagrees with the policy of the Government is respectfully asked to pack his bags," and invited the Governor General "to pack his bags."

I still recall the tension which prevailed in the Congo following the decision of the Governor General to allow the Congolese entry to public premises. Fortunately, this tension was eased when the Africans, with great reasonableness, withdrew from these places voluntarily.

I must add that a number of public premises were, and still are, glad to welcome Congolese.

"M. Buisseret continues to be the object of malicious partisan criticism, not because he is administering the Colony badly but because he attaches a great deal of importance to the social factor; because he never ceases to preach and defend the principle of equal rights and equal prestige; because he invites the Africans to come and discuss their problems in Belgium instead of confining them to the Congo and leaving all matters which concern them to be decided on the spot; be-

cause he wants to "go quickly" with the Africans instead of crawling along at a snail's pace and slowing up the emancipation of the natives by excessive delays; and because he introduced state education for the Congolese. But the establishment of state education for Europeans (the Royal Athenaeums) roused no protests; protests only come when Africans are concerned, and yet this education is giving great satisfaction to Congolese parents. The reason why protests are made against this education is that French is taught from the first year of the primary school. The curriculum is similar to that of the European schools, so that the Africans will soon have enough education to compete with the Europeans. There is opposition to M. Buisseret because he has won the hearts of the Congolese who regard him not as a Minister, a Belgian, a Catholic, a Liberal, a Socialist or a Communist, but a sincere FRIEND of the Blacks, just as they do in the case of all other Belgians who champion their cause. Some people are afraid that the unanimous liking which the Congolese of all shades of opinion, Protestants, Catholics and pagans, show for a Liberal Minister, and their great confidence in him, will lead all the Africans of the Congo to become Liberals; but this is completely false, since the African masses are not interested in the label—Liberal, Catholic, Socialist or Communist,—but in their *material, intellectual and moral welfare.* We will turn to anyone who can secure these benefits for us, or help us to obtain them, and we ignore questions of dogma or freemasonry, which are of little interest to us as they will bring us no material advantages. Finally, there is opposition to M. Buisseret because he wants the Blacks to advance instead of leaving them as servants of the Whites." These opinions have been expressed to me by ninety per cent of the Congolese, and I do not wish to make any comment on them.

24 CRISTOPHER NYANGONI AND GIDEON NYANDORO (Eds.)
ZIMBABWE INDEPENDENCE MOVEMENTS: SELECT DOCUMENTS

ZIMBABWE DECLARATION OF UNITY
Lusaka, 7 December 1974

ZANU, ZAPU, FROLIZI, and ANC, hereby agree to unite in the ANC.
2. The Parties recognize the ANC as the unifying force of the people of Zimbabwe.
  (a) They agree to consolidate the leadership of the ANC by the inclusion into it of the presidents of ZANU, ZAPU and FROLIZI under the chairmanship of the President of the ANC.
  (b) ZAPU, ZANU and FROLIZI shall each appoint three other persons to join the enlarged ANC executive.
4. The enlarged ANC executive shall have the following functions:
  (a) To prepare for any conference for the transfer of power to the majority that might be called.
  (b) To prepare for the holding of a congress within four months at which—
    (i) A revised ANC constitution shall be adopted;
    (ii) the leadership of the united people of Zimbabwe shall be elected;
    (iii) a statement of policy for the new ANC will be considered.
  (c) To organize the people for such conference and congress.
5. The leadership of the ZAPU, ZANU and FROLIZI call upon their supporters and all Zimbabweans to rally behind the ANC under its enlarged executive.
6. ZAPU, ZANU and FROLIZI will take steps to merge their respective organs and structures into the ANC be-fore the congress to be held within four months.
7. The Leaders recognize the inevitability of continued armed struggle and all other forms of struggle until the total liberation of Zimbabwe.

Signed:
ABEL TENDEKAYI MUZOREWA
President of ANC
Signed:
JOSHUA MQABUKO NKOMO
President of ZAPU
Signed:
NDABANINGI SITHOLE
President of ZANU
Signed:
JAMES ROBERT CHIKEREMA
President of FROLIZI

State House, Lusaka

SALISBURY DECLARATION
11 December 1974

Recognizing the paramount need for unity in the Zimbabwe liberation struggle, the executive committees of ZAPU, ZANU, FROLIZI and ANC have met in Lusaka to discuss the aims, objectives, and methods to be pursued. Full agreement was reached on the following points:
1. We have agreed to unite under one organization with immediate effect. We have agreed further, that this organization shall be the African National Council [ANC].
2. We shall be working for the independence of our country. We assume that on this demand for independence there is no difference among Rhodesians of all races. But there has until now been a difference on the kind of

independence which Zimbabwe must have. The Rhodesian Front has, in the past, sought independence on the basis of minority rule. We reject that. The independence we still seek, is independence on the basis of majority rule.

3. For the purpose of achieving that objective we have always been ready to enter into negotiations with others concerned. Now that some of us have been released from detention, we believe the time is ripe for us to repeat this offer. Without pre-conditions on both sides we are ready to enter into immediate and meaningful negotiations with leaders of the Rhodesian Front, and with the British government in Britain, on the steps to be taken to achieve independence on the basis of majority rule.

4. As a demonstration of our sincerity, all freedom fighters will be instructed, as soon as a date for negotiations has been fixed, to suspend fighting.

5. We are not racialists. We accept the right of white Rhodesians to live in Rhodesia and share the same rights and obligations of citizenship as their fellow Rhodesian of the majority community, without any discrimination on grounds of race, colour or creed.

6. We call upon all Rhodesians, and all who reside in Rhodesia, to remain calm, maintain peace and to go about their normal business, while these matters are being considered, and while any negotiations are proceeding.

7. We call upon all Zimbabweans, wherever they are, to remain united behind the demand for independence on the basis of majority rule, and to give full support to the African National Council.

8. We appeal to all our friends in Africa and abroad to continue their support for our struggle until independence is achieved on the basis of majority rule.

Signed:
ABEL TENDEKAYI MUZOREWA
President of ANC
Signed:
JOSHUA MQABUKO NKOMO
Former President of ZAPU
Signed:
NDABANINGI SITHOLE
Former President of ZANU
Signed:
JAMES ROBERT DAMBADZA CHIKEREMA
Former President of FROLIZI

From Christopher Nyengoni and Gideon Nyandoro, eds., *Zimbabwe Independence Movements: Select Documents* (N.Y.: Barnes and Noble, 1979). Reprinted by permission.

SECTION II

SOUTH AFRICA

SOUTH AFRICA

BY ROBERT O. COLLINS

EUROPEAN BEGINNINGS AT THE CAPE

Although the Portuguese were the first Europeans to round the Cape of Good Hope, their contact with South Africa and its inhabitants remained slight and hostile. The Orient was the destination of the Portuguese captains, who soon learned that a wide sweep far from land through the storm-tossed waters off the Cape was the best route to East Africa and India. Occasionally, homeward bound ships put in at the Cape to revictual, but after *Khoikhoi* (Hottentot) pastoralists—who, with the *San* (Bushmen), inhabited southern Africa—killed the Viceroy of India, Francisco d'Almeida, at Table Bay in 1510, the Portuguese tended to sail clear of the Cape to more secure anchorages along the coasts of eastern and western Africa. At the end of the sixteenth century, the Portuguese monopoly of the Indian trade was challenged by English and Dutch merchants venturing into eastern waters. In 1580 Sir Francis Drake rounded the Cape of Good Hope, and in 1591 James Lancaster landed at Table Bay. The Dutch were not far behind. In 1595 Cornelis de Houtman circumnavigated the Cape on his way to Java, soon to be followed by the organized expeditions of the newly founded Dutch East India Company. Since their goal was the East Indies, neither the British nor the Dutch ever displayed much interest in East African ports, preferring to sail south of Madagascar and directly across the Indian Ocean. Thus the Cape became the last and consequently an important landfall for Dutch and English captains, and as early as 1619 an Anglo-Dutch station at Table Bay was proposed by the Dutch East India Company. Nothing came of the proposal, however, since English interest soon shifted to India and the seaway to the Asian subcontinent that swung south of the hazardous coast of the Cape of Good Hope.

The Dutch, however, continued to require a refreshment station in southern Africa, and after the shipwreck of the Haarlem in 1647 had dramatized this need, Jan van Riebeeck arrived at Table Bay in 1652 on instructions from the Dutch East India Company. He built a fort, planted a vegetable garden, and sought to obtain cattle and sheep by barter in order to supply the company's ships (Jan van Riebeeck and Z. Wagenaar, *Of the Native Tribes of South Africa*). The results were at first disappointing. The station failed to provide adequate foodstuffs or livestock so that the company, hoping to stimulate production, began to offer land grants for settler farming in 1657. Settlers, however, were restricted to company servants, and certain crops and prices were strictly regulated. As a result, the growth and transformation of the Cape from a commercial outpost to a colony of free settlers remained imperceptible until the last quarter of the seventeenth century, when colonists were recruited from Holland and given free passage and free land. Thereafter, the number of colonists steadily increased. By 1707 there were over 1,600 free burghers at the Cape, producing more food than could be consumed internally or sold to the company for revictualing. Economic difficulties were compounded by settler discontent over the favoritism displayed by Governor Willem Adrian van der Stel, and although the company agreed to recall him, the directors blamed the political unrest on the colonists and terminated their assistance to immigrants from Holland. Thereafter, the growth of the free burgher population was determined more by natural increase than by immigration, weakening the settlers' links with Europe on the one hand and placing greater reliance on slaves to meet the farmers' labor requirements on the other.

Slaves had been present in the Cape colony almost since its inception, but the company practice of fixing prices on farm commodities encouraged the colonists to employ slave labor in order to produce crops cheaply enough to make a profit. The first slaves were not taken from the indigenous Khoikhoi population but were obtained from the traditional slave markets of West Africa and occasionally from Madagascar and the East Indies. The number of imported slaves increased steadily throughout the early decades of the eighteenth century, and since slave labor was three times cheaper than that of European farmhands and more manageable, white settlement was given no encouragement by either settlers or company. As the decades passed, the institution of slavery was not only accepted as the proper relationship between white man and black, but was regarded as necessary to the colony's economy, and the slave population, by importation and internal increase, soon came to outnumber the free burghers.

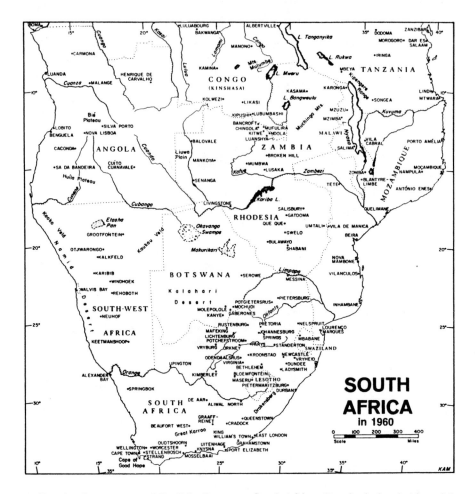

SOUTH AFRICA in 1960

Scale 0 100 200 300 400 Miles

Despite the presence of English, Danish, Swedish, and even French Huguenots among the colonists, the various European nationals were gradually assimilated during the eighteenth century and the character of the colony remained predominately German and Dutch. There was no restriction on the teaching of national languages, but the company insisted that Dutch be taught. However, the Dutch language that was used and invariably taught in the colony was more the vernacular of Dutch seamen than the language of the great cultural centers of Holland. When infused with elements from French, German, English, and African languages, South African Dutch gradually evolved into the Afrikaans language of today. The unifying force of South African Dutch, the inevitable social intercourse, intermarriage, and the pervasive influence and popularity of the Dutch Reformed Church (which was Calvinist in theology and fundamentalist in practice) produced not only a homogeneous settler class but one whose isolation from the rapid and profound changes taking place in seventeenth- and eighteenth-century Europe contributed to the development at the Cape of a unique white settler community.

THE EUROPEAN ADVANCE INTO THE INTERIOR

At the same time that the Europeans were evolving a distinctive folk nation, they were also challenging the indigenous societies of the Cape—the San and the

Khoikhoi. Perhaps because of their lack of centralized institutions, but certainly because of their propensity for cattle rustling, the San were relentlessly driven from the frontier by Europeans and Khoikhoi alike. The more numerous Khoikhoi fared little better, however, and their society steadily disintegrated in the face of European presence and disease. Like the San, many Khoikhoi retired to the frontiers of white settlement, where they conducted limited trade. Others remained behind in a servile capacity, adopting European customs while forgetting their own. Within the European community the dearth of white women soon resulted in a mixed class of "Cape Coloured" people—the products of the intercourse between white settlers and nonwhite slaves and indigenous peoples, which came to occupy a unique and not undistinguished place in the colony. By the eighteenth century, the black Africans no longer remained a threat to European expansion from the Cape.

The European advance into the hinterland followed the search for cattle pasturage. At the beginning of the eighteenth century, cattle raising became widely practiced by those farmers who, regarding Cape Town and its officials with deep suspicion, moved into the interior. In addition, the inability of the local market to absorb agricultural produce, as well as the steady increase in population, always producing more foodstuffs than could be consumed, encouraged more farmers to become frontier cattlemen, particularly as Khoikhoi resistance dissipated in the interior. Thus throughout the eighteenth century, a slow but steady stream of colonists, comprising a substantial part of the population increase, moved away from the administrative authority at Cape Town.

The colonists first went northward along the western coastal belt until they were blocked by the arid regions of Namaqualand. A second and more popular route took them along the southern coast, across the Hottentot Holland Mountains, and then eastward. In 1745 the importance of this eastward advance was acknowledged when the Cape authorities established a magistrate at Swellendam. Later, pioneers continued up over the mountains to the plateau, spurred on by company land grants of 600 acres. The promise of land encouraged the pioneers and drove them on, thus creating a pastoral people, accustomed to isolation, self-reliant, contemptuous of authority, and intensely individualistic. Not surprisingly, these Boers, as they came to be called, were difficult people to govern, and the company's failure to check their dispersion produced only contempt for its authority (Andrew Sparrman, *The Boers*). In the end the company was forced to extend its control, thereby acknowledging the expansion it had vainly sought to prevent. In 1778 Governor van Plettenberg established the eastern boundary of the colony at the Great Fish River, hoping that such a demarcation would act as a barrier not only to the Boers but also to the Bantu, with whom the colonists were coming in contact for the first time.

The Boers were not the only group to disperse. Bands of Cape Coloureds, acculturated to white society but unable to find a place within it, drifted north to the Orange River and then eastward along its course at the same time that the Boers were pressing on to the Great Fish River. Here on the Orange River the Griqua, as these Cape Coloureds were known, established several small states not unlike the abortive Boer frontier republics except that the European missionaries exerted considerable influence within them.

Thus in 150 years the revictualing station of the Dutch East India Company had grown from a small commercial outpost into a colony half again as large as England and Wales and inhabited by some 15,000 European colonists. Cape Town was the company's headquarters, and Table Bay was its port. Beyond this administrative capital were the agricultural areas of the coastal belt where, despite the monopolistic practices of the company, the settlers prospered from the produce of their farms. Finally, in the remote regions of the coast and on the interior plateau lived the pastoral population, which was difficult to rule in its isolation from the organized state, the established church, and the formal education of the settled regions around Cape Town. Despite differing national origins, the members of the European population had attained a homogeneous character and culture unique and even distinct from its Netherlands origins. Everywhere the Europeans employed slaves and menial laborers from the indigenous population. As a product of interracial intercourse, a third group of people with mixed blood had emerged to form the Cape Coloured folk. At the end of the eighteenth century, however, two new elements were soon to appear that changed dramatically, if not tragically, the course of South African history—the Bantu and the British.

THE BANTU

The first to appear were the Bantu. Although their initial appearance south of the Limpopo remains uncertain, they probably had arrived there by the end of the first millennium and certainly by the fifteenth century. By 1800 the two principal divisions of the South African Bantu—the *Nguni* and the *Sotho-Tswana* —had established numerous independent chieftaincies among whom the *Xhosa* had pressed westward to the Great Fish River. At this point the river formed an uncertain frontier between the volatile Bantu societies on the one side and the restless Trekboers on the other, and the clash of cultures soon led to open disputes all along the eastern frontier. Differing conceptions of land tenure and political authority combined with outright competition for control to precipitate numerous Kaffir (as the Bantu were called) wars throughout the last quarter of the eight-

eenth century (Thomas Pringle, *Boer Meets Bantu*). These frontier wars were fought mainly by the colonists themselves, who would hastily band together to repel Bantu raiders and seize their land and cattle. Occasionally, the authorities at Cape Town assisted the colonists, but the declining fortunes of the Dutch East India Company, which declared bankruptcy in 1794, did not enable its officials to provide adequate protection from the Xhosa raiders who remained in disputed territories. Infuriated at its failure to defend them, the colonists on the Zuurveld frontier rebelled against company rule in 1795 and established their own government at Graaff-Reinet. The burghers of Swellendam quickly followed their example in June 1795 and the colony broke into three parts.

THE BRITISH

The revolt at Swellendam coincided almost to the day with the arrival at Table Bay of nine British men-of-war. The great confrontation between Britain and France during the wars of the French Revolution and the Napoleonic Wars had drawn the British to South Africa. The Cape was still the halfway port between Europe and the eastern empires of Britain and France. Throughout the eighteenth century, Britain and France had struggled for supremacy in the East, and the outbreak of war in Europe only intensified this conflict for trade and dominion in the Orient. In the past the Cape had been in Dutch hands, but now the Dutch East India Company was in liquidation, Holland was dissolved, and the Cape was about to fall within the French sphere of influence. With the sanction of the Prince of Orange, whom the French had driven from the Netherlands into exile in England, a British naval force set sail for South Africa to secure the Cape against French annexation. After a short struggle the company officials capitulated on June 11, 1795, and the rule of the Dutch East India Company in South Africa came to an end.

In this way the British came to South Africa—at first as temporary rulers, representatives of the Prince of Orange, guardians of the passage to India. Although the Cape was restored to the Batavian Republic (the former kingdom of the Netherlands) after the Peace of Amiens in 1803, after the resumption of war in Europe the British returned and occupied Cape Town in 1806. This time the British did not retire, and as part of the European peace settlements concluded at Vienna in 1815, the Netherlands formally ceded the Cape to Great Britain.

Thus the British and the Dutch were brought together in South Africa. At first their relationship was that of ruler and ruled, but the arrival of British settlers introduced a distinct element into the homogeneous European society of South Africa. The political predominance of the British, as well as their Olympian preference for the English language and their intense national pride, prevented their being absorbed into the South African European community as readily as the French and the Germans had been assimilated earlier. At the same time, the British were never sufficiently numerous to absorb in turn the Cape Dutch, whose traditions and characteristics were as sharply delineated as their own. Briton and Boer were to discover that they possessed many common sentiments that might serve as the basis for cooperation and friendship. They were also to find, however, that the great strengths of their traditions and the divisive nature of their respective individualities hindered the inclusion of both groups into a larger white community of southern Africa.

BRITISH RULE AT THE CAPE: SLAVERY, MISSIONARIES, AND ENGLISHMEN

British rule at the Cape was not unwelcome during the early stages of first occupation. The new government began with the advantage of its predecessor's unpopularity. It abandoned the system of commercial monopoly, stimulated trade, and enjoyed the prosperity of a war economy. On the frontier, however, the British were less successful, proving to be every bit as vacillating as the company and nearly as unpopular. The second British occupation began less auspiciously than the first, yet the rulers and the ruled found they had much in common. The Europeans at the Cape were a conservative people, as were their British rulers. At first both the institutions and personnel of government remained virtually unchanged, and there was little interference with the customs and traditions of the Boers. In spirit the Cape remained a Dutch colony, and there was no policy of deliberate Anglicization. Even on the frontier the popularity of the government reached unprecedented heights when the Xhosa were finally driven from the Zuurveld to satisfy the insatiable land hunger of the white settlers at the expense of Xhosa needs for pasturage. In fact, cooperation between the Dutch and the British might very well have grown into confidence and acceptance if not for their different attitudes toward and treatment of the black South Africans.

In 1807 Great Britain abolished the slave trade throughout her empire, and although attempts were made to evade the law, the supply of slaves to the Cape dwindled to insignificance, and the European population, bolstered by the arrival of English immigrants, soon outnumbered the slaves. Diminished in number, the slaves increased in value as did the solicitude of the owners for their welfare. As an institution, slavery at the Cape had always been comparatively free from the abuses that prevailed on the slave plantations of the Americas. In fact, the abolition of the slave trade aroused little opposition at first but was ultimately to create much ill feeling. For without slaves, the farmers became increasingly dependent on the labor of free Khoikhoi or Cape Coloureds, and in the master-employer and servant-employee relations were the origins of exploitation that precipitated the righteous indignation of the English missionaries.

The early nineteenth-century missionaries were the religious by-products of the eighteenth-century Enlightenment. Just as the philosophes conceived of the natural rights of *all men,* so too did the missionaries preach the equal rights of *all men* before God. The disparity between the theory and practice of this doctrine as applied to the blacks of South Africa was self-evident to the English missionaries, particularly Dr. John Philip of the London Missionary Society, who soon came to regard themselves as protectors of their people against their Boer employers. But to the farmers suffering from a shortage of labor in the years after abolition, the mission stations became an annoying if not subversive sanctuary for unemployed blacks. It was not a difference between a specifically Dutch and a specifically British conception, for as British settlers came to South Africa they quickly adopted the farmers' point of view. But the missionaries were mostly British and the farmers were mostly Dutch, and consequently the issue sowed the seeds of future bitterness between Briton and Boer.

The preaching of the missionaries found its secular counterpart in the law, which was applied equally by British magistrates to both white men and black. But if the white colonists could not accept equality before God, they were not likely to accept equality before man. Thus, in one incident, when a frontiersman was summoned to court for maltreating a black servant, he resisted arrest and was shot to death. His friends vainly sought to raise the frontier in retaliation and revolt, but the rebels were seized and seven ringleaders were hung at Slachter's Nek. Although this frontier incident was relatively unimportant at the time (since most Boers appear to have agreed with British rule and its enforcement), Slachter's Nek became a vivid symbol of British oppres-

sion in the 1870s and its victims martyrs against British tyranny. The memory of Slachter's Nek has since remained a constant source of division between Briton and Boer.

The Slachter's Nek affair coincided with a change in the attitude of the British rulers toward the Cape colony. Until 1814 British occupation of the Cape remained uncertain; it merely checked innovations in government and discouraged British colonists from settling in South Africa. After the peace of 1815, however, immigration was actively encouraged, not only to relieve postwar unemployment in Britain but to place settler farmers on the Zuurveld frontier as a bulwark against the Bantu. Consequently, in 1819 the British government made available free passage and land on the frontier to parties of English immigrants that would settle in the Zuurveld, and in 1820 some twenty shiploads arrived at Algoa Bay. From there the immigrants scattered over the Zuurveld and beyond, and by 1821 nearly 5,000 English men, women, and children had arrived in the Cape colony. Although English settlers comprised only one-seventh of the European population, an active policy of Anglicization soon followed their arrival in the colony. The gradual substitution of English for Dutch as the official administrative and judicial language began in 1822. The judicial system of the colony was remodeled to conform to the English pattern. The old Burgher Senate ceased to exist, and even the Dutch rix-dollar was replaced by the British pound sterling. Clearly, the intention of the government was to make the Cape a British colony, administered by a centralized Anglicized British bureaucracy in the spirit of the Tory reaction of the 1820s. Although the Dutch inhabitants understood conservative government, they would not willingly abandon their language and traditions, to which they were deeply attached. Humiliated, the Boers soon had cause for even greater discontent.

The old established farmers of the western Cape met their labor requirements principally by the use of slaves. The eastern frontiersmen, however, possessed few slaves and were dependent for labor on Khoikhoi and Cape Coloured folk. These eastern farmers continually complained of the difficulties of securing labor and the depredations of those Khoikhoi who preferred to remain unemployed rather than labor on settler farms. The farmers therefore sought to impose checks on Khoikhoi freedom of movement by enacting vagrancy laws and legislation designed to force the blacks to labor on white farms. The English missionaries vigorously objected to this discriminatory legislation. Their object was to convert the Khoikhoi into landowners who were both equal before the law and in a position to bargain freely for their labor.

The struggle between the farmers and the missionaries was long and bitter, but in 1828 the missionaries triumphed with the passing of the famous Fiftieth Ordinance, which canceled the legislation restricting Khoikhoi freedom and secured the legal equality of the free black inhabitants of the Cape colony. Among the farmers in general, but among the eastern frontiersmen in particular, the passage of the Fiftieth Ordinance aroused great resentment. To them the ordinance meant scarcity of labor, the weakening of the white man's authority, and an invitation to vagrancy. But the effects of the ordinance went even further. It exacerbated the hostile feelings against the missionaries and brought into focus the fundamental differences between the missionaries' conception—a conception beginning to be widely accepted in Britain—of equal rights for all men, black, or white, and the view of the pioneer farmer who refused to admit such equality now or in the future. Once opened, the great gulf between the indiscriminate idealism of Exeter Hall and the intolerant but not unkindly pragmatism of the frontiersman could not easily be bridged.

THE GREAT TREK

The emancipation of the slaves in 1834 contributed to the growing resentment of the Boer farmers. Not only did the slave owners object to the legislation concerning the use of freed slaves passed in preparation for emancipation, but they were furious with the inadequate compensation paid for these slaves. Moreover, all claims had to be presented in London, where payment was to be made partly in cash and partly in bonds at 3.5 percent, so that many farmers, having no option but to sell their claims to agents, received only a small fraction of the value of their property. Humiliated by the regulations of emancipation and forced to take a considerable financial loss, the farmers received in return no law against vagrancy and little security against possible depredations by liberated slaves. To make matters worse, relations with the Bantu deteriorated into war on the frontier.

In 1834 the Bantu invaded the colony—burning, looting, and killing Europeans. The Governor, Sir Benjamin D'Urban, rushed troops to the frontier. In a short, sharp struggle the Bantu were defeated and driven back. D'Urban then sought to push the frontier eastward to the Kei River in the expectation of annexing the territory and granting the land to the frontier burghers both as compensation for their losses and as farms for their land-hungry sons. Although the D'Urban policy was popular in the colony, it was vigorously opposed by the missionaries and by their philanthropic supporters in London. D'Urban was overruled by the colonial secretary, Lord Glenelg, who had no intention of compensating the frontier burghers for damages incurred in a war that, in his opinion, the Bantu had ample justification for beginning. Frustrated at every turn within the colony and desperate for land, the Boers began to look beyond the boundaries of the colony for freedom from British control and for expansive farms to give their numerous sons. The Great Trek soon followed

(Anna Elizabeth Steenkamp, *The Great Trek*).

In one sense the Great Trek was but a continuation of the migration eastward from Cape Town, which had scattered European farmers over the interior plateau as far as the Great Fish River. Unlike the random, haphazard movements of the eighteenth century, however, the trek was undertaken only after considerable organization and planning. In 1834 three reconnaissances were made—one to Damaraland in what is now Southwest Africa, one to the Zoutpansberg in the northern Transvaal, and one to Natal. These investigations discovered good, thinly populated land to the northeast, and in the following year the first of two parties of Voortrekkers departed. The first group was destroyed by the Bantu; the second was decimated by fever. Undeterred, the main body of emigrants crossed the Orange River in 1836 just as the *Mfecane* had spent its terrible force.

THE MFECANE

The Nguni-speaking Bantu had inhabited Zululand and Natal since the sixteenth century. Here on the fertile grasslands between the Drakensberg Mountains and the sea the Bantu population rapidly increased; land became scarce, and intertribal fighting intensified as the eighteenth century came to a close. To compete effectively in these wars, the Nguni borrowed the use of age-regiments* from the neighboring *Sotho,* making warfare more efficient but also more intense. During this time of turmoil Shaka, the son of a chief of a small tribe known as the Zulu, began to train his followers in new methods of warfare, employing the short-stabbing spear, the assegai, for the traditional throwing spear, so that his warriors not only retained their weapons but could maneuver in close formation (Henry Francis

* Groups of young men of approximately the same age who, having passed through the initiation ceremonies together, remained together as a military unit.

Fynn, *Shaka*). By conquering neighboring tribes his forces increased, and by 1818 Shaka had become the dominant power in Zululand. Introducing the conception of total war, Shaka's victorious armies swept all before them, precipitating hordes of refugees northward where, by imitating Zulu military tactics, they absorbed the local inhabitants before breaking up into sections to found kingdoms in Zambia, Malawi, and Tanzania. Other Bantu tribes fled westward from Shaka's depredations into the high plateau country beyond the Drakensberg Mountains, which was inhabited by the Sotho-speaking Bantu. Destruction, upheaval, and death followed as tribes turned into wandering, pillaging hordes, that fought desperately with invaders and inhabitants alike and turned the plateau beyond the Orange River into a deserted land infested with bands of leaderless men, known indiscriminately as *Mantatees,* who preyed on the starving refugees of war. Two remarkable leaders soon emerged, however, to lead their people out of the chaos in Sotholand and to establish states in the upper Zambezi and the hill country of the upper Orange River. Sebetwane led his tribe, called the *Kololo,* to Barotseland, where he established a short-lived empire, while Moshweshwe founded a kingdom in Basutoland by bringing together the remnants of many tribes (Andrew Geddes Bain, *The Ngwaketse Defeat the Kololo*).

Refugees from Zulu armies were not the only peoples on the move. In 1821 one of Shaka's generals, Mzilikazi, defied his king and fled into the Transvaal with a section of the Zulu Army that came to be known as the Ndebele (or Matabele). Sweeping through the Transvaal, Mzilikazi's forces decimated the Tswana tribes, incorporating their young men into the Ndebele age-regiments. Meanwhile, in Zululand itself Shaka had become increasingly despotic, and after the deprivations that he had made his people undergo upon the death of his mother, he was assassinated by two of his brothers, one of whom, Dingane, made himself king of the Zulu. But the death of Shaka did not end the great upheavals of the South African Bantu—known as the Mfecane (the crushing)—which continued on into the decade of the Great Trek. Nevertheless, by 1830 the Mfecane had destroyed or driven away the Bantu inhabitants of wide areas of Natal, Trans-Orangia, and the Transvaal, while concentrating relatively dense populations in Basutoland and the coastal plains between the colonial frontier and Natal. The high veld of the interior of South Africa did not long remain empty, for soon the great ox-drawn wagons of the Voortrekkers appeared on the quiet grasslands.

BANTU AND BOER

One after another the Voortrekkers crossed the Orange River, traveling usually in small parties and dispersing to search out the land and graze their cattle. The only serious opposition came from Mzilikazi and his Ndebele, but Mzilikazi was ultimately defeated by Potgeiter in 1837 and headed north across the Limpopo River to establish his people in modern Rhodesia. Potgeiter and his followers remained behind to claim the high veld by right of conquest and to settle down to enjoy the fruits of victory. Meanwhile, the majority of the trekkers under the leadership of Pieter Retief turned eastward, crossed the Drakensberg Mountains, and appeared in Natal, where they requested permission from Dingane to settle. Dingane was at once alarmed by the appearance of the Voortrekkers and was determined to be rid of them. After agreeing to permit the Boers to enter Natal, he ordered Retief and his companions massacred at the royal enclosure. The murder of Retief precipitated a dramatic struggle between Bantu and Boer for control of Natal, the turning point of which was the Boer victory over Dingane's forces at the Battle of the Blood River on December 16, 1838. Dingane made peace

and promised to withdraw his people north of the Tugela River, but his defeat and willingness to evacuate divided the Zulu. One of Shaka's brothers, Mpande, refused to follow Dingane, placed himself under Boer protection, and defeated Dingane at the Battle of Magongo in February 1840. The Boers, however, were the principal winners of strife among the Zulu who, outgunned and divided, could no longer compete successfully for control in Natal.

BRITISH POLICY IN SOUTH AFRICA: ANNEXATION OR ABANDONMENT

Although the Great Trek had done much to resolve the difficulties that the Boers had faced in the Cape colony, it created more problems for the British government than it had solved for the Boers. On the one hand the Boers were British subjects, owing allegiance to the Crown, which was ultimately responsible for them, yet the British government was reluctant to incur the great expense of administering the vast and unproductive land into which the Boers had fled. On the other hand, if the Boers were left to create their own independent states, as they had already done in Natal, another European power might gain influence in southern Africa, endangering the route to India and undermining the fundamental purpose for British presence at the Cape. Moreover, the Boers regarded the Bantu with implacable hostility, and conflict between them, which seemed inevitable, would keep South Africa in turmoil, threaten the Cape colony, and require heavy military expenditure on punitive expeditions. If the Cape colony could not dominate frontier policy, the colonial government would undoubtedly have to intervene with military force. The dilemmas of South Africa were not easily resolved, and British policy vacillated wildly between ruling and abandoning the interior regions. As a result, all parties were ultimately alienated and British influence in South Africa was greatly diminished.

The Great Trek immediately presented the British with these great issues. No sooner had the Boers arrived in Natal than they declared an independent republic, to the alarm of the British authorities, who were concerned about the defense of the route to India, and the consternation of British philanthropists, who were angered by Boer expropriation of Bantu land and cattle. In 1842 a British force was sent to occupy Port Natal, and although it was besieged by the Boers, British reinforcements arrived and the republican government collapsed. In 1845 Natal was officially annexed to the Cape colony, and many Boers trekked back over the Drakensberg Mountains to the high veld. Here on the plateau the Boers could disperse over a much wider area than was possible in the comparatively restricted region of Natal. The Boers possessed two centers—one at Winburgh south of the Vaal, and the other at Potchefstroom north of the river—but their dearth of political experience, their resolute individualism, and their impatience with restraint, all the products of the isolated life on the frontier of the Cape colony in the eighteenth century, militated, against the development of settled government. Winburgh and Potchefstroom possessed loose links with the Natal republics, but when Natal was annexed, the ties disappeared and the Boer communities on the plateau fragmented into detached units.

At first the British authorities tried to bring about order without expense to the interior by recognizing the authority of the chiefs–in the hope that they would maintain control over black and white in their territories in return for a small British subsidy and British protection. Thus agreements were signed with the Griqua Chief, Adam Kok, and with Moshweshwe of the Basuto in 1843, but the policy soon appeared bankrupt. No Boer was about to submit to black authority, and British forces had to be rushed to the defense of Adam Kok in 1844. Then the British authorities tried another device. Governor Maitland sought to resolve the conflict between black and white by dividing the land into that portion over which the chief would exercise his direct authority, and those portions in which powerful white settlers would be under the control of a British resident. Although the system worked well at first, it was soon undermined by the insatiable demands of the Boers for land, and ended in yet another frontier war that dragged on until December 1847.

Having failed to resolve frontier conflict by recognizing and protecting the indigenous authorities, Sir Harry Smith, the new Governor, tried outright annexation. Dashing madly from the Cape to Natal, he annexed the eastern frontier and the whole area between the Orange and the Vaal rivers. The Boers were furious. They had trekked into the interior to escape British control and now found it suddenly imposed upon them. They rebelled, but were soon overpowered by British forces, who reinstated British officials in Trans-Orangia.

Although Sir Harry Smith's precipitate annexations seemed to have resolved the problem of frontier control, his policy had neither the resources to support it nor authorization from London. His representative in Bloemfontein, Major H. D. Warden, sought to reconcile the incompatible interests of Boer, Griqua, and Bantu. In this effort Warden was dependent on the goodwill of the white farmers who had already been alienated. Not surprisingly, he failed, and although Boer rebellions against the government were suppressed, the British government was prepared to abandon its attempts to control the wild interior of South Africa. The fluctuations of British policy reflected important changes occurring in mid-nineteenth-century Britain. Philanthropic humanitarianism had gone into decline after the emancipation of the slaves in 1834. Moreover, in the free trade atmosphere of the times, colonies were regarded as a burden to be avoided if possible and abandoned at the first opportunity. Even the indignation that had been aroused at the thought of leaving Bantu alone to face Boer gave way to a cynical acceptance of the view that concern for distant natives was a sentimental luxury Britain could no longer afford. In 1852 the Sand River Convention was signed, granting independence to the Transvaal, followed in 1854 by the Convention of Bloemfontein, which created an independent Orange Free State. The fragmentation of South Africa begun by the Great Trek now seemed complete.

The British might reluctantly abandon the interior, but they could not forget it. The independent Boer states simply did not have the resources to maintain order on their frontiers without resorting to violence and intimidation against their non-European neighbors. Without cooperation and coordination, characteristics that ran counter to Boer attitudes, these same states would remain permanently insecure before the mass of Bantu tribes. Moreover, the dearth of resources prevented both security and education for the Boers, which might have produced a more enlightened approach toward race relations than the primitive assumptions derived from their simplistic religion and the wild land they inhabited. Just as the British could not control the Boers except by force, so too the Boers failed to live with the Bantu except by violence (James Chapman, *The Boers and Their Attack on Kwena*). By 1858 war had broken out between the Orange Free State and the Basuto, but the Free State could not maintain its forces in the field and was forced to ask the British Governor at the Cape, Sir George Grey, to arbitrate peace. Unable to remain aloof from conditions in the interior, Grey sought to avoid outright annexation by creating a federation of white states. But even federation required a greater commitment than any British government wished to assume. Grey's policy was repudiated, and without imperial overrule,

by 1863 frontier affairs had degenerated once again into war with the Basuto. Although the forces of the Orange Free State successfully exhausted Basuto resistance, they stirred the powerful supporters of Moshweshwe in England to protest against the break-up of Basutoland before the Boer invasion. Reluctantly the British government gave way, and permitted Governor Wodehouse to annex Basutoland and defend it with British troops. Elsewhere on the frontier the British authorities continued to encroach upon the traditional powers of the chief in their efforts to establish control (*The Governor and the Tembookies*). Thus, despite its official determination to limit its commitments, the British government became increasingly involved in the interior, where a new factor suddenly appeared to further complicate relations among Briton, Boer, and Bantu.

THE DISCOVERY OF DIAMONDS

In 1867 diamonds were discovered in Griqualand West, in an area disputed by the Orange Free State, the Transvaal, the Griquas, and the *Tswana* tribes. The discovery not only coincided with the revival of the scheme for federation, but led to the annexation of yet another interior region by the British government. But it was not the glint of profits from the diamond diggings alone that determined the government's occupation of the diamondiferous area. Clearly, the British did not wish to see a major shift in population from the Cape to an unsettled land on the frontier in Griqualand West, or the turbulent mining population free from the restraints of British authority. The philanthropists did not wish to see the Griqua fall under Boer domination, and of course no British government would want the riches of the Kimberley mines to strengthen the Orange Free State. In 1871 Griqualand West was unceremoniously added to Britain's expanding empire in South Africa.

The discovery of diamonds led to greater changes in South African life than the transfer of Griqualand West to imperial control. The diamonds could not be excavated without large amounts of capital, which soon poured into South Africa, transforming the country from a rural to a mining economy. The social effects of the mining industry were far-reaching. Diamond mining required large numbers of laborers who were recruited from the Bantu population and left their homes to work in the mines. The use of migrant labor not only resulted in serious social and economic adjustments in the tribal homelands, but brought the Bantu increasingly within the white-dominated economy of South Africa. Here in the mines the men of many tribes found a common identity and a common enemy.

The annexation of the diamond mines provided yet another reason for Britain to try once again to establish a confederation of white states in South Africa. A confederation would ensure British influence while relieving Britain of the expense of administration. Unfortunately, the annexation of Griqualand West had further alienated the Boers of the Orange Free State, who not surprisingly felt that they had been unjustly deprived of their rightful claims. To the north in the Transvaal the grievance over British rule in the diamond region was not nearly so acute, but there on the high veld dwelt the most conservative Boer farmers. Isolated, poverty-stricken, and devoid of education, they were firmly opposed to the racial egalitarianism implied by a British-dominated federation. Even in the Cape colony there was a strong minority against confederation, and when the British Colonial Secretary, Lord Carnarvon, sought to hold a conference in London, the interested parties refused to attend and the scheme collapsed.

THE FAILURE OF FEDERATION

Although Carnarvon pressed on with his plans for confederation, the problems of black and white in South Africa remained to frustrate them. In Zululand, Cetewayo, who had succeeded Mpande, had rebuilt the Zulu military system as it had been in the great days of Shaka and, restored the Zulu as the most powerful Bantu state in South Africa. His intentions were not aggressive, but the mere presence of his formidable fighting machine posed a serious threat to the farmers of Natal and the Transvaal. Caught between the appeals for protection against the Zulu and the demands of philanthropic opinion in Britain to end Boer mistreatment of the Bantu, Carnarvon sought to force the pace of confederation by annexing the Transvaal. In April 1877 the Natal Secretary for Native Affairs, Theophilus Shepstone, appeared in the Transvaal, raised the British flag, and declared the end of Transvaal independence. The annexation was a disastrous blunder, arousing Boer national feeling and deepening antagonism and distrust between Briton and Boer. The annexation was not only a flagrant violation of solemn treaty obligations, but a tragedy, since the Transvaal Republic would probably have ultimately consented to confederation of its own volition. Instead, the opposition steadily increased, and protest followed protest. The British tried frantically to win Boer good will by breaking the threat of Zulu power, gratifying Boer grievances with Bantu land, and disassociating British policy from the pro-Bantu philanthropists in order to sweeten the bitter pill of annexation. The policy was as opportunistic as it was unsuccessful. The British forces sent into Zululand were annihilated at the Battle of Isandhlwana by Cetewayo's *impis* (regiments), and although British arms were ultimately victorious, Zulu power was broken, and Cetewayo was taken prisoner to Cape Town, the British had failed to win the Boers, while alienating the Bantu and their supporters. Driven to desperation the Boers rebelled, besieged the British garrison at Pretoria, and defeated British relief forces at the Battle of Majuba Hill. With both their policy and practice in ruins, the British had either to crush the Transvaal by overwhelming force or to reach a settlement. The British Prime Minister, William Ewart Gladstone, who had campaigned in Midlothian against the suppression of Boer freedom, agreed to negotiate, and in the Pretoria Convention the Transvaal regained its internal autonomy while recognizing in return only Britain's ultimate sovereignty, control of foreign affairs, and a British resident at Pretoria to advise on the Transvaal's policy toward the Bantu. Virtually independent, the Transvaal, together with the Orange Free State, had come to form the bastion of Boer nationalism and intransigence. Dutch heritage had been awakened, and the sense of Dutch nationhood became a powerful motive and inspiration in political action, ultimately to drive Briton and Boer into sharper antagonisms and hostility. Confederation had failed.

CECIL RHODES AND THE WAY TO THE NORTH

No longer checked by the restraints of British imperial policy, the Boers resumed their expansion to drive the Bantu from the frontiers and to seize their land. In the east the defeated and divided Zulu lost nearly half their land to Boer encroachment. In the west white freebooters interfered in the tribal disputes of the Tswana. In return for their assistance, various chiefs gave their whites land on which they established two petty republics that the Transvaal would certainly have absorbed had not the British government intervened to place the territory under imperial control and declare a protectorate over the tribes of Bechuanaland (John Mackenzie, *Bushman Land*). As in Natal and Basutoland, the imperial factor had once again been employed to check Boer expansion.

Bechuanaland itself was of little importance, but its strategic position in southern Africa was critical. Not only did the Bechuanaland protectorate prevent any land link between the Transvaal and their cultural kin and sympathizers in German Southwest Africa, but it provided a corridor to the north, the logical direction of European expansion toward the fertile uplands of Rhodesia and Zambia. The principal advocate for retaining the way into the interior beyond the Limpopo was Cecil Rhodes. Rhodes had come out to Africa for his health and drifted to the diamond fields where, by buying up small bankrupt claims, he was able to consolidate a host of petty holdings into profitable mines. Soon his De Beers Consolidated Mining Company controlled almost the whole South African diamond production and Cecil Rhodes had become a very wealthy man. He regarded money not as an end in itself, but rather as a means to unite Africa, from the Cape to Cairo, under the British flag. He was determined to employ his vast financial resources to move more conservative men in the extension of British authority, sweeping aside the opposition with little concern for the morality of his means. Rhodes envisaged that the way north was to be pioneered by both Briton and Boer, who, working together in a united South Africa, would push the cause of civilization beyond the Limpopo. The African was to play only a minor role in this great drama, and although Rhodes frequently uttered philanthropic sentiments, he regarded the African either as an instrument to further his grand design or as an obstacle to be overcome.

THE DISCOVERY OF GOLD

Rhodes' hopes for a united South Africa in which Briton and Boer would participate together in the march to the north were compromised by the discovery of gold at Witwatersrand and destroyed by the Jameson raid. The discovery of gold in the Transvaal not only accelerated the industrialization of South Africa that had been begun by the discovery of the diamond mines, but dramatically altered the balance of power in that area. Hitherto the Transvaal had been a poor and petty state that sooner or later would probably have been absorbed by the rich, populous, British-dominated Cape colony. Gold changed all that. Overnight the Transvaal became the richest of the white states, capable of amalgamating the others under the banner of Boer nationalism and, possibly, in alliance with Germany, jeopardizing Britain's strategic position in the Cape and the world. Two principal obstacles, however, stood in the way of the Transvaal's efforts to carry out a forward course in southern Africa—the miners and Paul Kruger, President of the Transvaal.

The miners who came to dig Transvaal gold were not Boers. They were capitalists and mine workers from America and Europe–principally from Britain. They were a rough, tough lot, who had little use for the simple farmers of the Republic, whose symbol was Paul Kruger himself. Kruger had taken part in the Great Trek; he had been reared as an honest, brave, God-fearing adult concerned with his duty and the obligation to maintain the hard-won independence of his people. Unfortunately, he was also ill-educated and unable to understand either the world around him or the sophisticated English. In the end he proved ill-fitted to lead the Transvaal through the tumultuous period of social and economic change, which Cecil Rhodes soon sought to turn to his own advantage in his efforts to build a united South Africa.

By the mid-1890s Rhodes had reached the height of his career, having marched steadily from success to success. In 1888 he had entered Cape politics and had managed to win over Jan Hofmeyr, leader of the Afrikaner Bond, which had originally been anti-British, to his idea of British and Boer cooperation in South Africa. Rhodes became Prime Minister of the Cape in 1890, the same year that his British South Africa Company sent a pioneer column to acquire Mashonaland and, eventually, the rest of what is now Zimbabwe. Financial success accompanied these political victories. His economic empire by this time included the largest diamond business in the world, gold mines in the Transvaal, and the British South Africa Company with its growing colony in Zimbabwe. More than ever, Rhodes was ready to absorb an independent Transvaal into a united South Africa, single-handedly if necessary. To Rhodes, Kruger's government appeared an anachronism against which the alien mineowners and workers, who had been denied the vote by the republican government, would turn if presented with an appropriate opportunity. Rhodes was determined to provide that opportunity.

THE JAMESON RAID AND THE BOER WAR

Aware of the discontent with Kruger's regime, felt by mineowners and miners alike, Rhodes planned to precipitate a revolt by the miners, who would seize the Rand mines and hold them until relieved by an armed column from the Bechuanaland protectorate–which would accomplish the overthrow of the Transvaal government. Joseph Chamberlain, the British Colonial Secretary, gave his blessing to the conspiracy, and the British High Commissioner at Cape Town approved. In December 1895 the plot was set in motion, only to end in dismal failure. The miners failed to rise, and the raiders, led by Dr. Starr Jameson, were surrounded and forced to surrender. Rhodes resigned as Prime Minister of the Cape, his dream of a united South Africa in ruins, and rode north to put down the Bantu rebellion in Zimbabwe. This revolt had erupted when Jameson and his police withdrew from the territory in order to lead the raid into the Transvaal.

The greater consequence of the raid, however, occurred south of the Limpopo. For over a century the Boers had regarded the British with sullen suspicion at best, and open hostility at worst. These fears now seemed confirmed; throughout South Africa there remained only bitterness, recriminations, and broken friendships in the aftermath of the

Jameson raid (Jan Christiaan Smuts, *A Century of Wrong*). The clash of interests appeared insoluble except by force, and in 1899 the British High Commissioner, Sir Alfred Milner, turned to British arms to carry out what British diplomacy and duplicity had failed to accomplish. The Anglo-Boer War lasted longer and entailed far greater expense than anyone, Briton or Boer, had foreseen. This conflict constituted the first modern antiimperial war. British forces were at first defeated by the tough farmers who comprised the Boer commandos, and even after Lord Roberts and Lord Kitchener had occupied the towns of the Transvaal and the Orange Free State, Boer guerillas continued to resist in the countryside. In order to prevent them from supporting the guerrillas, the Boer population was methodically herded into concentration camps, where some 20,000 women and children died from disease and unsanitary conditions. Unbeaten, but without victory, both sides were overcome by war weariness, which ultimately brought them to the conference table, where a negotiated peace was signed at Vereeniging on May 31, 1902. The Boer republics lost their independence but in return the Boers insisted that the blacks be denied the franchise. Both Briton and Boer then began to rebuild the devastated land with large sums from the British Treasury.

The task of reconstruction was directed with skill and efficiency by Lord Milner, who seized the opportunity to tie South Africa closely to Great Britain. He encouraged English settlers to immigrate to South Africa, and hoped to Anglicize the Boers by expanding public education in the English language. To carry out this policy, Milner first had to revive the Transvaal economy. Although Bantu labor had been sufficient during normal times, there developed an acute shortage of laborers during the period of reconstruction, which Milner dealt with by importing Chinese workers from Asia. Economically, the introduction of the

Chinese was a great success, and the mines were soon back in production. Politically, however, the arrival of Asians was intensely unpopular in South Africa, and even more so in England. There the Liberals rallied to the cry of Chinese slavery, and when they came to power in 1906, members of the Liberal government hastily gave the former republics responsible government. The Chinese were subsequently repatriated, but the British government had surrendered its power to influence the development of South African society.

THE UNION OF SOUTH AFRICA

Ironically, the combination of Milner's policy of Anglicization with the granting of responsible government by the Liberals produced results opposite to the intended objectives. Neither Milner nor his subordinates were in South Africa long enough to carry ou their policy of Anglicization successfully, while the representative government granted by the Liberals enabled the Afrikaners† to acquire power in South Africa within a few years after their military defeat. Although the Afrikaners were at first determined to cooperate with the British, the increasing influence of Afrikaners in the political life of South Africa advanced the status of Afrikaner culture and language, from which Afrikaner nationalism sprang as a political movement.

Although the Boers had been conscious of their distinctiveness since the time of W. A. van der Stel, this feeling could not be called a nationalist one for many generations. The Free State had many English-speaking citizens, and many Boers to whom state boundaries meant little. The English language was generally spoken at Bloemfontein, even by people of Dutch descent, and Free State farmers had farms and kinship ties in the Cape and Natal. This ease of intercourse with the British was less noticeable in the Transvaal, but here the Boers themselves were so deeply divided

†White South Africans of Boer extraction.

that national consciousness was slow to develop. Meanwhile, in the Cape, Anglicization continued. Schools and churches were filled with the British, and Dutch Reformed services were often conducted in English. Portraits of Queen Victoria were venerated even in farmhouses where English was not understood. The Cape Boers were led and represented by a squirearchy and by townsmen who were partly Anglicized and who deplored the Great Trek and all its consequences.

In the nineteenth century, particularly in the 1870s and 1880s, British policy in South Africa began to direct these diverse groups in the Boer population toward a common sentiment. The annexation of Basutoland and Griqualand West encouraged the process. The feeling that the Free State had been cheated of the diamond fields made the Boers aware that the Free Staters were their own people. The British annexation of the Transvaal, followed by the victory of Majuba and the granting of independence, fed the smoldering fires of Afrikaner nationalism, which blazed forth in the Boer War. Although a British subject, the Boer of the Transvaal regarded the British attack as an assault on his own land and his own people. In the Cape colony, Afrikaner nationalism was symbolized more by the fact that the Cape Boers were subject to an alien regime than by the vacillations of British policy on the frontier. English was the official language, and those who were not fluent in it were excluded from public life. Few Boers sat in the Cape Parliament or held positions in the civil service. To the simple Boer farmer, the whole apparatus of the state appeared to be an alien institution imposed from abroad without his consent. Boer resentment was first formalized by the creation of the Afrikaner Bond in the late 1870s. Under the leadershp of Jan Hofmeyr, the Bond remained studiously loyal during the Boer War, though deeply sympathetic to the cause of the Afrikaners.

The problem of language symbolized the political differences. To the Boer the Dutch language had become nearly as alien as English. Most literate Boers had difficulty translating their vernacular into written form of High Dutch, which, as a spoken language, was quite foreign; after the mid-nineteenth century a movement was begun to promote Afrikaans as a written language. Rules of spelling and grammar were laid down, and the language was formalized, so that by the end of the Boer War Afrikaans proved to be a fluent medium of communication and a powerful instrument for promoting Afrikaner nationalism.

The granting of representative government to the colonies provided the opportunity for Afrikaner nationalists, tempered in the crucible of war and given literary legitimacy, to seize political power. In the Transvaal a Boer party, the *Het Volk* led by Louis Botha and Jan Christiaan Smuts, won a large majority. In the Orange River colony, control passed into the hands of the Orangia Unie Party under J. B. M.. Hertzog. Even in the Cape the strongly pro-British administration was defeated by the Afrikaner Bond, which installed the government of John Xavier Merriman. Although nationalist in sentiment, if not in action, none of these Afrikaner parties was prepared to break with the British. To them, seeking equal recognition of their own culture did not necessarily mean refusal to collaborate with the British. Just as Jan Hofmeyr and his Africaner Bond cooperated with Cecil Rhodes in the 1890s, Smuts and Botha and even Merriman were prepared to create a Union of South Africa in association with the British. In 1909 the South Africa Act was passed by the British Parliament, and the diverse regions of South Africa were politically united. Many of the provisions of the act were similar to those that other dominions had adopted from the British Constitution: a Governor General, a Senate and a House of Assembly, a Cabinet of Ministers responsible to Parliament, a single Supreme Court, and a permanent civil service. The crucial issue was the franchise. The Transvaal was adamant against extending the franchise to nonwhites, and even advocated revoking the limited franchise of the coloreds and blacks in the Cape. In the end a compromise was agreed upon whereby the Cape franchise was retained, but no nonwhite could vote in the former republics or sit in the Union Parliament. In addition, the rural areas, which comprised the heartland of Boer conservatism, were given higher representation than the more cosmopolitan urban centers. Although protests were made to the British government by Cape Liberals, the British had had enough of South Africa. So long as the country was united and within the British Empire, the government was unwilling to jeopardize these gains by insisting on an extension of the franchise to the blacks. The draft constitution was accepted with few amendments, and except for the Cape franchise, nonwhites remained without the vote in South Africa.

HOLISM AND HERTZOGISM

The force of Afrikaner nationalism became more visibly apparent soon after the creation of the Union of South Africa. In 1912 J. B. M. Hertzog broke with the South African National Party to form the National Party, on the principle of South Africa first, the empire second—and the proposition that the "two separate streams" of Anglo and Afrikaner nationalism should flow apart. The National Party was not formally a republican or secessionist party, but Afrikaner aspirations were its driving force. The extremists in the party hoped to turn South Africa against Britain during World War I, but even Hertzog would not go that far, contenting himself with benevolent neutrality. In any event, he could not command sufficient support to defeat the Anglo-Afrikaner cooperation personified by the ruling South Africa Party,

which, after Louis Botha's death in 1919, came under the leadership of Jan Christiaan Smuts.

Smuts had originally been an Afrikaner Cape lawyer who emigrated to the Transvaal. There he became an aide to President Kruger (a Boer general) and a participant in the Peace of Vereeniging. During World War I he was a key member of the Commonwealth's Imperial War Cabinet; he was later an architect of the League of Nations. Smuts attempted to apply the idealism of war and peace to the South African dilemma; he envisaged an amalgam of Anglo-Afrikaner culture—which he called Holism—that would provide paternal leadership to the blacks, while allowing South Africa to participate in the larger community of mankind beyond its borders. According to the philosophy of Holism, each race would develop its own distinctive characteristics and would acquire meaning only in its unique relationship to the whole community. Smuts' intellectual brilliance and his enormous prestige abroad tended to obscure the growing division between Briton and Boer that Holism sought to reconcile.

In 1924 Smuts and his South African Party were defeated by a coalition government led by Hertzog, but Hertzog did not have sufficient support, particularly among English-speaking workers, to press his policy of two separate streams to its logical conclusion. During and after World War I the Labor Party had become a powerful force in South Africa politics. Originally founded by English-speaking workers, the labor movement was increasingly influenced by landless Afrikaners who came to work in the mines. These poor white workers deeply feared the Bantu laborers, and as they came to dominate the trade unions, they sought to prevent the blacks, Cape Coloureds, and Indians from competing in the skilled labor market. The labor movement became the protector of the poor white. After Smuts' government broke up, the strikers, who had seized the Rand mines in 1922 in opposition to proposals by the mining companies to open more jobs to the blacks, labor, and the Afrikaner nationalists, combined to defeat Smuts and to obstruct his hopes for Anglo-Boer cooperation in South Africa.

From 1924 until the outbreak of World War II, Hertzog and his coalition ruled South Africa. The basis of their policy was segregation of black and white, equality among whites, and sovereign independence for South Africa. The segregation of black and white was based on the assumption that the Bantu were intruders, permitted in South Africa by the white man's leave. Consequently, they could be segregated into settlements on the reserves, removed from the common voters' roll in the Cape, and eliminated from certain nonskilled jobs in favor of white workers. Indeed, Hertzog's "civilized labor" policy involved not simply the denial of certain jobs to nonwhites, but the actual replacement by whites of those coloreds, Indians, and black Africans working as skilled laborers, or on the railways and in the postal services. Although much of the legislation passed to implement this program was virtually unenforceable, the principles of segregation were legally defined—particularly in the crucial Native Trust and Land Act—and—the Representation of Natives Act of 1936—and were later to be refined by the practices of apartheid (Jan Hendrik Hofmeyr, *The Representation of Natives Act, 1936*.)

While seeking to segregate black from white, Hertzog worked assiduously to make the Afrikaner equal to English-speaking whites. In 1925 Afrikaans officially became equivalent to English and took the place of High Dutch in South Africa. An official Afrikaans dictionary was commissioned, and in 1933 Afrikaans acquired religious legitimacy with the appearance of an Afrikaans translation of the Bible. The sense of inferiority that had often haunted those who used colloquial Afrikaans gave way to an increasing pride and the stronger sense of national consciousness that went along with it. Only in the field of Commonwealth relations did Hertzog refuse to force the issue of South African sovereignty. In fact, he seemed to accept the assurance of South African independence given at the Imperial Conference of 1926, as well as that given in the Statute of Westminster of 1931, which defined the dominions as equal and in no way subordinate one to the other. Great Britain had abandoned even theoretical power to rule, and although judicial appeals could still be taken to the Privy Council, constitutional sovereignty belonged strictly to South Africa. White South African nationalism had achieved this crucial goal within a generation after the Anglo-Boer War, and this achievement conditioned the internal struggle between Briton and Afrikaner for political dominance.

THE TRIUMPH OF AFRIKANER NATIONALISM

The crisis of the world depression hit South Africa very hard, and before this great economic threat to national survival, the smoldering issues of race and culture momentarily receded. Smuts even brought his South African Party into the Hertzog government in a grand coalition, entitled the United South African National Party, to rally the nation against economic decline. On the fringe of the United Party, which embraced the vast bulk of English- and Afrikaans-speaking voters, were two dissident groups—the Dominion Party, which hoped to resurrect direct ties with Britain, and the Nationalists, led by Dr. Daniel François Malan, who believed that Hertzog had sold out to Liberal British interests. Malan repudiated Holism, and even Hertzog's segregation, in favor of a nation ruled by the will of the Afrikaner folk. At the time, neither party appeared to be a threat to the great United Party, but the coalition was in fact a fair-weather government, which could not stand against the storms of war.

The outbreak of war revealed the deep divisions in South African society, which the United Party had temporarily obscured. To Smuts, the war was a world crisis in which South Africa should play its part in defeating Germany's bid for the mastery of Europe and the world. Hertzog, however, did not feel that the war concerned South Africa, and when the Parliament agreed by a very small margin to support the Allies, Hertzog resigned. As South African forces became increasingly committed during the war and Smuts once again began to participate in Allied war councils, the Afrikaner nationalists remained neutral at best and openly hostile to the Allies at worst. Gradually, the more moderate Afrikaner leadership gave way to the extreme nationalists—Malan at the Cape, Johannes Gerhardus Strijdom and Hendrik Frensch Verwoerd in the Transvaal, and Charles Swart in the Free State—who banded together in a political alliance to defeat Smuts and his United Party in 1948.

In 1948 the Nationalists campaigned on a policy of apartheid, or comprehensive apartness of black and white in South Africa. By the end of the war the basic institutions of Afrikaner nationalism had been consolidated in youth groups, cultural organizations, paramilitary militias, and even the trade unions to provide a strong political base from which to challenge the moderate ruling coalition. They attacked Smuts for devoting his time to international diplomacy while ignoring the problems that industrialization had created in South Africa, particularly the migration of black Africans to the cities. The demands of war had accelerated South African industrialization, which had been slowly recovering from the setback of the Great Depression. The discovery and extension of rich new gold fields stimulated demands for steel, cement, machinery, and a wide variety of manufactured products. New coal mines

were opened and the world demand for gems revived the diamond industry. Nor was the countryside unaffected by the rapid pace of industrialization. Everywhere black laborers left the reserves and Afrikaners abandoned marginal farms to drift into the cities, and around the white residential centers shanty towns sprang up to breed crime and disease in the slum conditions. The fundamental fact that large numbers of Africans were now present in the towns precipitated political reaction, which took its form in apartheid. Burglaries, assaults, and murders increased, as did the pressure of black workers for employment in jobs traditionally reserved for whites. Despite the success of the white trade unions in resisting this pressure, such unions could not allay the fears of white workers, particularly the Afrikaners who had recently arrived from the countryside. To them the National Party and apartheid had great appeal, and by the end of the war the unions were almost completely under Afrikaner control.

Apartheid was not new; its only claim to originality was its systematic application of old assumptions. The first of these was that individuals of Dutch origin who belonged to the Reformed Church had been singled out by God and placed above and separate from all nonwhites and non-Calvinist aliens. Second, the Afrikaans-speaking South African was unique in that he had no European mother country. Acting on these assumptions, the Nationalists argued that the voters must choose between (1) white rule, racial purity, and Christian civilization, or (2) gradual absorption by the black masses. Only apartheid, or separate existence, could prevent the assimilation and loss of white civilization in South Africa by black barbarism. Although the Nationalists did not precisely define how apartheid would work in practice, the electorate understood it to mean separation of the races into definite territorial reserves. The black would be removed to the reserves, where he could work out his own economic and political destiny while being permitted temporarily into the white man's towns so long as his labor was required. Certainly this doctrine reassured the white worker, concerned over the pressure from black labor, the rise of crime, riots, and the growing "truculence" of the black. The result was a slim victory for the Nationalists in 1948, which was soon confirmed in the subsequent elections of 1953 and 1958 as the opposition steadily diminished in size and power before the implacable logic of Afrikaner nationalism (M. D. C. de Wet Nel, *The Principles of Apartheid*).

Once in power, Malan and his successors began to reorganize South African life in accordance with their policies, and in the practice of apartheid new features of past segregation inexorably appeared. For the first time the Nationalists politically unified the scattered Afrikaner groups and brought together the Afrikaans' social and cultural organizations into a powerful and well-supervised organ of nationalist propaganda and control. Then the Nationalists began to apply apartheid. A host of apartheid legislation extended and systematized the practical segregation already in existence into a rigid and comprehensive separation. Everyone was required to carry a certificate of racial classification, and each race was restricted to the areas that it already occupied. The reserves were to be transformed into autonomous *Bantustans* ‡ in which the traditional life of the Bantu people would be revived and allowed to develop uninfluenced by European ideas and institutions (Nelson Mandela, *Verwoerd's Tribalism*). In 1956 even the Cape Coloured population lost the vote. But before this sweeping legislation could be enacted, the opposition, both black and white, was rigorously suppressed as the civil liberties of all the people were increasingly restricted. In Parliament only

‡ Autonomous geographical and political entities within South Africa in which the black Africans managed their own internal affairs.

a few lonely voices crying in the wilderness lashed out against apartheid and its implications (Helen Suzman, *Mrs. Suzman and Apartheid*). Those organizations that did not cooperate with the government were dissolved or banned. Indeed, the triumph of Afrikaner nationalism appeared fully confirmed when the final tie with Great Britain was broken by the Declaration of the Republic on May 31, 1961.

By the late 1970s, Afrikaner unity, which had enabled the National Party to stay in power for three decades, was beginning to break up. In 1978, John Vorster was succeeded as Prime Minister by P.W. Botha, who had held the defense portfolio. At the Ministry of Defense, Botha had come under the influence of several army generals who had some definite ideas about the best way to preserve the apartheid system; they felt the system could be strengthened by making certain adjustments to it.

These army officers were led by General Magnus Malan, who later succeeded Botha at the Ministry of Defense. They viewed Southern Africa in long-range strategic terms, rather than thinking in terms of election strategies. They realized that the collapse of white rule in Angola, Mozambique, and later Zimbabwe would sooner or later constitute a military problem for the regime. Together with P.W. Botha, therefore, they began to inform the public about alleged Soviet plots against South Africa, although they knew very well that Soviet aid to the ANC and other liberation movements in the region was minimal, and that the real threat to the regime was posed by their fellow black South Africans. The alleged Soviet danger was useful, however, in encouraging whites to support their policies.

Botha, together with his supporters in what had come to be known as the "verligte," or "enlightened," wing of the National Party, began to press for certain changes: a constitutional formula that would allow some colored and Indian representation in the government; the end to some forms of petty apartheid; and more rapid entry of blacks into semi-skilled and skilled jobs that had been held by whites in the past, for which there was now a shortage of manpower.

Support for the verligte policies was strongest among the "new Afrikaners," the better-off class of business and professional people who were coming to share the less crude racial attitudes of their English-speaking counterparts. During three decades in power, the National Party had helped improve the economic position of some Afrikaners dramatically, and the distinction between Afrikans and English business was blurring. Businessmen in general thought that the new policies were necessary to preserve the system in the long run, and so supported them. In November 1983 P.W. Botha managed to win a referendum among whites approving his proposals to bring colored and Indian people into the national Parliament in separate chambers.

Meanwhile, these proposals had provoked a large backlash in the Afrikaner community; two hostile groups emerged. One consisted of those who had been excluded from power and from the party as a result of the Information scandal. The other group, led by Dr. Andries Treurnicht from within the party, thought that the Prime Minister's liberalization policies threatened to go too far. He led a breakaway group and formed the Conservative Party, while the National Party now came to be regarded as centrist, or middle-of-the-road.

THE RISE OF AFRICAN NATIONALISM

In 1912 Pixley Ka Seme, a black lawyer trained at Columbia, Oxford, and the Middle Temple, set up, along with several other black lawyers, an organization that later came to be called the African National Congress (ANC). During its first three decades, the ANC conducted itself as a restrained and moderate organization. It sought to change the system and to improve conditions for blacks by peaceful means. In order to win international support, the organization sent delegations to Britain and to the post-World War I conference at Versailles. It also tried to distance itself from such mass actions as the 1919 anti-pass campaign, the 1943 bus boycott in Johannesburg's Alexandra township, and the 1946 mineworker's strike.

In 1944, however, a new generation of young men, including Nelson Mandela, Oliver Tambo, and Walter Sisulu, founded the ANC's Youth League. This group was much more militant than the older generation. They argued that the ANC should become more aggressive and more involved in nationwide mass protest. They also felt that the organization should present extremely vigorous resistance to the National Party, which had come to power in 1948 promising to reinforce the existing system of racial domination with the policy of apartheid. In 1949, the younger leaders persuaded the ANC convention to approve the Youth League's program of action, which called for strikes, civil disobedience, and non-cooperation with any of the regime's institutions. In addition to this change, the organization's president-general and secretary-general were replaced by more activist League members—Dr. James Moroka and Walter Sisulu respectively. Thereafter, the ANC moved toward closer alliances with other groups, such as the Indian Congress and groups of sympathetic whites which were opposed to the apartheid system. In 1952, with increased mass support, the ANC decided, in the Gandhian tradition, to conduct a campaign of defiance involving massive, nonviolent civil disobedience all over the country.

The reaction of the government was predictably harsh. Using the Suppression of Communism Act, it "banned" (detained) fifty-two ANC leaders, including Nelson Mandela. New legislation was passed which increased penalties for defiance. In 1956, a further crackdown took place, resulting in the arrest of 156 ANC leaders; their trial dragged on for five years.

During the 1950s, the ANC continued the spirit of defiance by working more closely with the Indian Congress, the Colored People's Congress, and the Congress of Democrats, a small but vigorous group of white radicals. In 1955, the Congress Alliance of these groups met at Kliptown to draw up a declaration of principles. They came up with a short document, called "The Freedom Charter," which stipulated that "South Africa belongs to all who live in it, black and white." The charter promised to repeal all apartheid legislation and replace it with a one-man, one-vote system, guaranteed human rights for all, and various social welfare measures. It also pledged to nationalize the mines, the banks, and major industries.

One faction within the ANC, the Africanists, was, however, opposed to the idea that "South Africa belongs to all who live in it." In their view, this guaranteed the creation of a multiracial society, an ideal which they refused to embrace. To them, South Africa belonged to Africans. The liberation struggle should therefore, they felt, be carried out by Africans only. Led by Robert Sobukwe, this dissident group broke away in 1959 and set up the Pan-African Congress (PAC), which accused the ANC of being timid and moderate. By this time, the ANC had already lost numerous struggles with the regime. Among other failures, it had been unable to prevent the introduction of Bantu education; the ANC had failed to save Sophiatown (a black community township in western Johannesburg) from being levelled. It had also failed to prevent the pass laws from being extended to women. The PAC realized that the masses, having been disappointed by the failure of the ANC's moderate tactics, and encouraged

by news of decolonization further north, were now prepared for militant action.

In 1960, both the ANC and the PAC declared war on the pass laws. Despite its militant tone, however, the PAC still pursued a policy of nonviolence. PAC followers gathered in several urban centers to destroy their passes. At Sharpeville, one of the townships outside the steel town of Vereeniging, the police opened fire and sixty-nine people were killed. There was immediate reaction across the country, and the nation seemed to enter a mood of insurrection. The government then decided to ban both the ANC and the PAC. Chief Albert Lutuli, the ANC President, was banned and restricted to his home in rural Natal; this action signaled the end of the nonviolent phase of resistance which Africans had carried out for fifty years.

After the banning and restriction of Chief Lutuli, Nelson Mandela became the ANC's *de facto* leader (Nelson Mandela, *Address to the ANC*). At this point, armed struggle seemed the only alternative open to the organization. Yet, the ANC hesitated. Mandela moved secretly around the country, organizing a peaceful nationwide protest strike for May 1961. The strike was only partially successful because of the government's counter-tactic of employing threats and intimidation against the workers. Meanwhile, the PAC, its leadership imprisoned following the anti-pass campaign, was thrown into a state of confusion. Some of its supporters in the Cape even staged a few random attacks on whites; they were imprisoned or hanged. The ANC was, however, much more scrupulous. Its leader, Nelson Mandela, had left the country secretly and toured Africa and Britain to present the objectives of the ANC. Along with other ANC leaders, he established the guerrilla organization called "Umkhonto we Sizwe" (the Spear of the Nation), whose objective was to commit specific, limited acts of sabotage against selected targets. The aim was to put pressure on the regime to negotiate. A little later on, another organization with similar goals, called the African Resistance Movement (ARM), and composed of young whites, was also formed.

Alarmed by these developments, the government pushed a bill through parliament which allowed detention without trial of apparent suspects. At the same time, the security police began to torture political detainees. By the mid-1960s, the government had crushed armed resistance. Much of the leadership of Umkhonto we Sizwe, including Walter Sisulu (Zwelakhe Sislulu, *Keynote Address to the National Education Crisis Committee, Second National Consultative Conference*), Denis Goldberg (a white engineer), Govan Mbeki, and Ahmed Kathrada (an Indian), were captured. Along with Nelson Mandela, who was already in prison on a lesser charge, they were all sentenced to life imprisonment. The other resistance movements were also suppressed. PAC's leader, Robert Sobukwe, who had been sentenced to three years' imprisonment, was kept on Robben Island indefinitely under special legislation designed solely for him. He died in 1978 while in prison. Many of the leaders of ARM were also incarcerated.

As the crackdown after Sharpeville was proceeding, the ANC directed Oliver Tambo to flee the country. Outside of South Africa he began to establish the movement in exile and to lobby for international support, as did some of the PAC leaders. Both organizations trained small numbers of guerrillas, but they found it impossible to penetrate the protective ring of white-ruled states.

Meanwhile, a black consciousness movement, much like the Civil Rights Movement in the U.S., had begun to develop in South Africa in the late 1960s. Its leaders included people like Steve Biko (Steve Biko, *Black Consciousness and the Quest for True Humanity*), A.O.R. Tiro, and Barney Pityana. The movement urged blacks to do away with their feelings of inferiority and despair, and to start again to organize for liberation. Black consciousness leaders urged blacks to boycott the Bantustan system and other government-sponsored institutions. They founded the Black People's Convention (BPC), which enlarged their following, and established self-help projects in health and education in the townships.

Although the government at first approved of the black consciousness movement—finding an echo in its program of its own ideology of separate development—the regime soon realized that the movement was dangerously successful in stirring up black political activism once again. Although the leaders of the movement advocated nonviolence, the regime began to restrict their activities. Tiro was killed by a parcel bomb; Biko and others were banned; still others were convicted of "terrorism" and imprisoned on Robben Island. In August 1977, Steve Biko was detained near King William's Town in the Eastern Cape. A few weeks later, he was dead.

On October 19, 1977, the government responded to the outcry over Biko's death by banning all the remaining black consciousness organizations. The movement had, however, already achieved its immediate goal of dispelling the fear, shame, and feelings of impotence that had prevailed among blacks. In 1976, for instance, students had marched through Soweto and other urban centers demanding an end to segregated education; the South African Students Movement, an organization of high school students strongly influenced by black consciousness, was behind the march.

The October 1977 repression left a temporary political vacuum inside the country, with the regime becoming increasingly intolerant of opposition. Even moderate leaders like Dr. Nthato Motlana and Bishop Desmond Tutu were arrested and harassed. All open-air gatherings were outlawed; hundreds of people were detained. As a result, many students and others fled South Africa to the independent countries of Lesotho, Botswana, and Swaziland, where they encountered the ANC. The organization then began to recruit guerrillas for "Umkhonto."

During 1977 and 1978 Unkhonto carried out a few scattered attacks inside South Africa. In 1979 small bands of Umkhonto soldiers attacked police stations in Soweto. On June 4, 1980, guerillas simultaneously struck three separate targets hundreds of miles apart with explosives. The most spectacular attack was the one on the Sasol refineries south of Johannesburg, where a predawn explosion destroyed about $7.2 million in supplies.

After the 1977 crackdown, the pace of activity slackened for a time. Then, late in 1979, a new organization, called the Port Elizabeth Black Civic Organization (PEBCO), was formed in the Eastern Cape's large motor industry. Some seven hundred members of the new organization carried out a series of strikes to demand better working conditions. Meanwhile, the March 1980 ZANU victory in the election in Zimbabwe aroused a mood of optimism and renewed determination among blacks and coloreds. In Cape Town, black and colored school children began to boycott their classes, protesting that the 1976 strike had brought no improvements in their education. The boycott spread to the Eastern Cape, Johannesburg, Bloemfontein, and Durban. Black political and religious leaders began to urge the regime to negotiate, and to release Nelson Mandela. Unrest, meanwhile, continued, and workers staged further strikes. In mid-June of 1980, a successful "stay-away" from work was organized to mark the anniversary of the 1976 uprising. About

forty-two people were killed in the ghetto of Elsie's River when police opened fire.

Active in the 1980 strike were black workers. As far back as the 1920s, black workers had organized themselves, but only a few unions had survived the repression of the mid-1960s. Then in 1973 a wave of strikes shook Durban, as more than 100,000 workers at some 150 firms walked out to demand higher wages. Activists across the country began to exploit the new situation by forming strong, well-organized unions. By 1980, half a dozen new labor federations had emerged: SAAWU, FOSATU (Joe Foster, *The Workers' Struggle–Where Does FOSATU Stand?*), CUSA, GAWU, GWU, etc. There was a corresponding growth in trade union membership— from a small number in the mid-1970s to 300,000 by 1982. That year alone, there were four hundred strikes in South Africa, compared to only seventy annually in the 1970s.

At first the government tolerated the new unions, fearing that repression might provoke repercussions from overseas. It was also felt that moderate unions could very well be a force for stability, guiding discontent on factory floors into safe institutionalized channels. When the unions became increasingly militant, however, the government began to detain some of their leaders. One of these was a white medical doctor named Neil Aggett, who died on February 5, 1982 while still in detention.

In August 1983, the United Democratic Front (UDF) announced its formation (Terror Lekota *Letter*). The idea for the movement had originally come from the World Alliance of Reformed Churches, and the Front acquired a figurehead in Dr. Allen Boesak, who had been recently elected president of that alliance. Boesak was mainly responsible for persuading the alliance to declare apartheid a heresy during its conference in Ottawa in August 1982. The UDF arose out of the distaste of many South Africans for constitutional proposals which were intended permanently to exclude the entire African population of South Africa and the Homelands from the central parliamentary structures of the state. Its membership of over two million spans all races and classes, and is distributed through trade unions, local educational, religious, and social groups, and sports clubs. The UDF has declined, however, to form itself into a political party, perhaps out of its reluctance to appear to compete with the ANC, with which many of its members sympathize. It has accepted the Freedom Charter of 1955 as its formula for a "unitary socialist state." It rejects the apartheid structures, and hence declined to participate in the politics of the white referendum in November 1983, or the colored and Indian elections of 1984.

Umkhonto soldiers continued their sabotage campaigns into the early eighties. In 1981 there were some fifty-five separate attacks, including a rocket assault against the big Voortrekkerhoogte army base near Pretoria. The same level of attacks continued through 1982 and 1983. In reaction to these attacks and the escalating war in Namibia, the government responded with a strategic military offensive against neighbouring African states. In January 1981, South African commandos raided the outskirts of Maputo, Mozambique, attacking three residences that allegedly housed ANC guerrillas. In July 1981, Joe Gqabi, the ANC's first representative in Zimbabwe, was assassinated. In December 1982 the South African army invaded Maseru, Lesotho. In 1983 Mozambique was again raided several times with warplanes. In addition to this, the regime used surrogate forces to destabilize the region: the

National Union for the Total Independence of Angola (UNITA) in Angola; the MRN (RENAMO, or National Resistance Movement) in Mozambique; and the Lesotho Liberation Army (LLA).

In South Africa itself, the violent political unrest triggered by the decision, in June 1976, to make Afrikaans the official language of school instruction for the Soweto district has continued, at various levels of intensity, ever since. Underlying the unrest are not just specific grievances, but fundamental problems inherent to a society which outwardly professes adherence to Western democratic ideals and yet denies, on the basis of ethnicity, a majority of its population elementary political rights. Over the years, economic and social reforms have created more economic equity and access to employment for members of all ethnic groups. A slow dismantling of the rules of apartheid has been effected, with, among other changes, the abolition of the pass laws and the legalization of mixed-race sexual relations and marriage. Communities have also been given a right to vote on the question of ending racial segregation. However, major political reform has not yet been undertaken on a level acceptable to the black majority.

Throughout the 1980s, the Republic of South Africa has shown its ability at times to absorb severe and violent internal unrest and a diffuse series of terrorist attacks, to keep its borders secure, and to exert military influence over neighboring countries. However, defiance of majority opinion at home and abroad has come only at the price of international ostracism and increasing domestic repression, to the point that the country has been under a general state of emergency since June 12, 1986.

25 JAN VAN RIEBEECK AND Z. WAGENAAR

OF THE NATIVE TRIBES OF SOUTH AFRICA

The first two governors of the Cape of Good Hope after it was annexed as a trading and revictualing station by the Dutch East India Company in 1652 were Jan van Riebeeck (governor, 1652–1662) and Z. Wagenaar (governor, 1663–1666). Among the documents that they wrote for their successors were the following descriptions of the Khoikhoi (Hottentot) population of the Cape. At this time the Khoikhoi still retained their traditional organization of chiefdoms. This organization was soon disrupted by the alien influence of the Europeans, and the Khoikhoi became a landless population that existed in outlawry or in servitude to white masters. The chiefdoms were incorporated under the law of the Cape and were given some rights and partial protection only in 1828 as the result of missionary agitation on their behalf.*

EXTRACTS OF MEMORANDUM LEFT BY COMMANDER J. VAN RIEBEECK, FOR THE INFORMATION AND GUIDANCE OF HIS SUCCESSOR Z. WAGENAAR

May 5. [The first paragraph merely refers to the several instructions and other papers explanatory of the objects in taking possession at the Cape. Then follow the several subjects here omitted, which are denoted by the following marginals, given in italics.]

Company's first object attained; in addition to other refreshments. A good prospect of fruit, particularly from the vines; also olives in time. The corn lands turn out much poorer than was supposed. Trade; and the condition of the Cape Tribes.

Coming now to the subject of the trade with these native tribes, the same is now, thanks to God! on a much better footing than ever, through the knowledge which we are gradually acquiring of various races of people in the interior, whose names, with their places of abode and mode of living are thus briefly stated, in order to convey a better idea of their cir-

cumstances. We have then, in the first place—

The GORINGHAICONAS,[1] of whom Herry has been usually called the Captain; these are strandloopers, or fishers, who are, exclusive of women and children, not above 18 men in number, supporting themselves, without the least live stock of any description, by fishing from the rocks along the coast, thus furnishing a great accommodation to the Company's people and freemen, and also rendering much assistance to those who keep house, by washing, scouring, fetching firewood, and other domestic work; and some of them placing their little daughters in the service of the married people, where they are clothed in our manner, but they must have a slack rein, and will not be kept strictly, such appears to be contrary to their nature; some of them, however, begin to be tolerably civilized, and the Dutch language is so far implanted among them, old and young, that nothing can any longer be kept secret when mentioned in their presence, and very little in that of the—

GORINGHAIQUAS, whose Chief is named Gogosoa, and who are the Capemans; they are, exclusive of women and children, about 300 men capable of bearing arms, supplied with about enough cat-

From D. Moodie, *The Record* (Cape Town: A. S. Robertson, 1838), I, 246–251, 290–293.
* Although these are the first reliable contemporary accounts of the Khoikhoi, others of the same period may be found in Isaac Schapera and B. Farrington (eds.), *The Early Cape Hottentots, 1688–1695* (Cape Town: Van Riebeeck Society, 1933), Vol. XIV.

[1] The Goringhaiconas and other tribes mentioned herein are all Hottentot peoples (ed.).

tle to provide for their own wants, but as they begin to be somewhat fond of mercantile gains, (coopmanachtige) they are rather increasing their stock, particularly as they have always been knowing enough, upon the approach of strangers from the interior with pretty good cattle, to act as brokers and guides to conduct the strangers to us; exchanging their leanest and worst cattle for the good, and then bringing those strangers to us, and insisting upon it that they have been the means of enticing and fetching them out of the interior, &c. in which manner they well know how to enrich themselves, becoming every day worse and more cunning; these are they who pretend that this Cape land has been theirs from all ages, and who, seeing that we were betaking ourselves to permanent agriculture, made war upon us in the year 1659, on account, according to their statements, of their harsh treatment by some of the free men; but on seeing, contrary to their expectation, that we, though assailed at the weakest, were not to be so easily driven away, and that, meanwhile, the chief or king of the Saldanhars, took the opportunity of that disturbed time, to form an alliance with us—which alliances they had always used every art to prevent, &c. they were induced two years ago to request and to conclude a peace with us, as also did—

The GORACHOUQUAS, or tobacco thieves, so called because they once stole, from the field, the tobacco belonging to some free men, and whose chief is named Choro. You have been in both their camps—they have, besides women and children, 6 or 700 men capable of bearing arms, and are fully 6 times as rich in cattle as the last mentioned tribe, and a few head are sometimes bought from them; but nothing of importance.

They have, since the war before mentioned, generally lived close to the Capemans, and about a day's journey to the N. E. behind the Leopards Hill, not far from, and as it would seem, under the wing of the Saldanhars; but this April both tribes have come back to live at the foot of the Bosheuvel, under our protection, in consequence, as it would seem, of some difference which has arisen between them and the Saldanhars, who are the—

COCHOQUAS, consisting of two divisions, under 2 chiefs, or choquees, (which means kings) the first is named Oedasoa, a quiet man, whose wife—last year deceased—was sister of the interpreter Eva, who is also a niece of Herry, and has from her childhood been brought up in our house, and can speak Dutch almost as well as a Dutch girl, and we thus derive much service from her in translation, although she does lead us a dance now and then . . . and some things must be received from her with caution.

The other chief of the Saldanhars, or Cochoquas, is named Gonnoma, and is often some distance apart from Oedasoa. They have, together, several thousand men, and generally occupy the middle of the country opposite to us, under the African mountains, extending from near False Bay, quite to Saldanha Bay, but not always remaining in one place, and moving about for change of pasture. With which Oedasoa and Gonnoma we appear to have a very firm alliance, and with whom we carry on a good, indeed a constant trade in live stock—chiefly in sheep—but not so many horned cattle that we have ever been able to spare so many as now for the refreshment of the Company's shipping; they have helped however; but we have never procured any stock whatever, deserving of the name, from the—

LITTLE CHARIGURIQUAS, a people about as numerous as the Goringhaiquas, who chiefly reside between Saldanha Bay, and midway between Robben and Dassen Island—about 4 or 5 hours' walk from the sea coast, subject to Oedasoa, though they have rebelled against him; they were accustomed to be his stock keepers, but appropriated his cattle to their own use; and therefore they are not recognized by any of the Hottentoos as a people who have a Choeque or Hunque, that is a hereditary king or chief; they seem, however, to be able to take their own part, as it now begins to appear, through the fear which Oedasoa entertains for the—

NAMAQUAS, with whom the great Chariguriquas have sought and formed an alliance; this people have recently been found by us, after long search; they are very rich in cattle, and very tall in stature, almost half giants, dressed in fine prepared skins, as may be seen at full by the notes kept by our travellers, and inserted in our Journal under date the 11th March 1661; where it may also be seen that they are very favorably disposed towards us, and that they seem to be a people who carry on trade with other tribes residing further inland, and through whom the way is now in so far opened, that it is only now that we can properly begin to discover any thing better than cattle. Of these people, to all appearance, more will come to you than you can wish; and thus after 10 years toil we hope that we have opened for you a fortunate road to the North side of this Africa; whither, towards the end of September, another journey must be taken, in order to be enabled to cross the dry country (which at that season will probably be still moist after the rains) to the river upon which there is laid down, in Linschoten's map, a town (vaste plaets) called Vigiti Magna, and where there is a race of people quite different from the Hottentoos, of whom we have been hitherto treating, and to whom we shall also return, namely, to those whom we have found to be the richest, almost all of whom reside to the Eastward, along the East coast of Africa, where they sometimes show themselves in some bays, as we can discover from their own statements.[2] We have only begun to know them well during the last two years, and they are the—

CHAINOUQUAS, whose Choque or King is named Sousoa, with whom we are upon very good, and rather firm terms of friendship, and who have since that time bartered to us a great number of cattle, and a good many sheep also. They are able to supply us abundantly, and on taking leave of us last year promised to come back with a still larger quantity; we sincerely trust that you may, on the Company's account, enjoy the fortunate result, and also that, as we are given to expect by the accounts of all the Hottentoos, you may be soon visited by the—

HEUSAQUAS, from whom a messenger was last year at the fort, with intelligence that his Chief also intended to come to visit the Sourye (that is the Lord of the Land, the name by which I have been generally known,) of the Dutch, with money and cattle, to try to procure, like his friends, the Chainouquas, a share of our merchandize, which will be a most desirable event, as they are very rich in cattle, and have a strong liking for the consumable tobacco, and for certain red beads in the Company's stores, for which the cattle are procured from those people at a very cheap rate. The Hottentoos who live near us, speak in high terms of this tribe, saying that now that Sousoa is gone, they will come with such great herds of cattle, that the merchandize will fall short. This, however, need not be feared, but hoped for, *item,* also for the arrival of the—

HANCUMQUAS, who, according to the hopes held out to us, and from all that we have been able to learn, are the greatest and most powerful of all the race of greasy Hottentoos, living in houses, which like their's, are covered with mats, but of a very large size, and living permanently on the same spot, where they cultivate and dry a certain plant which they call *Dacha,* this they chew and eat, and consequently become very light-headed, as in India from opium, and this is the reason why they are so eager for the strongest tobacco. The Chiefs of this tribe appear to be Chiefs over all the other Choques or

[2] Jan van Linschoten (1563-1611), a Dutch traveler, spent nine years in the Portuguese service in the East Indies and wrote a detailed account of the Indian Ocean. His *Voyages* was an important contribution to sixteenth-century Europe's knowledge of Africa and Asia (ed.).

Kings, being entitled Choebaha, which seems to mean Emperor, or at least Upper King, or Lord over all the others.

Those now who reside further than this Chief Lord of the Hottentoos, though of the same race, and much richer in cattle than all those who live on this side of this supreme Chief, are named first, the—

CHAMAQUAS, and next them the OMAQUAS, ATIQUAS, HOUTUNQUAS, and CHAUQUAS, all subsisting like the Hancumquas, besides their countless herds of cattle, by Dacha plantations, living on fixed spots, in large mat huts, dressed in skins like all the Hottentoos, and also equally greasy, &c.

After those, are said to begin, though beyond the river Vigiti Magna, and in an Easterly direction, another race of people, called by all the before mentioned Hottentoos—

CHOBOQUA or COBONA, residing in fixed houses constructed of wood, clay, and other materials, but at the same time maintaining themselves by cattle, and wearing clothes, whom we conjecture to be the people of Monomotopa, as Eva would often persuade us, and that—as we have also been informed, through her interpretation, by the said Sousoa—there is Chory or gold and white gems among those Choboquas, of which he has promised to bring proofs, and also some one of that people. We trust that you may, for the good of the Company, experience the success of this, and procure some further account of the people of whom the messenger from the HEUSAQUAS told us, that they keep lions as tame as we keep dogs, and among whom it is said that the gold and the white gems are to be found. I trust that diligent inquiry will afford us further knowledge upon all these matters, either through their own people coming to us, or through our men, who are sufficiently well disposed to visit them, as the roads have, through the alliances formed with the several tribes of the race of Hottentoos, become so safe that our people have nothing to look for, in any quarter, but the most friendly reception. In conse-

quence of this, had I remained here, we fully intended, as soon as the rains were over, and at the commencement of the dry season, to send out a party of volunteers to try whether we could not find out the said Choboquas, as we last year, as before mentioned, found the long sought Namaquas.

Jealousy of the Saldanhars. But there is no doubt that Oedasoa, who is the greatest among the natives who live near to the Cape, is as jealous upon this matter, as were the Capemans formerly, when we were endeavoring to become better acquainted with him; and equally fearful of falling into less esteem, in proportion to the extent of our discoveries; this may be fully relied upon, as we have already begun to perceive it from Oedasoa's demeanor, but we have endeavored to remove his apprehension by friendly and affable treatment; and this course must of necessity be continued, for, upon any coolness with him, we can see no prospect of profit for the Company, and deem the preservation of friendship the preferable course; although he (just like the Goringhaiquas or Capemans, who long kept us in ignorance of him) has had in view precisely the same object as to the other tribes, in hoodwinking us, and leading us to believe that he was the greatest *heer* of this country.

But now, seeing that we have at length discovered the Namaquas, (a different, and as before observed, a more active race than the Hottentoos) and hearing that we have been well received by them, and that they have promised to come hither, whether he likes it or not—they having, however, first shown their inclination to be reconciled to him, and for that purpose offering to send 2 or 3 with our party to express their disposition for peace, and to settle old disputes with him (for the Namaquas did not dare to attack him here, for fear of our assisting him)—the said Oedasoa allowed himself to be in so far guided by us, that on the 21st March last year he sent 3 of his people to them as commissioners, in company with our party who went thither, and who were to act between the parties as mediators. This endeavour succeeded according to our wishes, and the result has been that they not only now leave each other unmolested on journeys, and in trading with us, but the Saldanhars may carry on a friendly intercourse and traffic with the said Namaquas, who are, as before observed, a different race from these Hottentoos, of much larger stature, clothed in fine well dressed skins without hair and using rushes (ruyge) at night to sleep on. Their own hair, although like that of the Caffers, is worn long, and plaited in an ornamental manner like locks, with many ornaments of copper, iron, and red beads; also, *caurys* and *bougys,* for which they are very eager, as well as for red caps, and for the red cloth of which to make them.

Hopes of Elephants' teeth among the Namaquas, and why. It would seem also that ivory is much more plentiful among them than among the Hottentoos, from the very thick bracelets of that article which they wear, and from the very singular plates of ivory which they wear over a finely dressed skin, worn as an apron. A specimen of each has been sent to our masters in Holland, and 2 such plates are in the office here; it may therefore happen that a trade in ivory and other articles may yet be opened with them, which were much to be desired for the relief of the Company's expenditure at this place.

Whereabouts the Namaquas are to be found by sea. From a calculation of the courses and distances travelled by our land parties, we are led to conjecture that those people reside not far distant from the coast, and near the bay called by Linschoten, *Angra das Voltas,* between the 29th and 30th parallel to the Northward; and had I staid here, I had it in contemplation, upon a favorable opportunity, to send a Cape galiot, or any small vessel that could be spared, to ascertain that point, as well as whether that bay might not be found suitable, in respect of anchorage, water, and other refreshments,

for Company's ships to touch at, when occasionally blown to leeward of the Cape by the S. S. E. gales in February and March, when the ships arrive from India, and when those winds are usually most severe; or in the event of ivory or other merchandize being found (which might be too bulky for conveyance by land) to place a trading station there, or otherwise, according to circumstances. I therefore bring the subject under your notice in order that you may, at a fitting opportunity, improve upon the suggestion in as far as you may deem it to be practicable, and serviceable to the Company; but the vessel must first be sent to Madagascar for rice and whatever else our masters have directed, or may hereafter direct to be done there.

Nothing more serviceable to the Company than peace with the Hottentoos. It being, above all things necessary, that you always endeavour to live in constant peace with the Hottentoos—one tribe as well as the other, not only that the roads may be every where safe, to facilitate further discoveries, but also that the tribes above named may always be able to come down without apprehension, with their cattle, for the refreshment of the crews of the Company's ships. To this object—in the first place, a more than usually liberal reception will much contribute, and especially if little squabbles occurring between our people—particularly the ship people —and them, be not too seriously taken up, but rather passed over occasionally, as if in ignorance, especially at first, or otherwise they would become so shy that they would fly inland with all they possess, making the other tribes so shy also, that they would keep away altogether; and you would thus find yourselves in a moment deprived, not only of the daily barter with the Saldanhars, but also of the trade with all the other tribes before named. The best advice, therefore, that I am able to give you in this matter is—that you keep your attention constantly fixed—steadfast as a wall, to this point: to live without any of the slightest estrangement from your neighbours here, the Capemans or Goringhaiquas, and the tobacco thieves or Gorachouquas, as well as with Oedasoa, the king of the Saldanhars; which may be effected—besides the friendly treatment aforesaid—by keeping so sharp and strict a watch, by mounted and other guards, (already brought so far into order) over the Company's live stock, and that belonging to the freemen, that a fair opportunity of driving them off is never left open to the natives, without exposing their lives to danger. For, should they have even the least chance of success, they could not refrain from the attempt; and on this account a very close watch will be always required here. *Au reste,* that when they sometimes perceive some simple green horn from the ships going to some retired spot and rob him of his tobacco, bread, and brass, or iron buttons from his clothes, is not a matter of such mighty importance, but that it may be easily arranged. The quarrels also, which occur between them and the ship people, more than those who are resident here, and which proceed perhaps to the length of pelting each other with stones, ought not to be too gravely regarded, for, our men, who, when playing and wrestling (stoeyende) with them, sometimes get a thump a little harder than they will bear, and are thus provoked to abuse them, and call them black stinking dogs, &c.—are themselves in a great measure the cause. For the natives fully understand these, and other Dutch words, and reply, that they are men as well as the Dutch, and so forth—so that I will add that our common people are often found, when out of our presence, to be the first cause of many disputes (questien) which are sometimes attended with trouble, in order to restore tranquillity among these natives; and this may be best accomplished by a show of injustice towards our own people, paying the others by a friendly promise of inflicting some kind of punishment on our men on board of their ships.

And although this course appears to many of our people somewhat improper, it is nevertheless most absolutely necessary, in order that we may live in peace and quiet; and I have therefore always pursued this line of conduct, and enforced it upon others; and whatever better course you may be able to adopt, cannot fail to be still more serviceable to the Company; for, in the event of disagreement, you will not be able to keep a single Hottentoo here or hereabouts; and therefore friendship, with those who have been herein named, should be kept in mind as one of the principal maxims; in which case the trade will not only continue to flourish more and more, but the roads also will be safe for travelling in every direction, to search for what has not been hitherto found; and, as before observed, the Directors [of the Dutch East India Company—ed.] and their Honors at Batavia will be thus best satisfied; for it may be seen from the public and private letters from both quarters, that journeys for the purposes of discovery are not disapproved, but expressly ordered to be prosecuted with every assiduity; and therefore—so far from dissuading you from continuing them at fitting seasons of the monsoon—I would most earnestly recommend their being prosecuted with vigor at the seasons before mentioned.

And to give out any lands beyond the Company's enclosure, is, on account of the attendant expense of protecting the freemen, quite unadvisable; even should they be disposed to live out there at their own risk, we have never dared to venture upon it, for they would instantly lose their cattle, and would be robbed of them, even by our best friends—unless indeed any one were mad enough, and rich enough to hazard his own capital—but with the Company's means—upon which all the farmers here have been set up—this would be entirely wrong, and ought never to be thought of; for the Hottentoos, upon seeing the least opportunity, could not abstain from stealing the cattle, as we have, at full length and breadth, explained to the Directors. And for the same reason I would not venture to sell cattle, even for ready money, to any one who was about to farm there, for he would forthwith lose them, and would then be troubling the Company for more.

The slaves here learn nothing but Dutch, and also the Hottentoos, so that no other language is spoken here, and if this can be continued it will be a desirable thing, as it always will keep the Portuguese and others from communicating with these tribes, so that they will be the less able to mislead them, &c. Herry and Doman live chiefly here at the fort, as interpreters or advocates, the first, as it were, for the tobacco thieves, and the other for the Capemans. They get their food and drink from us, and they should continue to be thus supported, to bind them to the Company, and to keep mischief out of their heads; though indeed, now that we are so well supplied with horses, I do not think that they will easily be inclined to undertake any thing against us, so long as good attention is paid to the mounted guard and the outposts.

How the interpreter Eva is retained and treated has been already mentioned, and verbally communicated. She acts chiefly for the Saldanhars, and others who come from a distance.

As I cannot but think that every thing has now been detailed at sufficient length, I do not know what more I can say, than to repeat briefly the most advantageous, and the chief rules to be attended to, for the service of the Company, namely,

1st. That you always endeavour to live, and trade, in peace with these tribes, at the same time and for the same purpose, to penetrate—by parties of volunteers—further and further into the interior.

2d. To have constantly in readiness sufficient refreshments for the shipping.

3d. The necessary increase of the stock of cattle and sheep, and also of pigs, &c.

4th. To keep up the cultivation of corn, and as far as practicable to extend it more

and more, for the purpose of provisioning this Residency, and that the less food may be required from abroad.

5th. The cultivation of the olive, as urgently recommended by the last letter from the Directors.

And now, trusting that I have sufficiently explained the objects of our Honorable Masters. I shall conclude by recommending you to the merciful protection of the Almighty, and by recommending to you the command and management of affairs here in the manner most serviceable to the Hon. Company. In the Fort the Goede Hope, adij 5th May Ao. 1662. JAN VAN RIEBEECK

EXTRACTS OF A MEMORANDUM LEFT BY COMMANDER Z. WAGENAAR, BY ORDER OF THE DIRECTORS, FOR THE INFORMATION OF HIS SUCCESSOR, MR. C. VAN QUAELBERGEN, &C.[3]

.   .   .

Respecting these aboriginal inhabitants. And although Mr. van Riebeeck has written very clearly upon every point, and in particular, has given so good a sketch of the disposition, character, and habits of these greasy Africans, commonly called Hottentoos, that I might be well excused from making any allusion to the subject, I shall, nevertheless, take a brief view of these savages, *en passant,* that I may let you know, by way of warning, from what kind among that people, the Company has to look for the greatest advantage in that very essential point, the cattle trade, (without which, there would be very little for us to do here,) and who, on that account, ought to be gratified and well treated in preference to others.

The said Hottentoos then, who usually reside inland within a space of 40 or 50 mylen to the east and north of this Afri-

[3] This memorandum is dated September 24, 1666 (ed.).

can Cape, and are in the habit of wandering from one place to another with their cattle, for the sake of pasture, are, (in so far as they are, for the greater part, known to us,) divided into 9 hordes, or assemblages of families, or rather of villagers, or members of the same kraal: they are named

Goringhaiconas, Goringhaiquas, Gorachouquas, Cochoquas, Charequriquas, Namaquas, Chainouquas, Heusequas, and *Hancumquas.*

The Cochoquas bring us the greatest number of cattle. Of all these tribes we procure the greatest quantity of live stock, chiefly sheep, from the Cochoquas, they live to the north, towards Saldanha Bay, whence their name of Saldanhars. They consist of two divisions, under separate *Choques* or Chiefs, Oudasoa and Gonnoma; they were formerly, with the kraals under their authority, so strong, that both together might have mustered three thousand men capable of bearing arms; but they were, some time ago, very much diminished and melted away by a sickness which prevailed among them. The others, who are nearer to us, and are in the habit of bringing their cattle close to us for good pasture, are the Goringhaiquas, or the Capemans, thus called because they at first made pretensions to a right of property in this Cape land; with the Gorachouquas, nicknamed the tobacco thieves; but at present both kraals, exclusive of women and children, can scarcely make out 800 men. The last, namely, the Gorachouquas, are however, much richer in cattle than the first, and bring us for sale, now and then, a lean ox or cow, or a few sheep equally lean; and although such supplies are of little use to us, we receive, notwithstanding, all they offer us, whether it be large or small, young or old, fat or lean.

What is commonly given for their cattle. Neither do we allow them to stand long waiting, but give instantly what they desire in exchange, such as copper in plates, or brass in bars, various kinds of beads,

but chiefly a small blood red sort, or tobacco, the first thing they ask for; and when they have received for each cow, calf, or sheep, such a quantity of those articles of merchandize as has been long since brought into train, we give to each of them a dram (pimpeltje) of brandy, and occasionally, to such as bring us many, or very fine fat cattle, a little biscuit or boiled rice besides; and thus dismiss them well satisfied. In this, or in some such manner, it will be necessary to attract these strangers to us, and to keep the trade alive. But to sell them thin square bar iron, as the Cochoquas or Saldanhars would have recently wished, is by no means advisable, as they know how to beat it into *pickysers,* or sharp points for their arrows and assagais, and to harden it very tolerably; so that, should they again come to ask for this iron, you should, upon one pretence or other, decline supplying it.

The Goringhaiconas subsist in a great measure by begging and stealing. Among this ugly Hottentoo race, there is yet another sort called Goringhaiconas, whose chief or captain, named Herry, has been dead for the last three years; these we have daily in our sight and about our ears, within and without the fort, as they possess no cattle whatever, but are strandloopers, living by fishing from the rocks. They were at first, on my arrival, not more than 30 in number, but they have since procured some addition to their numbers from similar rabble out of the interior, and they now constitute a gang, including women and children, of 70, 80, or more. They make shift for themselves by night close by, in little hovels in the sand hills; in the day time, however, you may see some of the sluggards (*luyoerts*) helping to scour, wash, chop wood, fetch water, or herd sheep for our burgers, or boiling a pot of rice for some of the soldiers; but they will never set hand to any work, or put one foot before the other, until you have promised to give them a good quantity of tobacco or food, or drink. Others of the lazy crew, (who are much worse still, and are not to be induced to perform any work whatever,) live by begging, or seek a subsistence by stealing and robbing on the common highways; particularly when they see these frequented by any novices out of ships from Europe.

Bold attempt of these Hottentoos. This was evident enough last year, when some men were ordered to go to the wood to assist in dragging out some timber; for, the corporal of the party being a little way behind with two soldiers who were carrying the provisions, and being attacked by seven or eight of those thieves, scarcely $1/4$ of a myl from the fort, stood up bravely in his own defence, not being inclined to part with his bread and cheese so cheaply; at last, however, he was so fearfully assailed from all sides with stones, that he was driven back and compelled to return to the fort with a bleeding pate.

In the same manner, shortly before, those vagabonds broke open a house at Salt River, belonging to a certain poor fisherman, and stole from it 200 guilders in cash, and all his little stock of tobacco, and food, and drink.

And although these, and similar daring acts require that an appropriate punishment should be inflicted upon those who commit them, or at least that this good for nothing gang should be denied a free access to the fort or the burgers' houses in the country, or entirely turned away from us; yet still we could not well dare to do so hitherto, for several reasons, but have winked at it all, and suffered it to pass unnoticed; for our masters in the Fatherland, in their letters from time to time, recommend to us nothing more earnestly than to deal with these men in a kind and peaceful manner; and not be too easily led to apply to them terms of opprobium, still less to kick, push, or ill use them, upon every slight cause of offence, so that they may not acquire any dislike towards us.

This was also the course followed by Mr. van Riebeeck, as you may see in several parts of the memoir left by him.

Who should one day be severely punished. But as, subsequently to his departure, this crew (*gespuys*) have not only (as before stated) increased in number, but have daily become more impudent and daring in the commission of every kind of mischief, we have deemed it as improper, as it is impossible, any longer to put up with such violence, breaches of the peace, and theft; but, ever since that time we have intended to have the first person that we can get hold of, who may be convicted of housebreaking or highway robbery, bound to a whipping post in front of the fort, and there to have his greasy hide so well rubbed down with good rods, that all his mischievous countrymen who might witness the punishment, should be frightened from the commission of the same offence; for to this it must come (would we live in peace and quiet) if we are annoyed by these *rappaille;* particularly because our honorable masters, upon our representations upon the subject, have been pleased to give their full approval and consent; but at the same time it will be much better and safer for us all if they will take a turn of their own accord, or if the greater part of the males could be induced to go away, without violence, than that the proposed punishment, or any kind of banishment should be resorted to. You will however be able to ascertain what may be hereafter the best course in this respect, with the aid of time and good counsel.

A close watch should also be kept on them. Meanwhile it will do no harm to keep a strict eye upon those idlers, while they are allowed to pass freely in and out, particularly now that all our soldiers are daily working upon the ditch of the new castle, and only 10 or 12 sick or lame men are on guard at the gate; for it has been seen already what these dirty creatures have dared to undertake against the Fort. It has been well apprehended and remarked by Commissioner Overtwater, (as you may see by the *memorie* he left here) that the maintenance of peace and concord with these tribes, should be attended by a proper degree of caution.

We also procure many cattle from the Chainouquas. For the last six years we have begun to be acquainted with the tribes who live to the Eastward, named the Chainouquas; and have always lived in perfect friendship with them, as we still do; they are very rich in cattle, for upon two missions which I sent to them in 1663 and 64, the first under fiscal Lacus, and the second under secretary Cretser, we procured 170 fine cattle and 400 sheep; and I would have sent a third party last year, but that we were then without tobacco, the merchandize chiefly in demand; we have however recently sent thither a party of 12 men under Mr. Cretser, and I hope that before my departure he may return with a good herd.

Which excites the jealousy of the Cochoquas. In consequence of Sousoa the chief of the Chainouquas not only inviting us into his country, but sending oxen to carry our provisions and merchandize; and of our availing ourselves of his invitation and assistance, the Saldanhars—and particularly the chief Oudasoa [*Oudasoa's proposal*]—conceived such a jealousy of them, that he came to the Fort and apprised us that he meant to make war upon Sousoa (who is since dead) as he could no longer suffer him to play the master every where; and requesting, not only the aid of some troops, but that we would take charge of 2500 of his cattle during the war, promising to send us, in 3 or 4 days, 600 cattle in payment, and an equal number in the event of his getting the victory; but after mature consideration, it appeared to us that the proposal would lead to much embarrassment, and perhaps eventually to some dispute, and we civilly declined his offer, allowing him to go away rather dissatisfied. The Directors have fully approved of our conduct in this respect, as may be seen by their letter of Oct. 8, 1664, in which they state their desire, that we should not concern ourselves with the mutual disputes or wars of these inland tribes; which will serve as a rule for your guidance under similar circumstances. Meanwhile it would appear that Oudasoa still feels much vexed, for it is more than 2 years since he has been in the Fort.

The Namaquas recently discovered. Of the Namaquas whom we first discovered in 1661, and who are a very *robust* people; as also of the tribes bordering on them to the Eastward, and who are all very rich in cattle, I am unable to add any thing to the remarks of Mr. Van Riebeeck, as contained in his memoir, to which I will merely refer, and pass on to some thing else.

26 ANDREW SPARRMAN
THE BOERS

Andrew Sparrman was a Swede who studied medicine at the University of Uppsala and subsequently accompanied Captain James Cook to the Antarctic as assistant naturalist. Between 1772 and 1776 he traveled in the Cape Colony, and although he was primarily concerned with its fauna, he provided the first complete description of the character, manners, and attitude of the Boer settlers at the frontier. The following selection was written in January 1776.

From Andrew Sparrman, *A Voyage to the Cape of Good Hope from 1772 to 1776* (2nd ed.; London: Robinson, 1786), pp. 164–169.

All the colonists who follow the grazing business, and particularly those at *Agter Bruntjes-boogte,* lead an easy and pleasant life. One of these boors usually puts to his plough eight or ten of his fat, or rather pampered oxen; and it is hardly to be conceived, with what little trouble he gets into order a field of a moderate size; and in consequence of his feeding so great a number of cattle, how easily he can render it in the highest degree fertile. So that, always sure of a rich harvest from a soil not yet worn out, and ever grateful to the culture bestowed upon it, he may be almost said merely to amuse himself with the cultivation of it, for the bread he wants for himself and his family; while many other husbandmen must sweat and toil themselves almost to death, both for what they use themselves, and for that which is consumed by others, who frequently live in ease and indolence. By his extensive pastures, and by throwing a sufficient quantity of land into tillage, he rears a considerable number of horses, which frequently are used only a few days in a year, for the purpose of treading out and threshing his corn. With pleasure, but without the least trouble to himself, he sees the herds and flocks, which constitute his riches, daily and considerably increasing. These are driven to pasture and home again by a few Hottentots or slaves, who likewise make the butter; so that it is almost only with the milking, that the farmer, together with his wife and children, concern themselves at all. To do this business, however, he has no occasion to rise before seven or eight o'clock in the morning; and notwithstanding his having enjoyed his bed so long in the morning, he can afford, without neglecting any thing of consequence, to allow himself an afternoon's nap, which the heat of the climate renders more agreeable than it is in our northern regions.

That they might not put their arms and bodies out of the easy and commodious posture in which they had laid them on the couch, they have been known to receive travellers lying quite still and motionless, excepting that they have very civilly pointed out the road, by moving their foot to the right or left. Professor THUNBERG, who has had greater opportunities than I had of exploring the warmer *Carrow* districts, where the inhabitants were still more indolent, has given me an account much to the same purpose.

The leaning of their arms on the table at meal times, is a custom very common with the colonists, and considered by them as a very laudable one, and in this particularly I followed my host's example; but I could not sufficiently admire the inventive spirit of idleness, exhibited in the voluptuous posture in which they universally indulge themselves when they smoke their pipes. Sitting on a bench or a chair without elbows, with their backs moderately bent, they lay their left leg over their right knee, and upon the left knee again thus raised, they rest their left elbow, while with the hand on the same side they support their chin, or one of their cheeks, at the same time holding their pipes in their mouths. Their right hand is then at liberty to grasp the small of their left leg with, or else to convey now and then to their mouth a cooling draught of tea. Let the reader represent to himself several people sitting together in this posture, and he will readily conceive what an elegant figure they would make in a group. I never saw any of the fair sex, however, in a posture of this kind. Among a set of beings so entirely devoted to their ease, one might naturally expect to meet with a variety of the most commodious easy chairs and sofas; but the truth is, that they find it much more commodious to avoid the trouble of inventing and making them.

I remarked as a very singular circumstance, that a wealthy farmer at *Agter Bruntjes-boogte,* who had plenty of timber to sell, had nevertheless only a ricketty elbow-chair in his house, and a few scanty stools of the most simple construction, made of a single board, with four rough-hewn ill-shapen legs. What, however, was still more singular was, that notwithstanding that one of these stools had lost a leg, yet it was frequently made use of to the endangering of the person's limbs who sat upon it, without either the master of the house or any of his three sons, who were otherwise all alert enough at the chase, having ever once thought of mending it. Nor did the inhabitants of this place exhibit much less simplicity and moderation, or to speak more properly, slovenliness and penury in their dress than in their furniture; neither of which, therefore, were in any wise correspondent to the large flocks and herds possessed by these graziers, and the plentiful tables they could afford to keep in consequence of these possessions. The distance at which they are from the Cape, may, indeed, be some excuse for their having no other earthenware or china in their houses, but what was cracked or broken; but this, methinks, should not prevent them from being in possession of more than one or two old pewter pots, and some few plates of the same metal; so that two people are frequently obliged to eat out of one dish, using it besides for every different article of food that comes upon table.

Each guest must bring his knife with him, and they frequently make use of their fingers instead of forks. The most wealthy farmer here is considered as being well dressed in a jacket of home-made cloth, or something of the kind made of any other coarse cloth, breeches of undressed leather, woollen stockings, a striped waistcoat, a cotton handkerchief about his neck, a coarse calico shirt, Hottentot field-shoes, or else leathern-shoes, with brass buckles, and a coarse hat. Indeed it is not in dress, but in the number and thriving condition of their cattle, and chiefly in the stoutness of their draught-oxen, that these peasants vie with each other. It is likewise by activity and manly actions, and by other qualities, that render a man fit for the married state, and the rearing of a family, that the youth chiefly

obtain the esteem of the fair sex; none of whom likewise were ever known, for the sake of vying with each other in point of dress, to have endangered either their husband's property or their own virtue. A plain close cap, and a coarse cotton gown, virtue and good housewifery, are looked upon by the fair sex as sufficient ornaments for their persons; a flirting disposition, coquetry and paint, would have very little effect in making conquests of young men, brought up in so hardy a manner, and who have had so homely and artless an education, as the youth in this place. In short, one may here, if any where in the world, lead an innocent, virtuous, and happy life.

When in company with these plain artless husbandmen, I used frequently to start such questions and subjects of conversation, as tended to give them a proper sense of the happiness of their situation, and make them set a higher value upon it, than they perhaps had done before. Indeed, I thought I could not more properly or more agreeably employ the little Dutch I had learned, than in persuading the good people among whom I sojourned, to be content with their lot, and consequently to be happy. One day, when I was urging this point, I received the following pertinent, but kind reply, from a discreet sensible woman, who was daughter to an inferior magistrate at *Zwellendam,* and was married to a yeoman in this place.

"My good friend, said she, you talk like a prudent sensible man; I am quite of your opinion, and wish you every happiness that can attend you: why need you wander any longer up and down the world in quest of happiness? You find it here, and are welcome to enjoy it among us. You have already a waggon, oxen, and saddle horses; these are the chief things requisite in order to set up a farmer; there are yet uncultivated places enough in this neighbourhood, proper either for pasturage or tillage, so that you may choose out of an extensive tract of land the spot that pleases you best. Here are people enough, who will send you that part of their cattle to keep which they cannot conveniently look after themselves, on conditions that you shall have the young ones produced by them for your trouble. In this way, many young beginners have acquired a competency in a few years. With your knowledge of disorders and plants, you may render yourself serviceable to your neighbours, and now and then get a heifer or a calf. In short, I will venture to prophesy, that you will soon have cows and sheep in abundance. Yet there is still somewhat wanting, which is most essential to your happiness; this is, a prudent and discreet wife: take my advice and look about you, and I will take upon me to assure you, that you will not long be without one in this country."

This advice, so consonant to the voice of nature, and coming with such kind intention from the fair sex, could not but greatly affect me: it is remarkable, however, that the poor woman who gave it me, had herself a bad husband.

27 THOMAS PRINGLE
BOER MEETS BANTU

Thomas Pringle (1789–1834) was born in Scotland. Associated with various literary reviews as poet and editor, he emigrated from his homeland to South Africa in 1820 with the wave of British settlers and established his home in the Albany district of the Eastern Province. Finding the frontier too dull, he moved to Cape Town in 1822, where he became well known as the co-founder, with John Fairbairn, of the South African Commercial Advertiser, *as well as for the controversy surrounding the subsequent suppression of the publication for his outspoken comments on the autocratic actions of the governor, Lord Charles Somerset. Pringle returned to Britain in 1826 and a year later became Secretary of the Anti-Slavery Society. He published two volumes of poetry, the second of which included a description of his experiences in South Africa and some aspects of South African history. The following selection is taken from a republication of the prose section of this volume, entitled* Narrative of a Residence in South Africa, *in which Pringle provides his interpretation of the first contacts between the southern Nguni and the whites.*

The term *Caffer,* like that of *Hottentot,* is entirely unknown in the language of the people to whom it is applied. It was originally a term of contumely (being the Arabic word *Cafir* or *Kafir,* signifying *Infidel*) employed, by the Moorish or Arabian inhabitants of the north-eastern coast, to designate the nations of South-eastern Africa who had not embraced the Mohammedan faith; and from them the term was adopted by the early European navigators. The appellation, though sometimes still applied in a more extensive sense, is generally used, in the Cape Colony, to denote the three contiguous tribes of Amakosa, Amatembu, and Amaponda; of whom the last may be considered identical with the Mambo, or what used to be called the Mambookie, nation. These three tribes, though governed by several independent chiefs, are decidedly one people; their language, manners, customs, and polity being essentially the same. The Amakosa, whose territory borders with the colony from the Winterberg

From Thomas Pringle, *Narrative of a Residence in South Africa* (London: E. Moxon, 1840), pp. 92–95.

to the coast, is the tribe with whom our intercourse, both in peace and war, has been far the most frequent.

The Caffers are a tall, athletic, and handsome race of men, with features often approaching to the European or Asiatic model; and, excepting their woolly hair, exhibiting few of the peculiarities of the negro race. Their colour is a clear dark brown. Their address is frank, cheerful, and manly. Their government is patriarchal; and the privileges of rank are carefully maintained by the chieftains. Their principal wealth and means of subsistence consist in their numerous herds of cattle. The females also cultivate pretty extensively maize, millet, water-melons, and a few other esculents; but they are decidedly a nation of *herdsmen*—war, hunting, barter, and agriculture, being only occasional occupations.

In their customs and traditions, there seem to be indications of their having sprung, at some remote period, from a people of much higher civilisation than is now exhibited by any of the tribes of Southern Africa; whilst the rite of circumcision, universally practised among them, without any vestige of Islamism, and several other traditionary customs greatly resembling the Levitical rules of purification, would seem to indicate some former connexion with a people of Arabian, Hebrew, or, perhaps, Abyssinian lineage. Nothing like a regular system of idolatry exists among them; but we find some traces of belief in a Supreme Being, as well as in inferior spirits, and sundry superstitious usages that look like the shattered wrecks of ancient religious institutions. Of their superstitions, the belief in sorcery is far the most mischievous, leading, in the same way as among the negroes on the west coast, to many acts of revolting oppression and cruelty.

The clothing of both sexes consists entirely of the skins of animals, rendered soft and pliable by a sort of currying. Their arms are the assagai or javelin, a short club, and a large shield of bullock's or buffalo's hide. The wars between the contiguous tribes above-mentioned, or the several clans with each other, are seldom very bloody, generally arising from quarrels relating to their respective pasturegrounds or the stealing of cattle, and bearing little resemblance to the ferocious mode of warfare recently pursued with such destructive effect by the Zoola [Zulu —ed.] nations. The females are seldom slain in their internal wars; and in their conflicts with the colonists, there are many well-known examples of their humanity towards females who had fallen into their hands. They are *barbarians*, but not *savages*, in the strict and proper sense of the term.

It is a curious and characteristic circumstance that the earliest notice upon record of intercourse between the Cape colonists and the Caffers, is an account of a marauding expedition by a party of the former against the latter. In 1701, a band of Cape-Dutch freebooters, under the name of traders or barterers, marched to the eastward, and after an absence of seven months returned with a large quantity of cattle and sheep, which they had obtained by plundering a nation called Cabuquas, or Great Caffers, (probably Tambuquas, *i.e. Amatembu,*) together with two kraals of Hottentots. In the attacks made upon these then remote tribes, numbers of the natives had been slaughtered. The facts are stated in a despatch sent to Holland in 1702 by the Governor and Council of the Cape of Good Hope, who, while they deplore "the intolerable and continued excesses of some of the free inhabitants, in committing acts of violence, with robberies and murders, and by these abominable means depriving those poor people of their subsistence," declare at the same time their inability to punish the delinquents.

The impunity thus enjoyed by the colonial freebooters (who consisted for the most part of the very refuse of Europe, disbanded soldiers from mercenary regiments in the Dutch service, and the like), led, as was to be expected, to the frequent renewal of similar marauding excursions. By this means, and by the gradual occupation of all the best parts of the country, the Hottentot race were, as we have seen, at length either extirpated, reduced to thraldom, or driven to the northern deserts. The Caffers, a more numerous and warlike people, and acting together in large masses, were not so easily overwhelmed. They appear to have successfully resisted on many occasions the attacks of the colonists; but, having only their slender missiles to oppose to the musket, they also often suffered dreadfully from their aggressions.

The Caffers had been for several generations gradually pressing upon the Hottentot race from the eastward. This is not only known from traditionary memorials, but is manifest from most of the names of the rivers west of the Kei being of Hottentot etymology. The Hottentot hordes do not appear to have been extirpated by them, but to have been partly pushed farther westward, and partly incorporated with their frontier clans. The Ghonaqua tribe, once numerous and powerful, consisted of a people of mixed Caffer and Hottentot lineage; and the dialect now spoken by the frontier Caffers partakes to a certain extent of the Hottentot *cluck,* a peculiarity not to be found among the tribes farther back.

The country between the Camtoos and Great Fish rivers was, up to 1778, partly occupied by the Ghonaqua tribes and other hordes of Hottentots still enjoying a precarious independence, partly by Caffer clans, intermingled with the Ghonaquas, and partly by European colonists, who, in defiance of the colonial regulations, had taken possession of the choicest spots they could find beyond the nominal boundary—then Camtoos River. In 1778, the Governor, Van Plattenberg, having, in the course of an extensive tour which he made into the interior, visited Bruintjes-hoogtè, and finding a considerable number of colonists occupying tracts

beyond the frontier, instead of recalling them within the legal limits, he extended the boundary (according to the ordinary practice of Cape Governors, before and since), adding, by a stroke of his pen, about 30,000 square miles to the colonial territory. It was at this period that the Great Fish River was first declared to be the colonial boundary on the east. The rights of the Ghonaquas and other independent Hottentot tribes within the extensive region thus acquired, do not appear to have occupied a single thought; the Boors were left to deal with them as they had dealt with their brethren already extinct: but with the more formidable Caffers the *form* of an agreement was observed. Colonel Collins relates that Colonel Gordon was sent in search of Caffers as far as the Keiskamma, and that he conducted "a few" to the Governor, who obtained their consent that the Great Fish River should thenceforth be considered the boundary between the two countries.

Who were "the few" that concurred in this agreement, it would be vain to inquire; but it is certain that the principal Caffer chiefs who had an interest in the affair refused to recognize it. Jalumba, then chief of the Amandanka clan of the Amakosa, endeavoured to maintain his ground in Bruintjes-hoogtè. "The *inhabitants,*" says Col. Collins, "reminded Jalumba (in 1781) of the recent treaty, and required his immediate departure. Their remonstrance having been disregarded, a commando assembled, by which the intruders were expelled with the loss of Jalumba and a great number of his followers. His son Dlodlo perished two years afterwards, in a similar attempt." Such is the colonial account of the affair; but Col. Collins, who derived his information entirely from the Boors and local functionaries, has not mentioned that on this occasion the expedition (of which Adrian Van Jaarsveld was the leader) plundered the Caffers of 5,200 head of cattle, which he divided "after consultation with the Veld-wagtmeester and corporals, amongst the commando." Nor was this the worst. We have got from Mr. Brownlee the Caffer account of the transaction, which is at least as much deserving of credit as the reports of the colonists who had enriched themselves with the spoils of the slaughtered Caffers; and from this it appears, that Jalumba and his clan were destroyed by a most infamous act of treachery and murder. The details may be found in the works both of Thompson and Kay. Vaillant, who spent a considerable time in this part of the country in the following year (1782), gives an account of the spirit of the frontier boors, and of the oppressions perpetrated upon the Caffers, that but too well accords with the story told by Mr. Brownlee, from Caffer tradition, of the massacre of the Amandanka. "A mulatto colonist," he says, "informed me that the report of this nation being barbarous and bloody was industriously circulated by the colonists, in order to justify the atrocious thefts they were daily guilty of towards them, and which they wished to have passed for reprisals. That they often formed pretences of losing cattle, purposely to make inroads into the Caffers' settlements, exterminating whole hordes without distinction of age or sex, carrying away their herds, and laying waste the country; this means of procuring cattle appearing much easier than the slow method of breeding them. In this manner, Hans assured me, twenty thousand head had been obtained the last year." After giving some details of particular atrocities reported to him, and making some very pertinent remarks upon the flagitious impunity enjoyed by these barbarous backsettlers, Vaillant states that when he expressed to one of them his surprise that the governor did not send down a troop of soldiers to arrest those who committed such acts in defiance of all authority, the Boor replied, that if such a thing were attempted, they would kill half the soldiers, and send them back salted by those that were spared, as an earnest of what they would do to any

authority that should dare to interfere with them! Such were the men who rose in arms in 1796, and again in 1815, against the British Government, in order to vindicate their right to rob and murder the natives without control!

Nearly about the same period, Zaka, the head of the Gunuquebi clan, with some other bands of the Amakosa, had obtained possession of the Zureveld, by purchasing with a large number of cattle permission to settle there from Kohla (called by the colonists Ruiter), who was then chief of the Ghonaqua Hottentots, the original possessors of the country. The colonists at the same time advanced into the Zureveld from the west. For a number of years the Boors and the Caffers occupied that district together, with their habitations and herds amicably intermingled; until, in 1786, some differences arising between them, the colonists called in the chief Islambi, the enemy of Zaka, to their assistance. The latter chief, being attacked simultaneously by the Boors on one side and by Islambi with 3000 warriors on the other, was defeated and slain; and his tribe (the Gunuquebi) were plundered by the confederates of almost the whole of their cattle, and driven by necessity to plunder the colonists for means of subsistence. The Boors, however, did not by this means accomplish their object. Kongo, the son of Zaka, having been soon afterwards joined by Maloo, Toli, Etoni, and several other chiefs at enmity with Islambi and Gaika, and by the remnant of the Amandanka under Olila the brother of Jalumba, the Gunuquebi, with their allies, re-established themselves in the Zureveld, in spite of the colonists, and plundered them in their turn of many cattle; and it is from the period of this struggle, and from the destruction of the Amandanka in Bruintjes-hoogtè, that the bitter animosity of the border tribes, formerly friendly, and their extensive depredations against the colonists, are to be dated.

In consequence of the representations

of the colonists, a large commando of Burgher militia was collected in 1793, to chastise the Caffers. This force, under the command of Mr. Maynier, landdrost of Graaff-Reinét, marched through the Zureveld, and penetrated into the Amakosa country, four days' journey beyond the Great Fish River, driving the natives everywhere before them into the woods, and capturing some herds of cattle; but without obtaining any decided advantage over the enemy, who, as soon as the commando retreated, returned to their former position. A treaty was at length concluded, leaving things precisely as they were, and in which, as Colonel Collins remarks, nothing was mentioned about the retreat of the Caffers from the disputed territory. In a report made to Government by the landdrost, Maynier, respecting the causes of this war, he observes, "that the excursions of the Boors into Cafferland for the purpose of hunting, the trade carried on between them and the Caffers, and the improper treatment which the latter had experienced from the former when in their service, were the principal occasions of the rupture."

In 1795, the colony was captured by the British arms; and the Boors of the Graaff-Reinét district having in the following year driven away their new magistrate, Mr. Bresler, the whole of the eastern province was thrown into a state of the utmost anarchy. Some of the Caffer chiefs were instigated by the colonists to attack the British troops who had been sent down by Sir James Craig to maintain order. Many of the Hottentots, as has been already noticed, availing themselves of the crisis, rose against their masters, and prevailed on the Caffer clans of the Zureveld to join them in plundering and driving out the frontier Boors, who were thus caught in the net of mischief they had themselves spread; and devastation and bloodshed continued to prevail for several years, during which much misery and many barbarities were reciprocally inflicted by both parties.

Such was the state of affairs on the eastern frontier in 1797, when Earl Macartney assumed the government, and Mr. Barrow was sent on a mission to Cafferland, of which he has given so interesting an account in his able work on the colony. The policy of the British government towards the native tribes at this period was unquestionably characterised by a spirit of justice and benevolence. The firm repression by Sir James Craig of an audacious attempt by the Boors of Bruintjes-hoogtè to obtain permanent possession of the country on the Kat and Koonap rivers; the testimony of Mr. Barrow on that subject; and the tone of Lord Macartney's proclamation of July 14, 1798, in establishing a fixed boundary for the colony, afford satisfactory evidence of the enlightened sentiments by which those Governors were actuated. But some great and lamentable mistakes were also then committed. The unjust and mischievous policy was adopted of treating with *one* Caffer chief instead of those who were far more directly interested in the question of boundaries; and this, notwithstanding that Gaika, while he stated truly enough that he was the chief first in *rank* on the frontier (for he was secondary to Hinza in the Amakosa tribe), carefully informed Mr. Barrow at the same time that those who held possession of tracts of country west of the Great Fish River, "were chiefs as well as himself, and entirely independent of him." No consideration was had to the claims of the Caffer chiefs in the Zureveld, who absolutely refused to accede to the treaty with Gaika or to leave the country, which they considered, and not without good reason, as their own both by purchase and conquest. Still less consideration appears to have been given to the yet more indisputable rights of the aborigines of the soil, the Ghonaquas, and other Hottentot hordes, to whom had originally belonged the large tract of country usurped so unscrupulously by Governor Plettenberg in 1778. The limits then assigned to the colony were now reclaimed without qualification, by the proclamation of Earl Macartney.

For the details of the policy pursued towards the Caffers for the twelve years which followed Mr. Barrow's embassy to Gaika, I must refer to the works of that writer and of Lichtenstein, and to the more recent publications of Thompson, Bannister, and Kay. The Gunuquebi clan, under Kongo, kept possession of the fastnesses of the Zureberg and the adja-

cent country, to the mouths of the Bushman and Sunday rivers. Islambi, who was at war with Gaika, had also crossed the Great Fish River, and fixed himself in the Zureveld. Their alliance with the insurgent Hottentots has been already mentioned. With the Boors they were sometimes at war, and sometimes living in precarious truce.

28 HENRY FRANCIS FYNN
SHAKA

Henry Francis Fynn arrived in South Africa in 1818, and six years later went to Port Natal as leader of an expedition of the Farewell Trading Company that was sent to open up the eastern coast. Soon after his arrival he visited Shaka, ruler of the Zulu state. Fynn's accounts of the events of this time and of Nguni history are the earliest and most reliable surviving record. Fynn remained at Port Natal and traded with Shaka and his successor, Dingane, until 1834, after which time he became an interpreter to Governor Benjamin D'Urban and British Resident for various southern Nguni chiefdoms. In 1852 he returned to the British colony of Natal, where he served as a magistrate and was regarded as an expert on native affairs. He never published the book based on his experience that he had intended to publish because he lost the original of his journal, but his writings have been preserved in the works of other travelers and annalists and in government reports. Fynn died in Natal in 1861.

I may at once state that the distance from the port to Shaka's residence was 200 miles. Our progress was exceedingly slow, each day's journey being arranged by Mbikwana [Shaka's uncle—ed.]. We afterwards found out that he had not taken us by a direct route, but to kraals of minor chiefs and some of the barracks of Shaka's regiments. Cattle-slaughtering occurred sometimes twice and thrice a day. Numbers of Zulus joined our column in order to relieve Mbikwana's peo-

ple of their burdens. We were struck with astonishment at the order and discipline maintained in the country through which we travelled. The regimental kraals, especially the upper parts thereof, also the kraals of chiefs, showed that cleanliness was a prevailing custom and this not only inside their huts, but outside, for there were considerable spaces where neither dirt nor ashes were to be seen.[1]

Frequently on the journey we saw large parties seated with grotesquely dressed men apparently lecturing in their midst,

From Henry Francis Fynn, *Diaries*, edited by James Stuart and Daniel McKinnon Malcolm (Pietermaritzburg, South Africa: Shuter & Shooter (Pty.) Ltd., 1950), pp. 70–80. Reprinted by permission. Except for two insertions in the texts delineated by brackets, the notes are those of James Stuart and Daniel McKinnon Malcolm.

[1] One afternoon seeing a flock of vultures near us, I shot one and on going to pick it up found they were devouring dead bodies, of which there were five. They appeared to have been killed the day before. Author's MS.

and on several occasions saw individuals seized and carried off and instantly put to death. The grotesque characters we learned were "witch finders" whilst those singled out and put to death were said to be "evil doers." [2]

Messengers passed three or four times a day between Shaka and Mbikwana, the former enquiring about our progress and doubtless directing how we should proceed so as to fall in with his own preparations for our reception. We had thus dallied 13 days on the road in travelling 200 miles, when the locality of Shaka's residence was pointed out to us about 15 miles off. While encamped that night we saw much commotion going on in our neighbourhood. Troops of cattle were being driven in advance; regiments were passing near by and on distant hills, interspersed with regiments of girls, decorated in beads and brass with regimental uniformity, carrying on their heads large pitchers of native beer, milk and cooked food. The approaching scene we anticipated witnessing cheered us considerably that evening. Farewell and Petersen expressed extreme affection and attachment for one another, with mutual apologies for past small differences.

It was not until ten o'clock the following morning that a proposal was made about advancing. In about two hours we arrived at a ridge from which we beheld an extensive and very picturesque basin before us, with a river running through it, called the Umfolozi. [3]

We were requested to make a stand under a large euphorbia tree, from whence, about a mile before us, we saw the residence of Shaka, viz: a native kraal nearly two miles in circumference.

While in this position, messengers went backwards and forwards between Mbikwana and Shaka. At length one came and desired Mr. Farewell and myself to advance, leaving Mr. Petersen and our servants and native followers, who were carrying Shaka's present, at the euphorbia tree. Mbikwana and about 20 of his followers accompanied us.

On entering the great cattle kraal we found drawn up within it about 80,000 natives in their war attire. [4] Mbikwana requested me to gallop within the circle, and immediately on my starting to do so one general shout broke forth from the whole mass, all pointing at me with their sticks. I was asked to gallop round the circle two or three times in the midst of tremendous shouting of the words, "UJojo wokhalo!" (the sharp or active finch of the ridge). [5] Mr. Farewell and I

<hr />

[2] One day we arrived at a large kraal containing 190 huts, the barracks of one of Shaka's regiments. We had not been there many minutes before our attention was drawn to a party of 150 natives sitting in a circle with a man opposite them, apparently interrogating them. In reply, they each beat the ground with a stick and said, He-sa-gee! [Yizwa Zhi! Editor.] After they had been answering with the same word about an hour, three of them were pointed out and killed on the spot. This man, whom they called an inyanga, or as we should say a necromancer, was dressed in an ape skin cap; a number of pieces of different roots were tied round his neck; and a small shield and assegai were in one hand, and the tail of a cow in the other. He was an interpreter of dreams and thought capable of telling what has happened in any other part of the country, also if one has injured another by poison or otherwise. His decision is fatal to the unfortunate individuals pointed out by him. Author's MS.

[3] Evidently the Umhlathuze is meant, for the Umfolozi cannot be seen from the position the travellers had now got to. Editor.
[4] "On entering its gates we perceived about 12,000 men in their war attire, drawn up in a circle to receive us." The author here refers to warriors only, whereas in the text he includes regiments of girls, women, servants, etc., as well. Editor.
[5] Literally the words mean: Long tailed Finch of the Ridge, which implies that the person to whom the words are applied is quick and brave in attacking and overcoming his enemy. Editor.

It is customary for the principal warriors of each regiment, in their war dances, to dance forwards [i.e. each dances a pas-seul by rushing forwards, gesticulating as he does so with the shield and weapons he is carrying.—Editor.], when they are applauded by their own heroic names. They, therefore, on the occasion in question, considered I was adopting their own practice, hence cheered me by a phrase or name commonly found among their own heroes. On entering the kraal's gates . . . we were desired to gallop two or three times round, then twice more; then to return and bring the remainder of the party with us. We were desired to gallop four times more round the kraal and then stand all together about were then led by Mbikwana to the head of the kraal, where the masses of the people were considerably denser than elsewhere. The whole force remained stationary, as, indeed, it had been since the commencement of the reception.

Mbikwana, standing in our midst, addressed some unseen individual in a long speech, in the course of which we were frequently called upon by him to answer "*Yebo,*" that is to affirm as being true all he was saying, though perfectly ignorant of what was being said.[6]

While the speech was being made I caught sight of an individual in the background whom I concluded to be Shaka, and, turning to Farewell, pointed out and said: "Farewell, there is Shaka." This was sufficiently audible for him to hear and perceive that I had recognised him. He immediately held up his hand, shaking his finger at me approvingly. Farewell, being near-sighted and using an eye-glass, could not distinguish him.[7]

Elephant tusks were then brought forward. One was laid before Farewell and another before me.[8] Shaka then raised the stick in his hand and after striking with it right and left,[9] the whole mass broke from their position and formed up into regiments. Portions of each of these rushed to the river and the surrounding hills, while the remainder, forming themselves into a circle, commenced dancing with Shaka in their midst.[10]

It was a most exciting scene, surprising to us, who could not have imagined that a nation termed "savages" could be so disciplined and kept in order.

Regiments of girls, headed by officers of their own sex, then entered the centre of the arena to the number of 8,000–10,000, each holding a slight staff in her hand. They joined in the dance, which continued for about two hours.

Shaka now came towards us, evidently to seek our applause. [The following from Bird's *Annals of Natal,* contributed by the author, describes the scene.] "The King came up to us and told us not to be afraid of his people, who were now coming up to us in small divisions, each division driving cattle before it. The men were singing and dancing and whilst so doing advancing and receding even as one sees the surf do on a seashore. The whole country, as far as our sight could reach, was covered with numbers of people and droves of cattle. The cattle had been assorted according to their colour. . . . After exhibiting their cattle for two hours, they drew together in a circle, and sang and danced to their war song. Then the people returned to the cattle, again exhibiting them as before, and, at intervals, dancing and singing. The women now entered the kraal, each having a long thin stick in the right hand, and moving it in time to the song. They had not been dancing many minutes, when they had to make way for the ladies of the seraglio [harem—ed.], be-

---

20 yards from a large tree at the head of the kraal. Author's note.

The probabilities are that Fynn began galloping alone, hence he was acclaimed, his prowess as a pioneer doctor having already become known, as stated in the text, and that in the succeeding gallops he was accompanied by Farewell. *Editor.*

[6] Evidently the King, but Shaka was so surrounded by his chiefs that we could not see him. Author's note.

[7] A speech in answer to Mbikwana's was then made by a chief opposite. Author's note.

[8] Mbikwana now made another speech. Author's MS.

[9] "and springing out from amidst the chiefs." Author's MS.

[10] In another MS. Fynn has: The whole body then ran to the lower end of the kraal, leaving us alone, with the exception of one man who had been hidden

in the crowd. This man proved to be a native of the Cape Frontier, who had been taken prisoner in a war between the Colonists and Kaffirs and sent to Robben Island. Captain Owen of the *Leven* had taken him as an interpreter to attend him during his survey of the Eastern coast. Afterwards the interpreter had been given over to Farewell on his voyage to St. Lucia Bay. There he ran off and sought protection with Shaka, who gave him the name of Hlambamanzi, denoting one who had crossed (swum) the water. Among the colonists he had been known by the name of Jacob Sumbiti. He spoke good Dutch.

Further particulars about this man will be found in Isaacs, *Travels and Adventures in Eastern Africa,* II, 251–58, 264–69; Owen, *Narratives of Voyages to Explore Shores of Africa, Arabia and Madagascar,* I, 59, II, 222. *Editor.*

sides about 150 others, who were called sisters. These danced in parties of eight, arranged in fours, each party wearing different coloured beads, which were crossed from the shoulders to the knees. Each wore a head-dress of black feathers, and four brass collars, fitting closely to the neck. When the King joined in the dance, he was accompanied by the men. This dance lasted half an hour. The order observed and the precision of every movement was interpreted to us by his interpreter, Hlambamanzi. He desired to know from us if ever we had seen such order in any other state, assured us that he was the greatest king in existence, that his people were as numerous as the stars, and that his cattle were innumerable. The people now dispersed, and he directed a chief to lead us to a kraal where we could pitch our tents. He sent us a sheep, a basket of corn, an ox, and a pot of beer, about three gallons. At seven o'clock, we sent up four rockets and fired off eight guns. He sent people to look at these, but from fear did not show himself out of his hut. The following morning we were requested to mount our horses and proceed to the King's quarters. We found him sitting under a tree at the upper end of the kraal decorating himself and surrounded by about 200 people. A servant was kneeling by his side holding a shield above him to keep off the glare of the sun. Round his forehead he wore a turban [11] of otter skin with a feather of a crane erect in front, fully two feet long, and a wreath of scarlet feathers, formerly worn, only, by men of high rank. Ear ornaments made from dried sugar cane, carved round the edge, with white ends, and an inch in diameter, were let into the lobes of the ears, which had been cut to admit them. From shoulder to shoulder, he wore bunches, five inches in length, of the skins of monkeys and genets, twisted like

the tails of these animals. These hung half down the body. Round the ring on the head, [12] were a dozen tastefully arranged bunches of the loury feathers, neatly tied to thorns which were stuck into the hair. Round his arms were white ox-tail tufts, cut down the middle so as to allow the hair to hang about the arm, to the number of four for each arm. Round the waist, there was a kilt or petticoat, made of skins of monkeys and genets, and twisted as before described, having small tassels round the top. The kilt reached to the knees, below which were white ox-tails fitted to the legs so as to hang down to the ankles. He had a white shield with a single black spot, [13] and one assegai. When thus equipped he certainly presented a fine and most martial appearance.

While he was dressing himself, his people proceeded, as on the day before, to show droves of cattle, which were still flocking in, repeatedly varying the scene with singing and dancing. In the meantime, we observed Shaka gave orders for a man standing close to us to be killed, for what crime we could not learn, but we soon found this to be a very common occurrence." [14]

Mr. Petersen, unfortunately, at this moment placed a musical box on the ground, and, striking it with a switch, moved the stop. Shaka heard the music. It seemed to produce in him a superstitious feeling. He turned away with evident displeasure and went back immediately to the dance.

Those portions of regiments which had

[11] This word, often applied to Zulu head-dresses and especially Shaka's, seems to us inaccurate. Zulus do not wear turbans. They wear headbands or circlets cut out or made of various skins or other substances. *Editor.*

[12] This clearly proves that Shaka wore a head-ring (*isicoco*). We have sometimes heard doubts expressed on this point by Europeans. Well-informed natives, however, believe the King to have worn a ring, without, in these latter days, being able to prove it. The only portrait of Shaka we know of which can claim to be authentic (that in Isaacs' *Travels and Adventures in Eastern Africa,* I, 58) leaves one in doubt, for the band there shown round the head may well be the circlet or headband known as *umqhele. Editor.*

[13] Somewhat oval in shape (seven inches by five inches) about the size of a man's open hand. It was midway down the shield and on the right-hand edge thereof. *Editor.*

[14] Bird, *Annals of Natal,* I, 77.

separated prior to the dance now returned from the river and from behind the adjoining hills, driving before them immense herds of cattle. A grand cattle show was now being arranged. Each regiment drove towards us thousands of cattle that had been allotted to their respective barracks, the colour of each regiment's cattle corresponding with that of the shield the men carried, which, in turn, served to distinguish one regiment from another. No cattle of differing colour from those allotted to a given regiment were allowed to intermix. There were many droves without horns, others with pendulous projections, four or six inches long, which covered a considerable portion of the animal. The cattle of the other droves had four, six, and eight horns apiece. This show of cattle continued till sunset, with dancing at intervals, when we proposed to pitch the tents we had brought with us. A man was ordered to point out a spot for the purpose. Greatly to Farewell's astonishment, this man proved to be Jacob, his interpreter, who had landed at St. Lucia the year previous when he, Farewell, lost his boats and the sailors therein were drowned. Jacob had been taken to Shaka, who immediately appointed him one of the sentries for guarding his establishment.

Two oxen were slaughtered for us. After dinner we prepared to retire, but messengers from Shaka requested us to go to him, with Jacob the interpreter.[15] I was

then led into the seraglio, where I found him seated in a carved wooden chair and surrounded by about 400 girls, two or three chiefs and two servants in attendance.

My name Fynn had been converted into Sofili by the people in general; by this, after desiring me to sit in front of him, he several times accosted me in the course of the following dialogue:

"I hear you have come from um-George, is it so? Is he as great a king as I am?"

Fynn: "Yes; King George is one of the greatest kings in the world."

Shaka: "I am very angry with you," said while putting on a severe countenance. "I shall send a messenger to um-George and request him to kill you. He sent you to me not to give medicine to my dogs." All present immediately applauded what Shaka had said. "Why did you give my dogs medicine?" (in allusion to the woman I was said to have brought back to life after death).

Fynn: "It is a practice of our country to help those who are in need, if able to do so."

Shaka: "Are you then the doctor of dogs? You were sent here to be my doctor."

Fynn: "I am not a doctor and not considered by my countrymen to be one."

Shaka: "Have you medicine by you?"

Fynn: "Yes."

Shaka: "Then cure me, or I will have you sent to umGeorge to have you killed."

Fynn: "What is the matter with you?"

Shaka: "That is your business to find out."

Fynn: "Stand up and let me see your person."

---

[15] The first meeting of Shaka with Farewell, Fynn, and the rest of the party was manifestly a unique and memorable occasion. Instead of the formal, stiff and constrained ceremonial customary at such a moment, Shaka, whose heart had been mysteriously touched by the advent of British settlers to his shores, converted the occasion into a grand and dramatically planned festival. We cannot but think these warm-hearted exhibitions of regard should be attributed in the main to two influences seemingly trivial in themselves: (a) Jacob's previous lengthy contact with worthy officers of the Royal British Navy; (b) Fynn's discreet, courageous and humane bearing during the weeks he was striving to open up communication with Shaka. His spontaneous humanity straightway disarmed all suspicion and even caused him to be taken as typical of the race he belonged to. Thus, through the agency of Fynn

and Jacob, the British people henceforth began to stand in a favourable light. Shaka, despot though he was, one of the greatest the world has ever known, took them to his heart and, as will be seen, never failed to treat them as friends. More than this, the conviction then arrived at as to their friendliness has, after many sad and trying vicissitudes of later years, been honoured down to the present time. *Editor.*

Shaka: "Why should I stand up?"

Fynn: "That I may see if I can find out what ails you."

Shaka stood up but evidently disliked my approaching him closely. A number of girls held up lighted torches. I looked about his person and, after reflecting on the great activity he had shown during the day, was satisfied he had not much the matter with him. I, however, observed numerous black marks on his loins where native doctors had scarified him, and at once said he had pains in his loins. He held his hand before his mouth in astonishment, upon which my wisdom was applauded by all present. Shaka then strictly charged me not to give medicine to his dogs, and, after a few commonplace questions in which he showed good humour, I was permitted to retire for the night.[16]

Very few, if any, of the Zulu army had any sleep that night. Cattle were slaughtered in great numbers, and all the country round about was illuminated by the fires, around which the people sat in groups.

The following day had been appointed by Shaka for receiving our present, which, fortunately, had been well chosen by Farewell for presentation to so superior a chief as Shaka. It consisted of every description of beads at that time procurable in Cape Town, and far superior to those Shaka had previously obtained from the Portuguese at Delagoa. There was a great variety of woollen blankets, a large quantity of brass bars, turned and lacquered, and sheets of copper, also pigeons, a pig, cats and dogs. There was, moreover, a full-dress military coat, with epaulettes covered with gold lace. Though Shaka showed no open gratitude, we saw clearly that he was satisfied. He was very interested in the live animals, especially the pig, until it got into his milk stores where

it committed great havoc, and set all the women in the seraglio screaming for assistance. All this ended in the pig being killed.[17]

The showing of cattle and dancing continued during the day, whilst other regiments, which had come from a great distance, arrived and took part in the festivities. Among the articles we had brought were some Congreve rockets. These we kept back. On returning to our camp, as the evening was dark, we fired them off, having first informed Shaka, and asked him to order his people to look upwards. Their surprise was great; I, however, question if the showing of such wonders to ignorant natives is advisable after so short an acquaintance between white and black as ours had been. In conversation on our object in coming to Natal, this part of South Africa, Shaka showed great desire that we should live at the port. Each evening he sent for me and conversed with me through the Kaffir Jacob, the interpreter, for three or four hours.

On the first day of our visit we had seen no less than ten men carried off to death. On a mere sign by Shaka, viz: the pointing of his finger, the victim would be seized by his nearest neighbours; his neck would be twisted, and his head and body beaten with sticks, the nobs of some of these being as large as a man's fist. On each succeeding day, too, numbers of others were killed; their bodies would then be carried to an adjoining hill and there impaled. We visited this spot on the fourth day. It was truly a Golgotha, swarming with hundreds of vultures. The effects of this together with the scenes of death made Mr. Petersen decide at once to dissolve the partnership and leave for the Cape.

[16] I remained till ten o'clock when I left him with a promise that, agreeable to his request, I would remain with him a month after the departure of Messrs. Farewell and Petersen. Author's MS.

[17] The bringing of the live animals to Shaka was due to a suggestion by Shaka's uncle Mbikwana, who had returned with me to Natal to accompany us all to Shaka's residence. He asked us not to omit to take one of each species of domestic animals we had brought with us, among which was a pig. All were taken to the *isigodlo*, a seraglio, for the amusement of the women. Author's MS.

In the afternoon of the fifth day Shaka sent for me and requested me to proceed with some of his servants to a distant kraal where the chief Mupangazitha was very ill. I went and found him in high fever. I bled him, gave him medicine and caused him to be brought to a full perspiration. At midday on the following day he was able to report himself comparatively well.[18] As this captain was a great

favourite with Shaka, my success gave him much pleasure.

.   .   .

On taking leave of the King on the following morning, Shaka presented Farewell and myself with five elephant tusks each and 40 head of cattle, and promised he would send out his soldiers to kill elephants for us. I accompanied Messrs. Farewell and Petersen a few miles, returned to Shaka by sunset and sat with him two or three hours in the evening.

[18] Five days afterwards I heard of his final recovery. Author's note.

29 ANDREW GEDDES BAIN
THE NGWAKETSE DEFEAT THE KOLOLO

The rise of the Zulu under Shaka set in motion a chain of movements and wars known as the Mfecane *or, in Sotho, the* Difaqane. *These events were not often recorded by eyewitnessess who had seen them, so that any accounts dating from this time are valuable. Only on the eastern frontier, where British forces accidentally came into collision with the* Taung, *and in the western borderlands, where missionaries and travelers were just arriving, were such eyewitness accounts possible. Some of the best known of these accounts are of the Battle of Dithakong, during which the Griqua, armed with guns and mobilized on horses, defeated a large army of raiders that had been set on a career of destruction and killing by the Zulu eruption. Three years after the Battle of Dithakong, while traveling north from Kuruman and Dithakong to the country of the* Ngwaketse, *Andrew Bain and John Burnet Biddulph found the Ngwaketse driven from their capital by more of these raiders. Although the raiders were known indiscriminately as* Mantatees *(after the leader of one group who, in fact, never crossed the Vaal River), those that Bain and Biddulph encountered were the* Kololo, *led by Sebetwane. After the defeat of the Kololo by the Ngwaketse, Sebetwane gradually moved northward and eventually established the state north of the Zambezi where David Livingstone met Sebetwane in 1851, shortly before the death of the Kololo leader.*

Andrew Geddes Bain (1797–1864) immigrated to South Africa from Scotland in 1816 and settled in Graaff Reinet. He was apparently the first to take out a license to trade across the Orange River when this requirement was imposed in 1825. The following year Bain made a trip northward with John Biddulph. The following extract is from a journal kept by Bain of this journey in 1826. He made numerous other trips, participated in public affairs in the Cape, built roads, and fought in the frontier war of 1835; he seems always to have been a figure of controversy. The Bain's Kloof Pass not far from Cape Town was named after him.

From *Journals of Andrew Geddes Bain, Trader, Explorer, Soldier, Road Engineer, and Geologist,* edited by Margaret Hermina Lister (Cape Town: Von Riebeeck Society, 1949), XXX, 51–53, 56–60, 64–71. Reprinted by permission of the Van Riebeeck Society, South African Library, Cape Town.

We pursued our journey & in about an hour more reached the valley of Silaqualaly [1] which we found literally strewed with human sculls, it having been the theatre of a bloody battle between the Bawanketzie & the Mantatees in which Makabba, the celebrated King of the former & father of the present monarch, was killed. The sight of the sculls did not impress us with a great idea of the humanity of the natives, & we were not void of apprehensions that our own might bleach in the same spot in a few days. We met a great number of natives of both sexes as we rode up the valley, but it was dark before we reached the springs.

This evening at 7 o'clock we reached Siloquilaly, the springs which supply the town of the same name, at present the capital of the Wanketsie Kingdom & situated a mile & a half to the eastward. We were scarcely span'd out before the King's 2 brothers waited on us to welcome us to their country & brought a large bag of thick milk, as much as 2 men could carry, part of which they poured out in their hands & tasted to shew that it contained no poison. They placed sentinels round our waggons to prevent the mob from injuring anything & told us that Sibigho, the King, would visit us as soon as the moon should rise, which would be about 9 o'clock. We gave each of them a piece of tobacco with which they appeared exceedingly well pleased.

At 9 the King made his appearance attended by 5 or 6 of his principal people. He greeted us in a very friendly manner but with very little ceremony &, taking his seat on the ground close by us, entered cordially into conversation with us. His appearance is very prepossessing & would alone point him out as the Chief among all his subjects. He is above the common size, well made, & features more approaching the European than the Bechuana or negro. He was dressed in a jack-

alls Kabo, had his head wrapped in a large & beautiful snake's skin [2] & in his hand carried a handsome battle axe. On his legs, ancles & wrists he wore an unusual number of copper rings & bracelets of curious workmanship, some of which I was told were made by himself.[3]

As he had already testified his friendship for us by sending us a cow for slaughter & a large quantity of milk the moment we arrived at his place, we took the earliest opportunity of presenting him with some beads, a roll of tobacco, a tinder box & knife.

He said he was very glad we were come as he expected our assistance against the common enemy, the Mantatees, who killed his father & destroyed all their towns & had driven them about from place to place for the last 3 years. They were now living in miserable huts which he would be ashamed to shew us, instead of the comfortable dwellings they had been accustomed to. We told him we were sorry we were not in condition to contend with such formidable enemies as the Mantatees were represented to be, that our number was very small & besides they had not done us any harm; that we were peaceable people who had come to open a friendly trade with him & we trusted we might remain friends without espousing his cause against his enemies. "That cannot be," said he, "you have accepted of & given presents to us & we look upon you as our friends. If you are then what you pretend to be, you will join us

[1] Selokolela, near the present Kanye, BaNgwaketse Reserve, Bechuanaland Protectorate. Latitude 24 57. Biddulph's list.

[2] "As an antidote against the headache with which he was troubled." *Ibid.*
[3] "Round his ancles were four rows of beads of virgin gold which he said he had taken from a Mantatee chief whom he had killed in battle." From Extract from Bain's Journal, *S.A. Quarterly.* 1830, and *G.T. Journal.* Oct. 27th, 1855, and Bain's letter to *The S.A.C. Advertiser,* Nov. 14th, 1826. In a note for the *Quarterly* extract Bain writes, "That was the first and only time that I have ever met with that precious metal among the savages of Southern Africa." The omission of gold beads from the list of ornaments mentioned in the original journal may be accounted for by the fact that Bain first saw Sebego by moonlight and firelight, and probably mistook gold for copper.

against the common enemy of mankind. It is but a month ago that they drove us hither, robbed us of our cattle & took possession of our town which they now occupy about one day's journey to the N.E. of this, & we are in daily expectation of being again attacked by them here." To prevent which he intended risking an engagement with them in a couple of days in which he hoped (in self defence) we would assist him.

In vain did we represent our inability to assist him, that some of our people were sick & none of them accustomed to fight; that we did not wish to be enemies with any nation & that our King, who is a Mighty Monarch, would certainly punish us should we interfere with other people's quarrels without his consent. "You are now," resumed he, raising himself a little from the ground, "in my dominions and consequently under my orders. Every respect shall be shewn you & you shall be treated as great Captains, as you certainly are, but it is my pleasure that you join us to eradicate from the face of the earth, the plunderers of this & all the neighbouring kingdoms before you can again return to your own country."

This he spoke in rather an authoritative tone which did not please us, so we begged the subject might be dropped for the present thinking we could devise some method of avoiding the disagreeable alternative he left us. We then changed the conversation & chatted together till 11 o'clock when he left us in very good humour, leaving some people with us to guard the waggons.

. . .

Augt. 22nd. This day we bought a good many elephants teeth from Sibigho without anything of consequence happening, except his telling us that we must prepare ourselves to join in the attack against the Mantatees, as we could not otherwise leave his dominions, for as long as we were here we would be a protection to him, but he wished to drive them entirely

out of the country & then he would suffer us to go whenever we liked. This news rather disconcerted us as we were now entirely under his power. He had only to take possession of our oxen to secure us, which he hinted would be done if we did not resolve to join him. We again tried to laugh it off & succeeded in turning the conversation, but the respite was of very short duration.

At sunset the King & all the people left us except the guards who watched the waggons day & night, but in about 2 hours after Kooa, Malmanjana and three grave looking old men came with a message of great importance from Sibigho, which they said would require our immediate consideration. Their spies had brought them information that the Mantatees were preparing to attack them again & that the King had resolved to meet them, in which case it would be absolutely necessary that we should join them with a few muskets, which he did not doubt would put their enemies to the route. We had already urged every excuse that we could devise but to no purpose, so we now begged them to give us the night to think over the matter & they should have our answer in the morning.

Augt. 23rd. This morning Sibigho sent for us at sunrise, for which purpose we could easily guess. We found him as usual sitting under the large tree surrounded by his great folks. After a mutual pull of our noses, the two inverted dishes were brought & we were invited to drink a beverage called Bajalo or Beer made from the Caffer Corn. This stuff exactly resembled the sour wash with which in England pigs are supplied from the breweries but, out of compliment to the King, we were obliged to swig off a good draught & pronounce it *Munati* (excellent). It nearly turned Mr. Biddulph's stomach, but mine stood it tolerably well.

After sitting there a few minutes Sibigho, attended by his two brothers, who are his almost inseparable companions & councillors, & the other grave personages who formed the embassy to us the preceding evening, rose & beckoned to us to follow them, which we did, to the outskirts of the town where they all sat down on the ground bidding us follow their example. This party I suppose form the King's privy council, for we always found them consulted on every important occasion.

Sibigho then asked us if we had made up our minds, to which we replied in the affirmative. We had naturally considered his message of last night and found our only alternative was to join him with, at least, a seeming good will, in which case we would no doubt be well used during our stay, or be compelled to go, when we might not have that respect shewn us which we hitherto had had. We told him that we would join him, but as the Mantatees had done us no harm we would fire nothing but blank cartridges, & stipulated further that he should promise not to take more cattle from the enemy than they had plundered him of. They cheerfully consented to our terms though we had reason to doubt their sincerity. Their eyes glistened with joy & the whole party shouted with one impulse Sinkly! Munati! [4] (excellent! good!) & in the height of their transports nearly pulled our noses off our faces. Very few more words passed on this subject. He only told us his army was ready & they should march tomorrow morning.

.   .   .

Augt. 25th. The King requested one of us to come up to the Kraal to look out the oxen he had promised us to ride on, but we found they were not riding oxen but merely pack bullocks, which were of no use to us as we only wanted one for each of ourselves & people to ride on, knowing that we could not keep up on foot with the Wanketsie army. We were now put to our shifts; we had only one horse left & that very poor, & we dreaded the fatigue of the march. We proposed at first that Mr. B. & myself should ride & walk alternately & the people would be forced to trudge it all the way, when one of them told us that one of our draught oxen was an excellent riding one, so Mr. B. had it saddled up for himself & I mounted the horse.

When everything was ready we could not help smiling at the ludicrous appearance which our little party made on this important occasion. Mr. Biddulph was mounted on his war ox with his double barrel on his shoulder & his boat cloak bound in front to prevent his falling forward, & I on my Rosinante with an old horse pistol (for I had only one) fastened to the bow of my saddle without a holster case. The rest of my thunder & lightning was contained in a trusty old fowling piece which I bore in proud pomp on my right knee. Behind us followed 3 Hottentots, each with a good musket on his shoulder, & next to them came our interpreters Ias & Poloholo, the one with a gun & the other with an old Blunderbuss which closed our rear.[5]

The cloaths of our people, from the length of the journey and the bushy country thro' which we had passed, were reduced to tatters &, waving gracefully in the wind, answered all the purposes of Banners. Thus Hudibrastically equipped did we sally forth to conquer a mighty & warlike people who had been for upwards of 3 years the scourge & dread of all South Africa.

When we reached the top of Golgotha we found the army waiting for us. They rose and greeted us with becoming acclamations of joy & we advanced at their head in company with Sibigho. We could not help admiring the good order & discipline which prevailed among those people & the alacrity with which the Chief's orders were executed.

Their dress consisted of a panther's hide thrown carelessly over the shoulders;

[4] Sentle! Monate!

[5] "Our mustachios would have done honour to any officer in the Cape Corps." Bain's letter to *S.A.C. Advertiser.*

a lynx's skin, suspended round the neck & cut in an oval form, covered the lower part of the body. A white tuft of goat's hair made up in the shape of a sun & a plume of ostrich feathers crowned their heads which, from the way they were covered with Sibilo & fat, a good deal resembled a steel helmet when exposed to the rays of the sun. Each had a shield of white ox hide, generally with a black or brown spot in the middle, to which were fastened 3 to 6 assagais. It is suspended from the Chacka or Battleaxe which they carry over their left shoulders & dangles at their backs, the shafts of the assagais being upwards & the blades fixed in a pocket at the bottom of the shield.

.   .   .

Augt. 27th. The bags being filled with water we started at sunrise in the same manner as yesterday morning, & only proceeded a short way when the usual halt & semicircle were made, only with the difference that we observed small parties of men at regular distances from the main body seated under the trees. They were now preparing for battle, not the Chase. All being assembled Sibigho rose & called out Hey! to which a sort of suppressed grunt or hem (a sound difficult to describe) was coughed out by all the men at once as a mark of attention to the speaker. He then said "Silence, warriors!" & the grunt was repeated. Then waving his assagais over their heads pronounced "Maroomo!" [6] (which literally signifies Assagais, but is used on such occasions, according to our interpreter, metaphorically to express that nobody shall throw one away without making sure of killing an enemy). A whistle of applause thrilled thro' the ranks which was [undecipherable] succeeded by a dead silence, leaving us gazing at one another in admiration & surprise.

He commenced his harangue in words (as I imperfectly gleaned from our inter-

preter) something to the following effect:

"Bawanketsie warriors! The honor of your country is now at stake & you are called upon to protect it. Long, long have the scum & dread of the earth had possession of our finest fields, driven us from our once flourishing towns & are still feeding on the fattest of our flocks & herds. They have killed your late king, my father, who was the love of his subjects & the dread of his enemies. Shall we longer live in continual fear of such a scourge? No! the time is now come when we must rid ourselves of them for ever, that we may again restore peace to the world & claim its admiration as we were wont to do.

Fortune has favoured us by sending the Makooas to our country just as we were preparing to strike this decisive blow; but let not the brunt of the battle fall on them. Their thunder & lightning will strike terror on the enemy, but on your bravery alone do I trust. The Macooa are great Captains and have passed thro' our enemies to visit us; let them be witnesses of your courage that the fame of your glory may reach the most distant nations.

The Mantatees are numerous as the locusts of the field, but let not that discourage you, for the Bawanketsie have the hearts of lions." Here he was interrupted by a whistle of applause & he again proceeded: "Yes, the Bawanketsie alone have stemmed the torrent of the Makarie [7] (Mantatees) which swept from the face of the earth our once powerful neighbours, the Bamorootzie [8] and Bakweenie,[9] whose very names are now almost forgotten. Let them no more enter the territories of the sons of Meleta [10] where they butchered

[6] Marumo.

[7] Makgare, another name for Mmantatisi.
[8] BaHurutshe, a Tswana tribe who once owned the country round Zeerust, Transvaal. Skilled workers in iron. Kurrechane (Kaditshwene) their capital was a very large town. Campbell, in *Travels in South Africa,* London, 1822, gives an attractive picture of the tribe before it was destroyed by the Mmantatisi and MaTebele.
[9] BaKwena, Tswana tribe. Settled north of the BaNgwaketse.
[10] Moleta, father of Makabba II and grandfather of Sebego.

my renowned sire, Makkabba. Yes, his glorious name must rouse our hearts to vengeance! Revenge! Revenge! Revenge!"

So saying, with his eyes gleaming fire & in a fine theatrical attitude, he twirled his battleaxe in the air amidst the shrill plaudits of his host.

.   .   .

At sunset we bivouaced in a thick wood at a short distance from the enemy's town & no fires were allowed to be lit until the King returned about midnight from reconnoitring the position. Few of the people, however, availed themselves of this privilege, as they had no game to grill & were doubtless fatigued with their day's march & the gastronomical exercises of the preceding night.

The King was, notwithstanding, always on his legs examining everything of consequence with his own eyes, & indeed we were astonished at the precautions, foresight & military skill used by this intrepid Chief, which indicated a practical knowledge of his profession that would not have disgraced any European general. He slept none the whole night but conversed privately with his Captains on the best method of attack. In vain did we request him to inform us of his plans, our knowledge of which we said might prevent a deal of confusion in the hurry of battle, but the wary Chief, perhaps doubting the sincerity of the part we would play from our lukewarmness in joining him at the beginning, merely replied with a smile: "There will be no confusion but always time to execute my orders when I give them." Then turning coolly round continued his conversation in a whisper to his friends who surrounded him.

Augt. 28th. At 4 o'clock this morning we resumed our march in perfect silence &, leaving the thicket, entered a beautiful open vale that leads to the town of Letubaruba, whose vicinity became evident by the numerous tracks of cattle taking [the] place of those of elephants, etc.

Here the King sat down and formed his favourite semicircular phalanx. By the glimmering light of the waning moon their white shields & plumes were alone perceptible along the inside of the crescent. After the usual preliminaries of calling to order, Sibigho rose &, in an animated speech of some length but of purport similar to that of yesterday, addressed his army, to which they frequently testified their approbation, not by noisy shoutings or clapping of hands, but their usual singular note whistled thro' their teeth. After the King had concluded, several Captains harangued them & each in his turn received the whistle of applause.

Orders were now given for the attack. One division, headed by a brother of the Chief, was dispatched thro' a defile to the left, to which two of our men were attached much against our will, as we wished to be all together. Our will, however, was not taken into consideration by the despotic Chief, he very coolly telling us that he knew what he was doing & it was our duty now only to obey his orders!

I must own that I felt a little melancholy that our people, who had hitherto served us so faithfully, should thus be taken from us perhaps never to see them more, for we were as yet perfectly ignorant of the nature of the warfare which we were destined to take such an active part in.

Every pass was quietly taken possession of before we, with the main body headed by his majesty, commenced our movement in breathless silence down the valley. My friend & self were dismounted, as Sibigho ordered our ox to be kept in the rear lest its bellowing on smelling the cattle of the town might, like the geese in the Roman Capitol, warn the inhabitants of the presence of their enemies. We passed thro' a small kloof &, on reaching its summit, the faint streaks of dawn now becoming visible dimly discovered to us the devoted town of Letubaruba at our feet. It is situated in a hollow valley surrounded on all sides by hills of inconsiderable height.

One glance at its situation shewed the wisdom of the general, for the Wanketzee white shields were now plainly perceptible in every outlet with a large body in their rear, so that it was impossible for any one to escape. Our orders were to remain steadfastly by the King & not to fire until a signal should be given from the party that our two men accompanied.

When I looked round on the scene before me I could scarcely persuade myself that it was reality, but only the "baseless fabric of a vision." A shot from the opposite side, reverberating among the hills like thunder, & a most hellish war whoop simultaneously uttered by the whole Bawanketzee host soon convinced me to the contrary. A sudden rush was made upon the town, warriors enough being left to guard every pass, & with their battleaxes in hand they butchered every unhappy wretch which the terrific sound of our musketry caused to emerge from their huts.

We kept up a brisk fire & doubtless the King thought we did great execution, but I had told our people by no means to kill any of the poor wretches except in self defence & therefore our balls passed over the town which was now on fire in several places. The shrieks of the women & children were most heart-rending, for wherever they turned they were met by a bloody battleaxe or the dreadful sound of our thunder.

Sibigho stood by us calmly looking on and giving directions to his numerous *aides du camp* about securing of the cattle, which seemed on the whole to be the only aim in storming the place. Very little resistance was offered on the part of the enemy as they were taken so aback as to be quite unprepared, which shews great improvidence in such a marauding people then living in an enemy country. When the cattle were driven out the confusion in the town became great on account of the thick clouds of dust & the smoke from the burning huts, for the whole town was now in flames, that in endeavouring to avoid the fury of the assailants they jumped thro' the burning element where, in all probability, they were met by an uplifted Chacka [ax—ed.] which cleft their scull in twain. One poor boy about 8 years of age, having lost his mother, came running towards us as if to seek protection & my blood freezes still in my veins when I think of his reception. Our interpreter, a Bechuana doubtless inured to scenes of blood, advanced in front of our line & clapping his blunderbuss to the child's head shot him dead on the spot.

The cattle being now secured & the enemy, who had the good fortune to escape the Bawanketze Chackas, clambered up the hills glad to get off with their lives, casting a desponding look behind on the town, now a heap of ashes, the greatest part of their cattle and effects in the hands of the conquering Bawanketzie.[11]

[The manuscript journal ends here, but the following extract supplies further information.]

EXTRACT FROM THE LETTER WRITTEN BY BAIN TO THE SOUTH AFRICAN COMMERCIAL ADVERTISER

The victory was complete and was ascribed entirely to us; and we were hailed as mighty gods (Moonris Zoora) and their deliverers from the scourge of the Mantatees. Our noses were pulled at such a rate that I really thought they would have sent us home without them. Had fortune turned against them I make no doubt they would have murdered us on the spot as the cause of it. The Bakwain country, as laid down by Burchell, as well as the Bankwet and several others which he

---

[11] "The Bawankets did not follow the fugitives, but were content with the rich booty which consisted of at least 2,000 head of cattle and a vast number of shields, assegais and battle axes, and a few sheep." From fragment of manuscript of Bain's letter to *S.A.C. Advertiser.*

merely had from hearsay are quite incorrect. Litabaruba is situated in the 24th degree of S. Latitude and the 7th of East Longitude. Makabba, the late king of the Bawankets, gave the unfortunate Mr. Cowan an escort to this town and the Bakweens escorted him to a powerful nation lying to the north east, called the Maglazielies, from which they proceeded to a tribe described as being near the coast and having long hair. The Bakween and the Bawankets suppose that they were murdered by the long-haired people as the murderers are described as being exceedingly savage.

On our return to Siloqualali we entered in triumph—the women singing and shouting for joy on hearing of our success —and we found everything right about our wagons, which we left in charge of the guard set over them by the king.

They sent us 82 head of cattle as our share of the spoil which we declined accepting, telling them we had merely assisted them through motives of friendship. This rather displeased him [Sebego] and he did not afterwards show us so much respect as before, no doubt taking it as a great affront.

After a journey of two months, in which we were frequently in danger with all our cattle dying of thirst from the great scarcity of water, we arrived here [Graaff-Reinet] safely on the 19th ultimo.

30 ANNA ELIZABETH STEENKAMP
THE GREAT TREK

Anna Elizabeth Steenkamp was a member of the famous Retief family. Pieter Retief was the foremost of the Voortrekkers—those Boers who moved from the Cape Colony inland to the high veld of the Transvaal and the plains of Nata in the decade after 1835. This article written by Anna Steenkamp first appeared in Cape Monthly Magazine *in September 1876 and has since become one of the best-known manifestoes of the Greek Trek. The reader should remember, however, that this account was written some forty years after the events.*

This record is written for the sake of my relations, children and grandchildren, now still residing in the interior, in order that they may know for what reason their parents and grandparents have forsaken their mother country, and what anxiety and anguish, grief and pain, destitution and distress, by reason both of foes and fire, have befallen us, and have been the cause of many a sad sigh and bitter tear; whilst, nevertheless, amidst these trying

Anna Steenkamp, "Record or Journal of Our Migration from Our Mother Country to Port Natal," *Cape Monthly Magazine.* September 1876. Reprinted in John Bird, *Annals of Natal* (Pietermaritzburg: P. Davis and Sons, 1888), I, 459—468.

circumstances, we were being guided and guarded by our faithful God, our Father.

The reasons for which we abandoned our lands and homesteads, our country and kindred, were the following:
1. The continual depredations and robberies of the Kafirs [black South Africans —ed.], and their arrogance and overbearing conduct: and the fact that, in spite of the fine promises made to us by our Government, we nevertheless received no compensation for the property of which we were despoiled.
2. The shameful and unjust proceedings with reference to the freedom of our slaves: and yet it is not so much their

freedom that drove us to such lengths, as their being placed on an equal footing with Christians, contrary to the laws of God and the natural distinction of race and religion, so that it was intolerable for any decent Christian to bow down beneath such a yoke; wherefore we rather withdrew in order thus to preserve our doctrines in purity.

3. But it is unnecessary to mention anything further just now about these questions, as I am aware that you are acquainted with these matters; but I shall rather relate to you what occurred to us on our expedition. Two bodies of people had left before us. The foremost were the Taljaards and Liebenbergs, among whom the first sad massacre was perpetrated by the great Kafir king (Masilikatzi).[1] At this battle, Potgieter with forty men defeated fully a thousand Kafirs, but we were ourselves not in that band. The rumours of this massacre, however, were the cause of our leaving the colony all the sooner, in order to hasten to the assistance of our brethren. The massacre committed by Masilikatzi took place on 2nd September, 1836. Another troop under the leadership of G. Maritz, as well as my aged father, François Retief, departed from the colony on 15th November, 1836, and I and my family had to stay behind, as my husband was very ill; but on 5th May, 1837, we also left the colony, alone with our children, servants, four wagons, and cattle. Our departure from Zeekoe River was accompanied with many troubles; for I had a sick husband and a sick child to attend to, and was myself suffering from a bad cold. The most difficult part of all still was, that we had to bury our lead and gunpowder under ground every day, and to send for them by night with a wagon. The reason of this was that we had a great deal of ammunition, and there was a prohibition against leaving with it. At length with great danger and much trouble we crossed the Orange River, and

there I offered my thanks to God, because thus far He had helped us. Then to our misfortune we arrived among the Bastards [people of mixed blood—white Europeans and black Africans—later known as Griquas—ed.], who received us very brutally, saying they had the right and orders to rob and despoil us of everything: for this tribe has since long ago been known to be the greatest thieves and robbers in the world. Our servants deserted us, and the girls, although weak and delicate, were obliged to lead and drive the wagons, nay even to drive the cattle on through all these ungovernable tribes. Our company was not increased: we were only with four wagons. Nevertheless we were cheerful, cherishing the hope of better days, consoling our hearts and longing for gladder times. We had, however, still to travel through two kinds of Bastards, the Korannas and Boschjesmans, with the loss of a number of our cattle and horses. With joy and gladness we reached the Riet River, and there we found a multitude of people, who were the first Christians whom we had seen on our long journey. Here we delayed twenty days on account of my husband being too ill to proceed further on the journey; but scarcely was he better than we set out with our four wagons. We then came into a desolate country, without any wood or manure (for fuel), where the grass was so high that we could hardly find the children and the cattle. Here also we had bitterly cold weather, and heavy rains.

At last we reached King Maroko, and the Kafirs came to meet us by hundreds, surrounding our four wagons like two walls. At the mission-house we delayed a little, and the great King Moshesh, with his servant and the clerk of Maroko, came to look if we had any slaves or apprentices by us, in order to take them away from us. After we left Maroko we had to experience severe trials, as we could find no road, and for that reason we had to wander hither and thither, and could find no one to show us the right way and give us

[1] Umsilikazi.

instructions; but we saw abandoned kraals and encampments, and our cattle died in great numbers; and above all we were in a country destitute of wood, but full of deserted kraals, and here and there heaps of bones of tribes murdered and destroyed by Masilikatzi. Here there was an abundance of game of all kinds.

At length after four months' travelling we reached Sand River; but as we were quite on the wrong road, my son rode forward on horseback to see whether he could find anybody to show us the way, and to our great joy he succeeded on 24th August, 1838, to meet people; and on 25th I was delivered of my youngest child. Herein I perceived the truth of the word of the Lord, that when our needs are sorest He is nearest. Nevertheless we had not yet found the formed company of which Maritz was the leader, nor my father; but three days after the birth of my child, 28th August, Commandant Potgieter proceeded on his journey with all his company, and then we all came together.

It was, however, still too troublesome for us to travel forward with so many people, and for that reason we were compelled to pass through a burning country, where we were in great anxiety lest our children should be burned. A number of our cattle, and of others whole herds, were burned. In the course of our journey we travelled through the country of two kinds of Bastards, Korannas and Bushmen (Maroko and Moshesh). Now we had to go through the country of the great Masilikatzi, but as his power had been broken by Mr. Maritz we had nothing to fear from him.

When we had left the Sikonyela behind us, we met Mr. Piet Retief in the neighbourhood of Drakensberg with the first emigrants, as well as my aged father, François Retief, and the Rev. Mr. Smit. This caused us great joy, as we had in the first some one to execute our existing laws, and in the last-mentioned a minister to give instruction in God's word, to administer baptism and the holy sacrament, so that our religious service flourished.

Every Sunday and every evening there were public services, and this made our journey through the wilderness pleasant, seeing that the Lord had not forsaken us.

Mr. Maritz had gone on with a part of the emigrants; but we soon after left, under the command of Mr. Retief, as far as the great Drakensberg; and from there Mr. Retief departed, with five men, for King Dingaan [Shaka's successor—ed.], to get the land from him, by purchase or by exchange, and in this he succeeded.

I must now relate to you something about Sikonyela. Whilst we remained on the Drakensberg, Sikonyela was found guilty of theft and robbery; for he had sent his people, on horseback, with guns and clothed, to Dingaan to steal cattle. We were not aware of this; but when Mr. Retief came to the king, the latter asking him whether he was not afraid to visit himself, as he had stolen his (the king's) cattle, Mr. Retief replied, "No; I have not done so." "Then," said the king, "you have fired on my people; they tell me it is the Malungus (white people) who have done so." After Mr. Retief had cleared himself of guilt, Dingaan entertained him in a friendly manner. This was mere hypocrisy, as you will see from the sequel.

Mr. Retief then started for the Bay. When he left King Dingaan, the latter gave him two chieftains and some of his people to see if any of his cattle were with Sikonyela. Mr. Retief then rode with the Kafirs and a portion of his men to Sikonyela, and found the cattle with him, and delivered them to the two chieftains to hand them over to the king.

With great difficulty we passed over the Drakensberg, and we encamped before the Great Tugela, when the emigrants under Mr. Maritz had collected together. Then the council resolved that Mr. Retief, after having convinced the king of the above-mentioned robberies, should go to acquire the land from him, which was done. He left us, accompanied by sixty-three men and three children, besides the "after-riders."

When Mr. Retief came to the king, the

latter willingly gave him, as he had found the cattle at Sikonyela's, the country from the Tugela to the Umzimvubu as a present, according to the contract which was afterwards found with the persons who were murdered. Nevertheless, all the friendliness of Dingaan proves that he intended carrying out a cruel and fearful murderous design, which he actually accomplished on 11th February, by the tyrannical murder of Mr. Retief and sixty-six other men; and on 17th February, the Kafirs attacked us also. Oh! dreadful, dreadful night! wherein so much martyred blood was shed; and two hundred innocent children, ninety-five women, and thirty-three men were slain, and hurled into an awful eternity by the assagais of those bloodthirsty heathens. Excluding the servants, the number was over four hundred souls. Oh! it was unbearable for flesh and blood to behold the frightful spectacle the following morning. In one wagon were found fifty dead, and blood flowed from the seam of the tent-sail down to the lowest. Ah! how awful it was to look upon all those dead and wounded. The following day we fled altogether to another encampment at Doornkop, between the Tugela and the Bushman's River. The massacre was perpetrated between Blaauwkrantz and Bushman's River. Mr. Maritz was at Doornkop with the first emigrants. The Kafirs came in in force in the daytime, but were gallantly repulsed and driven off by Mr. Maritz; and as the river was full, and the Kafirs had to go across, a large number was killed, so that the river ran as red as blood.

I must also tell you, my dear children, how it was that the Kafirs could so easily perpetrate the massacre that night. It was on account of disobedience and imprudence: the greater portion of the people were on the mission, and others engaged in buffalo-hunting; others, moreover, were on the road to the Drakensberg to assist their families in coming down: so that the Kafirs found the women and children quite alone, and sleeping peacefully. Mr. Retief had cautioned us at Doornkop to remain by each other till he came back, as he was ill at ease. He also wrote to us afterwards that we should not separate from each other; but the trouble we had with the cattle obliged many to proceed down the river with their families in small troops. We were alone, feeling secure and contented. Mr. Retief left his wife at Doornkop with Mr. Smit, and the Kafirs did not come there.

The day after our arrival there, the wounded (the women and children who were left) came; some on foot, some on horseback, and a portion in wagons. Our field-commandant, Mr. Piet Greyling, carefully provisioned and strengthened our encampment. He also took back our cattle from the Kafirs; that is to say, our sheep, as the oxen were across the river, which was full.

The commandant had the dead buried and the wounded attended to. On all sides one saw tears flowing, and heard people weeping by the plundered wagons, painted with blood; tents and beds torn to shreds; pregnant women and little children had to walk for hours together, bearing the signs of their hasty flight. Oh! how weary and fatigued were those women and children, and how terrible it was to see unborn children rent asunder by the murderous Kafirs. When the women came up to us, they fell upon their knees and thanked God for their deliverance out of the hands of the cruel tyrant. In our encampment there was nothing but lamentation and weeping. Every day we had to bury the dead bodies of the wounded. This spectacle, and the terrible circumstances, cannot be described by my pen.

In April our encampment was at Blaauwkrantz. There Field-commandant Piet Uys arrived. He went out with a commando, and perished with ten other men on the 10th May, 1838. The men who betrayed us, Stubbs and Blanckenberg, also went out on a marauding expedition to the Bay at the same time that our commando left; but the Kafirs flew round and murdered seventeen Englishmen, a number of Natal Kafirs, and also Stubbs; so that our betrayers fell into their own toils.

Thereafter, our whole force was assembled at the Blaauwkrantz River. Oh! my children, to live in so large a "laager" [encampment—ed.]" of a thousand wagons is hard, and it is also injurious to cattle. In July our laager went as far as Bushman's River. Listen now, my children, to my sad misfortunes.

On 2nd February your beloved younger sister died. On the 11th February the commission was murdered, amongst whom were my uncle Retief, his two sons, and other relations. On the 17th February the great massacre occurred. On the 10th May Piet Uys, with ten of his men, perished. On 23rd July your dear father died, and many other of our nearest relations and acquaintances. The last cases of death were probably caused by the dampness of our encampment, for nearly every day we had rain, and we could wear no shoes on account of the mud.

On the 10th August we were again attacked by the Kafirs at Bushman's River. Their bands were stretched out by thousands as far as the eye could see. It was a terrible sight to witness. I cannot describe their number, for one would have thought that entire heathendom had gathered together to destroy us. But thanks and praise are due to the Lord, who so wonderfully has rescued us out of the hands of our numberless and bloodthirsty foes, and granted us the victory. Their foremost band wore clothes and had the guns of the killed, and swarmed down upon us, whilst the others surrounded us. Our number of fighting men was considerably diminished, for a portion was with Maritz at Tugela, and another portion had gone ahead to Port Natal, so that our strength consisted of only two field-commandants and two field-cornets, with their men. The names of the field-commandants and field-cornets were Joachim Prinsloo, Jacobus Potgieter, Johannes du Plessis, and Johannes de Lange. Thirty

of Plessis' men and also a portion of Prinsloo's were with our cattle at the Drakensberg, so that we had only a few men capable of bearing arms at our laager, and the heathen had entirely overwhelmed us had God suffered them to do so. Now you may imagine, my dear children, in what a state of anxiety we women were when we beheld the onslaught of the enemy. The majority of the women consisted of widows and orphans. For we could not imagine that so few people would gain the victory; but the Lord strengthened us and weakened our enemy. They rushed down on us in a circle till almost within range of our guns. Then they attacked us at different points, so that our men were obliged to walk one behind the other to shoot down the enemy, now at one and then at another corner of the encampment. We had arranged our cannon so that they could not break into it. The Kafirs kept us busy for two days and two nights, and constantly fired at us, but not one of our men received any injury from their bullets, and seeing that a multitude of theirs were killed in that conflict, and that they were severely defeated, they left us with a war-song, and fired charges as far as we could hear them. The second day our men went in pursuit of them with the view of recovering our cattle, but the horses were too few and almost too famished in the encampment, so that they were obliged to return, and the enemy retained our cattle; but we thanked God for the preservation of our lives, with the exception of the loss of one man, who was murdered whilst with his sheep, and my faithful female slave who had fled from the encampment. After this occurrence we departed for Tugela, as Maritz wished his men to get out of the mountain. We remained together, however, for six months. In the meanwhile your brother, François Marthinus Hattingh, had left for the interior in order to collect a commando, and also to get horses in order to take away our cattle from the enemy, for there was famine among those who had been ruined by the enemy; but we assisted each other until we were entirely deprived of means of subsistence.

I was also married a second time to a stranger, a widower, named Thomas Engenaar Steenekamp. Mr. Maritz died; Mr. Retief had been murdered; Mr. Uys had been slain. All our leaders had been killed, and we were as sheep without a shepherd. On 10th November my son arrived with his uncle, Andries W. J. Pretorius, who was then by the general vote appointed head-commandant. He thereupon collected a commando, and had a fight with the Kafirs. Through God's blessing the Kafirs sustained a defeat, whilst a large number of them perished, and five of our men were killed. After the battle we left the Tugela in January, 1839, and arrived here at Pietermaritzburg. I must tell you what occurred to me on this last journey.

We left on the 20th January, and on the 23rd of the same month, my son, François Marthinus Hattingh, was killed by lightning during a violent thunderstorm, while he was with his cattle, at the age of twenty-eight years, and left a widow and two children behind to deplore his loss. Oh! what a blow it was for me and his whole family when he was snatched away by death. He was a peaceful man, respected and esteemed by everyone, and deplored by all. But the hand of the Lord doth what He willeth, and with death there is no respect of persons.

Since our arrival here we lived a whole year in laagers, and in the last of them a sad misfortune occurred to us. On the 28th August, 1839, at nine o'clock in the evening, our encampment caught fire through a little servant girl lighting a candle; and some had already gone to bed when the fire broke out, but we were still busy, teaching the children. Suddenly a cry was raised of "Kafirs!" and we did not think otherwise than that our enemies had put the encampment on fire. As soon as the first house stood in flames, all the rest caught fire. The laagers were plentifully

supplied with lead and gunpowder; for our father, Steenekamp, alone had a barrel containing six hundred pounds of powder, and the other houses were full of the same article, so that it was very dangerous to remain within the encampment. I fled with my twelve children out of the gate, as I was afraid of the fire and of the reported Kafirs, and went as far as the first hollow; further I could not go. Afterwards the other women followed me, and there we remained until the fire was burned out. Then I received information who the persons were that had perished in the fire; and people also told me that my husband was amongst the number: but this message gave me no anxiety, as I thought that it was impossible that the whole of us should have our lives spared. That night I had still more terrible thoughts: it was, in short, like unto the Day of Judgment; and the words of St. . Peter occurred to my mind, when he says: "The day of the Lord shall come as a thief in the night: in which the heavens and earth shall pass away with loud noises, and the elements shall burn and be destroyed; and the earth and the works which are within it shall be burnt." The most terrible part still of that night was to see when the gunpowder caught fire, and the pieces of the wagons around us flew about in all directions. As soon as the danger was passed, we betook ourselves again to the laager to assist the injured and bury the dead. When the first house caught fire, there were ten men to quench the flames, and when the gunpowder ignited three of them were killed, and the others severely injured. A trading wagon containing a large quantity of powder also caught fire. Two men attempted to save it, whereby one was so severely injured that he died immediately afterwards, and the other lived a short time. The gunpowder wagon was in the middle of the encampment. Two white children and two little Kafirs were burned to death in the house. The following day we found nine dead and twelve wounded, lying in the ashes. The heat was so intense that we could not take out the dead that night. Everything belonging to us was roasted and broiled: four wagons, nine "salted" fat oxen, as also fat, soap, salt, sugar, &c., were consumed, for we were wealthy, and provided with everything. Thirteen houses also were burned down. We had to sit by the fire the whole night, without clothing or bedding. Some of the wives and mothers were weeping, for they had seen their husbands and sons perishing in the fire. We, poor women and little children, had to struggle through many serious trials on account of the cold and the enemy, as we lay by night beside the houses; but to remain by so great a fire, wherein so many people were burned, was a still greater hardship; and the night was bitterly cold. In the morning of the following day, we bound the bones in a counterpane and buried them in a hole. There were three Steenekamps, two Potgieters, one Deventer, two children, and two Kafirs burned: and two Steenekamps severely injured, of whom my husband was one, but by God's goodness he recovered.

Here now, my dear children and friends, you may see with what sad misfortunes I had to struggle in my journey of twenty months before we had a home or a shelter. Shortly after the fire we were visited by measles, through which a great many deaths occurred. My old husband and myself had alone to provide for twenty-three children and grandchildren who were laid up, and who had to be attended by us, without house or tent, in only a wagon. Several days I was so weak through these exertions that I could hardly endure it; but God be praised, who has strengthened me in body, so as to bear the burdens which He has laid upon us; so then I was able to perform my duties.

For about two years after this we lived quietly, securely, and at peace with all the surrounding tribes, so that every one was again beginning to acquire the means of subsistence; for the country is very fertile, so that one could very well make a living, if not visited by wars or other misfortunes. But to our grief and sorrow the peace was again disturbed, and all our dreams of prosperity and happiness vanished; for on 6th May, 1842, Captain Smith [the commander of British forces—ed.] arrived in the bay of Port Natal, and on the 25th of that month he attacked us. He came along the shore of the sea with pieces of cable twisted round the axles of his gun-carriages. Here, also, my darlings, I wish you to see how the Lord has visibly assisted our men; for in spite of all the treachery displayed in this war, and all the heavy ordnance brought to bear against us, five men only were killed, whilst two were murdered by the Kafirs. Women and children were stripped of their clothes, and had to fly naked. Farms and lands were laid waste by the heathens, and again much cattle was taken from us by the Kafirs, so that we, through the unceasing thefts of the Kafirs, again fell into poverty. On 15th July, the first Cloete [British commissioner—ed.] arrived at Pietermaritzburg, and made peace with eleven persons, and fixed that day to be celebrated as a festival of happiness for us and for our children. On 9th May, 1843, the second Cloete arrived here, and we were fated to be deprived of the land which we had earned and bought: that was the satisfaction promised us.

But, my dear friends and children, I may finally mention, that if everything remains in the same unfortunate position as it is already, we shall be completely ruined; and it is possible that, after a few months, you will meet with very few of your kindred at Port Natal, for we are entirely impoverished, and wish to travel inland, if God grants us health and His blessing.

Your affectionate Mother and
Grandmother,
(Signed) ANNA ELIZABETH
STEENEKAMP
(*née* RETIEF).

31 JAMES CHAPMAN

THE BOERS AND THEIR ATTACK ON KWENA

Shortly after the British and the Transvaal Voortrekkers concluded the Sand River Convention in 1852, by which the British renounced any alliances with African peoples north of the Vaal River and agreed not to provide them with firearms, the Transvaalers attacked the Tswana state of Kwena, then ruled by Sechele. The attack had repercussions in the Ngwato state to the north. James Chapman was perhaps the only white non-Afrikaner to see David Livingstone's quarters immediately after the destruction, because Livingstone himself was away at the time and never returned to them. Chapman's account is, therefore, of importance, in light of the extensive and partisan histories that followed the Boer attack. The argument might be advanced that Chapman had anti-Afrikaner prejudices, but he did have a fairly intimate knowledge of Afrikaner attitudes and way of life and had many friends among the Afrikaners.

James Chapman (1831–1872) traveled extensively in the western part of southern Africa in what is now Bechuanaland, South-West Africa, Zambia, and Rhodesia. In 1852 he almost forestalled Livingstone by three years in the discovery of the Victoria Falls, but African political disputes prevented his passage down the Zambezi. Chapman spoke Tswana and was a keen observer of the African political scene during his travels. He became a friend of Sir George Grey, Governor of the Cape, who acted as his patron. Chapman was elected a Fellow of the Royal Geographical Society in 1867, but by that time he was in poor health and was ruined financially. In 1870 he went to the diamond fields, where he died two years later.

On the 15th of October we were delighted to be under way, steering for Sechelli's Town, which, after several days' march through heavy sands and dense forests, in parts well stocked with game, we reached on the 28th. Wirsing and I proceeded to Sechelli's residence on horseback, riding forward the last stage through rugged glens and among rocky hills, never venturing to move faster than a walk. We found the chief at his residence, perched on a hillock composed of blocks of sandstone, loosely piled upon each other, a fit abode for baboons only.

Sechelli, chief of the Bakwains, a tribe mustering about 500 men, stands about 5 ft. 10 in. high, has a pleasing countenance, and is rather stout. He was dressed in

From James Chapman, F.R.G.S., *Travels in the Interior of South Africa, Comprising Fifteen Years' Hunting and Trading; with Journeys Across the Continent from Natal to Walvisch Bay, and Visits to Lake Ngami and the Victoria Falls* (London: Bell and Daldy; Edward Stanford, 1868), I, 112–124.

moleskin trousers, a duffel jacket, a wide-awake hat, and military boots. In address and behaviour Sechelli is a perfect gentleman. He can read and write, having learnt within the last few years, and is an accepted member of the Kuruman [mission station—ed.] church. He was instructed by Dr. Livingstone, who lived with him for four or five years. Sechelli is said to be very quick at learning, and anxious to substitute more civilized customs among his tribe in the place of their own heathenish practices. He is also said to be good-natured and generous. He presented us with a fat ox for slaughter, a custom prevailing among all the tribes that can afford it.

Sechelli at once pronounced us to be Englishmen; and having corroborated the intelligence we had already heard from Sekomi respecting his disasters, he apologised for not being able to receive us as he would like; but he entertained us with roast beef, sweet and sour milk, served in clean dishes, and with silver spoons, also with sweet earth-nuts; and while we were doing justice to his hospitality, a man stood fanning away the flies with a bunch of white ostrich feathers. His loss, he informed us, was sixty-eight men killed of his own tribe, besides a number of women, and between 200 and 300 children carried away captives. He lost, also, about 1500 head of cattle, and several thousand sheep and goats. For his cattle he seemed not to care so much, although his people were starving. He hoped to be able to replace them by the profits of huntings for ivory; but his people felt sorely the loss of their children. Ninety wagon-loads of corn had been carried off by the Boers, and the rest they had burnt in his town. Besides his own property, they had carried off several wagons, oxen, and other property belonging to English gentlemen at that time travelling to the lake.

From Sechelli we learnt that the war originated with Maselleelie, chief of the Batkatla tribe at Mabotoa, who had often been promised by the Boers that if he supplied them with a number of servants he would be exempted from further demands; but on giving one supply after another, still more was demanded, in spite of the promises made him. At length he refused, and became surly, thinking probably, with many others of the natives, that the late fever had so diminished the numbers of the Boers that he could successfully resist their authority. The Batkatla chief having ascertained, however, that the Boers intended to punish him, and being an arrant coward, fled to Sechelli for protection, it being a custom amongst those races that when one tribe flies to another and solicits protection it must be given; so that on the Boers demanding that Maselleelie should be delivered up, Sechelli refused, saying he "could not do it unless he was to cut open his own bowels and let them fall out."

Most of the people of Sechelli's tribe were out during the day grubbing for roots, their only food at present. Famine, "the meagre fiend," that "blows mildew from between the shrivelled lips," had already made great havoc among them. Several mothers had followed the Boers home, and, hiding themselves during the day, endeavoured at night to steal away their children; a few only had succeeded and returned.

On the 1st of November we obtained a guide from Sechelli to conduct us to the main road, our wagons having been brought since our own arrival up to his town. We accordingly departed, and at night overtook some emaciated Bakwains, roasting the roots they had gathered during the day. I ate one of these roots, but I thought I should have died from the effects it produced, creating a lather like soap, and blistering the inside of my mouth in a few minutes. I drank water to cure it, but that only aggravated the symptoms. The pain I suffered was at last allayed by putting some fat into my mouth.

Next day we travelled still south, and reached Kolobeng in the forenoon. This is the site of the town where Dr. Livingstone lived with the tribe. His house had been pillaged, and presented a melancholy picture of wanton destruction. The Boers had taken away everything that was valuable to them in the shape of furniture, utensils, and implements, and destroyed some hundreds of volumes of Sechuana Testaments, and other religious works and tracts, the leaves of which still lay scattered for nearly a mile in every direction. Even the window and door frames had been taken out, and the floor was strewed with bottles of valuable medicines, the use of which the Boers did not understand. The town where Sechelli was attacked, and which was burnt to the ground, a few miles from Kolobeng, presented a melancholy scene of desolation, bestrewn with the unburied carcasses and bleaching bones of the natives who fell.

In the afternoon we started from Kolobeng, and, traversing the side of a very high mountain, the next day pushed on again.

By the fountain, and about some hundred yards from where I lay, stood a solitary but dense bush of the Waght-en-beetje (wait-a-bit) kind, and about ten minutes after, to my great surprise, about thirty savages, armed with spears, shields, and knobkerries, emerged from the bush. They came on, eyeing me with great suspicion, and inquiring whence I came; but on learning that I came from Sechelli's, they seemed satisfied; and from what I could understand they had heard of our being on the way from "Old Booy," whose wagon had preceded us a couple of days. Otherwise these fellows would probably have put an end to my travels, having been placed here by the chief for the purpose of cutting off spies or straggling parties of Boers.

The next day Wirsing and I left the wagons to follow, and proceeded on horseback to Mr. Edwards's station at Mabotoa, where, arriving in the afternoon, we were hospitably entertained with the first food we had eaten for three days, except a few gwarrie berries, which had made us sick. Having heard the news, and been shown all the damage done to Mr. Edwards's property by the Boer commando, we passed on to Mr. Inglis's station at Matebe, where we were also kindly received, and reached Vilgoen's place on the 5th of November, greatly to the astonishment of the Boers, who had long given us up as dead, and who overwhelmed us with inquiries about the movements of the natives, of whose attacks they were under great apprehension—wondering by what miracle we, having ventured to go to Sechelli's, had come away unhurt.

.   .   .

Having conveyed incidentally the results of some of my observations on the habits and manners of the Boers, I leave the reader to review in his own mind, as well as he is able to do from these inadequate notes, their past and present condition, and the degenerating tendency their daily course is taking. This arises partly from their nomadic life, their natural taste for that wild and roving state of existence in preference to any other, and their frequent collision and hostilities with the natives, for whom their hatred and contempt seems to have become quite inherent, and has been and is exaggerated in proportion as the tribes meet with sympathy from the Christian world.

It must I think be admitted, if such a man as Judge Watermeyer is an authority, that the first trekking of the Boers was not an act forced upon them by the British government, but the spontaneous inclination of a people fond of a roving life, and wishing to escape the control of law—a feeling which was already in operation during the time of their own Dutch government, and from the very beginning of the colony, and that in those days already inroads were made upon the territory of Hottentots and Kaffirs.

According to Judge Cloete, it will further be seen that the great impetus given to the trekking of the Dutch farmers commenced seriously after the merited condemnation to the gallows, by British authority, of some of their countrymen for acts of a criminal nature. These and other acts admit of no palliation. However much we may regret the necessity of such extreme measures, nobody will dare to dispute the legality of the punishments inflicted, which were only similar to many that have at various times occurred in England and Ireland, and which would very likely have been dealt more stringently upon rebellious Englishmen. The act of hanging the Boers on "Slagter's Nek" was a very painful necessity, but at the same time will never reflect dishonour on the British name, although it may excite pity for the sufferers, and their unfortunate relations who saw the sad end of their foolish and misguided countrymen.

It will probably not be denied that, on the part of the many Boers who have left the colony since [1835—ed.] the British administration, there were some *real* causes of complaint amongst many fancied grievances. Through a change of ministry in England, or a change of governors in the colony, it has happened that faith has not always been kept with some of the colonists, British as well as Boers, but it has been the peculiar failing of succeeding governors, as well as secretaries of state for the colonies, to upset, upon first coming into office, all the good work their predecessors have done.

Cases of unwarranted aggression on the part of Kaffirs towards the colonists have also transpired, such as may well wring the heart of many an honest farmer —English as well as Dutch. But even in these matters, when we come to look back into the first causes of things, and to review the many injustices that have been done to the native tribes of South Africa in the beginning, and take into consideration the unforgiving and unforgetting disposition (the great characteristic) of a savage, we cannot wonder at his persevering hatred towards the white man, however much we may pity the innocent, and, as it were, modern colonist, made the scapegoat for the sins of a former generation, and suffering grievously in the loss of their property and their friends at the hands of a savage and ruthless but, it has been asserted, in many respects still a noble enemy. The native races, it must in justice be allowed, have had cause for their hatred to the white man, and, as I have before remarked, a Kaffir may forget an injury for a time, but he never forgives. It is a national characteristic, and until their nationality is utterly destroyed this prominent feature will never be eradicated.

Vacillating as the government of this colony has ever been, there was one remarkable feature which had hitherto always pervaded British rule, and that was, the earnest solicitude it evinced for the welfare of the native tribes, as well as the desire it had shown to regain their confidence, and the inclination to redress their wrongs; but in one short year a blow was struck that has proved, as it will continue to prove, an injury to British subjects, a disgrace to a civilized and Christian gov-

ernment, and the bane to the British name in South Africa. A high commissioner, inexperienced in the affairs of the colony, in the person of Sir George R. Clerk, was entrusted to break up Her Majesty's government in the Sovereignty (now Free State)—a task which he is said to have performed with a tact and precision that did him great credit. This was in truth the greatest act of cruelty and injustice, not alone towards natives, but towards Europeans, that any government could have been guilty of, and was virtually equivalent to the discarding a great number of Her Majesty's faithful and loyal subjects! These men strongly remonstrated against the act, but too late, and their voices were too feeble. They indeed sent to England two delegates to represent their grievances, in the persons of Dr. Frazer and the Rev. A. Murray, jun., but it has never transpired satisfactorily in what the labours of these gentlemen resulted. It may be asserted that the orders Sir George R. Clerk received were imperative; but if he had represented the feelings of the people to the home government, and remonstrated with them, he would have done humanity a service, saved a jewel in the British crown, and gained honour for himself by advocating the retention of the Sovereignty. By leading people to believe that he was, if anything, in favour of retention, he misled them, so that they had no chance of remonstrating until the act was done; and this piece of injustice, unprecedented in the history of civilized nations, has not even been equalled by the Trans-Vaal Boers. From such humiliating injustice and pusillanimous behaviour on the part of a government to its own people—an act perpetrated by a government which, above all others, makes pretension to be the most humane and just towards its subjects, the protector of the oppressed, and the defender of the whole world against slavery—we must recoil in horror and hide our faces with shame. It is indeed a pity that the fair fame of our beloved sovereign should be compromised by a transaction which, to those who regard it from a distance, may seem of so trivial a nature, and should thereby receive in this colony an enduring blemish, brought about, we believe, by the misrule or misrepresentations of the individual or individuals employed to carry out this cruel and unwise policy.

Having alluded to the great change of feeling on the part of all the native tribes in South Africa—unfavourable to the English—I may mention that it is principally resulting from the injustice of the treaties made with the Boers, by which the natives are debarred from getting gunpowder and firearms (to them the *necessaries* of life as well as to the Boers), while every provision is made for the Boer getting as much as he requires. Native tribes within and out the colony, who are known only by their fidelity to Britain in her time of need, and were taught by us to fight against those very Boers who had rebelled against their queen and given so much trouble, are now spurned for their loyalty, and not alone spurned and discarded most ungraciously, but oppressed in the most arbitrary and ungrateful manner that ever a people were.

As soon as the tenor of the Sand River Treaty became known to the natives, and the subsequent abandonment of the Sovereignty, the news spread like wildfire from tribe to tribe, not alone along the whole border of British and Boer dominions, but even into the interior to the Bamanwato, Lake Ngami, and even to the Zambesi river, and meetings were held between the Griqua, Basutos, Barolong, Batlapies, Bakwain, Bahurutsi, Bamanwato, Baselika, and many other tribes: treaties were made between them for mutual protection and defence against the white man—Englishmen in particular—who seemed now to prove themselves the true oppressors of the black. By these treaties they are still bound to each other, nearly from one side of the continent to the other, and if any Kaffir war had unfor-

tunately broken out after this crisis, woeful would have been the consequences to the northern parts of this colony, and the Trans-Vaal and Free State in particular. As it was, many travellers were handled roughly, and, being questioned about the strange and dishonest policy of their government, were overwhelmed with shame. Much is due to the missionaries of Kuruman and other parts for the part they took, not in palliating or exculpating the policy of government (which they could not in justice do), but in seeking to alleviate the pain it inflicted, by expressing a conviction, prompted by their own hopes, that these proceedings would be disapproved of at home: they were, however, grievously disappointed. Time has, indeed, softened the feeling of the natives to a considerable extent, and much praise is due to the more enlightened and liberal rule of the present government, which has in many cases, by its acts, given the natives reason to hope for better days: and but for this some sad tragedy would have darkened the pages of modern South African history.

To return, however, to the Boers of the Trans-Vaal, on whose probable future, their prospects of an improved state of civilization, and the chances of a prosperous and useful career, I may perhaps be expected to say something. This I shall briefly enter upon, but with great diffidence, as it is a subject that ought much rather to come from one skilled in politics and prophecy than myself.

In the present state of society in the Trans-Vaal, it seems to me that as there are many ways (although sometimes uncertain) of easily attaining a livelihood and a competency, emigrants will find their way thither from the colony; but the treatment hitherto has been such as to exclude enlightened foreign immigration, and rather to encourage the introduction of disaffected Dutch farmers from the colony, many of whom have recently sold their farms there, and, with their flocks and servants, trekked into what they consider a free country (because exempt from British rule, which gives equal rights to white and black—an equalization which they cannot conceive to be just), where they can obtain a title to a 6000 acre farm for 2s. 6d. Beyond this, they give only encouragement to British deserters from Bloemfontein, or from Natal, because these are often useful as bricklayers, carpenters, or schoolmasters, and are compelled by their peculiar position to work for almost any terms offered to them, which generally consist of little more than their wretched food, a hut to sleep in, and concealment from their pursuers, if any should be in search of them. Hollanders were at one time in great favour with them; but since the defalcations of one or two, who imposed seriously upon the credulity of the Boers by representing themselves emissaries from the King of Holland, &c., they are utterly at a discount.

I have often thought that as European immigrants, and especially missionaries to the native tribes, have met with so much opposition from the Boers in these quarters, it is a pity that missionary societies, instead of quarrelling with the Boers in their endeavours to instruct the natives, have not rather turned their attention and their means to the advancement and instruction of the Boers themselves, who at the time I speak of had not one permanent clergyman amongst them, and generally no better schoolmaster than a British deserter fresh from the ranks to teach their progeny the *Dutch* language. In other countries missionaries have become willing martyrs to the Christian cause; and if the missionary societies had but taken half the pains to instruct the Boers first, and spent as much money in edifying and enlightening them during the last twenty years as they have done for the natives, they would now have reaped by this time a glorious harvest, not alone from the white populations thay had reclaimed from a retrograding state, but in the good fruit that that glorious harvest would

again have yielded. The Boers of the Trans-Vaal then would not only have by this time been perfectly civilized themselves, but many of them might have gone forth pioneers of civilization, carrying the Gospel into the dark regions, and have proved a blessing to South Africa, instead of carrying destruction and desolation through the land. Real Christianity infused into the bosom of the Boers would have done away with that feeling of superiority with which the white man is prone to look down upon the black races, their contempt for whom would thus be eradicated, and, as a necessary result, slavery in every form would be abolished. Until this is done, it appears to me that no real substantial improvement will take place. They must be taught to believe first. At present ninety out of every hundred will not believe that the soul of a black man is esteemed by the Creator equal to a white man's, and a feeling of this kind was manifested only a few days ago, even within the borders of this colony, when some white men declined sitting on a jury with men of colour; but the judge, though a descendant of a Dutch colonist himself, to his honour be it said, reproved them in a very laudable and becoming manner.

In the present unsettled state of the Trans-Vaal country, missionary influence will do great good if exerted first to promote the refinement of the Boers themselves, and soften down their peculiar prejudices. In this manner they will gain the confidence of the natives, and break that chain of alliance which, since the giving up of the Sovereignty, has been formed amongst the native tribes on their immediate borders. Their *real* position needs but, I am sure, to be made known to their fellow-countrymen and relations in the Cape (amongst whom we have so many noble examples of the great and powerful advantages of education), and they will, I feel confident, use their utmost exertions and influence amongst the many members of the Dutch Reformed Church, to whom they are bound by the ties of faith and relationship, to aid in promoting the education of the Trans-Vaal youths, by sending thither the necessary means, ministers, and teachers. In so fruitful a region, every description of farmers and mechanics can do well, and such people would find their way into a peaceable country, but that in the present state of things they are never certain of what they possess, for various reasons, which will have been gleaned throughout the perusal of this journal. Missionaries to preach to the Boers, and to instruct their children, might make them in a few years all useful and intelligent members of society, and thus we might, at no distant period, hope to see these very men, now so narrow and selfish in their ideas, confer benefits upon the natives by teaching and instructing them, and sending missionaries from among themselves (as some of the native tribes have long done) into the dark regions beyond. In the hope that this may yet be their destiny, we may look forward trustfully to happy days for our expatriated fellow-colonists.

32 NEWSPAPER ACCOUNT
THE GOVERNOR AND THE TEMBOOKIES

This account, published in the newspaper Queenstown Representative, *is less important as an example of Cape frontier policy, whose twists and turns were highly complex and confusing at the time, than as a verbatim recording of the dialogue between white officials and Africans on the question of the role of the chieftain under European rule.*

Wednesday, November the 22nd, 1865, will be remembered by the Tembookies as long as they remain a people; for that day witnessed the deposition of their chiefs, the substitution of English for native law, and the abolition of the office of Tembookie agent. This startling revolution, which, however, only concerns the Tembookies within, and not those beyond the boundary of, the colony, was effected by the civil commissioner of the district, C. D. Griffith, Esq., who quietly declared that this was the will of the governor, and henceforth it would be law.

As soon as the civil commissioner received his final instructions from Capetown, he communicated with Inspector Gilfillan, of the Frontier Armed Mounted

"The Governor and the Tembookies." *Queenstown Representative.* November 1865. Reprinted in W. C. Holden, *The Past and Future of the Kaffir Races* (London, 1866), pp. 393–402.

Police, at present stationed at Glen Grey, who immediately sent messages to the different chiefs and head men, calling upon them to attend at Glen Grey, and receive a message from the governor. At first it was intended that the gathering should take place on last Saturday; but it was found that it would be impossible to get the people together so speedily, and Wednesday was the day ultimately fixed upon.

From the first streak of dawn, the people in all parts of the location were in motion, forming into companies under their respective chiefs and head men, mustering as imposing a force as possible, and hastening to the place of rendezvous. One of the first of the natives to arrive on the ground was the great chief—or perhaps it would be more correct to say chieftainess—Nonesi, who was attended by a goodly cavalcade, by several of the inferior chiefs, and by an umbrella bearer, who was busily engaged in shielding her sable majesty's delicate complexion from the rays of the sun, which on Wednesday were extremely fierce. As it is usual to describe the dresses worn by royal personages on great occasions, we may state, for the information of the curious, that Nonesi was attired in a sky-blue dress, which had evidently seen better days; a mantle, also of sky-blue, and also somewhat faded; a black riding hat, trimmed with brown ostrich feathers; and Balmoral boots. The royal petticoats were of white, rendered somewhat dingy by use; and, unless her Majesty's stockings were of the very hue and texture of her skin, we may safely affirm, from certain glimpses of the royal understandings with which the wind favoured us, that she wore none at all. The effect of Nonesi's somewhat magnificent "get-up" was slightly marred by the fact that she insisted on riding astride, instead of in the orthodox feminine fashion; but this gave a dash of piquancy to the affair which partially redeemed its want of dignity.

Very soon after the arrival of the great chief the plain in front of the old Mission station and school buildings began to swarm with life. Troop after troop of Kaffirs galloped up, all having some appearance of military discipline, and all armed with formidable knobkerries, with the exception of the head men and chiefs, who generally carried assagais. The majority of the natives were extremely well mounted, many of them, nevertheless, on mares that had recently foaled. The foals in these cases followed their dams, and, as they ran, set up a whinnying that, although dissimilar, in some way reminded those who listened to it of the cries of children parted from their mothers, and longing to reach them.

At one time, the scene was not only animated, but highly interesting. Nonesi, surrounded by her immediate followers, was engaged in earnest conversation; the troops of Kaffirs that had already arrived were knee-haltering their horses; others were galloping up at full speed; while others again were pouring down a mountain pass at some distance from the station: those at the bottom of the pass appeared to be but a few inches in height, while their comrades at the top were mere dark specks thrown out into strong relief by the deep, dark, beautiful blue of the unclouded sky.

The footmen were not by any means as numerous as those who came on horseback; but they formed a goodly company nevertheless, and probably numbered five hundred men; of the horsemen there could not have been less than a thousand; and, by some people, this estimate was nearly doubled. For our own part, we think that a total of fifteen hundred natives will be somewhere near the mark. Of Europeans, there were, perhaps, five-and-twenty on the ground; but not one of them bore the slightest mark of authority, with the exception of Inspector Gilfillan, and one or two of his subordinates, who were in uniform.

At about half-past twelve o'clock, the civil commissioner took his seat in the porch of the church. He was supported by Inspector Gilfillan and Mr. Liefeldt—the latter acting as interpreter; the remaining Europeans grouped themselves about him; and the Kaffirs were invited to draw near. Nonesi, for whose accommodation a chair was provided, came first, and was speedily followed by her chiefs, counsellors, and people. The chiefs and counsellors sat on forms, placed right and left of Nonesi; the people, squatting on the ground, formed themselves into a huge semicircle, while at the rear of all were a few who stood upright to listen to the message of the great chief, the representative of their "mother," Queen Victoria.

To persons used only to meetings of whites, to crowds of English people, or of colonists, it was strange to observe the decorous silence, the apparent indifference of this crowd of half naked savages, who, armed with knobkerries as they all were, listened with perfect gravity and respect to the fiat that dethroned their chiefs, and at one blow declared unlawful all their cherished customs. The natural courtesy of these barbarians would put to shame half of the polished but constrained civilities of nations long accounted civilized, refined, and polite.

When all, chiefs and people, had taken their respective places, the civil commissioner, addressing the great multitude before him, said: "I have sent for you Tembookies, that I may make you acquainted with the governor's instructions as to your position in the Tembookie location on this side of the Indwe [River —ed.]. The governor's instructions to me are as follows: 'All chiefs remaining on this side of the Indwe are no longer to have any authority in their tribe.' "

At this portentous announcement there was a movement of surprise, slight almost as the motion of the leaves of the forest when touched by the softest breath of the summer wind; but this evidence of emotion almost instantly subsided, and a profound stillness took its place.

The civil commissioner went on: "I have to tell you also that all alike, chiefs and people, without exception, are to be dealt with under the colonial law, and treated in every respect as British subjects; and therefore all matters in dispute among you are to be decided by the magistrate in Queenstown, and not by your chiefs at all. This is the message which I have to communicate to you from the governor with regard to the position of those of you, whether chiefs or people, who choose to remain in the location on this side of the Indwe."

There was a long pause here; the people were still perfectly quiet; the chiefs apparently utterly indifferent to the whole matter. Nonesi, perplexed and thoughtful, took some long pulls at her pipe, and occasionally exchanged a few words in a low tone with her counsellors.

"And now, Nonesi," said the civil commissioner, addressing the great chief, "it is to you I speak. A complaint has been lodged with me by a Tembookie, who says that you sent some of your people to seize an ox of his, and had it slaughtered. You had no right to seize that man's property under any plea. Your customs are abolished. You have no authority to take anything belonging to any man without an order from a judge, or from a magistrate, or from a police officer. And those people who were sent by you to take the ox will have to appear in Queenstown, to answer the charge of robbing the man who was the owner of the ox. I want all the people to understand that it will be no excuse for them to say that they were sent by the chief to do any act contrary to the colonial law. The law will not recognise that as an excuse; and any man who commits a crime under any circumstances will be tried for it, and will suffer the penalty the law imposes. This is the message that I have to give you."

This announcement was succeeded by a long pause. At length an old man, in the thick of the crowd, exclaimed: "Your speech is about two or three matters. Cut them up and let us talk about them separately."

The civil commissioner: "I have explained that no one in the location has any right to exercise authority: that Nonesi did exercise authority; and was wrong in doing so."

An old man: "Who ate that man up?"

The civil commissioner: "I do not know; but you must understand that there can be no other chief but the governor in the colony. As you remain in the colony you must put up with colonial law, which is to recognise no other authority but that of the governor, and of the people he appoints to act under him."

A head man: "What is the cause of this sudden change? What have we done that we should be visited with the governor's anger?"

The civil commissioner: "All the chiefs agreed to accept the governor's terms, and go across the Indwe, and afterwards nearly all refused to do so; still I have not come here to answer any questions that you may put to me in this way, but simply to tell you what are the governor's instructions. If you have anything you wish to say to the governor, tell me, and I will represent it to him, and get his answer: but I will not argue with you."

Zenzwa, a chief, addressing the people, said: "You have heard what the magistrate has told you; and if you have anything to say against it, you had better go home and think it over, and then get ready your reply."

At this juncture, a long conversation took place between the principal Kaffirs as to whether they should reply at once, or delay their answer. Nonesi spoke with some energy, and her temper was plainly ruffled. Eventually the chief Lumko asked: "What offence are we guilty of, that such a thing as this should happen to-day? We have always thought, for years past, that we were under English rule; why are we thus treated?"

The civil commissioner: "I have told you that I cannot answer your questions. I have not come here to argue the matter, but to carry out the governor's instructions."

Umlanjane: "I cannot see my way through this. Mr. Griffith has come here to give us our new law, and why cannot we ask any questions?"

One of the crowd: "Why should our chiefs be taken from us? Why should they be deprived of their authority? We have lived a long time in the country. Some little chiefs and their people have gone away; but why then should authority be taken away from the chiefs who remain? This is the country of our fathers. The fathers of the chiefs were chiefs in the time of our fathers; and why, then, should we be so hardly treated?"

Nonesi: "I am an old chief, one of an old race. I was Umtirara's mother, and I belong to government. I have always been loyal. I was here under Warner; and when he left us he left his son behind.

When his son was going away, I tried to prevent it; but the governor would not listen. I am the mother of the great chief Queya; he is away from here, but I do not want to go away. I never agreed to cross the river; and it is not known to any one what I have done that the governor should be angry with me. Why, magistrate, do you speak in such a manner to me? If I have been guilty of any fault, let me know my fault, and then tell me that you will drive me over the river, or deprive me of my authority. I am a chief; why should I be less than a chief? Why should I be driven across the river? I am an old woman; I have been here since I was a child; I have brought up children here; and some of them have died before me, and their graves are here. I have been living with my own people in my own country, and have done nothing to make the governor deal so harshly with me. What have I done? The Tembookies are a large nation. My own people, the people over the river, and the people of Queya, my son, all consider themselves under the English government. Why, then, are we called together here to receive this particular report to-day? I have been loyal to the British Government always. I was loyal when other chiefs were fighting against it. In the time of the cattle slaughtering I was on the English side. I have all the country down to the Indwe, and have kept it loyal. I had always, till now, some one to look after me, and see that I was properly dealt with. When the governor took Warner away, I hoped that some one would be sent in his place; but no one is sent. We do not deny being under government; the Tembookies, wherever they may be, are, as we all know, under government. We do not wish it otherwise. Who among us said that we were willing to go over the river? I never agreed to go over. Some have crossed; others remain here. Those who have crossed the river were not sent across by me. I cannot say anything about them; they pleased themselves. That is all that

I have to say to-day—to ask the question why I am treated in this manner, and to deny that the Tembookies as a tribe ever agreed to cross the Indwe. I and all my people have been expecting a successor to Warner, and we are still looking for one to come after. Let some one follow Warner. I have said all now."

A native, addressing Nonesi, said: "Who is it that you are expecting in Warner's place? Where is the man?"

Nonesi: "I do not know the man; I am waiting for him."

The civil commissioner, turning to the chiefs, said: "You and your people are not to occupy any of the kraals vacated by those who have gone through the Indwe, without permission from me."

Nonesi: "There are no kraals empty in this part of the Tembookie country."

The civil commissioner: "I am not talking to you, Nonesi, alone, but to all the chiefs of your tribe."

Nonesi: "There may be vacant kraals, but I know nothing of them. Is not this place vacant now that Warner has gone?"

The civil commissioner: "Where there are vacant kraals, they are not to be occupied without my permission. I have not come here to answer any questions; but anything you may have to say I will take down, and send to the governor."

Nonesi: "There are no vacant kraals."

The civil commissioner: "Very well, then, it is all right."

Nonesi: "Who is to take Warner's place, and rule here on my ground?"

The civil commissioner: "There is no ground that belongs to you. It is government ground."

Nonesi: "I am the child of the government, but the ground is mine."

A Kaffir (to the crowd): "There is nothing to be done that will help us; but if you want to do anything at all, sit down and cry."

This terminated the conference on the principal business of the meeting, and the civil commissioner now called Carolus and Seelo to come forward. The men,

who were both decently dressed in European attire, having placed themselves in front of their brethren, the civil commissioner said: "Carolus and Seelo, you were both paid head men in the government service; and it has been reported to the governor that you objected to carry out the instructions of the agent residing with the Tembookies, and that you have also done all in your power to prevent the Tembookies from accepting the governor's offer of land beyond the colonial boundary. At the time you did this, you were drawing salaries as government servants; and because you did so, I am to tell you that you are no longer in the government service, and no longer to get government pay."

Carolus, whose tone and manner were both respectful and dignified, said: "I thank you, magistrate, for your words. I am thankful for what the government has done for us. We are all thankful; but there were head men and chiefs before the government paid us; and there will be head men and chiefs still, even if they are without pay."

The Chief Viezi: "I thank you, magistrate, for calling your children together that you may see them. We have been your children for a long time, and have always been under your protection; but you have come to say something to us that we do not understand. You say you take us under government rule. We thought we always were under government rule. Still, for what you have said, I thank you to-day with my hat in my hand; and I speak the word for all who are here. They have always wanted to belong to the government, and the governor has to-day kindly taken them under his protection, so that they may live properly under his rule! We cannot understand this thing, but we thank you! The Tembookies as a tribe have not crossed the river. Nonesi belongs to government. She stays with her tribe in Tembookie land. Those who have crossed the river are young men who had no huts and no land here, and wanted some. Nonesi always was the governor's, and will be so still. Her children were always your dogs, and will remain so."

The Chief Telle: "I have only a small word to say, which you may take as Nonesi's also. All the chiefs are here, and none have moved. Those who have moved are not held as chiefs, and have no land." Chief Telle said, "We want to know again what we have done to be treated as you are treating us to-day. There is one thing we want from the government: a magistrate to rule in Warner's place, and to be as he was. We thought the meeting to-day was to show us the new magistrate. Let him come. We wish to see him."

The civil commissioner terminated the meeting by telling the natives that he was very glad at having seen them all together, to hear what they had to say, and that they were at liberty to go home again.

As soon as Mr. Griffith left the place of meeting, the Tembookies broke up into scattered groups, who were speedily engaged in loud and animated conversation.

This, however, did not last long. In a very short time they began to catch and mount their horses; the different parties were formed under their chiefs and head men—chiefs and head men no longer, according to Sir Philip Wodehouse; and, in less than an hour, the whole of this numerous assemblage had dispersed, east, west, north, and south, and every Kaffir who had taken part in the meeting was out of sight, and Glen Grey was as quiet as though it had never witnessed a gathering of such great moment.

Two or three accidents happened in the course of the day. One Kaffir was thrown from his horse, but escaped with a severe shaking; a restive horse that seemed to have a great objection to being ridden, managed to fall in the course of the struggle with his owner, and singularly enough broke his neck—of course dying on the spot. Another horse was likewise accidentally killed, but under what circumstances we are unable to state.

33 JOHN MACKENZIE
BUSHMAN LAND

The eastern Tswana states—the Ngwato, Kwena, *and* Ngwaketse—*were scattered over the Kalahari Desert, a wilderness of scrub and thorns broken only by a few seasonal waterholes. The Kalahari was inhabited only by the* Sarwa, *a people of Bushman extraction, and the* Kgalagadi, *probably descendants of the earliest* Sotho *migrants to southern Africa. The following selection describes the relationship between the Tswana and the inhabitants of the desert.*

The Reverend John Mackenzie (1835–1899) spent most of his life as a missionary among the Tswana. Ordained in 1858, he left for South Africa later in that year and, after a time of uncertainty as to where he would take up mission work, settled at Shoshong, capital of the Ngwato state, in 1864. Between 1870 and 1871 he made a trip to Britain, where he wrote Ten Years North of the Orange River. *During a second term at Shoshong (1871–1876) and Kuruman (1876–1882), he became increasingly involved in the political aspects of British-South African-Tswana relationships. In 1883 and 1884 he returned to Britain to campaign for the annexation of Bechuanaland. In subsequent years he served briefly as the British Deputy Commissioner in southern Bechuanaland and as a political adviser and propagandist. In 1891 he retired from his position as pastor to a mission station for Negroes on the eastern Cape, where he died.*

. . . There are two distinct races held in subjection in this country, and we now met with specimens of both at every fountain. Those called Bakalahari are Bechuanas, whose tribes have been worsted in former contests, and who, not able to preserve their own independence, "khetha" or pay tribute to a powerful neighbouring chief [the state of the Bamangwato or Ngwato, a Tswana (Bechuana) people—ed.]. Like their rulers, these vassal-Bechuanas are not all of one tribe, nor do they all speak the same dialect of Sechuana. Within the memory of those now living, tribes once independent have been reduced to the condition of Bakalahari; while others who had been long Bakalahari, have been called, through the grace of their chief, to the privileges of citizenship, and appointed a place in the town of the tribe. The other subject race is that of the Bushmen, called Barwa by the Bechuanas in the south, and Masarwa by those in the north of the country. The relationship between the Bakalahari and their masters is much more friendly than that between the same masters and their Bushmen. The helplessness of the Bakalahari excites the contempt of their owners, and they are usually spoken of with the diminutive form of the word —Bakhalahatsane; but otherwise they are regarded as "bathu hela"—"like other people." The master therefore, knowing that he can trust to instincts and traditions similar to his own in the mind of the Bakalahari, sends his flocks and sometimes his herds to be taken care of by his vassals. The children of the Bakalahari luxuriate in goats' milk, while their father imagines himself considerably elevated in society as he gazes night and morning on

From John Mackenzie, *Ten Years North of the Orange River: A Story of Everyday Life and Work Among the South African Tribes* (Edinburgh: Edmonston and Douglas, 1871), pp. 128–139.

the cattle as they enter and leave their pen. When the owner of the stock now and then makes his appearance at the post, he speaks of the cattle as if they belonged to the Bakalahari; and when it is his intention to sell or to slaughter a certain animal he usually announces it, and sometimes even goes through the form of asking permission to do so, although all the cattle belong to himself. The pastoral instincts of the Bakalahari thus find full occupation, to the satisfaction of their lord, and to the advantage of the vassals. Then the master provides dogs for hunting—the ivory and ostrich-feathers, the furs and skins, to be his, the meat to belong to the Bakalahari. And when he visits the little settlement, it is usually with a little present of some tobacco or wild hemp for smoking, or a clasp-knife or a few beads, which he has purchased from a trader. He now receives the "tribute" of his vassals, staying with them a longer or shorter time according to his taste. As among Europeans, there are some Bechuanas who are happiest when "out of town" and in the hunting-field with their vassals. It is only at the positive command of the chief in time of disturbance that such Nimrods reluctantly return to their houses in the town.

But the Bushmen seldom secure much liking or consideration from their Bechuana masters. "Masarwa a bolotsana thata"—"Bushmen are great rascals," "Masarwa ki linoga hela"—"Bushmen are perfect snakes," are remarks often heard among the Bechuanas. The fact is, there is less in common between the two. Their allegiance is never so genuine, and while they yield tribute they hardly conceal their contempt for their masters. The Bushman is of use only in hunting. When his Bechuana master arrives he takes possession of the little huts, and receives all skins, etc., which the family have collected. And now they hunt every day in company, the Bushmen with their spears, bows and arrows, and dogs—their master with his spears, or, in recent years, with his gun. Woe betide the Bushmen should it be found out that they have hidden away part of the produce, or that, instead of keeping the skins for his master, the Bushman has ventured to make with some of them a mantle for himself or his wife! Thus Bushmen are continually on the alert for the arrival of their masters in the country; and should they cross the path and see his foot-mark on it, they are able to recognise it at once, and if possible will hasten home before him to hide that which must not meet the eye of their lord.

Looked at in this connection, it is not difficult to account for the well-known reluctance of Bechuana chiefs to allow traders and travellers to pass through their country. . . . While the Bamangwato, in whose country I was travelling, participate in the advantages of the trade recently begun with Europeans, they have lost property to the value of many hundreds of pounds through the opening up of the waggon roads to the Lake and to the Zambese. Both roads lead through districts occupied by their vassals, and it is well known that the latter do not hesitate to keep back part of the produce from their masters, and barter with it themselves as soon as a European waggon makes its appearance. . . . It has been found impossible by the Bamangwato to stop this "contraband" trade. They began with severity, and put some of their vassals to death for daring to sell what belonged to their masters. But they found that severity did not answer their purpose, and so the masters now are in point of fact competitors with the European hunters and traders for the purchase of ivory and feathers from their own vassals. Of course they do not acknowledge that they occupy such a position, but the "presents" which they now give their vassals are every year more handsome, and the whole transaction assumes more the appearance of bar-

ter than the levying of tribute. In a few instances masters have intrusted their Bakalahari and Bushmen with guns. The latter take to this weapon at once. What with their skill in stalking, and their steady aim, they soon excel their master in its use. Public opinion is against putting such dangerous weapons into the hands of the "lower classes," as an unsafe proceeding. But as it is to the decided advantage of the masters it is increasingly practised.

It is very interesting to observe how this vassalage becomes all but impracticable, and melts away before the teachings of Christianity and the increasing intercourse which now obtains among tribes that were formerly isolated. The missionaries in the southern district of Bechuanaland did not preach directly against this system; but they taught that the love and mercy of God were toward all, and that God was no respecter of persons. It was the custom even in the olden time, and is still in heathen towns, that if a slave regarded himself as ill-used by his master, or thought that his life was in danger, he might flee to the chief, and cast himself upon his protection. If the master complained of was a favourite with the chief, he would formally reprove him, and persuade the slave to return to his service. But if a charge of cruelty was proved against a master with whom the chief had a quarrel, he would at once release the slave from his obligations to him, and provide for him another master. It can readily be seen that Christianity, finding the slave enjoying such an amount of liberty, would speedily secure for him more. Thus in the southern district, and especially where Christian churches exist, this vassalage exists in many cases more in name than in reality. In most cases, as long as the vassals remain with their masters they receive some kind of payment for their service; and when they go away, there does not seem to be any power which is able and ready to bring them back. It is one of the faults which the heathen prefer against the partially-Christianized district in the south, that there the "batlanka" or slaves are no longer under their masters' control, as in the times of undisturbed heathenism. Christianity thus quietly lets the oppressed go free, and breaks every yoke.

But while under this system of appeal to the chief, the lot of these vassals is just bearable in time of peace, it is beyond conception wretched in time of war. I do not mean war among themselves in the country; they are too poor to quarrel seriously, or for a long time: but they are deeply interested in all the political questions of the town, being part of the property of the head men—a quarrel among whom is often followed up in the country in a way which astonishes as it shocks the Christian man. The contest for the possession of certain villages of Bakalahari or Bushmen, is a fruitful source of strife in Bechuana towns. The vassals with all their belongings are the subject of litigation and endless jealousies; and it needs all the skill of a chief to settle these matters between greedy and plausible rivals. When a decision is come to, the poor people in the country are hastily "lifted" by the successful litigant, to be brought back again should he afterwards lose his case. When rival chiefs fight for supremacy in the same tribe, the condition of the harmless vassals is wretched in the extreme. They are then scattered and peeled, driven hither and thither, and mercilessly killed, as the jealousy, caprice, or revenge of their masters may dictate. It is quite fair in such a struggle to kill all the vassals, as it would be to lift the cattle, of him who cannot be displaced from his chieftainship. And so with the varying fortunes of a "civil war," the vassals might be attacked by both parties in turn.

Again, when one Bechuana tribe attacks another, the Bushmen and Bakalahari belonging to both are placed in the same category with cattle and sheep—they are to be "lifted" or killed as opportunity offers. In such cases, there-fore, all Bakalahari and Bushmen flee into wastes and inaccessible forests, and hide themselves until the commotion is past.

We found an illustration of the terror and mistrust in which these people live, when we reached the fountain of Lotlakane. A "civil war" was still going on, in an intermittent fashion, between Macheng and Sekhome, for the chieftainship of the Bamangwato tribe. It mattered little to these serfs who the chief was to be; with them the important question was, to escape both parties while the strife was going on. And so for the first night we saw nobody at Lotlakane; but in the morning my men told me that there were footmarks of Bushmen all round our camp. They had come in the night to satisfy themselves that there were no Bamangwate in my party, before they ventured to come amongst us. How they distinguished as the men lay asleep between the two Bakwena whom I had hired from Sechele and Bamangwato, I know not; but their midnight inspection was held to be satisfactory, and next day several made their appearance at our waggon. It was affecting to witness the earnestness with which they asked if the Bamangwato were still fighting among themselves.

.   .   .

On all subjects lying within the range of the Bushman's observation you will meet with extreme shrewdness and intelligence. The Bushman has the most extensive knowledge of the *materia medica* of the country. If my own medicines were not available, I would trust myself sooner to the care of a Bushman than to any other native doctor. Nothing can exceed the skill and intelligence of the Bushman as a hunter, and an observer of the habits of the wild animals. And as to religion, if I am not greatly mistaken, the Bushmen are the most "superstitious" race in Southern Africa. The fact that they are so peculiarly dependent for subsistence upon what is beyond their control will perhaps account for this. With other natives the chief season of praying and necromancing begins when they have sown their corn, and stand in need of rain. But all seasons are the same to the Bushman. Therefore whilst he is most accomplished in everything belonging to his own way of life, and by general consent the guide and leader of every hunting party of which he is a member, he constantly seeks by charms and by spells to supply his own deficiencies. Whether the European has bent his knee in prayer or not before he springs to the saddle in the morning of a hunt, the Bushman has not failed to consult his "oracles." Approaching with mysterious and confident mien, he announces to the hunters that if they will only proceed in a given direction they will find the game they seek. In short, he has assumed the office of "seer" for the party. He has been inquiring of his dice or charms, and announces to you their verdict with confidence. If you still hesitate, he explains to you that Morimo [god —ed.] has told him where the game is, and at the same time shakes the dice which he carries round his neck. If you smile, and say that these are merely bits of ivory or bone, he assents at once, and would readily dispose of them to you for a few beads. But then at the earliest opportunity he would repair the deficiency, and replace them by another set. The bits of bone are nothing, he will admit, but through them he "makes inquiry" of the ex-human if not super-human. No party of Bushmen would consent to take the field without these charms. Whoever fancies he is self-contained, and able in himself, without prayer, or without divining, to cope with the difficulties of human existence, the Bushman in Bechuana-land is not. I believe life to a Bushman without this professed addressing something out of and beyond himself would be complete misery.

The relics of a tribal rite are also to be found among these Bushmen. If you point to the pierced cartilage of the nose, he will explain to you that that was done when he was introduced to Bushman manhood. He here uses the word "rupa," which in Sechuana means the introductory ceremony of circumcision. This, then, is to him what circumcision is to the Bechuanas. You point to certain marks on his face, or bits of wood on his hair, or tied round his neck. These are medicines or charms to be taken in sickness, or proximity to lions, or in other circumstances of danger. This is the fetichism which is common throughout Africa at the present time, as it was in Europe in past ages, and which is not unknown in our own day in rural districts of England and Scotland. If you point to the dice, the Bushman will say that they are "Lilo tsa Morimo oa me,"—"Things of my God." He will add, "Lia impuléléla mahuku," —"They tell me news." If he does not know much Sechuana, he will point to them and say, "Se se Morimo, se,"— "This is God." As in the other cases, this explanation is to be regarded in its connection with such views of Morimo as are known to these Bushmen. The Bushman means to say that what Morimo is to the Bechuanas and to you his dice and charms are to him. To affirm from such data that the Bushmen have a definite notion of Morimo (God) would be to say too much; to say that their God is a bit of ivory or bone would be equally incorrect; while to affirm that they have no religion or superstition to distinguish them from the brutes that perish is entirely false. . . .

In sleeping at the same fire with Bushmen or Bakalahari you are sure to be roused twice in the course of the night, or oftener, by the rising of one after the other of your companions. Their first stretchings, yawnings, and gruntings over, they assume a sitting position in a row round the fire, which they replenish with fresh logs. Sometimes they fall asleep in this position, and you see them nodding over the flames. When they lie down again you take notice that it is always in the opposite position with reference to the fire from that which they last occupied. Thus if they had their backs to the fire before they got up, they now turn their faces to it. Having no blanket or covering whatever, except a little skin mantle, which just covers their shoulders, it is only by repeated "turnings" that they are able to keep up heat in their bodies during the cold winter nights. Thus their bodies are always scorched and scarred, and generally "over-done" on both sides, by the fire at night. Before the day is fairly broken you again hear the yawning and other demonstrations—now in a louder tone. As the light increases the restless eye of the Bushman scans the heavens with a close scrutiny. On the ground also, as far as the eye can reach, he seems to notice every living thing. The process of roasting meat on the live coals now commences; and as this early breakfast goes on each one parenthetically mentions what he observes. At length one starts to his feet. What has he descried? After great effort you can just see "manong" or vultures in the distance sweeping over a certain spot. Seizing their weapons two or three men start at once in that direction; they hope to get there before the lion has finished the antelope or zebra, which has been his midnight meal. If they find the killer of the prey still at his repast, with a jackal venturing to approach the opposite end, while hyenas or younger lions bide their time at a distance—the Bushmen, who have been talking loudly as they approached, to give due notice of their arrival, now shout at the top of their voice, rattle their spears, break off decayed branches from trees, or shake their mantles, to frighten the lion and his courtiers, who retire into the adjoining thicket. Everything is now collected which is at all edible, and carried to the encampment. Should their visit be too late, and they find only bits of bone and hide and hoofs to reward them for their trouble, all these are collected and brought away; the vulture and the hyena or jackal finding little to pick up after the visit of the Bushman. Thus although Bakalahari object to lions in their vicinity, on account of the live stock which they are rearing for themselves and their masters, the Bushmen do not at all object to this proximity, for they have a good deal to gain from it, and if they only keep up a good fire at night in self-preservation they have nothing whatever to lose.

.   .   .

34 JAN CHRISTIAAN SMUTS
A CENTURY OF WRONG

First issued in Dutch in 1899 under the authorship of the State Secretary of the Transvaal Republic, F. W. Reitz, A Century of Wrong *was translated into English in 1900 and was published with a preface by W. T. Snead, himself an opponent of the Boers, or Afrikaners. A biased and polemical account of nineteenth-century South African history, particularly the relations between the Afrikaners and the English, this book was in fact written by Jan Christiaan Smuts (1870–1950), then an official in the government of the Transvaal. Smuts was later a general in the Anglo-Boer War (1899–1902), and Prime Minister of South Africa (1919–1924, 1939–1948). As a member of the British Imperial War Cabinet in World War I and as one of the major architects of the League of Nations and the United Nations, Smuts acquired an international reputation. In spite of, or perhaps because of this reputation, Smuts was never able to implement the same universalistic ideas at home that he proclaimed abroad.*

From [Jan Christiaan Smuts] *A Century of Wrong*, issued by F. W. Reitz, State Secretary of the South African Republic, with a preface by W. T. Stead (London: Review of Reviews, 1900), pp. 89–98.

I have now reviewed all the facts connected with the history of our oppression and persecution during the past hundred years. The allegations I have made are not invented, but are based upon the statements of the most reliable witnesses, nearly all of them of British nationality; they are facts that have been declared incontestable before the tribunal of history. As far as the more recent occurrences since 1898 are concerned, I may state that I have had personal knowledge of all the negociations and questions at issue above referred to, and I can only declare that I have confined myself to facts; these will stand out in a much clearer light when the curtain is raised and the events of the last two years in this sorely afflicted part of the world are revealed.

In this awful turning point in the history of South Africa, on the eve of the conflict [the Anglo-Boer War—ed.] which threatens to exterminate our people, it behoves us to speak the truth in what may be, perchance, our last message to the world. Even if we are exterminated the truth will triumph through us over our conquerors, and will sterilise and paralyse all their efforts until they too disappear in the night of oblivion.

Up to the present our people have remained silent; we have been spat upon by the enemy, slandered, harried, and treated with every possible mark of disdain and contempt. But our people, with a dignity which reminds the world of a greater and more painful example of suffering, have borne in silence the taunts and derision of their opponents; indeed, they elected out of a sense of duty to remedy the faults and abuses which had crept into their public administration during moments of relaxed vigilance. But even this was ascribed to weakness and cowardice. Latterly our people have been represented by influential statesmen and on hundreds of platforms in England as incompetent, uncivilised, dishonourable, untrustworthy, corrupt, bloodthirsty, treacherous, etc., etc., so that not only the British public, but nearly the whole world, began to believe that we stood on the same level as the wild beasts. In the face of these taunts and this provocation our people still remained silent. We were forced to learn from formal blue books issued by Her Majesty's Government and from dispatches of Her Majesty's High Commissioner in South Africa that our unscrupulous State Government, and our unjust, unprincipled, and disorderly administration, was a continual festering sore, which, like a pestilential vapour, defiled the moral and political atmosphere of South Africa. We remained silent. We were accused in innumerable newspapers of all sorts of misdeeds against civilisation and humanity; crimes were imputed to us, the bare narration of which was sufficient to cause the hair to rise with horror. If the reading public believe a hundredth part of the enormities which have been laid at the door of our people and Government, they must be irresistibly forced to the conclusion that this Republic is a den of thieves and a sink of iniquity, a people, in fact, the very existence of which is a blot upon humanity, and a nuisance to mankind. Of the enormous sums which we are alleged to have spent out of the Secret Service Fund in order to purchase the good opinion of the world there has been no practical result or evidence, for the breath of slander went on steadily increasing with the violence of a hurricane. But our people remained silent, partly out of stupidity, partly out of a feeling of despairing helplessness, and partly because, being a pastoral people, they read no newspapers, and were thus unaware of the way in which the feeling of the whole world was being prejudiced against them by the efforts of malignant hate.

The practical effect has been that our case has been lost by default before the tribunal of public opinion. That is why I feel compelled to state the facts which have characterised the attitude of the British towards us during the Nineteenth century. Naboth's title to his vineyard must be cancelled. The easiest way of securing that object, according to the tortuous methods of British diplomacy, was to prove that Naboth was a scoundrel and Ahab an angel. The facts which have marked Ahab's career have been stated. I shall now proceed to draw my conclusions, which I submit must appeal irresistibly to every impartial and right-minded person.

During this century there have been three periods which have been characterised by different attitudes of the British Government towards us. The first began in 1806, and lasted until the middle of the century. During this period the chief feature of British policy was one of utter contempt, and the general trend of British feeling in regard to our unfortunate people can be summarised by the phrase, "The stupid and dirty Dutch." But the hypocritical ingenuity of British policy was perfectly competent to express this contempt in accents which harmonised with the loftiest sentiments then prevailing. The wave of sentimental philanthropy then passing over the civilised world was utilised by the British Government in order to represent the Boers to the world as oppressors of poor peace-loving natives, who were also men and brethren eminently capable of receiving religion and civilisation.

It may seem inexplicable that the Power which stood up boldly at the Treaty of Utrecht [1713—ed.] as the shameless champion of negro slavery was the very one which was celebrated in South Africa for its morbid love of the natives; the explanation, however, is that it was not so much love for the native that underlay the apparent negrophilistic policy as hatred and contempt of the Boer. As a result of this hatred of the Boer, disguised under the veneer of philanthropy in regard to the aborigines, the natives were employed as police against us; they were provided with arms and ammunition to be used against us; they were incited to fight us, and, wherever it was possible, they murdered and plundered us. In fact, our people were forced to bid farewell to the Cape Colony and all that

was near and dear to them, and seek a shelter in the unknown wilderness of the North.

As an ultimate result of this hatred, our people had to pursue their pilgrimage of martyrdom throughout South Africa, until every portion of that unhappy country has been painted red with the blood, not so much of men capable of resistance as with that of our murdered and defenceless women and children.

The second period lasted until the year 1881. The fundamental principle then underlying British policy was no longer one of unqualified hatred. Results had already proved that hatred was powerless to subdue the Africander; it had, on the other hand, contributed largely to the consolidation of Africanderdom and to the fact that they spread over the whole of South Africa, thus forming the predominant nationality almost everywhere. In a moment of disinterestedness or absent-minded dejection England had concluded treaties with the Boers in 1852 and 1854, by which they were guaranteed in the undisturbed possession of certain wild and apparently worthless tracts of territory.

The fundamental sentiment which governed the policy of the second period was a feeling of regret at having made this mistake, coupled with the firm determination to set aside its results. These wild and useless tracts, which had been guaranteed to the Boers, appeared to be very valuable after the Boers had rescued them from barbarism, and opened them up for civilisation. It was felt that they ought to gleam amongst the jewels of Her Majesty's Crown, notwithstanding the obstacle in the treaties that had been concluded with the Boers. This was the concealed intention. As far as the means were concerned—they were, from the very exigency of inborn hypocrisy, partly revealed and partly concealed; the one differing from the other, as light from darkness. The secret means consisted in arming the Kaffir tribes against us in the most incredible manner, and in inciting them to attack us in violation of solemn treaties and promises. If this policy succeeded the real objects and means could be suppressed, and England could then come forward and pose openly as the champion of peace and order, and as the guardian angel of civilisation in this part of the world. The Republics could then be annexed under cover of these plausible pretexts. This policy failed as far as the Orange Free State was concerned, because the brave burghers of the neighbouring Republic succeeded, after great difficulty, in overcoming Moshesh [the great Basuto king —ed.], notwithstanding the fact that their arms and ammunition had been illegally stopped by the British Government. England was compelled in that case to confine itself to the protection of its "Basuto" tools. The British, however, succeeded in preventing the Boers from reaping the legitimate fruits of their victory, and in annexing the Diamond Fields— a flagrantly illegal act.

As far as the South African Republic is concerned, it was unfortunate that the burghers were not vigilant enough to foresee and prevent the crafty policy of the enemy. As the Transvaal Boers had subdued the most powerful Kaffir tribes, they never dreamt that the insignificant Kaffir wars in which they had been involved through English intrigue would have been seized as a pretext to annex their country to the British Crown. They had been remiss in not putting their full force into the field so as to bring these little wars to a speedy conclusion. And so the Magato and Socoecoeni campaigns were conducted in a protracted and half-hearted way, much to the satisfaction of Sir Theophilus Shepstone [Secretary for Native Affairs in Natal—ed.], and those who were at his back.

The Annexation was brought about. It was announced that the extension of Her Majesty's sway and protection over the South African Republic could alone secure unity of purpose and trade, as well as open out a prospect of peace and prosperity. In these words of Shepstone's proclamation we see in all its repulsive nakedness the hypocrisy which openly masqueraded in the guise of the disinterested and pitiful Samaritan, while its true and secret object was to inflict a fatal wound upon the burgher Republic.

The third period of our history is characterised by the amalgamation of the old and well-known policy of fraud and violence with the new forces of Capitalism, which had developed so powerfully owing to the mineral riches of the South African Republic. Our existence as a people and as a State is now threatened by an unparalleled combination of forces. Arrayed against us we find numerical strength, the public opinion of the United Kingdom thirsting and shouting for blood and revenge, the world-wide and cosmopolitan power of Capitalism, and all the forces which underlie the lust of robbery and the spirit of plunder. Our lot has of late become more and more perilous. The cordon of beasts of plunder and birds of prey has been narrowed and drawn closer and closer around this poor doomed people during the last ten years. As the wounded antelope awaits the coming of the lion, the jackal, and the vulture, so do our poor people all over South Africa contemplate the approach of the foe, encircled as they are by the forces of hatred and revenge, and by the stratagems and covetousness of their enemies. Every sea in the world is being furrowed by the ships which are conveying British troops from every corner of the globe in order to smash this little handful of people. Even Xerxes, with his millions against little Greece, does not afford a stranger spectacle to the wonder and astonishment of mankind than this gentle and kindhearted Mother of Nations, as, wrapped in all the panoply of her might, riches, and exalted traditions, she approaches the little child grovelling in the dust with a sharpened knife in her hand. This is no War—it is an attempt at Infanticide.

And as the brain of the onlooker reels,

and as his thoughts fade away into uneasy slumbers, there arises before him in a dream the distant prospect of Bantu children playing amongst the gardens and ruins of the sunny south around thousands of graves in which the descendants of the European heroes of Faith and Freedom lie sleeping.

For the marauding hordes of the Bantu are once more roving where European dwellings used to stand. And when the question is asked—why all this has happened? Why the heroic children of an heroic race, to which civilisation owes its most priceless blessings, should lie murdered there in that distant quarter of the globe? An invisible spirit of mockery answers, "Civilisation is a failure; the Caucasian is played out!" and the dreamer awakens with the echo of the word "Gold! gold! gold!" in his ears.

The orchids of Birmingham are yellow. The traditions of the greatest people on earth are tarnished and have become yellow.

The laurels which Britannia's legions hope to win in South Africa are sere and yellow.

But the sky which stretches its banner over South Africa remains blue. The justice to which Piet Retief appeals when our fathers said farewell to the Cape Colony, and to which Joachim Prinsloo called aloud in the Volksraad of Natal when it was annexed by England; the justice to which the burghers of the Transvaal entrusted their case at Paarde Kraal in 1880, remains immutable, and is like a rock against which the yeasty billows of British diplomacy dissolve in foam.

It proceeds according to eternal laws, unmoved by human pride and ambition. As the Greek poet of old said, it permits the tyrant, in his boundless self-esteem, to climb higher and higher and to gain greater honour and might until he arrives at the appointed height, and then falls down into the infinite depths.

Africanders, I ask you but to do as Leonidas did with his 300 men when they advanced unflinchingly at Thermopylae against Xerxes and his myriads, and do not be disturbed by such men as Milner, Rhodes, and Chamberlain, or even by the British Empire itself, but cling fast to the God of our forefathers, and to the Righteousness which is sometimes slow in acting, but which never slumbers nor forgets. Our forefathers did not pale before the terrors of the Spanish Inquisition, but entered upon the great struggle for Freedom and Right against even the mighty Philip, unmindful of the consequences.

Nor could the rack and the persecuting bands of Louis XIV tame or subdue the spirit of our fathers. Neither Alva nor Richelieu were able to compass the triumph of tyranny over the innate sentiment of Freedom and Independence in our forefathers. Nor will a Chamberlain be more fortunate in effecting the triumph of Capitalism, with its lust for power, over us.

If it is ordained that we, insignificant as we are, should be the first among all peoples to begin the struggle against the new-world tyranny of Capitalism, then we are ready to do so, even if that tyranny is reinforced by the power of Jingoism.

May the hope which glowed in our hearts during 1880, and which buoyed us up during that struggle, burn on steadily! May it prove a beacon of light in our path, invincibly moving onwards through blood and through tears, until it leads us to a real Union of South Africa.

As in 1880, we now submit our cause with perfect confidence to the whole world. Whether the result be Victory or Death, Liberty will assuredly rise in South Africa like the sun from out the mists of the morning, just as Freedom dawned over the United States of America a little more than a century ago. Then from the Zambesi to Simon's Bay it will be

"AFRICA FOR THE AFRICANDER."

35 JAN HENDRIK HOFMEYR

THE REPRESENTATION OF NATIVES ACT, 1936

Jan Hendrik Hofmeyr (1894–1948), son of Jan Hofmeyr, leader of the Afrikaner Bond, was one of South Africa's most brilliant minds and, in the fifteen years before his death, was the most prominent spokesman for the liberal philosophy in South Africa. A university graduate at the age of fifteen and principal of the University of the Witwatersrand at twenty-four, he became a minister in the fusion government of Prime Minister Hertzog and Jan Christiaan Smuts in 1934. Although he resigned temporarily from his Cabinet post in 1938, Hofmeyr was closely associated with Smuts during World War II and was widely regarded as his successor. Hofmeyr died, however, in the same year in which the Nationalist party defeated Smuts' United party (1948). The following speech, made by Hofmeyr during the debate on the second reading of the Representation of Natives Bill on April 6, 1936, is regarded as one of the great speeches of South African parliamentary history.

I regret that I cannot vote for this Bill. I can hardly make that vote a silent one, and, therefore, I must ask the indulgence of the joint sitting to give my reasons for that vote. Circumstances have prevented me from doing so at an earlier stage, as I had fully intended to do. Those circumstances kept me away from this joint sitting during the whole of the second reading debate, and during the discussion of nearly all the vital points in Committee. I had intended to vote and speak against the second reading. This Bill has emerged from the Committee practically the same as it was when read a second time. Therefore, I have no option but to vote and to speak against it now.

I used the word "regret" in all sincerity. I do very sincerely regret that I cannot, on this occasion, align myself with my leader, the Prime Minister's sincere desire to further the best interests of White men and Black in this country. I recognise that his knowledge and experience of Native affairs are far greater than mine, and that this Bill represents a life-work to him. I am most grateful indeed to him for his forbearance and his tolerance in this mat-

From "Third Reading of Representation of Natives Bills [J.S.1 and 2, 1936]," *Joint Sitting of Both Houses of Parliament, Union of South Africa, 13 February to 7 April 1936* (Cape Town: Hansard, 1936), cols. 1082–1091.

ter to an errant colleague. But for all that, there is a fundamental difference in this matter between my outlook and that which underlies this Bill. While that is so, I can do no other than oppose it, and I must do so regardless of what the political consequences for myself might be.

It is not the first time, Mr. Speaker, that a government of the Union has been divided on a franchise Bill. Five years ago the Prime Minister also introduced a franchise Bill for the enfranchisement of women. Two of his colleagues opposed that Bill at all stages. That Bill dealt with some 400,000 to 500,000 persons. This Bill deals with some 10,000 to 11,000 persons. But there is this further difference. By virtue of the seven points of coalition, those who entered into coalition specifically reserved to themselves the right to their own opinions in regard to this matter. The seven points contained this sentence—

This does not imply that an agreement has been attained in regard to the principle of separate political representation.

In the party programme again, that was stated to be a matter to be left to the individual party member. It was in that knowledge that some of us went into the present Government. It was with the knowledge of that fact that the country gave its endorsement to that Government. I claim today for myself that right to differ. But I want to make it very clear that in doing so I am neither directly nor by implication criticising anyone with whom I have been in agreement in the past but who today takes a different attitude from my own. I am merely asserting an individual right for myself.

I want to ask the joint sitting to view this Bill in its true setting. There is a right setting and a wrong setting in which this Bill can be viewed. Many hon. members have supported this Bill because they have viewed it against the background of its immediate predecessor, Bill No. 1. That is the wrong setting. The right setting in which to view this Bill is the two previous Bills of the Prime Minister, the Bill of 1926 and the Bill of 1929.[1] Those two Bills and this Bill represent a legitimate succession. The other Bill which I have mentioned, why, sir, that was left at the Prime Minister's doorstep by the hon. member for Roodepoort (Colonel Stallard) and by the hon. member for Zululand (Mr. Nicholls), and very gallantly adopted by him, fortunately only temporarily.

Let us look back upon those two Bills. The 1926 draft legislation provided for the representation of Natives on a communal basis to the extent of seven members in the House of Assembly. It provided for the representation in the House of Assembly of Natives in all provinces. It provided for the extension of Coloured representation to the north. It reconstituted the Native Council on a definite basis, making it a body meeting annually and giving it also legislative power. The 1929 Bill reduced the number of Native representatives in the Union House of Assembly from seven to three. It left the northern provinces to be represented in the House of Parliament only in

the Senate. The 1929 Bill, therefore, from the point of view from which I am speaking, marked a retrogression on the Bill of 1926.

This Bill marks a further retrogression on the Bill of 1929 and that is why I want the Bill to be viewed in its true setting. Let me mention four points.

In the first place this Bill, unlike its predecessors, creates what is virtually a colour bar in the Cape Provincial Council. The right hon. Senator Malan on Friday quoted a letter written by Onse Jan in 1909.[2] He might also have quoted the fact that Onse Jan at that time protested, amongst other things, against the creation of a colour bar in the Union House of Assembly. We are now going further and we are creating a colour bar in the Provincial Council.

In the second place we are laying down a definition of "Native" which is going to degrade an ever-increasing number of Coloured people and place them for ever among the ranks of Natives.

In the third place, this Bill not only provides for a separate Cape voters' roll but it also provides for the immediate removal of all existing voters to that roll. To me that seems in conflict with the spirit of the Act of Union. If we look at Section 35 of the Act of Union, we find that there are two sub-clauses. The one deals with existing qualifications and says that any change in those qualifications leading to a restriction shall not be made except by a certain procedure. Existing qualifications are entrenched, but there is laid down a method by which they may be altered. But the second sub-clause of the same section lays down absolutely and in definite terms that as a result of any such change of qualifications no single Native already on the voters' roll shall have his name taken from that roll and in this case no procedure is laid down for an amendment. I contend that in this new provision in this Bill we are acting against

[1] Earlier attempts by General Hertzog which did not get the necessary two-thirds majority of both Houses sitting jointly.

[2] Mr. J. H. Hofmeyr (Snr.), Leader of the Afrikaner Bond in the Cape.

the spirit of the Act of Union and I may say that I have very high authority for that statement of mine.

Then there is another point. It is now proposed to put up an entrenchment of a two-thirds majority not only against any deterioration in the Natives' position but also against any improvement in the Natives' position. The National Convention did not think such a double entrenchment necessary. Why not? Because the White man was put in the constitution into an impregnable position. They thought there was no necessity to protect the White man. They did not think it necessary to protect the White man against the possibility of his own generosity. Today we are asked to do both. I have heard one of my friends say that it is only just and fair that, if we give entrenchment on the one side, we should also give it on the other, and that reminded me of the first recorded definition of justice. "Justice is the interest of the stronger." I am afraid it is from that conception of justice that a good deal of the support of this Bill is derived. I think it is clear then that this Bill is less acceptable than its predecessors.

I shall be told, however, that there is another side of the account—that this Bill creates a Native Representative Council. Let us remember that the 1926 Bill put on a definite basis the Union Native Council, making it in some respects a weaker, in other respects a stronger body than the body which we are now creating, giving it legislative powers, which we are not doing today. But apart from that, I want to say that I have always had hopes for this Native Representative Council, but I have always realised that everything is going to depend on the attitude towards it of Government and Parliament, during the first critical formative years of its existence; and when I consider the spirit in which these changes which I have been mentioning have been brought in the present Bill, when I think of the attitude of mind which underlies them, when I know how it has been said again and again that this

Bill is only accepted for the present, when I realise that there will be powerful influences to make that Native Representative Council a futile body, then I find it difficult to maintain my hopes. I know that high hopes have been expressed during this session in regard to the Native Representative Council, but high hopes were also expressed in 1920 in regard to the Native Council created then. I find it difficult to discover ground for confidence that the hopes expressed at this time are not destined to similar discomfiture as were the hopes expressed in 1920. And so I again assert that this Bill is no more acceptable than its predecessors. It is called a compromise, but if we look back to 1926, then from the point of view of the Natives, it is the Natives who have done all the giving and none of the taking.

Let us see what this Bill does. The central feature is to give to the Natives an inferior, a qualified citizenship, a citizenship which has the marks of inferiority in clause after clause of this Bill and which bears the added stigma that whatever may be the advance of the Native in civilisation and education, to all intents and purposes, he is limited for all time to three members in a House of 153. That surely is a qualified, an inferior citizenship. May I make my own position clear? I am not one of those who would necessarily stand or fall by the ideal of common citizenship as an absolute thing. I do not go with the right hon. Senator Malan to that extent. If we were starting with a clean sheet, I think it would certainly be possible to devise a system of separate representation in separate assemblies which would be fair and just and sound. I am not saying that it is impossible to do so even today. But we are not starting with a clean sheet. We are starting with the existence of a vested right which has been in existence and which has not been abused for more than 80 years. And I want to say this, that once franchise rights have been given and exercised by a section of the community, then no nation save at the cost of honour and ultimate security should take away those rights without adequate justification. The Prime Minister, when he substituted this Bill for its predecessor, either in definite terms or by implication admitted that fact. He admitted that you could not take away franchise rights without justification and that there was no justification today for that absolute removal of the existing Cape Native franchise rights. This Bill does not absolutely remove franchise rights but it does replace those vested rights by an inferior, a qualified right. I contend that the same principle applies in this case, and I say that no nation save at the cost of honour or ultimate security can take away these rights without adequate justification.

Well, we are taking them away and we are replacing them by a qualified and inferior right. We have then to ask, what is the justification for this proposal? Attempts have been made to answer that question. Some have sought to find that justification in terms of high ethical or political principle. Some have used those blessed word phrases, segregation, trusteeship, the Native developing along his own lines. The Native developing along his own lines—that means for most who use the words the same as the Native being kept in his own place. Segregation— well, what a thing of shreds and patches this Bill makes of political segregation, just as my hon. friend over there pointed out, territorial segregation has become a thing of shreds and patches. And as for trusteeship, I would only say this: I have always regarded trusteeship as implying that at some stage or another, the trustee is prepared to hand over the trust to his ward. I have yet to learn that the European trustee in South Africa contemplates any such possibility. And that being so, I find it very difficult to reconcile the use of the word trusteeship in relation to a Bill for which it is claimed that it is going to make South Africa safe for European civilisation.

But we are also told that we can justify this Bill because once the political question is removed the Native will receive better treatment. There will be more sympathy with their development. I know that that is sincerely meant, but I know too that, in the case of many people, that is simply a conscience-salving argument which they are laying to their souls. I say that because I have sat for five years in the Transvaal Provincial Council. There was no question of Native political representation there. There was no such bogey, but I know how desperately difficult it was to get any consideration whatever for any question of Native development. Let me put it concretely—before long, we shall have to face up to the question of the inadequacy of Native education. I wonder how many after the first flush of enthusiasm over this Bill is passed, how many of those who support this Bill will be any more ready to repair the present inadequacy of Native education than they would have been if this Bill were not passed.

There is another justification adduced, and that is the justification of danger. We have heard so much, especially in the past, of the Cape Native vote being a danger. It is certainly not an immediate, urgent danger. In 1926 when the Prime Minister introduced a much more liberal Bill than this one there were 300,000 European voters on the roll of the Union and 16,500 Natives, but today there are 925,000 Europeans and 10,600 Natives. My department in 1933 and 1935 was instructed to do all in its power to get every qualified Native voter on to the rolls. In spite of that the figures dropped from 12,-715 to 10,628 today. Today there are only 14 constituencies in the Cape with more than 250 Native voters. There are only four with a more than 10 per cent Native electorate. Surely there is no immediate urgent danger. But we are told there is that danger in the uncertain future, that danger of which my colleague, the Minister of Mines, was speaking. It is the fear of that danger which is the only real justification which has been advanced in favour of the act of deprivation in this Bill. Well, here I agree with my hon. friend the member for Wonderboom (Mrs. Malherbe), who said a wise and timely word on Friday when she declared that no sound policy can be based on fear. No sound policy can be based on fear, and if that is the only justification for this Bill, the only justification for this act of deprivation, the fear of what may happen in an uncertain future, then, sir, I say there is no adequate justification.

Well, sir, I object to the Bill for that reason. I object to it also because I regard, as I have always done, the principle of communal representation as an unsound one, and a dangerous one not least of all from the point of view of the European in this country. Communal representation of different races implies a divergence of interests, and in South Africa there is no real ultimate divergence of interests between Europeans and non-Europeans. There is a far greater community of interests in this land. We have on both sides a contribution to make to the welfare of South Africa, and the weakness of this Bill, from my point of view, is that it emphasises the differences, it stimulates hostility, and it pays no regard to the ultimate community of interest. After all, sir, this principle of communal representation is no new one. It has been tried before, and verdicts have been pronounced upon it before. Here I have what the Donoughmore Commission wrote about it in regard to Ceylon—

Communal representation, they said, was devised with a view to assisting the development of democratic institutions in countries of different races and religions, and in the hope of eliminating the clash of those various interests during elections. Unfortunately, the experiment has not given the desired results, but has had, if anything, the opposite effect. The representatives of the various communities do not trust one another. The introduction of communal representation into the constitution with good intentions, has had unfortunate results.

A year after, the Hilton-Young Commission [of 1927—ed.] in regard to [the closer union of—ed.] East Africa wrote these words—

The surest foundation for a stable constitution is community of interests. The communal system where it has been tried has tended to accentuate differences and prevent the creation of a healthy political life.

The Simon Commission [of 1927—ed.] in regard to [the constitutional problem in—ed.] India similarly condemned it. They only allowed it to pass as a temporary expedient, in view of the deep religious cleavages in that unhappy land. What justification have we with these warnings before us for accepting and applying that system here? Surely we are deliberately accepting the worse course and incurring grave dangers for the future.

What, sir, is the chief objection to communal representation which emerges from these quotations? It is that it makes not for friendship, but for hostility. In the last resort, there is greater danger, there is more real cause for fear in this Bill than in anything we have today. By this Bill we are sowing the seeds of a far greater potential conflict than is being done by anything in existence today. Let me explain. To my mind, as I have always felt, the crux of the position is in regard to the educated Native. We have many educated and semi-educated Natives in South Africa. Many of them have attained to and many more are advancing towards European standards. They have been trained on European lines, they have been taught to think and act as Europeans. We may not like it, but there are the plain facts. Now what is the political future for these people? This Bill says that even the most educated Native shall never have political equality with even the least educated and the least cultured White or Coloured man. This Bill says to these educated Natives: "There is no room for you, you must be driven back upon your own people." But we drive them back in hostility and disgruntlement, and do not let us forget this, that all that this Bill is doing for these educated Natives is to make them the leaders of their own people, in disaffection and revolt. No, the introduction of this principle in this Bill will not make for peace and safety but for hostility and conflict and strife. I would put it in this way. This Bill is a Bill the acknowledged aim of which is the self-preservation of the European. It starts out from fear, and its underlying conception is the interests of the stronger. I do not believe that, in those circumstances, you can attain self-preservation. I do not believe that you can, in this country, have a safe Native policy which is not based on consent. I do not believe that we can assure the future of White civilisation in South Africa, save with the consent and the goodwill of the non-European people.

When I hear the Christian principle of self-preservation invoked in connection with this Bill, then I am reminded of the eternal paradox that whosoever will save his life shall lose it. It has been said recently, and I think we all acclaim it, "that the spirit of inequality and subjection in which the Peace of Versailles was concluded could only lead to great trouble. We are passing through days of division and strife, we have had them for years, and they are the result of that peace." I can only hope that the same division and strife is not going to be the result of the spirit of inequality and subjection which is largely at the root of this Bill.

I said that this Bill is born largely of fear. I know people don't like that word. Let me be perfectly frank. It is a perfectly natural fear, it is a fear we all have whether we oppose or support this Bill. We have all got that fear of the White man being drowned in a Black ocean, and we have all got that fear of race mixture and miscegenation.

AN HON. MEMBER: A justified fear.

MR. HOFMEYR: No, it is an unreasoning fear, it is largely an illogical fear. Let

me put this to my friend. We are told that political equality must make for social equality, and, therefore, for race intermixture. We are told that in regard to the Natives, but many of those who tell us that in regard to the Native have no fear at all of political equality in regard to the Coloured man. There, apparently, political equality will not make for social equality. I do not believe that the principle applies necessarily in either case, and I shall say why. Because the facts show that you get most miscegenation where you have White and Black people side by side, and where the Black people are kept in subjection. You get least race intermixture in such countries where the development of the Black people is encouraged and their race consciousness, their pride and their self-esteem are stimulated.

Let me give you the facts in South Africa. Here in the Cape we have a measure of political equality, which we have not got in the rest of the Union. Now take the figures in regard to offences against the Immorality Act [of 1927—ed.] for the last three available years. The figures in the Cape, where you have political equality were 3.2 per 100,000 of the Native population. In the rest of the Union where you have no political equality, they were 6.4 per 100,000, or twice as many. I have taken out the figures in regard to crimes of violence with sexual intent. In the Cape the figure is .6 per 100,000 of the Native population. I am now dealing with crimes of violence with sexual intent, committed by Natives on Europeans, and the figure in the Cape is .6 per 100,000 of the Native population. In the rest of the Union the figures are 2.4 per 100,000.

MR. C. R. SWART:[3] That proves nothing.

MR. HOFMEYR: No, sir, the fear is an unreasoning fear but, it is there for all that, and we cannot get away from it. It is that fact together with the sentiment based on tradition that is to a large extent

[3] National Party.

behind this Bill. These are the facts that made the Prime Minister recede from the relative liberalism of the Bill of 1929 (which was) worse than the Bill of 1926, and made this Bill again worse than the Bill of 1929. And there is no finality. There is no more finality than there was in 1892, when Sir James Rose-Innes supported the Bill of that date because it might bring finality. That tide of reaction is still flowing forward. I know that those of us who are opposing that tide cannot hope to check it. The puny breastworks that we put up must be swept away, but I do believe that the mere putting up of those breastworks is going to accelerate the day when the tide will turn, as turn, I believe, it some day will.

Let me repeat then, I oppose this Bill. It is a Bill which replaces a vested right by a qualified and inferior citizenship, and which creates a system of communal representation. I oppose it because for that act of deprivation no adequate justification has been advanced. I oppose it because in that system of communal representation there are the seeds of hostility and strife, and I oppose it also because of those forces of reaction behind this Bill which, if left unresisted, are inevitably bound to do us greater harm than anything can do us today. I know perfectly well that I am speaking against the feeling of the overwhelming majority of this House. I know I am speaking against the feeling of the great mass of the people of this country, I know how my remarks will be described as "academic" and quixotic and unrealistic. I am accustomed to that. I can see all the adjectives that will be used. But these are matters on which the future must be left to judge. I expressed the belief that the tide of reaction will turn, and I base that belief on what I know of what is going on in the minds of some at least of the younger people in South Africa, especially in the universities. I believe that there is also a rising tide of liberalism in South Africa. It is mostly the younger people who are in the forefront of that tide. It is they who are the custodians of our future. And whatever we may or may not do today, it is by them that the ultimate issues in connection with this matter will have to be decided.

36 M. D. C. DE WET NEL
THE PRINCIPLES OF APARTHEID

The Honorable M. D. C. de Wet Nel (1901–) was formerly Bantu Commissioner General for the ethnic units of Venda and Tsonga (in the upper Transvaal). He was formerly Minister for Bantu Administration and Development in the South African government, and a principal Cabinet spokesman for the ideal form of apartheid—separate development of black and white South Africans, including segregation of the Bantu peoples into their own states, called Bantustans, where they might run their own affairs and preserve their own culture. Wet Nel has a degree of Doctor of Philosophy from Pretoria University and was secretary of the Nationalist party between 1939 and 1948. The following selection is an extract from his speech in the House of Assembly on May 18, 1959, explaining National Party policy during the debate on the second reading of the bill promoting Bantu self-government.

From *Debates of the House of Assembly (Hansard), Union of South Africa* (Cape Town: Hansard, 1959), CI, cols. 6006–6011, 6018–6024.

I want to say that it is my deep and honest conviction that we have reached the stage where serious attention should be devoted to actually giving the Bantu the opportunity to manage their own affairs; because that is one of the elementary and the most moral rights to which every person is entitled. It is the legacy demanded by every nation in the world, and the Bantu eagerly demands it just like the White man and every other nation. Every nation in the world finds its highest expression and fulfilment in managing its own affairs and in the creation of a material and spiritual heritage for its successive generations. We want to give the Bantu that right also. The demand for self-determination on the part of the non-White nations is one of the outstanding features of the past decade. Outside Africa more than a dozen non-White nations have already obtained their freedom. In Africa it is the greatest phenomenon of the time. There are a number of people in Africa who have already received their freedom, and others are on the way to receiving it. This desire to manage their own affairs exists in the hearts of the Bantu population, just as it exists in the hearts of all other nations in the world. It is therefore our duty to approach these matters soberly and realistically. It is no use putting our heads in the sand and pretending to see nothing. We have to face the real facts. These matters lie near to the soul of the nation, and no safety valve in the world can smother them forever. The late Dr. Malan described it very pithily in this House once when he said that one might just as well try to stop the Southeaster with a sieve as to suppress the national sentiments of a nation. That applies to the Bantu also.

I say we must approach these matters soberly and with clear minds. If we close our eyes to them we are heading for self-destruction and death. People who are reckless in that regard are committing treason to their own people and digging the grave of the nation. We hear so many provocative remarks about Bantu nationalism and Black nationalism, but it is my conviction that there is nothing of the kind. If it exists, then there is also something like White nationalism. But what does exist in fact is hatred on the part of the Black man for the White man. That is the monster which may still perhaps destroy all the best things in Africa. But I want to ask whether this monster has not to a large extent been created by the White man himself? The fact that he has ignored the existence of national enmities,[1] that he has ignored their own forms of government and that he has ignored their own cultural assets, has led to the growth of this monster, and that is the reason why we plead that this monster must not rear its head in South Africa. That is why we want to give them these opportunities.

Mr. Speaker, I want to say frankly that I believe in the existence of nationalism on the part of the Bantu population groups. We cannot deny it; it is there. Amongst the Zulus there is a feeling of nationalism which can serve as an example to more than one of us, but it is not a Bantu nationalism; it is their own racial nationalism, just as it exists amongst the White people of South Africa and of the world. I grant them that nationalism. If the White man is entitled to it, I ask what right we have to say that those people should not be entitled to it also? Let us be honest and fair. Moreover, nationalism is one of the forces which puts into motion the best things in the spirit of the human being. Nationalism is one of the forces which has led to the most beautiful deeds of idealism and sacrifice and inspiration. Should the Bantu not have it? It is the Nationalist who has learned to appreciate the cultural assets of other nations, and as someone once put it very strikingly, a Nationalist is the best citizen of the world. That is my belief in regard to this matter. For that reason I want to

[1] Entities?

say this. It will always be my task to respect these things of the Bantu, but to assist them to develop it as something beautiful and something which is in the interest of South Africa. It is our task to provide the opportunities for developing these matters, so that we may have co-operation instead of racial clashes. To think that we can solve this problem by lumping together in one community everything which is Bantu is nothing less than a crime towards the Bantu. One of the good things contained in this Bill is that it formally recognises these national units among the Bantu, and to give them the right and to encourage them to continue along this road of national development.

The question may be put in all fairness: Will it not be better, in the interest of South Africa, rather to continue building on the pattern we have now? I want to deal with a few considerations only.

In the first place, I stated the proposition that the overwhelming majority of the national groups in South Africa, including the Bantu, have rejected the ideal of a multi-racial community and have chosen separate development on their own. If we continued to build further on the present pattern, it would be nothing else but a negation of the will and the desires of the overwhelming majority of the population groups in South Africa, White as well as Bantu. In the second place we must be fair and honest and admit that the present state of affairs is very unsatisfactory to the Bantu and very uncertain for the Whites. If we continue building on the present pattern the position of the Whites will be very uncertain and the Bantu will not be satisfied. Let us remember that in this House there are three representatives who represent only the Bantu population of the Cape Province. The rest of the Bantu in South Africa are not represented in this House. Do hon. members want to tell me that the Bantu population takes no notice of that and that they are satisfied with it? It is

an injustice which rankles in the minds of the Bantu in the other parts of the country. That is one of the main factors which engenders a spirit of suspicion and doubt regarding the honesty and the fairness and the justice of the White man. It is a political state of affairs which can no longer be tolerated. If hon. members want to be fair and logical, they should ask that at least the rest of the Bantu population in South Africa should be represented in this House on an equal footing with those in the Cape Province, and if they do that, I ask: Where will it end? We would then be setting in progress the same process which is being experienced in Kenya, Nyasaland and Northern Rhodesia today. We just cannot foresee the results of it.

In the third place, it is my honest conviction that these Bantu population groups can best be guided on the road to progress if their whole development is Bantu orientated, which means that all the administrative bodies from the highest to the lowest should be linked up and the whole of the Bantu population should be concerned in them. It must form part of the whole structure. The present pattern was White orientated, because it was coupled to the White man. The result was that there was a flight from the Bantu community. The developed Native no longer sought the satisfaction of his ambition to develop amongst his own people, but in the White areas. Surely that is a very sad state of affairs. There was a migration going on, not only of migrant labourers from the Bantu areas, but also of educated people from the Bantu areas, that most essential material for building up of a community. In my opinion every nation in the world is entitled to benefit from the efforts of its best sons and daughters and a policy which is calculated to deprive them of it is immoral; it is human erosion. A policy like that cannot be tolerated. Such a policy is one of the chief causes of racial hatred.

In the fourth place, I am convinced in

my mind that the expansion of the present system will have the result that the White population of South Africa will be dominated by the political power of the Bantu population. If this pattern is extended logically in the future, I say that the White people will be dominated by the political power of the Bantu. Surely it must be a very stupid politician who cannot appreciate the logical consequences of this.

The present system of Bantu representation has really made no contribution in any way towards creating sound racial relations in South Africa. I challenge any person to deny that. All it has done is to increase racial tension. That is the only result which can today stand as a monument for those people, with few exceptions. If we extended the present system, what would the result be? It would create a racial hatred which South Africa simply cannot afford, because, in the course of years, we would then have a bitter struggle on the part of the White man to ensure that he is not ploughed under politically by the non-White groups of the population, but, at the same time, it must be remembered that if we accepted that principle today, then the Bantu would have to accept this Parliament as his Parliament, and he would then become involved in a struggle in which he would demand representation in this House on at least the same basis as the White man. That is the trouble which awaits South Africa, and I say that anybody who does not realise that, must be stupid. Mr. Speaker, if there are people who say that the Bantu will always be satisfied to be represented in Parliament by a few people, I say to them that they are living in a fool's paradise. No nation in the world would agree to it, and still much less the proud Bantu.

Reference has been made here to "White leadership with justice." Mr. Speaker, this whole outlook is so unrealistic and childishly naïve that it amuses one. It is pathetic. Show me one nation in our modern history which would be prepared to agree to such a thing. Even the Bushmen rejected it in respect to the Bantu. Do members of the United Party want to tell me that the proud Bantu would agree to it? They can go and tell that story to political baboons but not to intelligent people. It is a hallucination!

Mr. Speaker, the African states are giving their reply today to this issue with which we are dealing. We are getting an object lesson with regard to this same issue in various territories of Africa. Are we politically blind or politically deaf? Are we going to learn no lesson from that? In places like Kenya, Nyasaland and Northern Rhodesia we saw that the British Government was prepared to go very far in giving the Bantu, on this same sort of basis, a say together with the White man in the government of the country, and what were the results? Did it produce peace? No, it created greater dissatisfaction. On this very same basis, they wanted to give greater rights to the Native population of other territories, and the result was simply that those people, once they had been given these rights, demanded that the sole say should be in the hands of the majority of the people. They are not going to be satisfied with anything less than the sole say. Why then should South Africa be an exception? No, Mr. Speaker, this political pattern does not create racial peace, but racial tension; it does not produce harmonious relations but clashes; it does not produce confidence but fear; it does not bring peace but strife; it does not produce order but chaos.

Mr. Speaker, in the light of South Africa's fundamental choice and standpoint, on the basis of our experience extending over generations, having regard to the salvation of South Africa and the happiness of all groups of the population, there is only one way—the traditional way, the way which is embodied in this Bill which I am submitting to the House for its consideration.

I want to pause for a moment to deal with the recognition of Bantu homelands.

In the White Paper [Promotion of Bantu Self-Government—ed.] I put forward a few propositions which I do not want to repeat here, but I just want to make this submission again that in setting aside Bantu territories both before and after the establishment of Union, the object was not purely and simply to set aside land for them; the great object was to give that land to the various communities as their homelands. The object was not simply to set aside that land; the main object was to assist those communities with their development, to link them up with their land. This setting aside of land was undertaken not only by the British Government, but also by the Republican Governments. As from 1878 the Bantu territories of the Ciskei were deliberately demarcated by the British Government, and that was done in the region between the Great Fish and the Kei Rivers. The constituent parts of the present Transkei, with the retention of their identity as Bantu territories, were incorporated into the Cape Colony by means of a series of acts and proclamations as from 1879. In 1839 the Voortrekkers started with territorial demarcation in Natal, and that was continued by the British Government in 1843. Separate areas were demarcated and given to the Natal Native Trust in 1864. In 1897 Zululand proper, with the retention of its identity, was incorporated into Natal by legislation. In the Transvaal a start was made in 1853 with the granting of land to the tribes, and in 1881 a standing Native Location Commission started defining those areas. The republic of the Orange Free State, by means of grants and resolutions, also recognised Bantu areas. So, for example, in 1867, with a further extension in 1873, Witzieshoek was granted to two tribes, while in 1884 Thaba'Nchu was set aside for the Barolong. With the establishment of Union, the British Government kept the three large Bantu territories, Bechuanaland, Basutoland and Swaziland—which jointly represented one-third of the surface area of

British South Africa, outside the Union and thereby indicated that these territories should be maintained as Bantu territories. After the establishment of Union the Union Government, by legislation, immediately entrenched as Bantu territories the areas which had been recognised by its predecessor as Bantu territories, and it did so by incorporating them in terms of the Native Land Act of 1913. But the Union Government did not leave it at that. Subsequently, a further 7,250,-000 morgen [a morgen is 2.116 acres —ed.] of land were released for systematic addition to the Bantu areas and since then nearly 5,000,000 morgen of land have been added. But I say again that the main task was neglected, and that is the development which should have accompanied that. In the case of the Transvaal, the Free State and Natal the main object was perfectly clear.

I just want to pause for a moment to deal with the aims which it was intended to achieve in setting aside Bantu areas. The main aim was to create homelands for the Bantu. In the case of the Cape Colony there was a two-fold policy. The first aim coincided with that of the Transvaal and Natal, and the other was to establish a number of small locations which were to serve as a means of breaking up the tribes, of introducing civilisation to the Bantu, and, as an historian put it, as labour reservoirs for the Whites. Here we really had a difference between the opinion of the people and that of the authorities, but the mass of the population in South Africa regarded these areas as the homelands of the Bantu and the Bantu accepted them as such.

One of the fine things that we are doing in this Bill is to give formal recognition to the various Bantu population groups. That is a desire that we find on the part of all the groups of the population. In the short time during which I have had some dealings with them, one of the questions which has been put to me everywhere is this: "Can't you give us recognition; why are you tearing us asunder?" In this Bill formal recognition is being given to the existence of those population groups, but particularly to the process of national development by and in the population groups themselves. I think by this time hon. members will concede that you cannot start a process of development by simply linking it up with the White man's way of life. That would be nonsensical. No process in which the Bantu's dignity is not acknowledged can form the basis on which development can take place, and in refusing to appreciate his own system of government and his own rights we slight the dignity of the Bantu himself. But hon. members will also concede a second thing, Mr. Speaker, and that is that that process cannot be started by creating an artificial unit, in other words, by bundling all the Bantu together in one common society, as many hon. members on the other side want to do, because there are only two bonds which bind them together: The first is their colour and the other is their hatred of the White man. But there is something greater than that, something higher than that which binds people together, and that is their spiritual treasures, the cultural treasures of a people. It is these fine things which have united other nations in the world. That is why we say that the basis of our approach is that the Bantu too will be linked together by traditional and emotional bonds, by their own language, their own culture, their national possessions. I am convinced that for this measure I shall receive the gratitude of the Bantu throughout South Africa.

This Bill also gives the various population groups their own territorial authorities. That is very important. Where there are no territorial authorities as yet, a Territorial Council will be established in the meantime, but I am convinced that within a year or two all these matters will be disposed of.

But the most important consideration is that this Bill makes it possible for the Governor-General to transfer his legislative powers systematically to those Territorial Authorities. Because of the nature of our national structure it is not possible today to see this in clear perspective, but I am convinced that once these Territorial Authorities have all been established, and these powers have been systematically transferred to them, we are going to achieve excellent results. This is an act of faith in the Bantu such as we have never had before in South Africa, and it is something which is going to satisfy him and for which he is already very grateful today. I readily concede that many of these things will take a little time before they can all be arranged and before all these powers can be granted, but once all the Territorial Authorities are in operation, it is my intention to review this whole matter and to see how we can best shape it in the interests of every population group and in the interests of the whole of South Africa. But the Bantu himself will have to help in extending this system. He will be called upon to extend it, and that is one of the fine principles contained in this Bill, because now it will no longer be the White man who will be doing these things; it will be the Bantu himself.

In the second place I want to mention another important aspect, and that is that we envisage that the Bantu will develop his own courts. Let me put it this way: The Bantu has developed a very fine legal system which ensures a high degree of justice. That is why it has also been recognised by the authorities, but the mistake that was made was that no attention was given to the question of allowing the courts to develop together with the development of the community. It was looked down upon and jeered at. After all, according to the United Party it was just a court conducted by barbarians. Mr. Speaker, that is not fair towards the Bantu; it is not reconcilable with the general development of the Bantu. That is why this Bill provides for special attention to be given to this matter so that it will become possible for them to administer their own system of justice. They will be assisted actively to extend their own courts, and I anticipate that the time will come when they themselves will have their own supreme court in their own territories with their own judges on the Bench. I propose to give very serious attention to this matter.

But this Bill goes further. It holds out this prospect that the Territorial Authorities are going to look after their own education. I just want to announce that the Department of Bantu Education is ready, as soon as the Bantu Territorial Authorities are in operation, to place a large portion of the education in the areas concerned directly under the Territorial Authorities. That will mean that the Territorial Authority will exercise authority and control over all the school boards and committees in this area. In exercising that control it will have in its hands the most important means of building up its community culturally and economically. Just think what it will mean to the Bantu if he himself exercises control over his education. Welfare work and social services will also be placed under them in due course. We shall see to it that it takes place on a sound basis.

Then I want to mention another important matter and that is that in due course the Native Trust Lands will be transferred to the Territorial Authorities, a very important decision. It must not be forgotten that the land which has been set aside for them—7,250,000 morgen—falls under the Native Trust. The Native Trust is responsible for the development of that land, etc. We now envisage transferring this land in due course to the Territorial Authorities. They will then be responsible for the proper conservation of the soil and its development, etc. I need only say this, Mr. Speaker, that when we look at the results which are being achieved at the present time, there can be no doubt that it would be in the interests of the Bantu

and of South Africa as a whole to entrust that task to the Natives. It is a question of faith. They would be responsible for the allocation of that land and all that type of thing. Let me just say this: There are very few things which have caused so much dissatisfaction amongst the Bantu as the fact that the land which was purchased at the time—I refer to the land which was promised to them at the time by General Hertzog and of which a portion was bought—was placed under the Native Trust and not directly under the chiefs. Throughout the whole of South Africa I have heard this reproach. Under the system which is now being introduced it will fall under the Territorial Authority, which is a responsible body. This is an important step forward.

Then I want to mention another important principle which is contained in this Bill. Formerly the Governor-General could appoint or dismiss any chief at will. He will now be obliged to consult the Territorial Authority. I admit that in the past the Governor-General has always consulted the tribe, but the responsibility is now going to rest with the Territorial Authority. In this way it is being given status, it is being given the status in its own territory which our Government has in the territory of the White man. That is the basic approach in connection with this matter.

But there is another important principle embodied in this legislation, and that is that for the first time official links are being instituted between the Bantu territories and the Natives in the cities. For the first time! I admit at once that here we are facing a very great problem. I readily admit that there are many Bantu in the White areas. But I also want to make this further submission that very large numbers of those Bantu were not born in South Africa. There are many of them whose home is Basutoland. Do you know, sir, that there are approximately 1,000,000 Sothos in South Africa? Large numbers of them were born in the Protectorate of Bechuanaland, and Swaziland is the home of a large section. Do not let us overlook that factor. That is a factor which will have to be faced squarely sooner or later. But that does not detract from the fact that there are also large numbers of our own Natives in the cities, and that is a very important problem. The question which is frequently asked is this: What is to be their future?

Let me first say this—and in this regard I want to be explicit and clear. It must be quite clearly understood by the United Party and by the whole world that those Natives will never become part of the White community; we are not going to follow a policy which is going to lead to a common society in South Africa. Let us be perfectly clear and explicit on that point. But in the second place, I want to make this statement that the vast majority of those people have never lost their links with their own territories. I personally made some pilot surveys and the Tomlinson Commission[2] made a large number of pilot surveys over the whole country, and it was found that easily 80 per cent, if not more, of those Bantu had always retained some link or other with the Bantu areas. We are not faced here with a problem of displaced persons. Our practical experience has been that although a Bantu has been in the city for years, for perhaps two or three generations, he still knows where his tribe is, and you will be surprised to know, sir, how readily he is absorbed again into his tribe. Why do hon. members come along and make a mountain out of a molehill? The fact of the matter is that links will now be created between the Bantu areas and those people in the cities. I have no doubt that it will have a very salutary effect. It will also have a salutary effect on the moral standards of those people. It must not be for-

gotten that as far as customs, etc. are concerned, the Bantu in the cities constitute rather a loose population, and in those places where the different ethnic groups are already separately housed and where we have given them non-official recognition, it has already been shown that a new ideal has been created for these people, where they have their own links and their own mother-tongue and when we restore to them those emotional links which are of so much value to every nation in the world. I have no doubt that in this way we are going to create a very fine link as far as the whole Native population is concerned.

Then I just want to say that in this process we should at least concede to the Bantu what the English people did not begrudge themselves. Let me just remind the House that the whole democratic system of the British nation was developed round the Royal house and the nobility. Let them deny it. It took years, but that is the position. Today every Englishman is proud of that democratic system. But it must not be forgotten that it is only since 1832 that that system has actually taken definite shape. Why then do we begrudge this same process to the Bantu? Here we have the same process. What is contained in this Bill is something that the Bantu understands, something that is integrated into his life.

But hon. members may ask perhaps why we do not carry on with this matter and leave alone the question of Natives' representation; why we do not allow the Natives' representatives to remain in this House; why we do not first complete the whole pattern and then consider thereafter whether we want to abolish the Native representation in this House. I just want to say that that is an attitude which can only be adopted by a person who has no knowledge at all of the Native. Any person who has taken the slightest trouble to make a study of the approach of the Bantu population to these matters, could never adopt such an attitude. Because in

[2] Appointed in 1948 by the Malan Government. Chairman: Professor F. R. Tomlinson of Pretoria University. [The commission was to consider the implementation of separate development—ed.]

connection with this political issue, they have an axiom which runs as follows, that the idea of two bulls in one kraal never works. The Native does not want it; to him it is unthinkable. To have two political processes which are diametrically opposed to each other and which try to destroy each other, is something which the Native simply cannot understand, and he would regard that as the greatest dishonesty on the part of the White man. Sir, there are Natives who have asked me to abolish the Native representation immediately. If we want to be honest, then we must take into account the approach of the Bantu himself, and then we cannot start such a process; we must adopt the course that is acceptable and understandable and honest towards the Bantu population, a course which in their eyes is not a conflicting policy but which they regard as an honest policy.

The question may be put to me: What does the Native population think about this matter? How do they feel? I just want to say that after the introduction of this Bill I made it my business to make its contents known to all the Bantu population groups throughout South Africa. More than 3,000 copies of the Bill and of the White Paper were distributed amongst them. The full contents were also published in the journal *Bantu*, more than 30,000 copies of which were distributed. What was the reaction? The reaction was this, that I have here a large number of telegrams from all parts of South Africa, from all the important Bantu population groups, from Cyprian, from Victor Poto, from Botha Sigcau, from the Venda chiefs, from the Ciskei, etc. I have had telegrams from the responsible groups in every territory conveying their gratitude and congratulations and telling me to go ahead with this. And do you know, sir, that I did not have a single letter or telegram of protest? Do you know where I came across a protest? A moment ago at the entrance to Parliament, where there is a placard bearing the words "no taxation without representation." The Black Sash!

MRS. BALLINGER: Hear, hear!

MR. DE WET NEL: I agree, but that is one of the great principles embodied in this Bill, because here it is envisaged that in the future they will impose their own taxes, and the time will come when all taxes in the Bantu areas will be imposed by the Bantu themselves. That is the only protest that I received. Everywhere the Bantu have acclaimed this as a new day and a new era which has dawned for the Bantu in South Africa. That is their approach to this matter.

The aims of this Bill could be briefly summarised as follows:

1. It gives expression to the racial pattern and the philosophy of life of the people of South Africa in respect to the colour question. It is the product of a deep and honest conviction which flows from historical experience and which is based on the Christian principles underlying the approach of our people, because we do not begrudge those people what we claim for ourselves.

2. It rests on the conviction that it will ward off those factors which may possibly plough the White man under, but at the same time it also creates the possibility for the Bantu to bring to the fullest fruition his personal and national ideas within his own population group. What we demand for ourselves, we do not begrudge the Bantu. Our approach is not simply negative but also positive.

3. It converts the Bantu development which was formerly instituted under the direction of the White man, into a development which will be anchored in the Bantu community itself, a development in terms of which all the factors of nation and community building will be actively placed in the service of each group of the Bantu population, on the same lines as in the case of the White man. In this way the material and spiritual growth of the Bantu population groups will be set in motion, so that they will also be able to

make a contribution to the eternal and lasting values of South Africa and of the world as a whole.

4. It lays the foundation of a form of government in which all population groups, on a basis of honour and mutual respect, can be informed and consulted about the great problems of South Africa and where everyone's efforts can be harnessed in a spirit of mutual trust for the welfare of South Africa.

5. It creates, I am convinced, a future of hope and expectation for all population groups in South Africa, a future of peace and security, not only for the White population of South Africa, but also for the Bantu population groups. Now every group will know in which direction it is moving. It removes the mists of doubt and uncertainty, which are the greatest cause of mistrust of the White man. Those mists of doubt and uncertainty have now disappeared. Everybody will know in which direction he is heading, and it is that certainty which gives man the greatest satisfaction.

6. I am deeply convinced that this is the only basis on which a great and happy South Africa can be built for all population groups.

37 NELSON ROLIHLAHLE MANDELA
VERWOERD'S TRIBALISM

Nelson Rolihlahle Mandela (1918–) is one of South Africa's foremost African nationalist leaders. He had been serving a sentence of life imprisonment on Robben Island when, in February 1990, he was released by the government of South Africa and resumed the leadership of the African National Congress. The son of a Tembu chief, Mandela left the University of Fort Hare in 1940 and went to Johannesburg, where he became involved in the formation of the Youth League of the African National Congress (ANC), a radical "ginger-group" within South Africa's oldest African nationalist organization. When the ANC launched its passive resistance campaign in defiance of apartheid legislation, Mandela was Volunteer-in-Chief and was later elected to the National Executive of the ANC. Restrictions were subsequently placed on him by the government, and in 1956 he was arrested and was one of the defendants in the abortive treason trial (1956– 1961). He rose to prominence in the white community in 1961, when South Africa declared itself a republic. Mandela went underground to organize a stay-at-home campaign and became known as the "Scarlet Pimpernel." While underground he also acted as one of the leaders of a sabotage group known as Umkhonto We Sizwe (Spear of the Nation). Many of the leaders of this group were arrested in 1963 at Rivonia and in 1964 some of them, including Mandela, were sentenced to life imprisonment.

During the 1950s, Mandela wrote a number of analytical articles on the South African situation, which have recently been collected into a book entitled No Easy Walk to Freedom, *edited by Ruth First.*

South Africa belongs to all who live in it, black and white.—Freedom Charter.

All the Bantu have their permanent homes in the Reserves and their entry into other areas

From Chapter 8, *No Easy Walk to Freedom,* by Nelson Mandela, © Nelson Mandela, 1965, Basic Books, Inc., Publishers, New York. Reprinted by permission of Basic Books, Inc. and Heinemann Educational Books Ltd.

and into the urban areas is merely of a temporary nature and for economic reasons. In other words, they are admitted as work-seekers, not as settlers.—Dr. W. W. M. Eiselen, Secretary of the Department of Bantu Administration and Development. (Article in *Optima*, March 1959)

The statements quoted above contain diametrically opposite conceptions of this country, its future, and its destiny. Obviously they cannot be reconciled. They have nothing in common, except that both of them look forward to a future of affairs rather than that which prevails at present. At present, South Africa does not "belong"—except in a moral sense —to all. Ninety-seven per cent of the country is legally owned by members (a handful of them at that) of the dominant White minority. And at present by no means "all" Africans have their "permanent homes" in the Reserves. Millions of Africans were born and have their permanent homes in the towns and cities and elsewhere outside the Reserves, have never seen the Reserves, and have no desire to go there.[1]

It is necessary for the people of this country to choose between these two alternative paths. It is assumed that readers of *Liberation* [an anti-apartheid journal —ed.] are familiar with the detailed proposals contained in the Charter.

Let us therefore study the policies submitted by the Nationalist Party.

The newspapers have christened the Nationalists' plan as one for "Bantustans." The hybrid word is, in many ways, extremely misleading. It derives from the partitioning of India after the reluctant departure of the British, and as a condition thereof, into two separate states, Hindustan and Pakistan. There is no real

parallel with the Nationalists' proposals, for:

(a) India and Pakistan constitute two completely separate and politically independent states.

(b) Muslims enjoy equal rights in India; Hindus enjoy equal rights in Pakistan.

(c) Partition was submitted to and approved by both parties, or at any rate fairly widespread and influential sections of each.

The Government's plans do not envisage the partitioning of this country into separate, self-governing states. They do not envisage equal rights, or any rights at all, for Africans outside the Reserves. Partition has never been approved of by Africans and never will be. For that matter it has never really been submitted to or approved of by the Whites. The term "Bantustan" is therefore a complete misnomer, and merely tends to help the Nationalists perpetrate a fraud.

Let us examine each of these aspects in detail.

It is typical of the Nationalists' propaganda techniques that they describe their measures in misleading titles, which convey the opposite of what the measures contain. Verwoerd called his law greatly extending and intensifying the pass laws the "Abolition of Passes" Act. Similarly, he has introduced into the current parliamentary session a measure called the "Promotion of Bantu Self-Government Bill." It starts off by decreeing the abolition of the tiny token representation of Africans (by Whites) in Parliament and the Cape Provincial Council.

It goes on to provide for the division of the African population into eight "ethnic units" (the so-called Bantustans). They are: North and South Sotho, Swazi, Tsonga, Tswana, Venda, Xhosa, and Zulu. These units are to undergo a "gradual development to self-government."

This measure was described by the Prime Minister, Dr. Verwoerd, as a "su-

---

[1] According to the 1951 census, trust land locations and Reserves accounted for only $2^1/2$ million out of a total African population of, at that time, $8^1/2$ million. A further $2^1/2$ million, nearly, were on European-owned farms. The rest were mainly in urban areas.

premely positive step" towards placing Africans "on the road to self-government." Mr. De Wet Nel, Minister of Bantu Affairs, said the people in the Reserves "would gradually be given more powers to rule themselves."

The scheme is elaborated in a White Paper, tabled in the House of Assembly, to "explain" the Bill. According to this document, the immediate objects of the Bill are:

(a) The recognition of the so-called Bantu National Units and the appointment of commissioners-general whose task will be to give guidance and advice to the units in order to promote their general development, with special reference to the administrative field.

(b) The linking of Africans working in urban areas with territorial authorities established under the Bantu Authorities Act, by conferring powers on the Bantu Authorities to nominate persons as their representatives in urban areas.

(c) The transfer to the Bantu territorial authorities, at the appropriate time, of land in their areas at present held by the Native Trust.

(d) The vesting in territorial Bantu authorities of legislative authority and the right to impose taxes, and to undertake works and give guidance to subordinate authorities.

(e) The establishments of territorial boards for the purpose of temporary liaison through commissioners-general if during the transition period the administrative structure in any area has not yet reached the stage where a territorial authority has been established.

(f) The abolition of representation in the highest European governing bodies.

According to the same White Paper, the Bill has the following further objects:

(a) The creation of homogeneous administrative areas for Africans by uniting the members of each so-called national group in the national unit, concentrated in one coherent homeland where possible.

(b) The education of Africans to a sound understanding of the problems of soil conversion and agriculture so that all rights over and responsibilities in respect of soil in African areas may be assigned to them.

This includes the gradual replacement of European agricultural officers of all grades by qualified and competent Africans.

(c) The systematic promotion of a diverse economy in the African areas, acceptable to Africans and to be developed by them.

(d) The education of the African to a sound understanding of the problems and aims of Bantu education so that, by the decentralization of powers, responsibility for the different grades of education may be vested in them.

(e) The training of Africans with a view to effectively extending their own judicial system and their education to a sound understanding of the common law with a view to transferring to them responsibilities for the administration of justice in their areas.

(f) The gradual replacement of European administrative officers by qualified and competent Africans.

(g) The exercise of legislative powers by Africans in respect of their areas, at first at a limited scale, but with every intention of gradually extending this power.

It will be seen that the African people are asked to pay a very high price for this so-called "self-government" in the Reserves. Urban Africans—the workers, businessmen, and professional men and women, who are the pride of our people in the stubborn and victorious march towards modernization and progress—are to be treated as outcasts, not even "settlers" like Dr. Verwoerd. Every vestige of rights and opportunities will be ruthlessly destroyed. Everywhere outside the Reserves an African will be tolerated only on condition that he is for the convenience of the Whites.

There will be forcible uprooting and mass removals of millions of people to "homogeneous administrative areas." The Reserves, already intolerably overcrowded, will be crammed with hundreds of thousands more people evicted by the Government.

In return for all these hardships, in return for Africans abandoning their birthright as citizens, pioneers, and inhabitants of South Africa, the Government promises them "self-government" in the tiny 13 per cent that their greed and miserliness "allocates" to us. But what sort of self-government is this that is promised?

There are two essential elements to self-government, as the term is used and understood all over the modern world. They are:

1. *Democracy.* The organs of government must be representative; that is to say, they must be freely chosen leaders and representatives of the people, whose mandate must be renewed at periodic democratic elections.

2. *Sovereignty.* The government thus chosen must be free to legislate and act as it deems fit on behalf of the people, not subject to any limitations upon its powers by any alien authority.

Neither of these two essentials is present in the Nationalist plan. The "Bantu National Units" will be ruled in effect by the commissioners-general appointed by the Bantu Government, and administered by the Bantu Affairs Department officials under his control. When the Government says it plans gradually increasing self-gov-

ernment, it merely means that more powers in future will be exercised by appointed councils of chiefs and headmen. No provision is made for elections. The Nationalists say that chiefs, not elected legislatures, are "the Bantu tradition."

There was a time when, like all peoples on earth, Africans conducted their simple communities through chiefs, advised by tribal councils and mass meetings of the people. In those times the chiefs were indeed representative governors. Nowhere, however, have such institutions survived the complexities of modern industrial civilization. Moreover, in South Africa we all know full well that no chief can retain his post unless he submits to Verwoerd, and many chiefs who sought the interest of their people before position and self-advancement have, like President Lutuli, been deposed.

Thus, the proposed Bantu authorities will not be, in any sense of the term, representative or democratic.

The point is made with pride by the Bantu Affairs Department itself in an official publication:

The councillors will perform their task without fear or prejudice, because they are not elected by the majority of votes, and they will be able to lead their people onwards . . . even though . . . it may demand hardships and sacrifices.

A strange paean to autocracy, from a department of a Government which claims to be democratic!

In spite of all their precautions to see that their "territorial authorities"—appointed themselves, subject to dismissal by themselves and under constant control by their commissioners-general and their Bantu Affairs Department—never become authentic voices of the people, the Nationalists are determined to see that even those puppet bodies never enjoy real power of sovereignty.

In his notorious (and thoroughly dishonest) article in *Optima,* Dr. Eiselen draws a far-fetched comparison between the relations between the future "Bantustans" and the Union Government, on the one hand, and those between Britain and the self-governing Dominions on the other. He foresees:

A cooperative South African system based on the Commonwealth conception, with the Union Government gradually changing its position from guardian and trustee to become instead the senior member of a group of separate communities.

To appreciate the full hypocrisy of this statement, it must be remembered that Dr. Eiselen is an official of a Nationalist Party Government, a member of a party which has built its fortune for the past half century on its cry that it stands for full untrammelled sovereignty within the Commonwealth, that claims credit for Hertzog's achievements in winning the Statute of Westminster, which proclaims such sovereignty, and which even now wants complete independence and a republic outside the Commonwealth.

It cannot be claimed, therefore, that Eiselen and Verwoerd do not understand the nature of a commonwealth, or sovereignty, or federation.

What are we to think, then, in the same article, when Dr. Eiselen comes into the open, and declares:

The utmost degree of autonomy in administrative matters which the Union Parliament is likely to be prepared to concede to these areas will stop short of actual surrender of sovereignty by the European trustee, and there is therefore no prospect of a federal system with eventual equality among members taking the place of the South African Commonwealth . . .

There is no sovereignty then. No autonomy. No democracy. No self-government. Nothing but a crude, empty fraud, to bluff the people at home and abroad, and to serve as a pretext for heaping yet more hardships and injustices upon the African people.

Politically, the talk about self-government for the Reserves is a swindle. Economically, it is an absurdity.

The few scattered African Reserves in various parts of the Union, comprising about 13 per cent of the least desirable land area, represent the last shreds of land ownership left to the African people of their original ancestral home. After the encroachments and depredations of generations of European land-sharks, achieved by force and by cunning, and culminating in the outrageous Land Act from 1913 onwards, had turned the once free and independent Tswana, Sotho, Xhosa, Zulu, and other peasant farmers of this country into a nation of landless outcasts and roving beggars, humble "work-seekers" on the mines and the farms where yesterday they had been masters of the land, the new White masters of the country "generously presented" them the few remaining miserable areas as reservoirs and breeding-grounds for Black labour. These are the Reserves.

It was never claimed or remotely considered by the previous governments of the Union that these Reserves could become economically self-sufficient "national homes" for 9,600,000 African people of this country. The final lunacy was left to Dr. Verwoerd, Dr. Eiselen, and the Nationalist Party.

The facts are—as every reader who remembers Govan Mbeki's brilliant series of articles on the Transkei in *Liberation* will be aware—that the Reserves are congested distressed areas, completely unable to sustain their present populations. The majority of the adult males are always away from home working in the towns, mines, or European-owned farms. The people are on the verge of starvation.

The White Paper speaks of teaching Africans soil conservation and agriculture and replacing European agricultural officers by Africans. This is merely trifling with the problem. The root problem of the Reserves is the intolerable congestion which already exists. No amount of agricultural instruction will ever enable 13 per cent of the land to sustain 66 per cent of the population.

The Government is, of course, fully aware of the fact. They have no intention of creating African areas which are genuinely self-supporting (and which could therefore create a genuine possibility for self-government). If such areas were indeed self-supporting, where would the Chamber of Mines and the Nationalist farmers get their supplies of cheap labour?

In the article to which I have already referred, Dr. Eiselen bluntly admits:

In fact not much more than a quarter of the community (on the Reserves) can be farmers, the others seeking their livelihood in industrial, commercial, professional, or administrative employment.

Where are they to find such employment? In the Reserves? To anyone who knows these poverty-stricken areas, sadly lacking in modern communications, power resources, and other needed facilities, the idea of industrial development seems far-fetched indeed. The beggarly £500,000 voted to the so-called "Bantu Investment Corporation" by Parliament is mere eyewash: it would not suffice to build a single decent road, railway line, or power station.

The Government has already established a number of "rural locations"—townships in the Reserves. The Eiselen article says a number more are planned: he mentions a total of no less than ninety-six. Since the residents will not farm, how will they manage to keep alive, still less pay rents and taxes and support the traders, professional classes, and civil servants whom the optimistic Eiselen envisages will make a living there?

Fifty-seven towns on the borders of the Reserves have been designated as centres where White capitalists can set up industries. Perhaps some will migrate, and thus "export" their capital resources of cheap labour and land. Certainly, unlike the Reserves (which are a monument to the callous indifference of the Union Parliament to the needs of the non-voting African taxpayers), these towns have power, water, transport, railways, etc. The Nationalist Government, while it remains in office, will probably subsidize capitalists who migrate in this way. It is already doing so in various ways, thus creating unemployment in the cities. But it is unlikely that any large-scale voluntary movement will take place away from the big, established industrial centres, with their well-developed facilities, available materials, and markets.

Even if many industries were forced to move to the border areas around the Reserves it would not make one iota of difference to the economic viability of the Reserves themselves. The fundamental picture of the Union's economy could remain fundamentally the same as at present: a single integrated system based upon the exploitation of African labour by White capitalists.

Economically, the "Bantustan" concept is just as big a swindle as it is politically.

Thus we find, if we really look into it, that this grandiose "partition" scheme, this "supremely positive step" of Dr. Verwoerd, is like all apartheid schemes—high-sounding double-talk to conceal a policy of ruthless oppression of the non-Whites and of buttressing the unwarranted privileges of the White minority, especially the farming, mining, and financial circles.

Even if it were not so, however, even if the scheme envisaged a genuine sharing-out of the country on the basis of population figures, and a genuine transfer of power to elected representatives of the people, it would remain fundamentally unjust and dangerously unstable unless it were submitted to, accepted, and endorsed by all parties to the agreement. To think otherwise is to fly in the face of the principle of self-determination, which is upheld by all countries and confirmed in the United Nations Charter, to which this country is pledged.

Now even Dr. Eiselen recognizes this difficulty to some extent. He pays lip-service to the Atlantic Charter and appeals to "Western democracy." He mentions the argument that apartheid would only be acceptable "provided that the parties concerned agreed to this of their own free will." And then he most dishonestly evades the whole issue. "There is no reason for ruling out apartheid on the grounds that the vast majority of the population oppose it," he writes. "The Bantu as a whole do not demand integration, in a single society. This is the idea . . . merely of a small minority."

Even Dr. Eiselen, however, has not the audacity to claim that the African people actually favour apartheid or partition.

Let us state clearly the facts of the matter, with the greatest possible clarity.

NO SERIOUS OR RESPONSIBLE LEADER, GATHERING, OR ORGANIZATION OF THE AFRICAN PEOPLE HAS EVER ACCEPTED SEGREGATION, SEPARATION, OR THE PARTITION OF THIS COUNTRY IN ANY SHAPE OR FORM.

At Bloemfontein in 1956, under the auspices of the United African clergy, perhaps the most widely attended and representative gathering of African representatives, of every shade of political opinion ever held, unanimously and uncompromisingly rejected the Tomlinson Report, on which the Verwoerd plan is based, and voted in favour of a single society.

Even the rural areas, where dwell the "good" (i.e. simple and ignorant) "Bantu" of the imagination of Dr. Verwoerd and Dr. Eiselen, attempts to impose apartheid have met, time after time, with furious, often violent resistance. Chief after chief has been deposed or deported for resisting "Bantu authorities" plans. Those who, out of short-sightedness, cowardice, or corruption, have accepted these

plans have earned nothing but the contempt of their own people.

It is a pity that, on such a serious subject, and at such a crucial period, serious misstatements should have been made by some people who purport to speak on behalf of the Africans. For example, Mrs. Margaret Ballinger, the Liberal Party M.P., is reported as saying in the Assembly "no confidence" debate:

The Africans have given their answer to this apartheid proposition but, of course, no one ever listens to them. They have said: "If you want separation then let us have it. Give us half of South Africa. Give us the eastern half of South Africa. Give us some of the developed resources because we have helped to develop them." (*S.A. Outlook,* March 1959)

It is most regrettable that Mrs. Ballinger should have made such a silly and irresponsible statement towards, one fears, the end of a distinguished parliamentary career. For in this instance she has put herself in the company of those who do not listen to the Africans. No Africans of any standing have ever made the proposals put forward by her.

The leading organization of the African people is the African National Congress. Congress has repeatedly denounced apartheid. It has repeatedly endorsed the Freedom Charter [a manifesto of ideals for future South African society drafted by African nationalists and their associates of other races—ed.], which claims South Africa "for all its people." It is true that occasionally individual Africans become so depressed and desperate at Nationalist misrule that they have tended to clutch at any straw to say: give us any little corner where we may be free to run our own affairs. But Congress has always firmly rejected such momentary tendencies and refused to barter our birthright, which is South Africa, for such illusory "Bantustans."

Commenting on a suggestion by Professor du Plessis that a federation of "Bantustans" be established, Mr. Duma Nokwe, secretary-general of the African National Congress, totally rejected such a plan as unacceptable. The correct approach, he said, would be the extension of the franchise rights to Africans. Thereafter a National Convention of all the people of South Africa could be summoned and numerous suggestions of the democratic changes that should be brought about, including the suggestion of Professor du Plessis, could form the subject of the Convention.

Here, indeed, Mr. Nokwe has put his finger on the spot. There is no need for Dr. Eiselen, Mrs. Ballinger, or others to argue about "what the Africans think" about the future of this country. Let the people speak for themselves! Let us have a free vote and a free election of delegates to a national convention, irrespective of colour or nationality. Let the Nationalists submit their plan, and the Congress its Charter. If Verwoerd and Eiselen think the Africans support their schemes they need not fear such a procedure. If they are not prepared to submit to public opinion, then let them stop parading and pretending to the outside world that they are democrats, and talking revolting nonsense about "Bantu self-government."

Dr. Verwoerd may deceive the simple-minded Nationalist voters with his talk of Bantustans, but he will not deceive anyone else, neither the African people, nor the great world beyond the borders of this country. We have heard such talk before, and we know what it means. Like everything else that has come from the Nationalist Government, it spells nothing but fresh hardships and suffering to the masses of the people.

Behind the fine talk of "self-government" is a sinister design.

The abolition of African representation in Parliament and the Cape Provincial Council shows that the real purpose of the scheme is not to concede autonomy to Africans but to deprive them of all say in the government of the country in exchange for a system of local government controlled by a minister who is not responsible to them but to a Parliament in which they have no voice. This is not autonomy but autocracy.

Contact between the minister and the Bantu authorities will be maintained by five commissioners-general. These officials will act as the watchdogs of the minister to ensure that the "authorities" strictly toe the line. Their duty will be to ensure that these authorities should not become the voice of the African people but that of the Nationalist Government.

In terms of the White Paper, steps will be taken to "link" Africans working in urban areas with the territorial authorities established under the Bantu Authorities Act by conferring powers on these authorities to nominate persons as their representatives in urban areas. This means in effect that efforts will be made to place Africans in the cities under the control of their tribal chiefs—a retrograde step.

Nowhere in the Bill or in the various proclamations dealing with the creation of Bantu authorities is there provision for democratic elections by Africans falling within the jurisdiction of the authorities.

In the light of these facts it is sheer nonsense to talk of South Africa as being about to take a "supremely positive step towards placing Africans on the road to self-government," or of having given them more powers to rule themselves. As Dr. Eiselen clearly pointed out in his article in *Optima*, the establishment of Bantustans will not in any way affect White supremacy since even in such areas Whites will stay supreme. The Bantustans are not intended to voice aspirations of the African people; they are instruments for their subjection. Under the pretext of giving them self-government the African people are being split up into tribal units in order to retard their growth and development into full nationhood.

The new Bantu Bill and the policy behind it will bear heavily on the peasants in the Reserves. But it is not they who are the chief target of Verwoerd's new policy.

His new measures are aimed, in the first place, at the millions of Africans in the great cities of this country, the factory workers and intellectuals who have raised the banner of freedom and democracy and human dignity, who have spoken forth boldly the message that is shaking imperialism to its foundations throughout this great continent of Africa.

The Nationalists hate and fear that ban-ner and that message. They will try to destroy them, by striking with all their might at the standard-bearer and vanguard of the people, the working class.

Behind the "self-government" talks lies a grim programme of mass evictions, political persecution, and police terror. It is the last desperate gamble of a hated and doomed fascist autocracy—which, fortunately, is soon due to make its exit from the stage of history.

May 1959

38 HELEN SUZMAN
MRS. SUZMAN AND APARTHEID

Helen Suzman is the sole member of Parliament representing the Progressive party, which advocates a gradual evolution to a nonracial society. Her constituency is the wealthy Houghton district of Johannesburg. Mrs. Suzman was Assistant Statistician to the Accountants for the War Supplies Board from 1941 to 1944 and Part-Time Lecturer in Economic History at Witwatersrand University from 1944 to 1952. She is a member of the Council of the Institute of Race Relations. Mrs. Suzman's speech of January 28, 1965, which she made during the annual "no confidence" debate initiated by the opposition United party, follows.

Mrs. SUZMAN: Members on the Government side are always giving us impossible choices to make in South Africa. We have heard from the hon. Prime Minister that South Africa had to choose between being poor and White or mixed and rich; this afternoon we heard from the hon. Deputy Minister of Labour that South Africa has to choose between a shortage of labour and prosperity. Does it never occur to hon. members on the other side that these are not the only choices lying before this country? The country can be prosperous and does not have to suffer this shortage of labour. Indeed a little advanced planning would have seen to it that we would not suffer such a shortage of labour. What is more, I want to warn the hon. Deputy Minister that prosperity will disappear in South Africa and that we will have inflation unless steps are in fact taken, drastic steps, to overcome the shortage of labour.

I saw the hon. Deputy Minister of Labour in a new role this afternoon. Usually when one discusses job reservation, or any other of the methods that inhibit the full utilization of labour resources in South Africa, the hon. Deputy Minister comes along and defends the rights of the White workers in South Africa, proclaiming that people wish to undermine the standards which have been reached by White workers in South Africa, proclaiming that the

From *Debates of the House of Assembly (Hansard). Fourth Session. Second Parliament. Republic of South Africa. 22nd January to 18th June 1965* (Cape Town: Hansard, 1965), XIII, cols. 195–205.

removal of the industrial colour bar would spell doom for the White workers in South Africa. This afternoon, I am glad to say, the hon. Deputy Minister took a different line, a much more intelligent line; even if it was not completely accurate it showed that he is thinking on new lines.

The DEPUTY MINISTER OF LABOUR: We can deal with that further when we come to your motion.

Mrs. SUZMAN: I have got a lot in reserve for my motion as well. The hon. Deputy Minister and I will cross swords on that in due course, but I want to say that I am very glad to find this new pattern of thinking in the hon. Deputy Minister's mind, because he was trying to tell us to-day that in fact job reservation was not as serious as people were making out; that thousands upon thousands of Coloured workers were engaged in skilled trades in the Cape—which of course is true—but he forgot to add that there are other areas in the Cape Province where there are statutory barriers against the employment of Coloured workers in certain skilled trades, and most important, he forgot to remind us that although existing workers may continue in their skilled occupations in the Cape, new entrants to those occupations are in fact forbidden . . .

The DEPUTY MINISTER OF LABOUR: That is a very limited sphere, as you know.

Mrs. SUZMAN: It is true that it is limited, but it does exist. Then the hon. Deputy Minister gave figures which were accurate, but he used them in a misleading way. The hon. Minister told us, quite correctly, that 30 per cent of the workers in South Africa who are engaged in managerial, technical, administrative and other high standards of occupation are non-Whites. I think that figure comes from the Bureau of Statistics. But the hon. Deputy Minister did not tell us the other half of this equation and that is that Whites, who only represent 20 per cent of the total economically active population in South Africa (1960 figures) represent 70 per cent of the country's managerial, technical and skilled workers; the non-Whites representing 80 per cent of the country's totally economically employed population represent only 30 per cent of that higher class. These are equations that the hon. Minister should have given to the House for the sake of accuracy. What I am trying to point out is that 80 per cent of the working population, the non-Whites, represent only 30 per cent of any form of skilled workers, and this represents an imbalance in the country's economy.

Mr. F. S. STEYN: It may also be a question of ability.

Mrs. SUZMAN: Well, let us give them an opportunity to show whether they are less gifted. That is all I ask: equal opportunity. It is quite possible that the hon. member is right, but we do not really know if we deny them an equal opportunity to become skilled workers. We do not give them an equal opportunity because we do not give them the necessary education. There is no free education for non-Whites, and we do not allow them to enter skilled trades because they are not included in the definition of "employee." Therefore until the hon. member for Kempton Park is prepared to withdraw these very real barriers and restrictions to the full employment of non-White labour in this country, both he and I will be guessing in regard to the non-White's ability. But I say that the hon. member has less faith in the White workers than I have, because I am prepared to withdraw the superficial colour bar that protects the White worker, because I believe the White workers will be able to hold their own with non-White workers. Is the hon. member prepared to withdraw these restrictions? Is he prepared to allow the non-Whites to become apprentices, to join trade unions and get the necessary education? That will be the only way to see whether they can take full advantage of such opportunities. The hon. member of course is not prepared to commit himself on that. But I do commend the hon. Deputy Minister on the fact that at least he is not standing up defending the rights of White workers against the intrusion of non-Whites in their field.

I want to come back to the main trend of this no-confidence debate over the last three afternoons, and I must say that I have been profoundly depressed by what I have heard in this House. Both the Government and the official Opposition have been vieing with each other in pretending to be the main defenders of White supremacy, domination, in South Africa. The official Opposition now say that their policy is White leadership. It used to be White leadership "with justice." I am afraid I did not hear the words "with justice" uttered in this House over the past few days. I heard much talk about the maintenance of White leadership. They say that what they stand for is White leadership in the whole of South Africa. The Government on the other hand also claims to be upholding White leadership in South Africa, but with this difference: They claim White leadership over the whole of South Africa minus 13 per cent, and that 13 per cent of course represents the land allotment under the Land Acts for the Bantustans, for the Native reserves. In that 13 per cent of South Africa, the Government is prepared to set aside what it calls "White leadership," and at some distant time in the future it will be prepared to give independence to the Bantustans. On this basis the hon. member for Vereeniging (Mr. B. Coetzee) bluffs himself presumably, because he speaks with great sincerity, but he also imagines that he is bluffing the world that the Nationalist Party has a policy of non-discrimination and that indeed they are offering a fair *quid pro quo* to the non-Whites because they are giving them rights in 13 per cent of the country as against the deprivation of all rights in the White areas. The hon. member for Heil-

bron (Mr. Froneman) yesterday admitted that there is discrimination in the White areas of South Africa. He likened this to the discrimination suffered by immigrants who go to any country in the world. Well, I would like to find a country first of all which classifies persons born within its borders as "immigrants" and a country where immigrants who have been living there for one generation or two generations and are still classified as immigrants with no rights in the country where they are now living. In other words, all the Africans who have been in the so-called White areas of South Africa for two and three generations are in the mind of the hon. member for Heilbron still immigrants. But this he claims justifies the whole policy of the Government. The hon. member for Vereeniging had a vision in this House which he put across with his usual skill, of South Africa as the leading nation on the great Black continent of Africa, the leading light in Africa, in this Commonwealth of Nations. He was not very pleased for having to use the word "commonwealth," but at the moment he could not think of anything better. Now I ask him whether he can carry this vision a little further for us and tell us how he imagines this image measures up to the realities of the situation where South Africa is not welcome at international conferences held in the Black states of Africa, where she is denied air space and landing rights and airports throughout Africa, where South Africa has not got a single representative in any Black country in Africa and where South Africa is only prepared to accept diplomats from the rest of this Black commonwealth under the most stringent conditions. By virtue of what does the hon. member for Vereeniging bluff himself that South Africa is going to be the leading nation in Africa under such circumstances? Now the interesting thing about this vision is that it could indeed come to pass if South Africa made some very necessary adjustments in racial policies, and I want to put it to this

House that there has never been a time when White South Africa could more easily afford to make the necessary adjustments so as to make this country able to take what I do believe is its rightful place on the continent of Africa, as the leading light on the continent of Africa, with friendly neighbours and not hostile neighbours on our continent. I want to put it to the Government that without any sort of partnership policy there are still methods whereby it could in some way readjust its position in the eyes of the rest of Africa. I put it to the Government that now is the time to do this in a position of strength. Concessions which are made in a position of weakness are of no use at all, which is the main reason (I might add) why the partnership policy of the Federation failed. It failed because that Government did not make concessions at a period when the Government was in a position of strength, but waited and only in the last two years of the ten years of the Federation Government real concessions to partnership were made. For the first eight years of partnership a policy indeed of apartheid was practised. It was the old Huggins policy of the partnership of the man and his horse, with the man riding on the back of his horse as his partner. If the hon. member for Pinelands (Mr. Thompson) would speak to Rhodesians, they would tell him that during the last two years when concessions were forced on the Rhodesians, it was too late. By then the Black man had lost all faith in the White man's good intentions. Of course in my opinion the Government should go in a different direction, in the interests of common justice, viz., a multiracial partnership in South Africa, a country where merit and not colour would be the yard-stick. But while I do not expect the Government to go in this direction it could still make very important adjustments which would help us in our present position, and I want to tell the Government what I mean by that. I mean that the Government must stop some of

these devastating implementations of policy which are going on at the present time. Call a halt to them. After all it has been ticking over very nicely gathering White votes unto itself on the, shall I say, paper policy that it has been presenting. But now we are seeing the devastating effect of the actual implementation of these policies and I think the Government should call a halt. I am not talking about "petty apartheid," which really does not interest me very much. I am not talking about the sort of nonsense like the Adam Faith-Dusty Springfield debacle [English pop singers who wanted to perform before integrated audiences and quarreled with the South African government—ed.] which makes us ridiculous in the eyes of the civilized world because it is such a ridiculous example of the Government's obsession in regard to any sort of multiracial mixing. I am not talking about that nonsense, although heaven knows those incidents should never have occurred. I am not talking about the removal of notices which say "Whites only" or "non-Whites only," which certain people think would solve the trick right away. I am not doing that because to me they are just symbols of the deeper malaise of attempted separation. So what I propose goes much further than that but it still could be done and still could help this country without, as I say, the Government having to throw overboard all its prejudices. I am referring to the Government's senseless policy at the present stage in regard to the devastating group areas proposals, where one sees proposals to make the whole of the Western Cape bar small areas entirely White, spreading alarm and despondency amongst thousands upon thousands of non-Whites, the sort of group areas proposals for Durban, for Johannesburg, for the Transvaal, where one pattern evidences itself all the way through: Get rid of the non-Whites, out of the town, out of the suburbs, push them across the river, onto the veld, miles away outside the trading areas of our towns. These are devastating instances of the implementation of this policy of apartheid which I believe is spreading despair among our indigenous non-Whites and is making it absolutely hopeless for South Africa to play her part on the continent of Africa. I believe the implementation of the Bantu Urban Areas Act should be called off. It is having a most far-reaching effect on the family lives of the Africans in our cities. The hon. the Leader of the Opposition called this Act "a gesture to apartheid." I want to tell him that it is very much more than a gesture to apartheid, irrespective of whether economic integration is going on apace. It is going on apace, but this does not mean that Africans are not feeling the effect of the implementation of apartheid.

Indeed, they are feeling it in a more and more critical way every year, because they are now being integrated as migratory workers and not as permanent workers, and that means that family life is more and more adversely affected, and it means that Africans coming to work for Whites are tied to specific employers and are unable to take jobs where they can better their position. They run the risk of endorsement out if they lose their jobs. Now, however many additional Africans come in to towns as evidence of integration, I can assure this House that the effect of the apartheid legislation is felt in stark reality and these are things which the Government should score out at this stage of the history of Africa. Otherwise we are sowing a legacy of hatred for ourselves which we may be able to weather but which I can assure the House our children will certainly not be able to weather. I think that the Government, apart from taking what I will call a positive and they will call a negative step of calling off the devastating effects of the implementation of the apartheid policy, should be willing to take a far more positive step in tackling the very real problem of poverty among the non-Whites in this country. That is the overriding problem, and it does not

matter whether one allows Africans to come into the urban areas or applies influx control in order, as it is said, to protect the urban Africans, if those Africans are going back to the rural areas to starve. The problem is one of unemployment and of poverty, and of course I believe that industrialization will solve that problem if the Government would only allow it to. But nevertheless these are the problems to which the Government is not paying sufficient attention, and these are the factors which are sowing bitter despair among the non-Whites. We heard the hon. the Minister of Bantu Administration painting one of his charming pictures of satisfied Africans in the tribal areas. He is always coming to us with examples of people enjoying themselves in the tribal areas. If it is not a man walking along in the track £1,000 with tucked in his moochi, it is another one cycling along with his Hansard [parliamentary debates—ed.] tucked under his arm. But the realities of the situation are those of poverty and unemployment in those areas, and of Africans living at subhuman standards of living and the break-up of family life. [Interjection.] The Chairman of the Bantu Affairs Commission should be the last person to ask me where that happens.

The industrialization in the rural areas that he speaks of is a farce. There are two factories in the Transkei, which is after all the only Bantustan which now exists. We do not know when the others will come about [no other Bantustans have yet been established—ed.]. There are two factories employing between 200 and 300 people. The border industries are mostly in the established industrial areas. As I pointed out last year, the Witwatersrand could easily be a border area in terms of the argument that you simply declare Soweto to be a Black area. But none of these areas touch the fringe of the vast poverty of the non-Whites in this country, and there is poverty in the urban areas as well, because the Government refuses to introduce minimum wage legislation, which I asked for in a motion in this House the year before last and which was rejected, and which the White trade unions are now asking for in South Africa because they are beginning to realize that the prosperity of the non-Whites is the corner-stone of the prosperity of the Whites, and that unless we expand the productivity and the consumer power of the non-Whites, our present prosperity is not going to be of any lasting duration. The figures I want to quote emanate from the manager of the Non-European Affairs Department of the Municipality of Johannesburg. In a recent survey—he delivered this paper in December 1964—he found that most families are living below the poverty line. The average family income was calculated in Johannesburg at R58 a month, and the average income earned by the head of the family was R42 a month; 48 per cent of all the families in Soweto, which is a huge African township, depend on the income of the head of the family, and the calculated minimum budget is R48 a month, and therefore unless the wives and children go out to work the majority of the families are at least R6 below the poverty datum line.

Mr. FRONEMAN: Nonsense!

Mrs. SUZMAN: I do not know how the hon. member for Heilbron (Mr. Froneman) substantiates his idea of what is really going on in the country. I am talking about figures taken out by a responsible official who is hardly likely to produce figures simply for my benefit. As long as important members like the hon. member for Heilbron—and he is important, ex officio—persistently ignore the realities of the situation in South Africa, I for one am filled with despair. I am not interested in which side of the House is going to maintain White domination. I only know that unless real and important changes are made in South Africa, the future of the White man in this country will not be ensured either by the Government party or by the Opposition, nor even by the Security Police of the hon. the Min-

ister of Justice. None of these things will help, because there are genuine underlying grievances and injustices in this country which are not being set right. Therefore I ask these necessary adjustments, and not because I want to set us right in the eyes of the outside world. That is not my basic reason, and not even because I want to meet Black demands, but simply because of the demands of natural justice. I can see no justification for denying people rights simply on the basis of the colour of their skins, for not allowing a man to live a family life just because he is an African; for not allowing an Indian to continue to run his shop which he has been running for 20 or 30 years, just because he is an Indian; and for not allowing Coloured folk to go on living in Kalk Bay or District Six simply because they are Coloured. I can see no justification for not educating people to take full advantage of their potentialities, simply because they are not White. Not only do I see no justification for this, but I consider it incredibly short-sighted of White South Africa not to realize what a legacy of resentment and hatred it is building up against the White man in South Africa. That is why I ask for what I believe to be very necessary adjustments in this country.

Now I want to say a few words to the hon. the Minister of Justice. I am sorry he is not in the House now, but I must say it. The Minister has told the country that he has restored law and order in South Africa.

Mr. FRONEMAN: He has not restored it; he has maintained it.

Mrs. SUZMAN: Well, in that case it means that there never was any unrest in this country. I understood that there was a state bordering on an emergency some time ago when we had to introduce the 90-day law [indefinite detention without writ of habeas corpus—ed.]. I want to say right away of course that I never believed that there was any justification for that law. I believe that our Police Force and our Special branch should be quite competent to handle any such manifestation of subversion, without recourse to any law as far-reaching as this 90-day law. I want to warn the Minister that I believe, as I said earlier this afternoon, that there will always be unrest in South Africa unless the basic injustices are set right. I believe that there are injustices and I will not adopt the ostrich-like attitude of people in this country who say there are no injustices, and that it is all only the work of agitators and communists, and that everything is fine. Everything is not fine as long as there is poverty and there are group areas and such things. But I want to come back to this question of the 90-day law and I want to say that I believe this law has done more harm than any other single law that has ever been passed. It is not a law which a Western civilized country requires to maintain law and order. That should be possible if the Government is governing with the consent of the majority of the people, and if the Government takes cognizance of the injustices before it is too late. I believe that this law should be not suspended but repealed. I was against its introduction and I am against its continuation on our Statute Book. I think the Minister should not only suspend it but should repeal it. It is a law which lends itself to abuse, which allows people to be subjected to standing interrogation for long periods, the sort of thing done by the Ogpu, standing for hours while being interrogated by teams of officers. It kept people in solitary confinement week after week, a devastating form of torture. [Interjection.] Of course, I am not in favour of sabotage, but

I can tell the hon. member that it is no use trying to stop sabotage unless one tackles the basic underlying reasons for it. The 90-day law should be repealed.

In the few minutes remaining to me I want to raise a final matter, again with the Minister of Justice, and that is the banning of Professor Roux and of Professor Simon under the new use to which he is putting his anticommunist law; in other words, the prohibiting of these men, because they were listed as communists, from teaching at our universities. [Interjections.] Professor Roux in fact has not been a member of the Communist Party since 1936, when he resigned from it. [Interjections.]

An HON. MEMBER: Solly Sachs also resigned.

Mrs. SUZMAN: Professor Roux wrote a book which is a standard text-book for students and he is now prohibited not only from teaching but from publishing his work or from continuing with his research in plant physiology. I think this is the most absurd banning order on a man of science who has contributed a great deal to South Africa. As far as Professor Simon is concerned, he remained a member of the Communist Party until it was banned in 1950, and to the best of my knowledge since that time he has taken no part in political activity and, indeed, he has broken no law, because if he had broken a law one wonders why the hon. the Minister of Justice has not hauled him, as well as Professor Roux, into the courts of law, where they can be dealt with under proper procedure, and not simply by arbitrary banning by the Minister of Justice. [Time limit.]

BLACK CONSCIOUSNESS AND THE QUEST FOR TRUE HUMANITY

Steve Biko was a founder, leader, and major contributor to the ideas of Black Consciousness, a movement initially based among students, which emerged in the late 1960s and was banned in 1977. The movement called for a racially exclusive struggle, emphasizing the need for blacks to reject racial inferiority and submissiveness. Biko died while in prison in 1977. This essay, written for a book on Black Theology, is generally considered to be Biko's best work.

"Black Theology" is historically an American product, emerging from the black situation there. Its most articulate exponent in the U.S. is Dr. James H. Cone, Professor of Theology at the Union Theological Seminary, New York, author of Black Theology and Black Power *(Seabury, 1969) and, most recently, of* God of the Oppressed *(Seabury, 1975; SPCK, 1977).*

In mid-1970 UCM appointed Sabelo Stanley Ntwasa Travelling Secretary for 1971 with a special mandate to encourage thinking and writing on Black Theology. The book Black Theology: the South African Voice, *edited by Basil Moore (C. Hurst & Co., London, 1973) is the result of that year's endeavours, and this paper by Steve is perhaps the most eloquent contribution to that book and, in the present writer's view, the best thing he ever wrote.*

BLACK CONSCIOUSNESS AND THE QUEST FOR A TRUE HUMANITY

It is perhaps fitting to start by examining why it is necessary for us to think collectively about a problem we never created. In doing so, I do not wish to concern myself unnecessarily with the white people of South Africa, but to get to the right answers, we must ask the right questions; we have to find out what went wrong—where and when; and we have to find out whether our position is a deliberate creation of God or an artificial fabrication of the truth by power-hungry people whose motive is authority, security, wealth and comfort. In other words, the "Black Consciousness" approach would be irrelevant in a colourless and non-exploitative egalitarian society. It is relevant here because we believe that an anomalous situation is a deliberate creation of man.

There is no doubt that the colour question in South African politics was

From Steve Biko, *"Black Consciousness and the Quest for True Humanity,"* from *I Write What I Like,* edited by Aelred Stubbs, San Francisco: Harper and Row, 1986, pp. 87–98. Reprinted by permission.

originally introduced for economic reasons. The leaders of the white community had to create some kind of barrier between black and whites so that the whites could enjoy privileges at the expense of blacks and still feel free to give a moral justification for the obvious exploitation that pricked even the hardest of white consciences. However, tradition has it that whenever a group of people has tasted the lovely fruits of wealth, security and prestige it begins to find it more comfortable to believe in the obvious lie and to accept it as normal that it alone is entitled to privilege. In order to believe this seriously, it needs to convince itself of all the arguments that support the lie. It is not surprising, therefore, that in South Africa, after generations of exploitation, white people on the whole have come to believe in the inferiority of the black man, so much so that while the race problem started as an offshoot of the economic greed exhibited by white people, it has now become a serious problem on its own. White people now despise black people, not because they need to reinforce their attitude and so justify their position of privilege but simply because they actually believe that black is inferior and bad. This is the basis upon which whites are working in South Africa, and it is what makes South African society racist.

The racism we meet does not only exist on an individual basis; it is also institutionalised to make it look like the South African way of life. Although of late there has been a feeble attempt to gloss over the overt racist elements in the system, it is still true that the system derives its nourishment from the existence of anti-black attitudes in society. To make the lie live even longer, blacks have to be denied any chance of accidentally proving their equality with white men. For this reason there is job reservation, lack of training in skilled work, and a tight orbit around professional possibilities for blacks. Stupidly enough, the system turns back to say that blacks are inferior because they have no economists, no engineers, etc., although it is made impossible for blacks to acquire these skills.

To give authenticity to their lie and to show the righteousness of their claim, whites have further worked out detailed schemes to "solve" the racial situation in this country. Thus, a pseudo-parliament has been created for "Coloureds", and several "Bantu states" are in the process of being set up. So independent and fortunate are they that they do not have to spend a cent on their defence because they have nothing to fear from white South Africa which will always come to their assistance in times of need. One does not, of course, fail to see the arrogance of whites and their contempt for blacks, even in their well-considered modern schemes for subjugation.

The overall success of the white power structure has been in managing to bind the whites together in defence of the *status quo*. By skilfully playing on that imaginary bogey—*swart gevaar*—they have managed to convince even diehard liberals that there is something to fear in

the idea of the black man assuming his rightful place at the helm of the South African ship. Thus after years of silence we are able to hear the familiar voice of Alan Paton saying, as far away as London: "Perhaps apartheid is worth a try". "At whose expense, Dr. Paton?", asks an intelligent black journalist. Hence whites in general reinforce each other even though they allow some moderate disagreements on the details of subjugation schemes. There is no doubt that they do not question the validity of white values. They see nothing anomalous in the fact that they alone are arguing about the future of 17 million blacks—in a land which is the natural backyard of the black people. Any proposals for change emanating from the black world are viewed with great indignation. Even the so-called Opposition, the United Party, has the nerve to tell the Coloured people that they are asking for too much. A journalist from a liberal newspaper like *The Sunday Times* of Johannesburg describes a black student—who is only telling the truth—as a militant, impatient young man.

It is not enough for whites to be on the offensive. So immersed are they in prejudice that they do not believe that blacks can formulate their thoughts without white guidance and trusteeship. Thus, even those whites who see much wrong with the system make it their business to control the response of the blacks to the provocation. No one is suggesting that it is not the business of liberal whites to oppose what is wrong. However, it appears to us as too much of a coincidence that liberals—few as they are—should not only be determining the *modus operandi* of those blacks who oppose the system, but also leading it, in spite of their involvement in the system. To us it seems that their role spells out the totality of the white power structure—the fact that though whites are our problem, it is still other whites who want to tell us how to deal with that problem. They do so by dragging all sorts of red herrings across our paths. They tell us that the situation is a class struggle rather than a racial one. Let them go to van Tonder in the Free State and tell him this. We believe we know what the problem is, and we will stick by our findings.

I want to go a little deeper in this discussion because it is time we killed this false political coalition between blacks and whites as long as it is set up on a wrong analysis of our situation. I want to kill it for another reason— namely that it forms at present the greatest stumbling block to our unity. It dangles before freedom-hungry blacks promises of a great future for which no one in these groups seems to be working particularly hard.

The basic problem in South Africa has been analysed by liberal whites as being apartheid. They argue that in order to oppose it we have to form non-racial groups. Between these two extremes, they claim, lies the land of milk and honey for which we are working. The *thesis*, the *anti-thesis* and the *synthesis* have been mentioned by some great philosophers as the cardinal points around which any social revolution revolves. For the *liberals*, the *thesis* is apartheid, the *anti-thesis* is non-racialism, but the *synthesis* is very feebly defined. They want to tell the blacks that they see integration as the ideal solution. Black Consciousness defines the situation differently. The *thesis* is in fact a strong white racism and therefore, the *antithesis* to this must, *ipso facto*, be a strong solidarity amongst the blacks on whom this white racism seeks to prey. Out of these two situations we can therefore hope to reach some kind of balance—a true humanity where power politics will have no place. This analysis spells out the difference between the old and new approaches. The failure of the liberals is in the fact that their *antithesis* is already a

watered-down version of the truth whose close proximity to the thesis will nullify the purported balance. This accounts for the failure of the Sprocas[1] commissions to make any real headway, for they are already looking for an "alternative" acceptable to the white man. Everybody in the commissions knows what is right but all are looking for the most seemly way of dodging the responsibility of saying what is right.

It is much more important for blacks to see this difference than it is for whites. We must learn to accept that no group, however benevolent, can ever hand power to the vanquished on a plate. We must accept that the limits of tyrants are prescribed by the endurance of those whom they oppress. As long as we go to Whitey begging cap in hand for our own emancipation, we are giving him further sanction to continue with his racist and oppressive system. We must realise that our situation is not a mistake on the part of whites but a deliberate act, and that no amount of moral lecturing will persuade the white man to "correct" the situation. The system concedes nothing without demand, for it formulates its very method of operation on the basis that the ignorant will learn to know, the child will grow into an adult and therefore demands will begin to be made. It gears itself to resist demands in whatever way it sees fit. When you refuse to make these demands and choose to come to a round table to beg for your deliverance, you are asking for the contempt of those who have power over you. This is why we must reject the beggar tactics that are being forced on us by those who wish to appease our cruel masters. This is where the SASO message and cry *"Black man, you are on your own!"* becomes relevant.

The concept of integration, whose vir-

---

[1] Study Project on Christianity in an Apartheid Society. Set up by S.A. Council of Churches and Christian Institute in 1968. Editor's note.

tues are often extolled in white liberal circles, is full of unquestioned assumptions that embrace white values. It is a concept long defined by whites and never examined by blacks. It is based on the assumption that all is well with the system apart from some degree of mismanagement by irrational conservatives at the top. Even the people who argue for integration often forget to veil it in its supposedly beautiful covering. They tell each other that, were it not for job reservation, there would be a beautiful market to exploit. They forget they are talking about people. They see blacks as additional levers to some complicated industrial machines. This is white man's integration—an integration based on exploitative values. It is an integration in which black will compete with black, using each other as rungs up a step ladder leading them to white values. It is an integration in which the black man will have to prove himself in terms of these values before meriting acceptance and ultimate assimilation, and in which the poor will grow poorer and the rich richer in a country where the poor have always been black. We do not want to be reminded that it is we, the indigenous people, who are poor and exploited in the land of our birth. These are concepts which the Black Consciousness approach wishes to eradicate from the black man's mind before our society is driven to chaos by irresponsible people from Cocacola and hamburger cultural backgrounds.

Black Consciousness is an attitude of mind and a way of life, the most positive call to emanate from the black world for a long time. Its essence is the realisation by the black man of the need to rally together with his brothers around the cause of their oppression—the blackness of their skin—and to operate as a group to rid themselves of the shackles that bind them to perpetual servitude. It is based on a self-examination which has ultimately led them to believe that by seeking to run away from themselves and emulate the white man, they are insulting the intelligence of whoever created them black. The philosophy of Black Consciousness therefore expresses group pride and the determination of the black to rise and attain the envisaged self. Freedom is the ability to define oneself with one's possibilities held back not by the power of other people over one but only by one's relationship to God and to natural surroundings. On his own, therefore, the black man wishes to explore his surroundings and test his possibilities—in other words to make his freedom real by whatever means he deems fit. At the heart of this kind of thinking is the realisation by blacks that the most potent weapon in the hands of the oppressor is the mind of the oppressed. If one is free at heart, no man-made chains can bind one to servitude, but if one's mind is so manipulated and controlled by the oppressor as to make the oppressed believe that he is a liability to the white man, then there will be nothing the oppressed can do to scare his powerful masters. Hence thinking along lines of Black Consciousness makes the black man see himself as a being complete in himself. It makes him less dependent and more free to express his manhood. At the end of it all he cannot tolerate attempts by anybody to dwarf the significance of his manhood.

In order that Black Consciousness can be used to advantage as a philosophy to apply to people in a position like ours, a number of points have to be observed. As people existing in a continuous struggle for truth, we have to examine and question old concepts, values and systems. Having found the right answers we shall then work for consciousness among all people to make it possible for us to proceed towards putting these answers into effect. In this process, we have to evolve our own schemes, forms and strategies to suit the need and situation, always keeping in mind our fundamental beliefs and values.

In all aspects of the black-white relationship, now and in the past, we see a constant tendency by whites to depict blacks as of an inferior status. Our culture, our history and indeed all aspects of the black man's life have been battered nearly out of shape in the great collision between the indigenous values and the Anglo-Boer culture.

The first people to come and relate to blacks in a human way in South Africa were the missionaries. They were in the vanguard of the colonisation movement to "civilise and educate" the savages and introduce the Christian message to them. The religion they brought was quite foreign to the black indigenous people. African religion in its essence was not radically different from Christianity. We also believed in one God, we had our own community of saints through whom we related to our God, and we did not find it compatible with our way of life to worship God in isolation from the various aspects of our lives. Hence worship was not a specialised function that found expression once a week in a secluded building, but rather it featured in our wars, our beer-drinking, our dances and our customs in general. Whenever Africans drank they would first relate to God by giving a portion of their beer away as a token of thanks. When anything went wrong at home they would offer sacrifice to God to appease him and atone for their sins. There was no hell in our religion. We believed in the inherent goodness of man—hence we took it for granted that all people at death joined the community of saints and therefore merited our respect.

It was the missionaries who confused the people with their new religion. They scared our people with stories of hell. They painted their God as a demanding God who wanted worship "or else". Peo-

ple had to discard their clothes and their customs in order to be accepted in this new religion. Knowing how religious the African people were, the missionaries stepped up their terror campaign on the emotions of the people with their detailed accounts of eternal burning, tearing of hair and gnashing of teeth. By some strange and twisted logic, they argued that theirs was a scientific religion and ours a superstition—all this in spite of the biological discrepancy which is at the base of their religion. This cold and cruel religion was strange to the indigenous people and caused frequent strife between the converted and the "pagans", for the former, having imbibed the false values from white society, were taught to ridicule and despise those who defended the truth of their indigenous religion. With the ultimate acceptance of the western religion down went our cultural values!

While I do not wish to question the basic truth at the heart of the Christian message, there is a strong case for a re-examination of Christianity. It has proved a very adaptable religion which does not seek to supplement existing orders but—like any universal truth—to find application within a particular situation. More than anyone else, the missionaries knew that not all they did was essential to the spread of the message. But the basic intention went much further than merely spreading the word. Their arrogance and their monopoly on truth, beauty and moral judgment taught them to despise native customs and traditions and to seek to infuse their own new values into these societies.

Here then we have the case for Black Theology. While not wishing to discuss Black Theology at length, let it suffice to say that it seeks to relate God and Christ once more to the black man and his daily problems. It wants to describe Christ as a fighting God, not a passive God who allows a lie to rest unchallenged. It grapples with existential problems and does not claim to be a theology of absolutes. It seeks to bring back God to the black man and to the truth and reality of his situation. This is an important aspect of Black Consciousness, for quite a large proportion of black people in South Africa are Christians still swimming in a mire of confusion—the aftermath of the missionary approach. It is the duty therefore of all black priests and ministers of religion to save Christianity by adopting Black Theology's approach and thereby once more uniting the black man with his God.

A long look should also be taken at the educational system for blacks. The same tense situation was found as long ago as the arrival of the missionaries. Children were taught, under the pretext of hygiene, good manners and other such vague concepts, to despise their mode of upbringing at home and to question the values and customs of their society. The result was the expected one—children and parents saw life differently and the former lost respect for the latter. Now in African society it is a cardinal sin for a child to lose respect for his parent. Yet how can one prevent the loss of respect between child and parent when the child is taught by his know-all white tutors to disregard his family teachings? Who can resist losing respect for his tradition when in school his whole cultural background is summed up in one word–barbarism?

Thus we can immediately see the logic of placing the missionaries in the forefront of the colonisation process. A man who succeeds in making a group of people accept a foreign concept in which he is expert makes them perpetual students whose progress in the particular field can only be evaluated by him; the student must constantly turn to him for guidance and promotion. In being forced to accept the Anglo-Boer culture, the blacks have allowed themselves to be at the mercy of the white man and to have him as their eternal supervisor. Only he can tell us how good our performance is and instinctively each of us is at pains to please this powerful, all-knowing master. This is what Black Consciousness seeks to eradicate.

As one black writer says, colonialism is never satisfied with having the native in its grip but, by some strange logic, it must turn to his past and disfigure and distort it. Hence the history of the black man in this country is most disappointing to read. It is presented merely as a long succession of defeats. The Xhosas were thieves who went to war for stolen property; the Boers never provoked the Xhosas but merely went on "punitive expeditions" to teach the thieves a lesson. Heroes like Makana[1] who were essentially revolutionaries are painted as superstitious trouble-makers who lied to the people about bullets turning into water. Great nation-builders like Shaka are cruel tyrants who frequently attacked smaller tribes for no reason but for some sadistic purpose. Not only is there no objectivity in the history taught us but there is frequently an appalling misrepresentation of facts that sicken even the uninformed student.

Thus a lot of attention has to be paid to our history if we as blacks want to aid each other in our coming into consciousness. We have to rewrite our history and produce in it the heroes that formed the core of our resistance to the white invaders. More has to be revealed, and stress has to be laid on the successful nation-building attempts of men such as Shaka, Moshoeshoe and Hintsa. These areas call for intense research to provide some sorely-needed missing links. We

[1] Early nineteenth-century Xhosa prophet, sentenced to life imprisonment on Robben Island and drowned while escaping in a boat. Refusal by blacks to accept the truth of his death led to the mythical hope of his eventual return. Editor's note.

would be too naive to expect our conquerors to write unbiased histories about us but we have to destroy the myth that our history starts in 1652, the year Van Riebeeck landed at the Cape.

Our culture must be defined in concrete terms. We must relate the past to the present and demonstrate a historical evolution of the modern black man. There is a tendency to think of our culture as a static culture that was arrested in 1652 and has never developed since. The "return to the bush" concept suggests that we have nothing to boast of except lions, sex and drink. We accept that when colonisation sets in it devours the indigenous culture and leaves behind a bastard culture that may thrive at the pace allowed it by the dominant culture. But we also have to realise that the basic tenets of our culture have largely succeeded in withstanding the process of bastardisation and that even at this moment we can still demonstrate that we appreciate a man for himself. Ours is a true man-centred society whose sacred tradition is that of sharing. We must reject, as we have been doing, the individualistic cold approach to life that is the cornerstone of the Anglo-Boer culture. We must seek to restore to the black man the great importance we used to give to human relations, the high regard for people and their property and for life in general; to reduce the triumph of technology over man and the materialistic element that is slowly creeping into our society.

These are essential features of our black culture to which we must cling. Black culture above all implies freedom on our part to innovate without recourse to white values. This innovation is part of the natural development of any culture. A culture is essentially the society's composite answer to the varied problems of life. We are experiencing new problems every day and whatever we do adds to the richness of our cultural heritage as long as it has man as its centre. The adoption of black theatre and drama is one such important innovation which we need to encourage and to develop. We know that our love of music and rhythm has relevance even in this day.

Being part of an exploitative society in which we are often the direct objects of exploitation, we need to evolve a strategy towards our economic situation. We are aware that the blacks are still colonised even within the borders of South Africa. Their cheap labour has helped to make South Africa what it is today. Our money from the townships takes a one-way journey to white shops and white banks, and all we do in our lives is pay the white man either with labour or in coin. Capitalistic exploitative tendencies, coupled with the overt arrogance of white racism, have conspired against us. Thus in South Africa now it is very expensive to be poor. It is the poor people who stay furthest from town and therefore have to spend more money on transport to come and work for white people; it is the poor people who use uneconomic and inconvenient fuel like paraffin and coal because of the refusal of the white man to install electricity in black areas; it is the poor people who are governed by many ill-defined restrictive laws and therefore have to spend money on fines for "technical" offences; it is the poor people who have no hospitals and are therefore exposed to exorbitant charges by private doctors; it is the poor people who use untarred roads, have to walk long distances, and therefore experience the greatest wear and tear on commodities like shoes; it is the poor people who have to pay for their children's books while whites get them free. It does not need to be said that it is the black people who are poor.

We therefore need to take another look at how best to use our economic power, little as it may seem to be. We must seriously examine the possibilities of establishing business co-operatives whose interests will be ploughed back into community development programmes. We should think along such lines as the "buy black" campaign once suggested in Johannesburg and establish our own banks for the benefit of the community. Organisational development amongst blacks has only been low because we have allowed it to be. Now that we know we are on our own, it is an absolute duty for us to fulfil these needs.

The last step in Black Consciousness is to broaden the base of our operation. One of the basic tenets of Black Consciousness is totality of involvement. This means that all blacks must sit as one big unit, and no fragmentation and distraction from the mainstream of events be allowed. Hence we must resist the attempts by protagonists of the bantustan theory to fragment our approach. We are oppressed not as individuals, not as Zulus, Xhosas, Vendas or Indians. We are oppressed because we are black. We must use that very concept to unite ourselves and to respond as a cohesive group. We must cling to each other with a tenacity that will shock the perpetrators of evil.

Our preparedness to take upon ourselves the cudgels of the struggle will see us through. We must remove from our vocabulary completely the concept of fear. Truth must ultimately triumph over evil, and the white man has always nourished his greed on this basic fear that shows itself in the black community.

Special Branch agents will not turn the lie into truth, and one must ignore them. In a true bid for change we have to take off our coats, be prepared to lose our comfort and security, our jobs and positions of prestige, and our families, for just as it is true that "leadership and security are basically incompatible", a struggle without casualties is no struggle. We must realise that prophetic cry of black students: "Black man, you are on your own!"

Some will charge that we are racist but these people are using exactly the values we reject. We do not have the power to subjugate anyone. We are merely responding to provocation in the most realistic possible way. Racism does not only imply exclusion of one race by another— it always presupposes that the exclusion is for the purposes of subjugation. Blacks have had enough experience as objects of racism not to wish to turn the tables. While it may be relevant now to talk about black in relation to white, we must not make this our preoccupation, for it can be a negative exercise. As we proceed further towards the achievement of our goals let us talk more about ourselves and our struggle and less about whites.

We have set out on a quest for true humanity, and somewhere on the distant horizon we can see the glittering prize. Let us march forth with courage and determination, drawing strength from our common plight and our brotherhood. In time we shall be in a position to bestow upon South Africa the greatest gift possible—a more human face.

40 JOE FOSTER

THE WORKERS' STRUGGLE—WHERE DOES FOSATU STAND?

Joe Foster was in 1982 General Secretary of FOSATU (Federation of South African Trade Unions), then the largest union federation in South Africa. This speech lays out FOSATU's political policy, calling for an independent workers' movement which would not be under the control of more populist organizations, such as the exiled African National Congress. The speech was heavily criticized by the Charterists as being an extreme form of "workerism." In 1985, FOSATU implicitly abandoned its independent line by joining in the creation of the Congress of South African Trade Unions, the largest such federation in South African history.

The following document is the full text of the keynote address, given by the FOSATU General Secretary, Joe Forster, at the FOSATU Congress in April 1982.

INTRODUCTION

Three years ago—almost to the day—we met in this very same place to form FOSATU. Today we have set as our theme—the Workers Struggle—in a serious attempt to further clarify where we as worker representatives see FOSATU to stand in this great struggle.

That we are discussing this theme today and resolutions that relate to it is a justification of our original decision to form FOSATU and shows how seriously we take the new challenges that face us three years after that decision. Clearly any such discussion raises many very important issues and the purpose of this paper is to try and bring together these issues in ways that will help guide our discussions.

It is the task of this Congress to give a clear policy direction to our actions between now and the next Congress—we believe that the issue is raised in this paper are crucial to a political understanding of our policies and what we hope to achieve by them. We also believe that it is the task of Congress to add

From Joe Foster, *"The Workers' Struggle—Where Does FOSATU Stand?"* reprinted in the *South African Labour Bulletin*, volume 7, number 8, 1982, pp. 67–86.

and modify the views expressed through open and serious debate.

In the three years that FOSATU has existed there is little doubt that we have achieved a lot in terms of growth and gains made for our members. However, I believe that our greatest achievement is the fact that at this Congress we are determined to re-evaluate our policies. We are determined to respond to new challenges and set new directions if this is necessary. We could have made this Congress a great occasion open to all to parade our successes and hide our failures, however, we have chosen otherwise.

We have chosen to keep it closed and to once again self-critically examine our position. I believe that this shows our determination to take the great militancy of our members and use this to build a just and fair society controlled by workers.

We have no intention of becoming self-satisfied trade unionists incapable of giving political direction to the workers struggle.

Yet we would only be dreaming of change if we do not strengthen and build our unions into large and effective organisations.

At our Inaugural Congress we stressed certain policies and set ourselves the task of establishing a tight federation of non-racial, national, industrial unions, based on shop floor strength. We set ourselves the task of sharing resources between affiliates and of building up an educational programme. We further stressed our independence in regard to party political organizations and from international trade union organisations.

Now it is not my task to assess every success and failure of FOSATU. There are reports tabled that will allow delegates to draw their own conclusions. However, it is important to make certain assessments in order to go further and identify why we need to clarify our position and set new clearer directions.

I believe that we have to ask ourselves two crucial questions:

—have we established an effective organisation based on shop floor strength and national non-racial industrial unions?

—has our organisational activity developed worker leadership that can give guidance and direction to all workers?

In answer to both questions it would be wrong to expect a positive answer after only three years. However, we should be able to assess if we are going in the right direction.

Clearly in regard to the first question we made progress—it could even be said to be considerable progress—with NAAWU, NUTW, and MA beginning to be a significant presence in what are major industries. However, there is a long way to go both in these cases and more so in those of the other affiliates.

It is, however, the second question that poses more problems. As the unions grow and are faced with new challenges it becomes crucial that the leadership knows what direction it is going in. What are the organisational strategies that are necessary as the unions become larger and more effective? What dangers to worker militancy lie in recognition and stability?

As these unions grow then the question is what role do they play in the wider political arena. There has been a great upsurge in political activities over the last few years and many different political groups are looking to the union movement to state its position. We must be sure our organisation and our leadership can confidently state *its* position and continue to organise in the way that will strengthen and not weaken that position.

The purpose of this paper is to set out the issues we should debate if we are to meet the challenges.

WORKING CLASS MOVEMENT

As a trade union federation we are clearly concerned with workers and their aspirations. If we were to think in terms of our members only, we would have a very limited political role. If, however, we are thinking more widely of the working class then we have to examine very much more carefully what our political role is. In particular we need to look at this role in the South African context.

If we look at the advanced industrial countries then we see what can be called working class movements. There are a number of different organizations—trade unions, co-operatives, political parties and newspapers—that all see themselves as linked to the working class and furthering its interests. These working class movements are, therefore, powerful social forces in those societies.

In the capitalist economies these working class movements have power and organisation yet politically the working class is still subject to policies and practices that are clearly against their interests as the activities of Thatcher and Reagan show. This is increasingly leading to intense political and organisational activity to give the working class and the union movement a clearer direction so as to gather together the working class movement into a force that will more definitely put workers in control of their own destiny.

In the Socialist countries similar battles are being fought. Whilst social, political and economic relations in these countries have been greatly altered and there have been great achievements to the benefit of workers, there is still the need for workers themselves to control their own destiny. So Solidarity was not struggling to restore capitalism in Poland, its struggle was to establish more democratic worker control over *their* socialist society.

Now my purpose in briefly looking at the working class movement in the advanced industrial countries was twofold:

Firstly, so that we can be clear that worker activities such as strikes and protests do not in themselves mean that a working class movement or working class politics exist. These later are more than than that—they are large scale organisations with a clear social and political identity as the working class.

Secondly, I wished to show that the pure size of working class organisation is itself no guarantee that workers will control their own destiny. In fact as the struggle of Solidarity shows, even the fact that a country is said to be socialist does not guarantee that workers control their own destiny.

In short, it could be said that workers must build a powerful and effective movement if they are to succeed in advancing their interests against some very hostile forces, but they must also ensure that this movement is able to take a clear political direction.

The experience of the great working class movements in the advanced industrial countries is a very important guide and lesson to us. However, it cannot provide all our answers. Firstly, in South Africa we cannot talk of a working class movement as we have defined it above. Secondly, whilst there is undoubtedly a large and growing working class its power is only a potential power since as yet it has no definite social identity of itself as working class.

The questions we should, therefore, address ourselves to, are

—Why has no working class movement emerged?
—What are the prospects for such a movement emerging?
—What role can FOSATU play in such a process?

POLITICAL HISTORY AND WORKERS

It is not possible in a paper such as this to deal fully with all the developments in South Africa's history that have led to the non-existence of a workers' movement in South Africa.

South Africa's history has been characterised by great repression and the major political and ideological *instrument* for this repression has been *racism*. Yet the major effect of this repression has been to very rapidly establish a large capitalist economy.

Racism and the violence and injustices associated with it is a very stark and clear form of repression. Alongside this only about 5–10% of the population has ever had the franchise. Clearly, therefore, there is a very identifiable oppressive force and the major political task of the oppressed peoples has always been to attack that oppressive and racist regime.

So what has developed in South Africa is a very powerful tradition of popular or populist politics. The role of the great political movements such as the ANC and the Congress Alliance has been to mobilise the masses against the repressive minority regime. In such a situation mass mobilisation is essential so as to challenge the legitimacy of the State both internally and internationally.

Where virtually all the population is voteless and oppressed by a racial minority then a great alliance of all classes is both necessary and a clear political strategy. Furthermore, building such an alliance was a great task.

The ANC had to overcome racial division so as to rise above the divisive racism of the oppressors. They had to deal with opportunistic tribal leadership, to organise thousands upon thousands of people and they had to do all this in the face of harsh repression by the State. In achieving this there is little wonder that the ANC rose to be one of the great liberation movements in Africa.

In this context it is also easier to see and understand why the trade union movement acted in a particular way. The racial divisions in the working class, linked as they were to other objective factors, made it possible for capital to quite quickly suppress any serious challenge to their supremacy. It was possible to create the conditions that led to a politically tame union movement and thereby forced more militant and progressive unions to bear the brunt of State action, which in turn affected the politics of these unions.

Furthermore, at all times there were occasions when workers resisted by strike action, protest and organisation. Yet this by itself cannot constitute a working class movement. Whilst the unions were often prominent they were always small and weakly organised both nationally and in the factories. They could not provide an organisational base for a working class movement as we have defined it above.

Progressive and militant unions were continually the subject of State harassment, but, never managed to seriously challenge capital nationally or on a sustained basis. As a result the effective political role of progressive unions and of worker activity was to provide a crucial part of any popular struggle and that was to give it its "Worker Voice". No mass popular movement can be effective or be seen to be effective if it does not have some worker involvement or representation. By the 1950's with the growth of South Africa's industry and the size of the working class the need to include

workers became essential and as a result SACTU became an important element of the Congress Alliance.

In these circumstances the progressive trade unions became part of the popular struggle against oppression. They did not and probably could not have provided the base for working class organisation. There is of course no doubt that their activities have been very, very important in creating the conditions that led to the emergence in the last ten to fifteen years of the present progressive trade unions. However, these unions are operating in a different environment.

Workers and their struggle became very much part of the wider popular struggle. An important effect of this development was that capital could hide behind the curtains of apartheid and racism. The political energies of the oppressed masses and of international critics were focussed on the apartheid regime and its abhorrent racism. The government and Afrikaanerdom became the focus of attack. In fact the position was such that learned liberal academics saw in capital the great hope for change despite the fact that capital and its lackeys were undoubtedly the major beneficiaries of apartheid.

Capital did its very best to keep in the political background and as a result this helped prevent the creation of capital's logical political opposite which is a working class political movement. However, of crucial significance was that capital was growing rapidly and changing its very nature into a more monopolistic, technologically advanced and concentrated form. Its links internationally were also growing as was its importance for international capital.

We find, therefore, that behind the scenes of the great battle between the apartheid regime and its popular opponents that the capitalist economy has flourished and capital emerges now as a powerful and different force.

—is highly concentrated in truly gigantic corporations;

—has access to international information on how to deal with working class challenges;

—has access to the State's security information;

—is able to rapidly share and assess information;

—is able to use the objective circumstances in its favour such as unemployment and influx control to weaken worker organisations;

—is now an important part of international capital and cannot, therefore, be lightly discarded by international capital;

—is able to hide behind politics and as a result can hide sophisticated attacks on labour because no-one is paying any attention.

Yet as the upsurge of popular political activity emerged again in the 1970's some of its new forms such as Black Consciousness also place little emphasis on capital. So there is a growing gap between popular politics and the power of capital and as a result the potential power of workers. It is in this context we should look at the likelihood of a working class politics emerging.

NEED FOR A WORKING CLASS MOVEMENT

The growing size of the economy and the dramatic changes taking place in capital have created important new conditions in the economy. We also have to take into account the speed and manner in which the economy has developed. In discussing the working class movements in the advanced industrial economies, we have to bear in mind that in most cases they took about 100 years or more to fully develop. Industry started first by building larger and larger factories and bringing people together in these factories.

The new capitalists had to struggle

politically with the older ruling classes over labour, land, taxation policy, tariff protection, political rights and political power.

Then mechanisation became more important and there was a definite change in production processes. As this happened the skilled workers who had usually given leadership to the craft unions found themselves in a very difficult position. As a result leadership problems in the organisation of trade unions and the political environment developed in a complex and relatively slow way.

In South Africa this has been condensed into 60–70 years and from the outset large scale capitalist enterprises dominated. The birth of capitalism here was brutal and quick. The industrial proletariat was ripped from its land in the space of a few decades. At present capitalist production massively dominates all other production. There are no great land lords on their agricultural estates and there is no significant peasantry or collective agriculture. Virtually everyone depends for all or part of their income on industry or capitalist agriculture.

The working class have experienced a birth of fire in South Africa and they constitute the major objective political force opposed to the State and capital. There is no significant petty bourgeoisie or landed class with an economic base in our society.

In the economy capital and labour are the major forces yet politically the struggle is being fought elsewhere.

The existence of this industrial proletariat and the rapid transformation of capital are very powerful reasons why a working class movement could rapidly develop in South Africa. There are a number of factors that will assist in the organisation of workers:

—the great concentration of capital has also meant a greater concentration of workers. These workers generally have a higher level of basic education and skills than before and their links with the past are all but broken so that more and more a worker identity is emerging: —this is reinforced by the sophisticated strategies that are designed to "de-racialise" industry and some other areas of society. The effect of this is to divide off certain privileged members of Black society leaving workers at the bottom of the privilege pile:

—the concentration of workers in industry has also concentrated them in the great urban townships;

—the particular structure of the South African economy with its high degree of State involvement, price controls and heavy dependance on international markets has made it a very sensitive economy. As a consequence attempts to "buy off" the major part of the working class will fail. It is more likely that as some readjustments of privilege are attempted that it will have to be workers that suffer through inflation and lack of basic commodities;

—the above factors and South Africa's international economic importance are likely to force capital into the political open and as a consequence develop a worker response;

—although capital can at present hide behind apartheid it is also the case that if workers organise widely enough they can get great support from the international labour movement. Also international public opinion has to be very carefully watched by capital because both international and South African capital are dependent on the links with the rest of the world.

These then are some of the important factors that are favourable to the development of a working class movement in South Africa. However, this does not mean that this will automatically happen. To understand this, we need to look at the present political environment more carefully to see both the present political tendencies and to establish why some active leadership roles should be played by the unions and FOSATU in particular.

Workers need their own organisation to counter the growing power of capital and to further protect their own interests in the wider society. However, it is only workers who can build this organisation and in doing this they have to be clear on what they are doing.

As the numbers and importance of workers grows then all political movements have to try and win the loyalty of workers because they are such an important part of society. However, in relation to the particular requirements of worker organisation, mass parties and popular political organisations have definite limitations which have to be clearly understood by us.

We should distinguish between the international position and internal political activity. Internationally, it is clear that the ANC is the major force with sufficient presence and stature to be a serious challenge to the South African State and to secure the international condemnation of the present regime. To carry out this struggle is a difficult task because South Africa has many friends who are anxious to ensure that they can continue to benefit from her wealth. The fact that the ANC is also widely accepted internally also strengthens its credibility internationally.

However, this international presence of the ANC which is essential to a popular challenge to the present regime places certain strategic limitations on the ANC, namely;

—to reinforce its international position it has to claim credit for all forms of internal resistance, no matter what the political nature of such resistance. There is, therefore, a tendency to encourage undirected opportunistic political acitvity; —it has to locate itself between the major international interests. To the major Western powers it has to appear as anti-racism but not as anti-capitalist. For the socialist East it has to be at least neutral in the super power struggle and certainly it could not appear to offer a serious socialist alternative to that of those countries as the response to Solidarity illustrates. These factors must seriously affect its relationship to workers; —accordingly, the ANC retains its tradition of the 1950's and 1960's when because there was no serious alternative political path it rose to be a great populist liberation movement. To retain its very important international position it has to retain its political position as a popular mass movement. This clearly has implications for its important military activities.

Internally we also have to carefully examine what is happening politically. As a result of the State's complete inability to effect reform and the collapse of their Bantustan policy, they are again resorting to open repression. Since 1976 in particular this has given new life to popular resistance and once again the drive for unity against a repressive State has reaffirmed the political tradition of populism in South Africa. Various political and economic interests gather together in the popular front in the tradition of the ANC and the Congress Alliance.

In the present context all political activity, provided it is anti-State, is of equal status. In the overall resistance to this regime, this is not necessarily incorrect. In fact without such unity and widespread resistance it would not be possible by means of popular mass movements to seriously challenge the legitimacy of the present regime.

However, the really essential question is how worker organisation relates to this wider political struggle. I have argued above that the objective political and economic conditions facing workers is now markedly different to that of twenty years ago.

Yet there does not seem to be clarity on this within the present union movement. There are good reasons for this lack of clarity.

As a result of repression most worker leadership is relatively inexperienced and this is made worse by the fact that their unions are weak and unstable organisationally. The union struggles fought against capital have mostly been against isolated companies so that the wider struggles against capital at an industry or national level have not been experienced. This also means that workers and their leadership have not experienced the strength of large scale worker organisation nor the amount of effort required to build and democratise such large scale organisation. Again State repression and the wider political activity reinforce previous experience where the major function of workers was to reinforce and contribute to popular struggle.

Politically, therefore, most unions and their leadership lack confidence as a worker leadership, they see their role as part of wider struggle but are unclear on what is required for the worker struggle. Generally, the question of building an effective worker organisation is not dealt with and political energy is spent in establishing unity across a wide front.

However, such a position is clearly a great strategic error that will weaken if not destroy worker organisation both now and in the future. All the great and successful popular movements have had as their aim the overthrow of oppressive—most often colonial—regimes. But these movements cannot and have not in themselves been able to deal with the particular and fundamental problem of workers. Their task is to remove regimes that are regarded as illegitimate and unacceptable by the majority.

It is, therefore, essential that workers must strive to build their own powerful and effective organisation even whilst they are part of the wider popular struggle. This organisation is necessary to protect and further worker interests and to ensure that the popular movement is not hijacked by elements who will in the end have no option but to turn against their worker supporters.

Broad and complicated matters have been covered and it is difficult to summarise them even further. However, I shall attempt to do so in order for us to try and examine the role that FOSATU can play in this struggle.

1. That worker resistance such as strike action helps build worker organisation but by itself it does not mean that there is a working class movement.
2. There has not been and is not a working class movement in South Africa.
3. The dominant political tradition in South Africa is that of the popular struggle against an oppressive, racist minority regime.
4. That this tradition is reasserting itself in the present upsurge of political activity.
5. However, the nature of economic development in South Africa has brutally and rapidly created a large industrial proletariat.
6. That the size and development of this working class is only matched by its mirror image which is the dramatic growth and transformation of industrial capital.
7. That before it is too late workers must strive to form their own powerful and effective organisation within the wider popular struggle.

FOSATU'S OBJECTIVE

From what has been said we believe that FOSATU must set itself the task of giving leadership and direction to the building of a working class movement. Our efforts so far have equipped us to do this. Our organisation is nationally based, located in the major industries and the militancy of our members has generally developed a politically aware and self-critical leadership.

FOSATU as a trade union federation will clearly not constitute the working class movement nor would this place FOSATU in opposition to the wider political struggle or its major liberation movement.

FOSATU's task will be to build the effective organisational base for workers to play a major political role as workers. Our task will be to create an identity, confidence and political presence for worker organisation. The conditions are favourable for this task and its necessity is absolute.

We need have no fear of critics—our task will contribute to the wider liberation struggle and will also ensure that the worker majority is able to protect and further its interests. Ours is a fundamental political task and those who ask of workers their political support without allowing them the right to build their own organisation must answer for *their* real motives.

As was said above, capital has transformed itself and has a greater capacity to tolerate worker organisation because it is now more powerful and better able to deal with a worker challenge. Also because of its absolutely central position it will have the full support of the State in its actions and in the bitter struggles that are to come.

This requires a very much greater effort to establish worker organisation and requires thorough organisational work and ceaseless mobilisation of our members. The growth and transformation of capital has created the very preconditions for large scale worker organisation.

OUR CONCRETE TASKS AND CHALLENGES

If we set the above as our general direction then we must deal with concrete tasks and challenges.

Organisation:

What is crucial in organisation is the quality of that organisation—the quality that gives it its overall political direction and capability. As is clear from the experience of the advanced industrial countries that we looked at earlier, organisational size alone is not enough, yet without size there can be no effective counter to capital.

Broadly one can distinguish three factors that affect the quality of worker organisation—the structure of organisational strength and decision making; the location of organisational strength and the political qualities of its leadership structures.

Structure:

The structure of an organisation should be such that it correctly locates worker strength and makes best use of that strength.

FOSATU's experience in this has been very important. Our organisation is built up from the factory floor. As a result, the base of the organisation is located where workers have most power and authority and that is where production takes place. This also has the effect of democratising our structures since worker representatives always participate from a position of strength and authority in the organisation. By stressing factory bargaining we involve our Shop Stewards in central activities and through this they gain experience as worker leadership. It should be said that they do battle every day.

These factory-based structures are the key to transforming pure quantity of members into a flexible and effective quality. Capital's hostility to factory organisation forces members and Shop Stewards to struggle continuously or else to have their organisation crushed.

At the union level FOSATU has attempted to build broad industrial unions on a national basis. We, in effect, have a position of one affiliate per industry. We have chosen industrial unions because of the organisational advantages we gain in our struggle against capital. However, FOSATU's role is to link these industrial unions into a tight federation that is based on common policy and a sharing of resources. Our aim is to keep a unity of purpose among affiliates at all levels of their organisation.

Our task in the three years to come must be to consolidate and develop factory organisation, a national presence for our unions and to reassert unity of purpose among affiliates.

The structures we are developing are an essential basis for effective and democratic organisation and are the basis for greater worker participation in and control over production.

Location:

The question of location is closely related to structure. Without correct structures then the location of one's organisational strength is not as important.

We must accept that it will take many years to organise all workers and at present that should not be our aim. Our present aim must be to locate our organisation strategically. We need to look at the location of our organisational strength in relation to the industry, geographic area and the points at which we can most effectively carry out collective bargaining.

Our major affiliates should be located in the major industries. Within those industries we must become a substantial presence by carefully building our organisation in major factories, companies and areas.

Geographically we must clearly aim to

be a national presence both as FOSATU and as the affiliates. Our organisation should be able to dominate major industrial areas. By doing this we create the major means whereby worker organisation can play a significant if not dominant role in the communities that surround these industrial areas.

Successful collective bargaining requires that the organisation is capable of mobilising its members behind demands. Thus far our unions have only really been able to mobilise at the plant level. However, the experience of NAAWU which is exceptional in FOSATU has shown what can be gained by mobilising across companies. We have flexible structures and we must use them if we are to serve our members. We must be able to mobilise across factories and in local areas across industries. We must see industry bargaining or regional bargaining not as something to be feared but as the logical extension of our present structures and practices.

Worker Leadership:

Here we must be immediately clear that we are not talking about leadership in the sense that it is usually discussed—which is in terms of individuals and "great men". This view of leadership is not what is important for a worker organisation. What we are interested in is the elected representatives of workers and the officials they appoint to work within the organisation.

We are interested in how the leadership is elected or appointed; who it is answerable to and how this accountability is achieved; how experienced leadership is and how it gains this experience and how they develop means of training and educating leadership so that it remains self-critical and politically active.

The challenges facing worker leadership are undoubtedly different to other leadership groups. For worker leadership in a capitalist society, your everyday struggle is related to your job and therefore your wage and therefore your very ability to survive. The most appropriate comparison is with that of the guerrilla fighter who has to develop the strength to resist daily, the knowledge of his terrain that will give him every tactical advantage and the support of those for whom he is struggling. Probably most important because both the worker leader and the guerrilla are fighting a powerful enemy, is the development of a sense of when to advance and when to retreat.

These skills are not easily learnt and not easily replaced. So worker leadership cannot be wasted by opportunistic and overly adventuristic actions.

We are also concerned with worker leadership in a wider arena than only that of the union struggle. Giving leadership to the working class requires an organisational base. Without this base, then the poverty and the lack of education, information and time that workers are struggling against will be the very factors which will force workers to surrender leadership of the community to other stratas in society.

Our aim is to use the strength of factory-based organisation to allow workers to play an effective role in the community. Worker leadership will have:

—gained invaluable political experience from their factory struggles;
—organisation and resources behind them;
—organisational structures and location that will give them localised strength;
—the ability to speak with a clear and democratically established worker mandate.

The points made here should be our guide for action and we have a long way to go in building a larger leadership structure that has the political qualities of clarity, determination, discipline and the ability to be self-critical.

Working Class Identity:

The task of organisation outlined above and more important, the quality of that organisation will absorb most of our energies in the next three years, and is, therefore, our major priority. Yet to give leadership in the building of a working class movement we must start to build a greater identity for worker organisation.

In a very important way the building of effective trade unions does create a worker identity. However, there is the danger that the unions become preoccupied with their members and ignore workers generally. By establishing a clear political direction we can avoid this.

One answer that is often proposed is to be involved in community activities. That FOSATU should be involved in community activities is correct since our members form the major part of those communities. However, as we have argued above we must do so from an organisational base if we are truly to be an effective worker presence.

Without this base, it is more likely that we will destroy a clear worker identity since workers will be entirely swamped by the powerful tradition of popular politics that we examined earlier.

It is also the case that there has emerged into our political debate an empty and misleading political category called 'the community'. All communities are composed of different interest groups and for a worker organisation to ally itself with every community group or action would be suicide for worker organisation. Under the surface of unity community politics is partisan and divided. FOSATU cannot possibly ally itself to all the political groups that are contesting this arena. Neither can it ally itself with particular groups. Both paths will destroy the unity of its own worker organisation.

This simple political fact is the reason for one of our founding resolutions. It has nothing to do with not wanting to be involved in politics. Our whole existence

is political and we welcome that. Our concern is with the very essence of politics and that is the relation between the major classes in South Africa being capital and labour.

We need to state this more clearly and understand it ourselves more clearly. There is also no doubt that we must take our own newspaper very much more seriously as it can be a major instrument in building a worker identity.

At the level of organisation we have a sound base on which to work. Probably our main problem has been that we did not clearly state why we had chosen certain structures and what could be achieved by them.

As our political clarity and confidence grows, so we must state one position more clearly in our meetings, among our members and through our own newspaper.

Unity in the Labour Movement

Our first step must be to address ourselves to unity in the labour movement. If we are to create a working class movement then trade union unity has to be dealt with very early on in our struggle. Because we take working class politics seriously we must take trade union unity seriously.

At present there is a very great momentum to unity in the labour movement and we have to carefully consider and analyse what is happening.

The first point to understand is that all the unions involved in the talks are relatively weak in relation to their potential—some appallingly so. Many are too easily fooled by their own propaganda and the great interest shown by everyone into believing that they are now a strong force.

Furthermore, with a few exceptions (mostly in FOSATU), these unions are not yet a national or an industrial presence. Their strengths lie in isolated factories and very few have any real geographic concentration. As a result, both the leadership of these unions and their membership have no clear conception of the organised power of capital nor for that matter of its weakness. There is no real experience of the difficulties of large scale worker organisation nor of the difficulties in building democratic worker structures. The bulk of the present leadership has no clear conception of the needs of worker struggle or of a worker dominated society. There is all too often a contradiction between the political position and organisational practice. Radical political positions are adopted but the organisational practice makes little headway into the power of capital nor is it effectively democratic. A number of factors result from this—often capital is attacked in the 'abstract' by making it all powerful and accordingly seeing an attack on the State as the only answer, or political energies are spent in widespread campaigns. Actual worker organisation and advance is left weak and based on sporadic upsurges rather than on organisational strength.

As a consequence of these factors it is not possible for people to draw any distinction between worker struggle and popular struggle let alone understand the relation between the two in South Africa. The unity talks are therefore conceived of as being within the wider popular struggle and as another area where anti-State unity can be achieved. A formal unity rather than a working unity against capital is therefore seen as the prime object.

There are broadly speaking three forms of unity to the union movement at present and we should look at each fairly carefully:

"Ad hoc unity": this is what has occurred at present where unity is issue-located and there are attempts to take a common stand. At present this unity is significant in that it creates unity out of apparent disunity. However, its significance will rapidly decline. Such ad hoc unity can only achieve anything on specific issues and it is inevitably forced to take more and more concerted and concrete actions unless it merely wants to be the source of endless press statements. Such further actions require a more permanent organisational link.

"United front unity": here the organisations remain autonomous but they set up a permanent platform of contact. Some people seem to see the solidarity committees as such a platform. However, although this provides a more definite organisational link considerable new problems are posed. Again the movement is towards more and more significant gestures of protest and the problem now posed is how are decisions to be taken and on what mandate. Does each organisation have an equal vote or is voting by size? If decisions are on a consensus basis—then on what mandate? Should each organisation have a formal mandate on each issue and if they don't, how representative of rank and file membership is each decision? Is there not a greater than usual danger of decisions being taken by a few officials who have easy access to meetings?

A permanent organisational link requires a process for making decisions that is democratic and equitable. Furthermore, if solidarity actions are to be successful they require organisational co-ordination—this in turn requires the power to sanction. How can this be done if participants are entirely autonomous?

A further step in this type of unity can be a "loose federation" such as CSA, where the unions are now all in the same federal organisation and the symbolism of unity is far greater. However, such a federal body—not being based on any clear principles—is unlikely to generate working unity as it could contend with numerous problems of jurisdiction between unions and it is unlikely that organisational rationalisation could take place without firm policies and particular structures.

In fact "United front unity", with or without a loose federation, can destroy the hope of greater unity by creating unresolved differences and no acceptable way of resolving these.

"Disciplined unity": this requires common political purpose, binding policy on affiliates and close working links based on specific organisational structures.

If such a federation is based on industrial unions then FOSATU is the closest to being an example of such "disciplined unity"—in the present circumstances. If the federation were not based on an industrial structure but in a regional one, then it is more difficult to set out its working structures since there is no clear experience of how this would work. However, there is no doubt that some allowance would have to be made for industrial considerations and the industrial organisation of capital. In FOSATU we have argued that industrial unions in a "tight federation" allow for maximum flexibility and efficacy.

It is clear from this that unity means little unless these factors are taken into account. To talk lightly of unity is to keep it within the framework of ad hoc or united front unity. The effectiveness of such unity would rapidly disappear. So if that is what is meant by unity we have to imply certain possible motives of its proponents:

—inexperience and lack of thought on the matter;
—political expediency whereby this unity is for specific limited ends of embarrassing certain organisations;
—a preoccupation with popular politics and a lack of commitment to the building of a working class political position.

However, if we in FOSATU are to take our objective seriously and this ob-

jective is the building of a working class movement then we have to take unity very seriously. Clearly by unity we should strive for "disciplined unity" since it is only such unity that can possibly meet our objective.

We must ourselves work out a programme for unity and on the basis of that programme we should not hesitate to attack those who are impeding the development of a working class movement.

CONCLUSION

The issues that have been covered in this paper are important and complicated—they are the basis for an understanding of the true nature of the workers struggle in South Africa and the political role our organisation must play in that struggle.

We believe that in FOSATU we have a firm base on which to build organisationally. Our task in the three years to come is to firmly commit ourselves to a working class political position. With this greater political understanding we must:

—consolidate our organisational structures;
—give guidance and leadership in the building of a larger working class movement in South Africa;
—seek out comrades and allies who will join us in this struggle;
—and in this way make our fundamental contribution to the liberation of the oppressed people of South Africa.

In doing this we must all be clear that we shall never be so petty as to insist on our organisation's name as the only one in the trade union movement which can carry out this task. It is what the organisation does that is important—not what it is called. Yet equally, we shall never be so politically foolish as to abandon the worker struggle.

41 NELSON MANDELA
ADDRESS TO THE ANC

In January 1985, State President P. W. Botha offered to release Nelson Mandela after he had served more than twenty-three years of his life sentence if Mandela would renounce the use of violence. In this speech, read in public in February by Mandela's daughter, Zindzi, Mandela rejected the offer. This was the first time since his imprisonment that Mandela was permitted to be quoted directly addressing his followers. On February 11, 1990, Mandela was released unconditionally from the Victor Verster prison farm outside Cape Town by President F. W. de Klerk, who was convinced that the leader of the ANC was committed to a peaceful resolution of the racial conflict in South Africa. De Klerk succeeded P. W. Botha as President of South Africa in August 1989. In his historic speech on February 27, 1990, he removed crucial restrictions on groups opposed to the South African government.

My father and his comrades wish to make this statement to you, the people, first. They are clear that they are accountable to you and to you alone. And that you should hear their views directly and not through others.

My father speaks not only for himself and for his comrades at Pollsmoor prison but he hopes he also speaks for all those in jail for their opposition to apartheid, for all those who are banished, for all those who are in exile, for all those who suffer under apartheid, for all those who are opponents of apartheid and for all those who are oppressed and exploited.

Throughout our struggle there have been puppets who have claimed to speak for you. They have made this claim, both here and abroad. They are of no consequence. My father and his colleagues will not be like them.

My father says, 'I am a member of the African National Congress. I have always been a member of the African National Congress and I will remain a member of the African National Congress until the day I die. Oliver Tambo is much more than a brother to me. He is my greatest friend and comrade for nearly fifty years. If there is any one among you who cher-

From Mary Benson, *Nelson Mandela: The Man and the Movement* (N.Y.: W. W. Norton and Company, 1986), pp. 235–237. Reprinted by permission.

ishes my freedom, Oliver Tambo cherishes it more, and I know that he would give his life to see me free. There is no difference between his views and mine.'

My father says, 'I am surprised at the conditions that the government wants to impose on me. I am not a violent man. My colleagues and I wrote in 1952 to Malan asking for a round table conference to find a solution to the problems of our country but that was ignored.

'When Strijdom was in power, we made the same offer. Again it was ignored.

'When Verwoerd was in power we asked for a National Convention for all the people in South Africa to decide on their future. This, too, was in vain.

'It was only then when all other forms of resistance were no longer open to us that we turned to armed struggle.

'Let Botha show that he is different to Malan, Strijdom and Verwoerd. Let *him* renounce violence. Let him say that he will dismantle apartheid.

'Let him unban the people's organization, the African National Congress. Let him free all who have been imprisoned, banished or exiled for their opposition to apartheid. Let him guarantee free political activity so that the people may decide who will govern them.

'I cherish my own freedom dearly but I care even more for *your* freedom. Too many have died since I went to prison. Too many have suffered for the love of freedom. I owe it to their widows, to their orphans, to their mothers and to their fathers who have grieved and wept for them. Not only I have suffered during these long lonely wasted years. I am not less life-loving than you are. But I cannot sell my birthright nor am I prepared to sell the birthright of the people to be free. I am in prison as the representative of the people and of your organization, the African National Congress, which was banned. What freedom am I being offered while the organization of the people remains banned? What freedom am I being offered when I may be arrested on a pass offence? What freedom am I being offered to live my life as a family with my dear wife who remains in banishment in Brandfort? What freedom am I being offered when I must ask for permission to live in an urban area? What freedom am I being offered when I need a stamp in my pass to seek work? What freedom am I being offered when my very South African citizenship is not respected?

'Only free men can negotiate. Prisoners cannot enter into contracts. Herman Toivo Ja Toivo, when freed, never gave any undertaking, nor was he called upon to do so.'

My father says, 'I cannot and will not give any undertaking at a time when I and you, the people, are not free. Your freedom and mine cannot be separated. I *will* return.'

42 ZWELAKHE SISULU
KEYNOTE ADDRESS TO THE NATIONAL EDUCATION CRISIS COMMITTEE, SECOND NATIONAL CONSULTATIVE CONFERENCE
March 29, 1986

Sisulu is the son of imprisoned ANC leader Walter and United Democratic Front president Albertina, and a leading black journalist, most recently serving as editor of The New Nation. *In 1986, at the height of popular unrest and in the middle of a declared State of Emergency, Sisulu gave his address, entitled "People's Education for People's Power," to a major gathering held to discuss the continued school boycotts. Shortly thereafter, Sisulu was detained and held in prison for two years without charges.*

Friends, Comrades,
I welcome you to this historic gathering, a meeting of people from all over the country, from every province, from big and small towns, rural and urban areas. We gather here as a meeting of people drawn from all walks of life, from all sections of the people: students, teachers, parents, workers, community and political leaders. We bring together all sections of the oppressed community and all who detest apartheid. We have tried to ensure representation of all po-litical tendencies and all sections of our population, black and white.

This is a truly historic conference in the tradition of earlier national meetings such as the Congress of the People of 1955 and the 1961 All-in Africa conference.

It is an important lesson to the apartheid forces: The people stand united. Ten years after the 1976 rising we remain united in our demand for the ending of apartheid education and the establishment of a democratic, people's education. We also remain convinced that this can only be achieved with the eradication of the apartheid system and the establishment of a democratic people's South Africa.

Ever since 1976 the people have recognised that apartheid education cannot be separated from apartheid in general. This conference once again asserts that the entire oppressed and democratic community is concerned with education, that we all see the necessity of ending gutter education and we all see that this is a political question affecting each and every one of us.

Let us now turn to the critical question which concerns us all, all oppressed and democratic South Africans. The December Conference gave the government until today to meet the demands of parents, students and teachers. Has the government met the demands? We want to answer this loudly and clearly so that there can be no mistaking what we are saying: The answer is NO. They have not met our demands.

We are saying this for two reasons: firstly most of the demands which we made in December have not been met. Secondly any steps the government has taken have been sideways steps. They lifted the emergency because they were forced to do so, because they were afraid of the united mass action of the people which they know is coming after March 31. At the same time they said they were going to impose a *permanent emergency* by giving the SAP [South African Police] and SADF [South African Defence Force] powers throughout the country, whereas previously they have only had these in parts of the country.

In the meantime, the emergency in fact continues to exist throughout the country. There is little difference now from when the official state of emergency was in force. It was *after* the emergency was lifted that our children were shot in Kabokweni in the Eastern Trans-

vaal and that other atrocities were perpetrated. . . .

THE CURRENT SITUATION.

We stand today at a crossroads in our struggle for national liberation. We hold the future in our hands. The decisions we take at this conference will be truly historic, in the sense that they will help determine whether we go forward to progress and peace, or whether the racists push us backwards and reverse some of the gains that we have made, towards barbarism and chaos.

I want to make it clear that these aren't empty slogans. When we say that we have reached a decisive historical moment, this is based on a careful assessment of our current reality. In any struggle it is extremely important to recognise the critical moment, the time when decisive action can propel that struggle into a new phase. It is also important to understand that this moment doesn't last forever, that if we fail to take action that moment will be lost.

This moment has a number of important features:

—the state has lost the initiative to the people. It is no longer in control of events.

—the masses themselves recognise that the moment is decisive, and are calling for action.

—the people are united around a set of fundamental demands, and are prepared to take action on these demands.

Having said this, I want to strike a note of caution. It is important that we don't misrecognise the moment, or understand it to be something which it is not. We are not poised for the immediate transfer of power to the people. The belief that this is so could lead to serious errors and defeats. We are however poised to enter a phase which can lead to transfer of power. What we are seeking to do is to decisively shift the balance of forces in our favour. To do this we have to adopt the appropriate strategies and tactics, we have to understand our strengths and weaknesses, as well as that of the enemy, that is, the forces of apartheid reaction.

Having said this, let us describe some of the main features of the current situation. The government introduced the state of emergency because it was losing political control. It hoped that the emergency would achieve two objectives: firstly, to stop the advances of the democratic movement, and to destroy the people's organisations which were taking control in various parts of the country. Secondly it aimed to reinstitute the puppet bodies in the townships which had been destroyed since the Vaal uprising ten months previously. Through this two-pronged attack it hoped to regain control, regain the initiative, and impose its apartheid reforms on the people.

In fact, the state failed hopelessly in these objectives. Its brutal actions, and atrocities committed by the SADF and SAP, only angered the people more and mobilised them in evergrowing numbers. Puppet structures, instead of being restored, came under more widespread attack. In a number of areas people's organisations strengthened their structures and became more rooted in the masses. Struggle began to be waged in all corners of the country and new organisations sprang up daily. Where youth had previously waged the struggle alone, whole communities now involved themselves in united action against the regime.

Despite the heavy blows against our leaders and organisations, there was a real strengthening of the democratic forces, the people's camp; and a weakening of the forces of apartheid, the enemy camp. Let us first look at the situation in the enemy camp. When the regime declared the emergency, all sections of the white ruling bloc supported it, in the belief that the resistance of the people would be crushed, paving the way for a Buthelezi-Muzorewa option. Barely one month later this appearance of unity had crumbled. Mass resistance had spread and taken new forms. The regime stood more isolated than ever before at the international level; and the economic crisis reached new proportions with the loss of investor confidence in the stability of the South African regime.

This situation brought home to its allies that the regime was no longer able to rule in the old way. The people heightened contradictions within the ruling bloc by strategies such as the consumer boycott. The regime became increasingly divided and unable to act as greater pressure built up, locally and internationally, to meet the people's demands. The divisions reached right into the cabinet itself, as sections of the government differed with each other on the correct way to deal with the situation. The SPCC initiative created public divisions between the SADF and SAP on the one hand, and the DET on the other; something which previously would have been unthinkable.

The initiative passed into the hands of the people. The ANC, in particular, became seen as the primary actor on the South African stage. Not only the people, but sections of the white ruling bloc, began to look to the ANC to provide an indication of future direction.

Doubts amongst whites in the ability of parliament to provide a solution to the country's problems reached a peak with the resignation of Van Zyl Slabbert. Politically, therefore, the regime had become totally isolated, both locally and internationally. Morally, it had been exposed as totally bankrupt and without any legitimate right to rule. Economically, it faced its worst crisis ever.

It was in this context that they lifted the state of emergency. They did not do this from a position of strength. The people forced them to lift the emergency. They are trying to gain a breathing space before launching a new offensive against the people.

A number of pressures forced the regime to lift the emergency. But it was the deadline which was set at the December conference which was the decisive factor. They knew that the eyes of the whole country would be on the decisions of this conference, and they hoped that the lifting of the emergency would defuse a programme of united action. We know that they intend re-imposing the emergency in another form. But we must not let this happen. We must frustrate this scheme.

ADVANCES OF THE PEOPLE

When the emergency was declared, a situation of ungovernability existed mainly in two areas, the Eastern Cape and the East Rand. By the beginning of this year the situation was very different. Ungovernability had not only extended to far more areas. The people had actually begun to govern themselves in a number of townships.

The period of the emergency saw very important advances made by the people. Confronted by the terror of the SADF and SAP, the people, under the leadership of their organisations, closed ranks. Structures were built which would survive the period of the emergency and beyond it. In a number of townships, the area was split up into zones, blocks and areas, each of which would have its own committee, and some townships developed street committees.

As a result, in many cases our organisations matured and grew under the guns of the SADF. Action taken against the leadership didn't result in the collapse of our organisations. Not only did our organisations grow in strength, they often took over the running of the townships. So we saw the emergence of zones of People's Power in a number of town-

ships. This development is so important that I shall deal with it separately later.

Another feature of the emergency was the highly political character of the struggle we waged, and the tendency for the struggles to develop in a national direction. The masses linked up local issues with the question of political power. A set of national demands emerged which transcended specific issues or regional differences. The transformation of SPCC from a locally based education initiative into a national body combining educational and political issues is an important instance of this development.

Our struggle took on an increasingly national character in another sense too. From being youth-led, the struggle began to involve all sections of the population. Greater involvement of parents gave rise in turn to initiatives such as that of the SPCC. This development wasn't confined to education however. Parents and workers began to take a more active involvement in all issues concerning the community. There was a general recognition in the democratic movement that it was a major challenge to consolidate and accelerate this process. There was also a recognition that serious obstacles existed which had to be tackled. Our youth organisations began to play an important role in trying to channel the militancy of unorganised youth into disciplined action, responsive and accountable to the whole community.

Complementing this was the development of a close relationship between the trade unions and the rest of the democratic movement. The formation of Cosatu was of particular importance in this regard, since it took a strong stand supporting trade union involvement in community and political issues.

In terms of developing the struggle nationally, we made our most significant advance in the last months of the emergency. For the first time in decades, our people took up the struggle in the rural areas. People in a number of bantustan areas challenged the so-called tribal authorities, and in some instances even replaced these bantustan sellouts with people's village councils. Areas which the enemy could previously rely on as zones of subservience and passivity were now being turned into zones of struggle. In the midst of the emergency our people waged campaigns against these puppets in seven of the nine bantustans. Of course, the majority of our people in the rural areas have yet to challenge their oppressors. But the significance of these developments should not be underestimated. Everyday this process is being furthered as more and more people in the rural areas take up the cudgels of freedom.

In summary, then, a new situation developed in the course of the emergency, with a number of special features. On the side of the regime, they found themselves totally isolated, divided and unable to act effectively. On the people's side, organisations often matured, sprung up in new areas, and resistance took on an increasingly national character. We have isolated these as the most significant features of this period, as the features which characterise the special situation, or decisive moment in which we find ourselves.

This doesn't mean that the regime has no strengths and we have no weaknesses. If we overplay the regime's weaknesses and ignore their strengths we shall be fooling ourselves. More importantly, if we only concentrate on our strengths and ignore our weaknesses we shall commit serious errors. I have pointed to positive tendencies which have to be encouraged. But we must also be aware of the counter tendencies which threaten to reverse our struggle if we don't address them seriously. We need to consolidate, defend and advance the gains we have made in this period. In this way we can deepen the breakthroughs we have

achieved in the various parts, thereby ensuring that temporary gains are transformed into fundamental and long-lasting features of our struggle.

DEFEND, CONSOLIDATE AND ADVANCE

We have said that we must have no illusions about the type of regime we are dealing with. The increase in atrocities since the lifting of the state of emergency shows that we can expect no letup. The regime may be losing control, but as it gets more desperate, so its actions get more criminal. The advances which the people have made mean that the old methods of state repression are no longer effective. Detaining our leaders no longer frightens our people or breaks our organisations.

This is why the system is adopting new methods to try and destroy us. These methods are taking three main forms. What they all have in common is that they are illegal or semi-legal, and that they use secret terror or more open fascist methods. They all involve physical attacks or killing of our leaders and ordinary residents.

Firstly our people are being attacked by apartheid vigilante squads in areas where apartheid authority has been challenged or destroyed. From Moutse to Welkom to Lamontville these agents are operating to try and prop up the rejected community councils and tribal authorities.

Secondly apartheid death squads are operating to assassinate important leaders of the people. Since the killing of Matthew Goniwe a number of our leaders have fallen to these agents. Our people have foiled a number of other attempts on the lives of our leaders. Assassinations have happened in areas north of Leardre where our people are threatening to establish democratic control of their communities; or where the process of people's power has advanced such as in the Eastern Cape and Pretoria. It is not possible to say exactly who is responsible for such murderous acts, since these cowards strike under the cover of darkness. But we just have to ask ourselves, who has the capacity to mount these actions, and who stands to benefit from them?

Thirdly, the SADF and SAP hooligans are being given powers to act as they please, to use emergency powers, whether there is an emergency or not, killing and maiming our people. The government has said that it intends to make this legal by giving them permanent emergency powers throughout the country. This is a formal declaration of war on the people of South Africa.

The aim of these three methods is to frighten our people and break their morale, thereby leading to the disintegration of their resistance. So far they have only had this effect where our people are not strongly organised. In areas where we have developed strong people's committees, these attacks have been resisted and sometimes frustrated. The people have seen the need to defend their leaders, defend their organisations in order to consolidate and advance.

FORWARD TO PEOPLE'S POWER

Why do we use the slogan "Forward to People's Power"? Firstly it indicates that our people are now seeing the day when the people of South Africa shall have the power, when the people shall govern all aspects of their lives, as an *achievable reality* which we are working towards.

Secondly, it expresses the growing trend for our people to move towards realising people's power *now*, in the process of struggle, before actual liberation. By this we mean that people are beginning to exert control over their own lives in different ways. In some townships and schools people are beginning to govern themselves, despite being under racist rule.

When our people kicked out the puppets from the townships they made it impossible for the regime to govern. They had to bring in the SADF as an army of occupation. All they could do was to harass and use force against our people. But they couldn't stop the people in some townships from taking power under their very noses, by starting to run those townships in different ways. In other words the struggles which the people has fought, and the resulting situation of ungovernability, created the possibilities for the exercise of people's power. . . .

I want to emphasise here that these advances were only possible because of the development of democratic organs, or committees, of people's power. Our people set up bodies which were controlled by, and accountable to, the masses of people in each area. In such areas, the distinction between the people and their organisations disappeared. All the people young and old participated in committees from street level upwards.

The development of people's power has caught the imagination of our people, even where struggles are breaking out for the first time. There is a growing tendency for ungovernability to be transformed into elementary forms of people's power, as people take the lead from the semi-liberated zones.

In the bantustans, for example, struggles against the tribal authorities have developed into struggles for democratic village councils. These councils are actually taking over in some areas, thereby adapting the forms of people's power developed in the townships to rural conditions.

We must stress that there is an important distinction between ungovernability and people's power. In a situation of ungovernability the *government* doesn't have control. But nor do the people. While they have broken the shackles of direct government rule the people haven't yet managed to control and direct the situation. There is a power vacuum. In a situation of people's power the *people* are starting to exercise control.

An important difference between ungovernability and people's power is that no matter how ungovernable a township is, unless the people are organised, the gains made through ungovernability can be rolled back by state repression. Because there is no organised centre of people's power, the people are relatively defenceless and vulnerable. Removal of our leadership in such situations can enable the state to reimpose control. We saw, for example, the setbacks experienced by our people in the Vaal and East Rand. Despite heroic struggles and sustained ungovernability, the state through its vicious action was able to reverse some of the gains made in these areas. Where, however, people's power has become advanced, not even the most vicious repression has been able to decisively reverse our people's advances. If anything, their repressive actions serve to deepen people's power in these zones and unite the people against the occupying forces. In the Eastern Cape people's power forced the SADF *out* of the townships, if only temporarily.

The reason that people's power strengthens us to this extent is that our organisation becomes one with the masses. It becomes much more difficult for the state to cripple us by removing our leadership, or attacking our organisations. Instead they confront the whole population and occupy our townships. As our people make increasing gains through the exercise of people's power, experience the protection of our mass organisations, and frustrate the attacks of the regime, the masses tend to consolidate their position and advance. In other words, people's power tends to protect us and constantly open up new possibilities, thereby taking the struggle to a new

level. This explains why people's power is both defensive and offensive at the same time.

Struggles over the past few months demonstrate that it is of absolute importance that we don't confuse coercion, the use of force *against* the community, with people's power, the collective strength of the community. For example, when bands of youth set up so called "kangaroo courts" and give out punishments, under the control of no-one with no democratic mandate from the community, this is *not* people's power. This situation often arises in times of ungovernability. We know that this type of undisciplined individual action can have very negative consequences.

When disciplined, organised youth, together with other older people participate in the exercise of people's justice and the setting up of people's courts; when these structures are acting on a mandate from the community and are under the democratic control of the community, this is an example of people's power.

We have seen that people's power, unlike exercise of power by individuals, tends to be disciplined, democratic and an expression of the will of the people. It develops the confidence of our people to exercise control over their own lives and has the capacity to achieve practical improvements in our every day lives.

A very important, almost astonishing, achievement of our people in this regard has been in the area of crime control. Apartheid and crime make very good bedfellows. They thrive on each other. In fact, very often it is difficult to tell them apart! But people's power and crime cannot co-exist. I am not saying this lightly. Crime has thrived in all townships in the country. But in the areas where people are taking control, crime is being wiped out.

This shows that the people do have the power, if we stand united in action.

We can achieve things we would otherwise never imagine possible—if we are organised, if we use our collective strength. Where we have developed people's power we have shown that the tendency for one section of the community to lead, while the others remain passive, can be overcome. Therefore, those initiatives which overcome these divisions and bring our people together must be jealously guarded and developed to their full potential. The National Education Crisis Committee is one such initiative.

The NECC has opened the way for people's power to be developed in our struggle for a free, democratic, compulsory and non-racial education. The crisis committees have brought all sectors of the community together in the pursuit of this noble goal. Students, parents and teachers now have democratic organisations available through which we have begun to take some control over education. They provide the vehicles through which divisions between young and old, teachers and parents can be overcome. Not only this, but our democratic crisis committees can, and must be used to help tackle all the problems which we face, to develop and deepen people's power in the townships and in the schools. The education struggle is a political struggle in South Africa. We are fighting for the right to self-determination in the education sphere as in all other spheres.

PEOPLE'S EDUCATION FOR PEOPLE'S POWER

The struggle for People's Education is no longer a struggle of the students alone. It has become a struggle of the whole community with the involvement of all sections of the community. This is not something which has happened in the school sphere alone; it reflects a new level of development in the struggle as a whole.

It is no accident that the historic De-cember Conference took place at a time when our people were taking the struggle for democracy to new heights. At a time when the struggle against apartheid was being transformed into a struggle for people's power. In line with this, students and parents were no longer only saying "Away with apartheid, gutter education!" We were now also saying "Forward with People's Education, Education for Liberation!"

The struggle for people's education can only finally be won when we have won the struggle for people's power. We are facing a vicious and desperate enemy, an enemy which wants at all costs to maintain a system of racist domination and exploitation that includes Bantu Education. Any gains which we make are only finally guaranteed when that enemy is finally defeated, once and for all.

We are also facing an enemy which is unwilling to reason, which is unmoved by the hunger of children, or cries of suffering. It only understands power and that there are two types of power. Its own power and the power which comes from the organised masses, people's power. Therefore gains we make in the education struggle depend on our organised strength, on the extent to which we establish organs of people's power.

In the few short months since the December conference, we have already seen some of the things People's Power can achieve in our education struggle. We have also seen that the state will do anything it can to reverse these gains and turn them into defeats. In hundreds of schools students have established democratic SRCs, but the state is doing everything it can to frustrate and crush them. The state has conceded our demand for free text books, but tries to wriggle out of this by saying there aren't enough. Also, many detainees, student leaders, are being released, but then excluded from schools. These are only a few examples which show the kind of enemy we face.

But it is also true that where we are strongest, where people's power is most advanced, we are able to frustrate the state in *its* objectives. For example, in the Eastern Cape, they fired one of our democratic teachers. Through being organised, the people in that area were able to simply send that teacher back to school. They employed him. In fact they raised the funds among themselves, and said this is the people's teacher. If the state can't pay him, they said, we will pay him ourselves, because this is how important people's education is to us.

Of course the people shouldn't have to pay that salary. They are getting slave wages and the taxes from the profits they make for the bosses are going to Botha's army. But since they do not yet control the budget for People's Education, this was one way they could enforce the people's will. That teacher is now teaching in their school. . . .

Another area where we are demonstrating the possibilities of people's power is through the school committees. The December Conference took a resolution to replace statutory parents' committees with progressive parent, teacher, student structures. Although these government committees continue in name, they have been rendered unworkable in many parts of the country. Our democratic people's committees have been established and are preparing to take more and more control over the running of the schools. They are the ones who are putting forward the pupil's demands and negotiating with the school principals. The government committees are now being ignored. In effect they are falling away. In some areas their members have abandoned them and joined the people's committees.

Even the Regional Directors of Education are meeting with the people's committees. And finally, of course, the central government has been forced to recognise the people's crisis committees by meeting with representatives of the NECC. . . .

Of course we should mention here that teachers are also coming into the fold of the people. The decision by the traditionally conservative Atasa to withdraw from the structures of the DET reflects the beginning of this process. We now have to ensure that this process is accelerated, that teachers fully identify with the aspirations and struggles of the people. Gone are the days when teachers were forced to collaborate with apartheid structures. The people have opened the way. It is up to the teachers and the teacher's organisations to ensure that teachers follow the path of the people, the path of democracy. Our teachers need to follow the lead given by progressive teachers organisations such as Neusa and Wectu.

We call upon those teachers following the path of collaboration to abandon that path. Some teachers have allowed themselves to be used as tools to victimise student leaders and progressive teachers. Others have even been used as vigilantes against the struggles of their communities. It is our duty, parents, students and teachers alike to ensure that all teachers understand and are made part of the struggle for people's education. We cannot afford to allow any section of the community to be used against the struggles of our people. . . .

What do we mean when we say we want people's education? We are agreed that we don't want Bantu Education but we must be clear about *what* we want in its place. We must also be clear as to *how* we are going to achieve this.

We are no longer demanding the same education as whites, since this is education for domination. People's education means education at the service of the people as a whole, education that liberates, education that puts the people in command of their lives.

We are not prepared to accept any 'alternative' to Bantu Education which is imposed on the people from above. This includes American or other imperialist alternatives designed to safeguard their selfish interests in the country, by promoting elitist and divisive ideas and values which will ensure foreign monopoly exploitation continues.

Another type of 'alternative school' we reject is the one which gives students from a more wealthy background avenues to opt out of the struggle, such as commercially-run schools which are springing up.

To be acceptable, every initiative must come from the people themselves, must be accountable to the people and must advance the broad mass of students, not just a select few. In effect this means taking over the schools, transforming them from institutions of oppression into zones of progress and people's power. Of course this is a long-term process, a process of struggle, which can only ultimately be secured by total liberation. But we have already begun this process. . . .

The apartheid authorities are unable to accept the transformation that is taking place in the schools. That is why, unlike previously when the authorities were doing their utmost to get children back to school, they are now locking children out of schools. Lock outs have occured in a number of places including parts of the Eastern and Western Cape and Soshanguve and Witbank in the Transvaal. The regional director in the Western Transvaal simply closed all schools in his area recently. The response of students and parents has been to demand that the doors of learning and culture be opened, and there has been a move towards occupying the schools. People are claiming the schools as their

property and demanding education as their right. In P.E. last week the DET locked the students out of the schools. Over two thousand parents took their children to the schools to demand that they be opened. I understand that they successfully occupied the schools. This is in line with action workers are taking in certain parts of the country, where they are occupying factories in defiance of the bosses' attempts to lock them out. These school occupations give students the opportunity to start implementing alternative programmes, people's education.

STRUGGLES IN THE COMMUNITIES

The demand for free, democratic people's education we have said, is part of, indeed inextricably tied to the struggle for a free, democratic, people's South Africa. The struggle against apartheid education is not a question for students and teachers alone. A conference like this demonstrates the concern of the entire community with the problem of gutter education.

Likewise the enemy views education as a crucial political issue. To ensure that our demands are not met, to maintain the existing educational system, SADF and SAP are deployed against our children, shooting and teargassing them— driving them into and sometimes out of schools, detaining and harrassing them in numerous other ways.

It is for this reason that our demands at the December conference were against apartheid education and also the broader acts of war against our communities.

Now, three months later, we have noted that our demands have not been met. What should our response be? It is not for me to preempt the decisions of this conference. What might be useful, however, is for me to outline some of the strategies and tactics that our people have adopted and are using at present in their struggles against the enemy. It is important that we assess these and understand how best they can further some of the gains that we have made and how they can increase the crisis and disarray in the ranks of the enemy. What I am saying is that we do not choose tactics at random. Any tactic that serves to unite the entire community on as broad a basis as possible, involving as many sectors and areas as possible, must be encouraged.

Any tactic that is likely to be sustained and to help build our organisation; that consolidates our strength and our unity, must be encouraged. Any tactic that hampers this process must not be embarked on.

Against this background let us look at recent campaigns:

In many townships, community councillors have been forced to resign. We have noted that popular structures have often been erected to replace them. Through these democratic organs our people are starting to control their own lives. These organs are based on and simultaneously facilitate the development of organisation.

In many townships, especially in the Transvaal, successful rent boycotts have been instituted. Some of these have been sustained for more than two years. The value of rent boycotts is that they strike at the material basis of Black Local Authorities, while simultaneously relieving some of the economic pressures on the masses. Without drawing exorbitant rents from our people, the community council system cannot operate. It is reported, now, that every month that the boycotts continue, the system is losing R2 million.

Amongst our people, unemployment has reached a record figure and continues to increase. GST continues to impose a heavy burden. In this situation, the people, by refusing to pay rent, transfer part of the burden to the system.

In the rural areas, bantustan rule is under sustained attack. So-called tribal authorities are being forced to resign and are sometimes being replaced by village councils that enjoy confidence and ensure the participation of the community.

One of the key forms of struggle employed in recent years has been the consumer boycott. The weapon's potency lies in the fact that it requires the organisation of the entire community in order to be effective. To sustain it requires strong, deeply-rooted organisational structures. Its success in the Eastern Cape lay in the street committees which facilitated the effective participation of most residents. This proved very effective in the Eastern Cape in the people's campaign to get the troops out of the townships.

Where organisation has been weaker the consumer boycott has not only been less successful, but its implementation has sometimes weakened rather than strengthened unity amongst the people. In such situations, young people, often well-meaning, have tended to apply force instead of political education, to persuade the community to support the boycott. This has had the effect of alienating some people from the struggle.

Another dramatic and often-utilised weapon is the stayaway. Where it is based on strong organisation, it is powerful and builds unity not only within the community, but also between community and trade union organisations. Where such organisation is not present, where such stayaways are not adequately prepared, they tend to produce, as with consumer boycotts, intimidation instead of persuasion, disunity instead of growing unity of the people. The adequate preparation for such a tactic requires careful discussion amongst all sections of the community, including hostel dwellers, and especially between community and worker organisations. Only then is this weapon powerful and effective.

A crucial demand of the entire African people remains the abolition of the pass system. Sensing the continued popular anger and militancy, Comrade Barayi, president of Cosatu, made a call at the launch of the trade union federation, for the burning of the badges of slavery. Should such a call be implemented it is likely to capture popular imagination, to involve every section of the African community and enjoy the support of all democrats.

THE WAY FORWARD

The struggles which I have mentioned are the context within which, I think, we need to understand our education struggles. I do not want to in any way dictate or pre-empt the outcome of the discussions at this conference. However, I believe that we need to plan our future struggle on the education front in the context of the broader struggle against apartheid and in line with the general tasks of the anti-apartheid forces at present.

During the emergency, the National Education Crisis Committee was both a shield and a spear: the question which we must now ask ourselves is how do we advance our struggle on the education front and at the same time strengthen, consolidate, unite and deepen our organisations?

In answering these questions, we need to weigh up how we advance the gains of the Parents Crisis Committees over the last three months and at the same time overcome their weaknesses.

As organisation aiming at co-ordinated national response to the education crisis, NECC was able to unite parents, teachers, and students nationally around a single set of demands. This achievement was historic in the level of coherence it achieved in our organisations nationally

and in terms of the enormous pressure it placed on the regime.

When planning our future, we need to ask ourselves how do we deepen and broaden this national unity? In assessing different strategies, we need to ask ourselves whether they will reach out to communities not yet touched by our organisations, particularly those in the rural areas, bantustans and small towns.

We need to ask ourselves what actions, campaigns and strategies will overcome the uneven level of development of our organisations in different areas. In short, what action will pave the way for us to take even greater strides forward in all sections of the community, in all areas.

We also need to examine ways of making inroads into the white community. To break the stranglehold that apartheid education has on the minds of white children. We must show their parents that apartheid education provides no future for their children, or any of South Africa's children.

A significant achievement of NECC was its ability to begin building alliances between different sections of our oppressed people: between parents and students, between students and teachers, between parents and teachers. This has laid the basis for undermining the divisions which the state tried to create between youth and older people, between urban and rural communities, between professionals and other members of the community. We have already given examples of the achievements of these alliances so far. But we know that the bonds between these different sections of the community could be strengthened still further.

There are still areas where students are fighting the education struggle without the support of their parents or teachers. There are still areas where the struggle is led by the youth and the students and older members of the community are left behind or alienated.

There are still sections of the teaching profession who side with the apartheid government and promote its will. The question we face is how to strengthen the alliance between parents, teachers, and students. We will not defeat apartheid while the youth alone carry on the struggle against Bantu Education or other aspects of racist rule. We will not win while our ranks are split by teachers who have not yet thrown in their lot with the democratic movement. We will not win while parents remain alienated from the demands of their children. These weaknesses and divisions will only delay our victory.

Our task is to deepen the alliance between all sections of the community against Bantu Education and all aspects of apartheid rule. It is to look for strategies which continually strengthen and enlarge the ranks of the people and constantly weaken, divide and isolate the ranks of the enemy.

The December conference not only united different sections of the community, it also united all opponents of apartheid under a single banner against Bantu Education. The unity and hence the strength of the December conference shook the apartheid regime to its roots. Alone, isolated and disorganised it was unable to reassert Bantu Education in our schools. It lost the initiative and was only able to respond piecemeal to our demands. For this reason the government and all the forces of racism and exploitation in our country have a deep-seated desire to prevent the success of this conference.

They long to undermine us by disuniting us. Just as we need unity in order to advance, so we must understand that any act of disunity is an act against the struggle, against the people. Any act of disunity aids the enemy. To cast aside our unity at this time is to weaken our shield and blunt our spear. Our greatest weapon lies in our collective organised strength.

We must remember that the enemy is not sleeping while we plan our activities. We know that it openly attacks us. But it does not only operate outside our ranks. It also operates from within our ranks.

From within, the enemy takes advantage of any sign of indiscipline, any disunity, every sign of weakness. It does this in order to confuse our people, to increase disunity, and sow chaos in our ranks.

When we look to the future we need to remember that our task is not only to broaden our unity, but also to deepen our organisation. It was the people's organisation which built democratically controlled schools committees, SRCs and parents Crisis Committees. This organisation has taken us from opposing Bantu Education to organising the people's alternative. The building of democratic organisation is the priority. For those of you struggling on the education front, your task is to deepen people's control over education. This means strengthening democratic teachers organisations by recruiting all teachers into the ranks of these organisations, setting up SRCs in every school, and parent, teacher, student committees to control education in these schools. During the last months we have learnt that the state will not stand idly by and allow us to implement these actions. They will continue to harass us, to detain student leaders, to occupy our communities and to dismiss and transfer democratic teachers.

Our task is not only to build democratic organisations, but to build these in such a way that they can withstand the harassment of the apartheid government. We know that our greatest strength lies in the power of the people, in our mass based committees in the schools, streets and factories; in our co-ordinated strength in our national organisations, such as NECC.

Long live the struggle for democratic, people's education!

Long live the united popular struggle
against apartheid!
Forward to a free, democratic people's
South Africa!

Amandla Ngawethu!
Power to the People!

43   TERROR LEKOTA
LETTER

Terror Lekota was national publicity secretary of the United Democratic Front until he was arrested in 1984. These notes, written clandestinely by Lekota in prison in 1988, demonstrate his commitment to the ideals of the Freedom Charter, in particular to the need for a non-racial, populist, and non-violent struggle. The statement was smuggled out of prison in the form of a letter. In 1988, Lekota was convicted of treason and sentenced to fifteen years in prison.

Statement by Terror Lekota
February–April 1988

What is meant by change?

The concept of change in this question I have always found problematic. It seems to suggest rejection of the concept of black consciousness. I wish to point out here that if that is the connotation attached to rejection as employed in the above question, then the question fails to understand my position in relation to black consciousness.

Two facets apply to BC [Black Consciousness] in my view. There is the ideological (theoretical) facet and there is the practice of BC. In theory, BC is an articulation of black resistance of white racism. And the drive to reshape a black psyche free from the cobwebs of black inferiority and all other outgrowths of black oppression. It is for this reason that BC has been defined as an attitude of the mind and a way of life.

Now, in relation to this aspect of the matter, BC remains relevant for me. In fact, it remains an integral part of the struggle for South African freedom. For as long as there is a modicum of racism—and racism has always preyed on colonized black people—the struggle for its elimination necessitates BC. To that ex-

tent I remain deeply committed to BC thinking and I uphold its idiom.

But the second facet of the practice of BC in South Africa is what I reject. I reject the approach of those of our countrymen who would refuse white South Africans the right to join in the national effort to eliminate oppression. It seems to suggest that whites must be rejected for being white. It fails to realize that racism knows no racial bounds and that just as the ruling National Party of the thirties, forties, fifties and sixties taught racism on its upward momentum, so too can our own black organizations turn into racialist monsters of the future. Racism has so far preyed on the black oppressed but it has also begot itself in the ranks of its victims.

So the struggle against racism must not and should no longer be looked at from the side of black people alone. It must be looked at and fought from on both sides of the color line. That does not of course mean that the present set of circumstances should be ignored. A necessary balance must be struck to give sufficient leverage to those who fight the immediate evil of white racism. But those of us who shoulder the burden of struggle should not be swung around completely. We should not move over to the extreme of employing practices which may prove disastrous on the dawn of a new day.

Non-racialism and non-violence are inseparable twins.

It is my genuine desire that when freedom day comes it should not find reconciliation too far to attain. Our freedom day and reconciliation should be very close to each other. This immediately raises the question of the methods of struggle. The more jarring and shattering the methods, the deeper the alienation of our people and, consequently, the more difficult the process of healing the wounds and reconciling the people.

Non-racialism as a method embodies the process of pulling black and whites together so that they jointly dismantle apartheid. In the process they already have a chance of learning to know each other. And artificial suspicions, nurtured by years of apartheid myths and propaganda, are demolished. And when freedom comes it will not be the victory of blacks over whites but that of the people of South Africa over an evil system that has for so long set them up one against another.

In this context, it becomes clear that the non-violent path is the one that creates the greatest number of possibilities of bringing black and white South Africans together. And only then can one articulate this path of progress and allow the process to develop to maturity. Our organizations must be seen as the beginnings of the fully developed future non-racial and democratic South Africa. We cannot wait for freedom day to teach white and black South Africans to love and live with each other. We must begin today, now, because if we cannot do it now we shall not be able to do it some other day. The non-racial and non-violent paths are the right one.

As I understand and have always understood black consciousness, it is a demand for the recognition of the humanity of blacks. It is not a demand for the denial of the humanity of whites. No, what it says is this: that in a world in which the humanity of whites is already acknowledged and even exaggerated to the level of an icon, blacks' humanity must also be rediscovered and raised to acceptable levels. The worship of whiteness must be done away with. In this way an acceptable parity must be established.

What I am saying, therefore, is that there are two forms of black consciousness. For those who understand it as a simple demand for the recognition of black humanity and to hell with the humanity of whites, practice will assume one form. For us who seek the humanization of blacks while preserving that of our white counterparts, practice will assume yet another form, namely that of employing the movement as the theoretical and practical area of education and training in coexistence and mutual respect.

Those who doubt the correctness of our approach will do well to take a close look at the history of the National Party. For three or four decades they harangued their own people about "separate but equal". Today, as they try to advance in the face of hard political and economic realities they are caught up in the cobwebs and hang-over of the days of Verwoerdian apartheid euphoria. We shall not commit the same mistake.

Are the means to be the same as the end?

In political struggle, the means must always be the same as the ends. How else can one expect a racialistic movement to imbue our society with a non-racial character on the dawn of our freedom day? A political movement cannot bequeath to society a characteristic it does not itself possess. To expect it to do so is like asking a heathen to convert a person to Christianity. The principles of that religion are unknown to the heathen, let alone the practice.

It is important to keep in mind what we mean by reconciliation. It does not mean pampering and pandering to the grunts and groans of the oppressor. Certainly, it does not mean tinkering with an evil system. But it would be self-defeating to resort to patterns and grounds of action which trample under foot principle even though they take us forward faster. Whatever "harder" stance may be adopted should not disregard the crucial aspect of reconciliation. Our objective is to excise a cancer in the duodenum of our society; not to destroy or poison the entire society.

No the system is not vague. It is very real and experience has brought this home to us. The task of those who struggle for change is also to educate the greater majority. Only those who are lazy and seek short-cuts to freedom argue that the system is vague. It is very possible to explain the nature of oppression even by pointing out those groups and classes which constitute its pillars. But to (single out) individuals, groups, etc. is dangerous since one can quite easily create a followership that will forever be in search of particular visible enemies. What makes Dr. Treurnicht unacceptable to us is not that he is Dr. Treurnicht or white. It is that he stands for a particular system—apartheid—which relegates us to an inferior status. If he abandoned that stance tomorrow, if therefore white South Africans were to accede to a national convention tomorrow and a non-racial and democratic constitution were drawn up and accepted, the system of apartheid would be gone. Would it be necessary to struggle on? No. Would we still talk of vagueness? I do not think so.